ACCOMPLISHING NAGPRA

Accomplishing NAGPRA

PERSPECTIVES ON THE INTENT, IMPACT, AND FUTURE
OF THE NATIVE AMERICAN GRAVES PROTECTION
AND REPATRIATION ACT

Edited by Sangita Chari & Jaime M.N. Lavallee

FIRST PEOPLES
New Directions in Indigenous Studies

Oregon State University Press   Corvallis

The paper in this book meets the guidelines for permanence and durability of the Committee on Production Guidelines for Book Longevity of the Council on Library Resources and the minimum requirements of the American National Standard for Permanence of Paper for Printed Library Materials Z39.48-1984.

Library of Congress Cataloging-in-Publication Data

Accomplishing NAGPRA : perspectives on the intent, impact, and future of the Native American Graves Protection and Repatriation Act / editors, Sangita Chari and Jaime Lavallee.
  pages cm
  Includes bibliographical references and index.
  ISBN 978-0-87071-720-8 (alk. paper) -- ISBN 978-0-87071-721-5 (e-book)
  1. United States. Native American Graves Protection and Repatriation Act.
  2. Human remains (Archaeology)--Law and legislation--United States. 3. Human remains (Archaeology)--Repatriation--Law and legislation--United States.
  4. Indians of North America--Antiquities--Law and legislation. 5. Cultural property--Repatriation--United States. 6. Indians of North America--Material culture. I. Chari, Sangita, editor of compilation. II. Lavallee, Jaime, editor of compilation.
  KF4306.R4I47 2013
  344.73'094--dc23
                              2013013091

Oregon State University Press
121 The Valley Library
Corvallis OR 97331-4501
541-737-3166 • fax 541-737-3170
www.osupress.oregonstate.edu

Contents

Introduction

SANGITA CHARI AND JAIME M. N. LAVALLEE

The Native American Graves Protection and Repatriation Act (NAGPRA; 25 U.S.C. 3001 et seq.) marked its twentieth anniversary on November 16, 2010. At the time we both worked for the National Park Service in the National NAGPRA Program. Inspired by the significance of the anniversary, the National NAGPRA Program convened a small group of practitioners representing NAGPRA's main constituents—museums, federal agencies, Native Hawaiians, and Indian tribes—to develop a symposium to recognize the occasion. At the first meeting, it became apparent that before we could delve into the practical aspects of planning the event, we had to come to consensus about just how this occasion would be commemorated. Some saw the anniversary as a time of celebration and an opportunity to acknowledge the tremendous progress made since the 1990s. Others felt the occasion was more appropriately marked by recognizing the solemn reality that, after twenty years, a substantial number of human remains and cultural items are still in museums and federal repositories. We all agreed that the anniversary provided an important opportunity to share experiences and reflect on twenty years of NAGPRA implementation. The basis for this book grew out of our work with the symposium committee. It reflects our desire to acknowledge the tremendous work accomplished by NAGPRA practitioners and to elevate the voices of those who do the daily work of NAGPRA, in tribes, Native Hawaiian organizations, museums, and federal agencies around the country.

The intent of NAGPRA

The passage of NAGPRA was to end the centuries-old practice of removing human remains and cultural items from Native American graves, lands, and communities; treating them as collectibles to be stored, studied, and displayed in museums and repositories in the name of scientific study, education, and "cultural preservation." Such practices flourished because despite the existence of federal laws that protected gravesites and property, the laws did not extend to Native Americans.[1] Instead, their dead and cultural items were treated as property for the benefit of the American public. As a result, Native Americans were systematically disenfranchised and denied access and authority over their graves and cultural items, which were taken without permission or under duress. NAGPRA acknowledged that these collections were the result, directly or indirectly, of values and practices that conflated scientific discovery with ownership, and brought to light the questionable collecting practices that preyed upon impoverished or dispossessed Native Americans. It is this past that underlies why, at the time of its passage, NAGPRA was hailed as a significant landmark in civil rights, human rights, and Indian law. As Senator Daniel Inouye testified, "In light of the important role that death and burial rites play in Native American cultures, it is all the more offensive that the civil rights of America's first citizens have been so flagrantly violated for the past century. Mr. President, the bill before us today is not about the validity of museums or the value of scientific inquiry. Rather, it is about human rights."[2]

Twenty years later, the way museums and federal agencies view, interact, and care for Native American human remains and objects has undergone a significant change. Inherent in the NAGPRA process is an acknowledgment that every object and every set of human remains carries cultural, religious, spiritual, and social significance that is to be valued as much as (or more than) scientific analysis. No longer are they treated as discrete objects and specimens disconnected and irrelevant to present-day Native Americans. Rather, they are considered to be ancestors and objects of ongoing significance and meaning to their living descendants.

NAGPRA overview

In its most basic form, NAGPRA requires federal agencies and museums to repatriate the Native American human remains and objects in their collections. NAGPRA also requires federal agencies to work with Indian tribes[3] and Native Hawaiian organizations[4] when Native American remains and cultural items are discovered or removed from federal or tribal lands.[5] NAGPRA has two elements: the statute under 25 U.S.C. 3001 and the regulations at 43 CFR 10. The NAGPRA statute outlines the framework, but the NAGPRA regulations provide the implementation process, including timelines, procedures, and guidelines.[6] NAGPRA's reach is expansive. All federally recognized Indian tribes, which include Alaska Native villages and Native Hawaiian organizations, are allowed to repatriate under NAGPRA. Also covered is every federal agency except the Smithsonian Institution,[7] and every institution that meets the NAGPRA definition of a museum.[8] NAGPRA goes beyond the typical definition of a museum to encompass any institution that receives federal funds and possesses Native American and Native Hawaiian human remains or cultural objects. This includes, but is not limited to, universities, state or local governments, libraries, state historic preservation offices, community colleges, small historical houses, and local parks.

The Secretary of the Interior oversees NAGPRA. The National NAGPRA Program, housed at the National Park Service, has been delegated some of the Secretary of the Interior's NAGPRA responsibilities, including developing regulations and guidance, providing administrative and staff support to the NAGPRA Review Committee, managing a grants program, publishing notices, and assisting the Assistant Secretary for Fish and Wildlife and Parks with civil penalty investigations. Within NAGPRA, there are two distinct processes for administering the return of human remains and cultural items: one for museum or federal agency collections ("collection process"), and another for those removed from federal and tribal lands after November 16, 1990 ("land process").

Collection process

The collection process requires museums and federal agencies to conduct a thorough assessment of their Native American collections and consult with Indian tribes or Native Hawaiian organizations. Collections are divided into two categories: human remains and their associated funerary objects, and all other Native American cultural items. Native American cultural items that are determined to be unassociated funerary objects (funerary objects with no connection to a specific set of human remains),[9] sacred objects,[10] and cultural patrimony[11] are subject to repatriation under NAGPRA.

Native American human remains and associated funerary objects are further determined to be culturally affiliated or culturally unidentifiable, and follow a specific process based on their designation. NAGPRA defines "cultural affiliation" as "a relationship of shared group identity which can be reasonably traced historically or prehistorically between a present day Indian tribe or Native Hawaiian organization and an identifiable earlier group."[12] This recognizes that Indian tribes and Native Hawaiian communities are dynamic cultures that are connected to "those that were here before." The regulations state that cultural affiliation can be established when the preponderance of the evidence based on geographical, kinship, biological, archaeological, linguistic, folklore, oral tradition, historical evidence, or other information or expert opinion reasonably leads to such a conclusion. In the preamble to the regulations published in 1995, the use of evidence is discussed: "The applicability and strength of particular types of evidence must be determined on a case-by-case basis. It would be inappropriate to place stipulations on the applicability of various types of evidence in regulation."[13] This means that no form of evidence is weighted more than the other, but rather all lines of evidence are to be understood in their totality for that situation. In other words, Native American systems of knowledge, such as oral history evidence, cannot be undervalued or not considered, but rather should be equally weighted with western, scientific knowledge when coming to a decision. Thus, NAGPRA, as a human rights law, not only provided rights to the human remains and cultural objects of Native Americans, but also the right to have their knowledge equally recognized and considered.

Not all human remains are determined to be affiliated to a specific tribe or Native Hawaiian organization. These "unaffiliated" remains are defined under NAGPRA as "culturally unidentifiable." On May 14, 2010, the most recent section of the regulations went into effect as 43 CFR 10.11, also known as the culturally unidentifiable rule (CUI rule). This section articulated what the statute meant by "culturally unidentifiable" [14] and outlined the process in which museums and federal agencies could return these remains. This section was highly anticipated since there are over 123,000 individuals listed on the National NAGPRA Program database as culturally unidentifiable; accounting for approximately 75 percent of the individuals reported in museum and federal agency collections to date.[15]

Under NAGPRA, a determination of cultural affiliation or culturally unidentifiable must be made in consultation with all relevant tribes and Native Hawaiian organizations. Consultation is defined in the regulations as phone or face-to-face meetings between the museum or federal agency and the tribe(s) or Native Hawaiian organization(s). The process differs based on whether the museum or federal agency is trying to repatriate human remains or cultural items, as well as whether they are part of a collection process or the land process. However, the intent is the same: all parties must contribute to the decision-making process. The regulations outline the procedures for consulting with tribes and Native Hawaiian organizations as well as the penalties for either not consulting or not fully consulting.[16]

Every decision for repatriation or the return of Native American remains and objects reached by a museum or federal agency is made legal by the publication of a notice in the *Federal Register*. The National NAGPRA Program receives these notices from museums and federal agencies and manages their publication. Once this step is complete, museums and federal agencies can repatriate the human remains or cultural items. A quick look at published *Federal Register* notices showcases the broad reach of NAGPRA (as well as the extent of collecting that took place in the nation's past).

At NAGPRA's passage, there was estimated to be between 100,000 to 200,000 Native American human remains in museum and federal agency collections and about 10 to 15 million cultural items.[17] NAGPRA set ambitious deadlines for when museums and federal agencies would need to complete their assessment of the Native American human remains and cultural items in their collections. The first deadline was to produce a summary, a brief listing of Native American cultural items in museum or federal agency collections, and send a copy to the appropriate Indian tribes or Native Hawaiian organizations by November 16, 1993.

The next deadline was to produce an inventory of the human remains and associated funerary objects in museum and federal agency collections by November 16, 1995, and send copies to the appropriate Indian tribes and Native Hawaiian organizations. Unlike summaries, NAGPRA required museums and federal agencies to consult with lineal descendants and Indian tribes or Native Hawaiian organizations prior to creating the inventory. The inventory consists of a summation of the consultation efforts, as well as a detailed description of the human remains and associated funerary objects, including reasons for the cultural affiliation or culturally unidentifiable determination, and other relevant information such as the donor and geographic location.

Although many museums and federal agencies strove to meet these deadlines, not all of them were able to do so as fully and completely as outlined under NAGPRA. There are still updates, consultations, and corrections being prepared by museums and federal agencies today.

Land process

A separate process was created for federal agencies to facilitate the return of Native American human remains and cultural items found on federal or tribal land after November 16, 1990. Tribal land is defined under NAGPRA to mean: all lands within the exterior boundaries of any Indian reservation; all dependent Indian communities; and any lands administered for the benefit of Native Hawaiians pursuant to the Hawaiian Homes Commission Act, 1920.[18] In addition, federal land means "any land other than tribal lands which are controlled or owned by the United States, including lands selected by but not yet conveyed to Alaska Native corporations and groups organized pursuant to the Alaska Native Claims Settlement Act of 1971." This means that federal land could be broader than the almost 650 million acres of land under direct government ownership,[19] since it includes lands where the federal agency has a "legal interest sufficient to permit it to apply these regulations."[20]

Similar to the collection process, consultation with Indian tribes and Native Hawaiian organizations is central to the land process as federal agencies are required to consult with tribes to determine the transfer of the human remains or items. The federal agency can either consult with Indian tribes or Native Hawaiian organizations prior to excavation (intentional excavation) or after the discovery of human remains and cultural items (inadvertent discovery) about their return. In either instance, the federal agency is required to publish a notice twice in a newspaper (as opposed to the *Federal Register*) with the results of the consultation and the determination of which tribe(s) the human remains or cultural items will be returned to, and submit these finalized, published decisions to the National NAGPRA Program.

It is important to note that because state agencies are defined as museums under NAGPRA, state or private lands are not excluded. The agency may be subject to the collection process under the guidelines set out at 43 CFR 10.13 for removals from state or private land after November 16, 1990, if remains or cultural items come under the control of the state agency.

Impact of NAGPRA

At the time NAGPRA was passed, many underestimated the range of complexities, both practical and theoretical, associated with the implementation of the legislation. The past twenty years has required a substantial infusion of resources, including time, money, materials, training, travel, and expertise, from museums, federal agencies, tribes, and Native Hawaiian organizations to fulfill the goals of the act. Federal agencies and museums had to reassess (or assess for the first time) their Native American collections, determine their scope, train staff, and develop internal processes for consultation and repatriation. Many museums and federal agencies had not segmented their collection into the categories defined by NAGPRA. Furthermore, it was not unusual for a museum or federal agency to have incomplete or inaccurate information about the human remains or cultural items in their collection, making consultation and affiliation difficult. Federal agencies were especially challenged as their collections were spread across the nation in museums, universities and other repositories. Some agencies are still identifying collections long neglected and preparing them for NAGPRA implementation.[21]

Along with the practical challenges of implementation, the museum and scientific communities struggled with the cultural and ethical issues posed by repatriation. Have museums relinquished their ethical responsibility to the greater society by repatriating human remains and cultural items? Would scientific discovery be compromised by repatriating human remains and cultural items to Indian tribes and Native Hawaiian organizations? These questions are still being considered and debated.

Tribes and Native Hawaiian organizations were equally challenged with implementing NAGPRA. Anxious to bring home ancestors and cultural items long separated from them, tribes and Native Hawaiian organizations had the daunting prospect of receiving numerous summaries, inventories, and consultation requests from museums and federal agencies from around the country. Systems and procedures had to be developed to simply manage the sheer volume of information they received. Like museums and federal agencies, new staff positions, committees, policy guidelines, and databases had to be developed, all of which took significant—and often scarce—resources to accomplish. In addition to the practical reality of repatriation, NAGPRA presented a number of spiritual, cultural, and ethical challenges for tribes and Native Hawaiians. What ceremonies are appropriate for the reburial of ancestors or the return of cultural items? How do you handle items that are contaminated and could pose health risks for the community if used or reburied? What is the best way to deal with human remains that might be affiliated to more than one tribe? Where should the tribe rebury, especially if the tribe no longer lives on their ancestral lands?

Furthermore, museums, federal agencies, tribes, and Native Hawaiian organizations had to develop a process for communicating with each other. Most NAGPRA practitioners characterize the historical relationship between federal agencies, museums, and Native Americans as one based predominately on distrust. Could these distinct communities overcome differences in values, ethical obligations, and historical perspectives to build a new way of interacting with each other? The passage of NAGPRA was one thing, but the reality of seeing ancestors, sacred items, and other important cultural objects lined up in museum collections was and continues to be a difficult and emotional experience.

NAGPRA irrevocably changed the way the United States government understands its role as a steward of Native American graves and cultural items. The NAGPRA community continues to find creative and practical ways to improve the NAGPRA process. Programs have been developed, coalitions formed, and museums, federal agencies, tribes, and Native Hawaiian organizations continue to develop meaningful partnerships that extend well past the repatriation effort that drew them together.[22] Despite the many challenges that NAGPRA presented, there have been significant improvements in the documentation, communication, and interaction of tribes and Native Hawaiian organizations with each other and with museums and federal agencies. Yet, the numbers show that while much has been accomplished, there is even more left to do. At the end of twenty years, over 1,500 museums and federal agencies have submitted inventories representing over 160,000 individuals.[23] Of these, approximately 40,000 human remains and over one million associated funerary objects are accounted for in published notices and eligible for repatriation. Since a notice is required before repatriation can occur, this means that about 120,000 or three-fourths of all reported individuals cannot be repatriated yet. Currently, an average of 2,100 individuals are published in notices on an annual basis.[24] If this rate remains steady, it will take up to sixty years for the current number of remaining individuals to be published in notices.[25] Given the human rights imperative that underscores NAGPRA, is this an acceptable timeline?

Even if the rate of consultation and notice publication increases, another question regarding NAGPRA implementation arises: Is NAGPRA actually resulting in repatriations? Although the law requires a museum or federal agency to publish a notice to legally transfer control of human remains or cultural items to a tribe or Native Hawaiian organization, it does not require museums or federal agencies[26] to report whether or not the human remains or cultural items were actually transferred. In the past twenty years, only 10,000 individuals—or one-quarter of those in published notices—were (voluntarily) reported to the National NAGPRA Program as being transferred by a museum or federal agency to a tribe or Native Hawaiian organization.[27] Because of the voluntary nature of current reporting, this number probably does not reflect the totality of those that have been repatriated. It does provide an indicator that repatriation is not occurring at the rate of notice publication. The reasons behind the disparate numbers require further examination and contemplation. Are tribes and Native Hawaiian organizations choosing not to repatriate human remains and cultural items? If not, then why not? Are there other issues that are blocking their repatriation efforts, such as funding or adequate burial locations? How are museums and federal agencies adjusting to having human remains and cultural items that are no longer in their control but continue to remain in their possession? Is it accurate to say that NAGPRA is working if the human remains or cultural items are not being repatriated?

Purpose and organization of the book

We both came to the practice of NAGPRA from our respective fields through the National NAGPRA Program. Our time at National NAGPRA afforded us the unique ability to interact on a regular basis with NAGPRA practitioners across the country representing Indian tribes and Native Hawaiian organizations, museums, and federal agencies. On any given day, it was not unusual to speak with a tribe in Washington State trying to garner funding to support a repatriation, a museum in New York writing their first NAGPRA notice, and a federal agency needing clarification on a legal point. This bird's-eye view of the everyday questions and concerns of NAGPRA practitioners gave us a unique insight into the nuances of implementing NAGPRA.

What became clear to us was that despite the vast geographic, social, cultural, and economic differences inherent in a national program that covers multiple sectors of American society, NAGPRA practitioners make up a distinct community that shares many of the same challenges and frustrations. Examples of solutions to those challenges can be found throughout the country and can be transferred and modified to fit various local situations. However, a mechanism for sharing stories, navigating challenges, and collectively improving how we implement NAGPRA does not exist at a national level. We hope that the experiences described in this book serve as a conversation starter and initiate a much-needed national dialogue about the type of structures and common strategies required to support the efforts of those that carry out this vitally important work.

This book looks at the reasons surrounding NAGPRA's passage, and examines both the practical application of NAGPRA and NAGPRA's effectiveness as human rights law. NAGPRA implementation is considered through its three major constituent groups: Indian tribes and Native Hawaiian organizations, museums, and federal agencies. Situated primarily in case studies and personal reflection, this book seeks to examine the implementation of NAGPRA, and to showcase the grassroots, daily, practical application of NAGPRA throughout the country in tribes and Native Hawaiian organizations, museums, federal agencies, and the National NAGPRA Program. The contributors are drawn from a variety of backgrounds, including program staff, academics, museum personnel, attorneys, government officials, traditional religious leaders, and tribal NAGPRA representatives. There are those who helped enact NAGPRA, and those who arrived after NAGPRA, but all are concerned with implementation on a local or national level. Indeed, it is their first-hand experiences with the highs and lows of NAGPRA implementation that are so valuable.

The book is divided into three sections, starting with the historical background and a review of the law; moving onto the implementation of NAGPRA through the perspectives of NAGPRA practitioners from the major constituent groups; then finishing with a reflection on NAGPRA's impact and effectiveness. Each chapter lays the foundation for the next, and goes through in more detail what has been discussed and outlined in the introduction about the successes and challenges faced by the NAGPRA community. The chapter authors take a critical look at the result of what was, as Trope states in Chapter 1, "a compromise forged by representatives of the museum, scientific, and Indian communities." Does NAGPRA work? Has NAGPRA, as Indian law and human rights law, lived up to its promise to redress a historical injustice and give Native Americans back control and authority over their ancestors and cultural items? Has NAGPRA given tribes what Hemenway describes in Chapter 3 as "the opportunity to reclaim vital aspects of our culture, things that define who we are as a people, legally as well as in a cultural and spiritual sense"? His tribe has accomplished numerous repatriations, but he writes that it came at a price. "I have learned that you must possess the emotional and mental fortitude to deal with not having your beliefs taken seriously—with rejection, narrow ideas, and difficult personalities, all the while knowing that the spirits of the dead languish while their remains await reburial." NAGPRA is not without its paradoxes. Neller notes in Chapter 7 that the emphasis on federally recognized tribes has actually "taken away the rights of some who are culturally affiliated but have no 'standing' under the law," leaving non-federally recognized tribes with limited legal rights to repatriation. Greer goes further in her examination of NAGPRA's impact in Hawaii to state that, "Some would argue that the legal framework divides the Native Hawaiian community and undermines Native Hawaiian funerary traditions." The irony of legislation meant to support native sovereignty that places the decision-making authority with museums and federal agencies is not lost on tribal and Native Hawaiian practitioners. Peters writes, "It is ironic that NAGPRA does not require a museum to justify their decision to designate an individual as culturally unidentifiable, and yet tribes must produce the preponderance of the evidence in defense of our right to claim a connection to our ancestors." Keller O'Loughlin challenges the prevailing notion that NAGPRA was designed to "balance the interests" of tribes and museums; she asks, "How long will we continue to believe that a 'balance-of-interests' approach between spiritual responsibilities and institutional property rights will be successful?"

Few would argue that NAGPRA has not permanently altered the way museums and federal agencies engage with Native Americans and curate and exhibit Native American collections. Waldbauer goes as far as to state that "NAGPRA has affected federal agencies' approach to the preservation of the nation's cultural heritage." Indeed, Capone writes that NAGPRA has been for many a tool of "consciousness-raising." She notes that a museum visitor's encounter with objects "evokes a sense of wonder through the physical experience of being with the object and through thinking about the layers of meaning which objects induce." NAGPRA offers museums the opportunity to bring "a social and civil conscience to wonder, and in some cases, critical awareness of the dark side to wonder's baggage."

Bernstein reflects that "[t]he passage of NAGPRA was a major human rights victory ... [and] an opportunity for museums and federal agencies to begin to develop a new kind of relationship with Native Americans and Native Hawaiians ... " It is this sense of opportunity— the opportunity to address historical inequalities and heal past injustices, the opportunity to reclaim one's identity, the opportunity to reconsider fundamental societal beliefs and values that support one set of values to the detriment of another—which is echoed throughout the chapters in this book. Twenty years later, NAGPRA has become an integral part of the fabric of federal agencies, museums and Native American communities. The opportunities NAGPRA presents for all of us are only beginning to emerge.

Notes

1   25 U.S.C. 3001(9), "'Native American' means of, or relating to, a tribe, people, or culture that is indigenous to the United States."

2   136 Cong. Rec. S17174 (daily ed., Oct. 26, 1990). (Statement of Senator Daniel K. Inouye at the time of the enactment of the bill by the Senate).

3   25 U.S.C. 3001(7), "'Indian tribe' means any tribe, band, nation, or other organized group or community of Indians, including any Alaska Native village (as defined in, or established pursuant to, the Alaska Native Claims Settlement Act), which is recognized as eligible for the special programs and services provided by the United States to Indians because of their status as Indians."

4   25 U.S.C. 3001(11), "'Native Hawaiian organization' means any organization which (A) serves and represents the interests of Native Hawaiians, (B) has as a primary and stated purpose the provision of services to Native Hawaiians, and (C) has expertise in Native Hawaiian Affairs, and shall include the Office of Hawaiian Affairs and Hui Malama I Na Kupuna O Hawai'i Nei."

5   25 U.S.C. 3002.

6   As of September 30, 2010, there were only two sections of the regulations that remained to be developed: 43 C.F.R. 10.7, Disposition of unclaimed human remains, funerary objects, sacred objects, or objects of cultural patrimony, and 43 C.F.R. 10.15(b), Failure to claim where no repatriation or disposition has occurred.

7   The Smithsonian conducts repatriations under the parallel National Museum of the American Indian Act (NMAI Act), 20 U.S.C. 80q-1 et seq.

8   25 U.S.C. 3001(8), "'museum' means any institution or State or local government agency (including any institution of higher learning) that receives Federal funds and has possession of, or control over, Native American cultural items. Such term does not include the Smithsonian Institution or any other Federal agency."

9   25 U.S.C. 3001(3)(B), "'unassociated funerary objects' which shall mean objects that, as a part of the death rite or ceremony of a culture, are reasonably believed to have been placed with individual human remains either at the time of death or later, where the remains are not in the possession or control of the Federal agency or museum and the objects can be identified by a preponderance of the evidence as related to specific individuals or families or to known human remains or, by a preponderance of the evidence, as having been removed from a specific burial site of an individual culturally affiliated with a particular Indian tribe."

10   25 U.S.C. 3001(3)(C), "'sacred objects' which shall mean specific ceremonial objects which are needed by traditional Native American religious leaders for the practice of traditional Native American religions by their present day adherents."

11   25 U.S.C. 3001(3)(D), "'cultural patrimony' which shall mean an object having ongoing historical, traditional, or cultural importance central to the Native American group or culture itself, rather than property owned by an individual Native American, and which, therefore, cannot be alienated, appropriated, or conveyed by any individual regardless of whether or not the individual is a member of the Indian tribe or Native Hawaiian organization and such object shall have been considered inalienable by such Native American group at the time the object was separated from such group."

12   25 U.S.C. 3001(2).

13   Native American Graves Protection and Repatriation Act Regulations; Final Rule. 60 Fed Reg. 62133-62169 (December 4, 1995).

14   43 C.F.R. 10.2(e)(2).

15   *National NAGPRA Program FY 2010 Final Report, for the period October 1, 2009–September 30, 2010.* http://www.nps.gov/nagpra/DOCUMENTS/NAGPRA_FY10_Program_Report. pdf (hereinafter National NAGPRA FY 2010 report).

16   43 C.F.R. 10.

17   H.R. Rep. No. 101-877, at 22 (1990).

18   25 U.S.C. 3001(2).

19   "The Federal Government owns nearly 650 million acres of land—almost 30 percent of the land area of the United States. Federally owned and managed public lands include National Parks, National Forests, and National Wildlife Refuges. These are lands that are held for all Americans." National Atlas of the United States, U.S. Department of the Interior. http://nationalatlas.gov/printable/fedlands.html.

20   43 C.F.R. 10.2(f), "control," as used in this definition, refers to those lands not owned by the United States but in which the United States has a legal interest sufficient to permit it to apply these regulations without abrogating the otherwise existing legal rights of a person.

21   *Native American Graves Protection and Repatriation Act: After Almost 20 Years, Key Federal Agencies Still Have Not Fully Complied with the Act* (Washington DC: GAO-10-768, July 28, 2010).

22   *Journeys to Repatriation: 15 Years of NAGPRA Grants (1994–2008)* (Washington DC: National Park Service, U.S. Department of the Interior, 2009).

23   *National NAGPRA Program FY 2010 Final Report.* The Culturally Unidentifiable database lists 123,927 with 4,916 subsequently affiliated and 42,313 in the affiliated database (which should include the 4,916), equaling a total of 161,324 individuals.

24   According to the *National NAGPRA Program FY2010 Final Report*, 40,303 individuals have been published in notices since 1992, which amounts to an average of 2,121 individuals per year. http://www.nps.gov/nagpra/DOCUMENTS/INDEX.htm.

25   According to the *National NAGPRA Program FY2010 Final Report*, there are 121,021 remaining individuals in total. At the current rate of 2,121 individuals published annually, it will take approximately fifty-seven years for all those individuals who have been reported (but not yet published) to be eligible for repatriation or transfer. This number does not include any possible further additions or submissions by museums or federal agencies. http://www.nps.gov/nagpra/DOCUMENTS/INDEX.htm .

26   *Native American Graves Protection and Repatriation Act: After Almost 20 Years, Key Federal Agencies Still Have Not Fully Complied with the Act*, 44.

27   National NAGPRA report statistics, *National NAGPRA Program Midyear Report*, 2011. http://www.cr.nps.gov/nagpra/DOCUMENTS/Reports/NationalNAGPRAMidYear2011final.pdf, at 16.

Chapter 1
The Case for NAGPRA[1]

JACK F. TROPE

Introduction

The Native American Graves Protection and Repatriation Act (NAGPRA) was part of a larger movement to recognize and rectify government actions taking place over centuries that had the goal of destroying Native American religions and cultures. For most of American history, the United States government actively discouraged and even outlawed the exercise of traditional Indian cultures and religions. For instance, from the 1890s until the 1930s, the federal government outlawed the sun dance, similar dances and religious ceremonies, and the practices of medicine men.[2] It was not until the 1970s that Congress enacted the American Indian Religious Freedom Act (AIRFA).[3] Although not enforceable in court, AIRFA established a federal policy to protect and preserve the right of Native Americans to believe, express, and exercise their traditional religions, including access to sites, use and possession of sacred objects, and the freedom to worship through ceremonials and traditional rites.[4]

In the late 1980s and early 1990s, an effort was made by Indian tribes and national Indian organizations, with the support of traditional practitioners, to put teeth into this policy—to protect sacred sites and burial sites and the use of ceremonial objects such as eagle feathers, and to repatriate human remains, as well as funerary and sacred objects. In 1988, a broad-based national American Indian Religious Freedom Coalition (which became known as the AIRFA Coalition) was formed by the Association on American Indian Affairs (AAIA), Native American Rights Fund (NARF), and National Congress of American Indians (NCAI). Responding to the case of *Lyng v. Northwest Indian Cemetery Protective Association*,[5] in which the United States Supreme Court interpreted the First Amendment to the Constitution in a manner that essentially precluded Native religious practitioners from using the First Amendment to protect their sacred sites, the Coalition ultimately included numerous Indian tribes, Indian organizations, and non-Native organizations, including human rights, environmental, and religious organizations.[6]

At that time, I was a staff attorney with AAIA and worked closely with other tribal advocates and Congressional staff on this broad range of legislative issues, including what ultimately became NAGPRA. Simultaneously, I was working at the grass roots level with traditional tribal leaders to protect sacred sites from destructive development. Ever since, I have had the continued privilege of working on these profoundly important issues critical to the well-being of tribal communities and the continuation of tribal cultures.

Although the impetus for the creation of the AIRFA Coalition had been the *Lyng* case, laws mandating repatriation became the initial focus of the coalition. During 1989 and 1990, a concerted national effort to enact such laws took place. The result was the passage of NAGPRA and the repatriation provisions applicable to the Smithsonian in the National Museum of the American Indian Act (NMAI Act or Museum Act),[7] probably the most significant accomplishments that arose as a result of the efforts of this coalition.[8]

Historical background

Respect for the dead is a value shared by almost all cultures. It is an integral part of the philosophical and legal structure of the United States, just as it is throughout most of the world. As noted by one analyst: "[American cases] all agree in principle: The normal treatment of a corpse, once it is decently buried, is to let it lie . . . [No] system of jurisprudence permits exhumation for less than what are considered weighty, and sometimes compelling reasons."[9]

These principles are reflected in the laws of all fifty states and the District of Columbia in statutes that regulate cemeteries, prohibit grave robbing, and ensure the proper treatment of human remains. Many state laws seek to ensure that all persons are entitled to a decent burial, regardless of their economic or social status.[10] In addition, judicially created common law protects the sanctity of the dead.[11] Disinterment is allowed only in the most unusual circumstances and under strict conditions set by the courts.[12]

Unfortunately, this legal structure failed to protect the grave sites and human remains of Native peoples in this country, yet another aspect of historical discrimination against Native Americans. State laws did not protect unmarked Native graves like they protected marked graves.[13] The laws also did not recognize that an entire tribe may maintain a strong cultural connection with its ancestors; instead, the right to protect human remains and grave sites under most laws was limited to the immediate next of kin. The common law failed to take into account unique indigenous burial practices such as scaffold, canoe, or tree burials.[14] The law also failed to take into account that many tribes were removed from their historic homelands, leaving behind (involuntarily) their burial grounds.

For example, in *Wana the Bear v. Community Construction, Inc.,* the court held that a historic Indian cemetery was not a "cemetery" within the meaning of state cemetery protection laws.[15] In *State v. Glass,* the court held that older human skeletal remains were not considered "human" for purposes of an Ohio grave robbing statute.[16] In *Carter v. City of Zanesville,* the court held that a cemetery may be considered "abandoned" when no further burials are taking place—a holding that ensured that the burial places of relocated Indian tribes would not be protected.[17]

The results of these policies and the inadequacy of the legal system have been devastating to Native communities. Inventories prepared under NAGPRA have identified more than 180,000 human remains in the possession of museums and federal agencies[18] (and under the Museum Act, another 18,000 have been inventoried by the Smithsonian Institution).[19] Almost every Indian tribe has had their dead transported into collections held by well-known institutions all across the country.

The law also failed to protect against the transfer of huge quantities of cultural property—sacred objects and cultural patrimony. One historian explained this phenomenon:

> During the half-century or so after 1875, a staggering quantity of material, both secular and sacred—from spindle whorls to soul-catchers— left the hands of their native creators and users for the private and public collections of the European world. The scramble . . . was pursued sometimes with respect, occasionally with rapacity, often with avarice. By the time it ended there was more Kwakiutal material in Milwaukee than in Mamalillikulla, more Salish pieces in Cambridge than in Comox. The City of Washington contained more Northwest Coast material than the state of Washington and New York City probably housed more British Columbia material than British Columbia itself. . . . In retrospect it is clear that the goods flowed irrevocably from Native hands to Euro-American ones until little was left in possession of the people who had invented, made, and used them.[20]

The sordid history of how these human remains, funerary objects, and other cultural items were obtained has been documented in recent studies. One such study, the Bieder Report, was presented to Congress as an appendix to testimony submitted by the Association on American Indian Affairs at a Senate Select Committee on Indian Affairs hearing on NAGPRA.[21] It is worth summarizing some of the findings of that report.

Dr. Bieder found that there were two primary reasons that Native American human remains were collected by Euro-Americans. One purpose was to advance certain scientific theories about the nature of the different races, particularly through the now thoroughly discredited "science" of phrenology (the study of skulls).[22]

Dr. Samuel Morton, often thought of as the founder of American physical anthropology, authored *Crania Americana* in 1839, which analyzed the cranial capacity of the skulls of different races. He and like-minded scientists viewed this as a reflection of intelligence. Their conclusions were summarized by one phrenologist as follows, "The general size [of the Indian heads] is greatly inferior to that of the average European head; indicating inferiority in natural mental power."[23] In order to obtain these skulls, Morton and others actively sought assistance from "collectors" and this activity took place even though the objections of Native peoples were well known.[24]

Later, the search for Indian body parts became official federal policy with the Surgeon General's Order of 1867. The policy directed army personnel to procure Indian crania and other body parts for the Army Medical Museum, "the chief purpose ... in forming this collection is to aid in the progress of anthropological science by obtaining measurements of a large number of skulls of aboriginal races of North America."[25] These theories provided "scientific support" for the manifest destiny policies followed by the United States during the nineteenth century—policies that led to the relocation of Indian tribes and taking of tribal lands, and the aggressive policies that decimated tribal populations and suppressed tribal cultures and religions.

Bieder also documented that a second reason for the acquisition of Native human remains and cultural items was a competition between museums as to which could collect the most Indian bodies and "artifacts." These museums included many of the most prominent museums in the United States, including the Field Museum of Natural History in Chicago, the American Museum of Natural History in New York, and the Smithsonian Institution.[26]

The means for obtaining bodies and grave goods were often unethical and unsavory. The Bieder Report documents the stripping of whole villages of both artifacts and human remains in the dead of night with the contents carted off to museums. These actions were often taken with full knowledge that Indian people objected to such actions, and those seeking to "excavate or seize" Indian remains were forced to resort to surreptitious means to obtain them, because they knew that the affected Indian people would resist the desecration of their burial sites.[27] One 1892 account of a rainy-night grave robbing of fifteen Blackfeet Indian graves is typical of what took place:

> [T]he burial place is in plain sight of many Indian houses and very near frequent roads. I had to visit the country at night when not even the dogs were stirring ... after securing one [skull] I had to pass the Indian sentry at the stockade gate which I never attempted with more than one [skull], for fear of detection. .... On one occasion I was followed by an Indian who did not comprehend my movements, and I made a

circuitous route away from the place intended and threw him off his suspicions. On stormy nights—rain, snow or wind and bitter cold, I think I was never observed going or coming, by either Indians or dogs, but on pleasant nights—I was always seen but of course no one knew what I had in my coat . . . the greatest fear I had was that some Indian would miss the heads, see my tracks and ambush me, but they didn't.[28]

As Franz Boas, the famous American anthropologist, observed in the 1880s, "It is most unpleasant work to steal bones from graves, but what is the use, someone has to do it."[29]

Jerry Flute, a former tribal chairman of the Sisseton Wahpeton Sioux Tribe and a traditional practitioner of Dakota culture and religion, testified (as Assistant Director of the Association on American Indian Affairs) about the Bieder Report at the Senate hearing. In his words, "This is a very difficult report for an Indian to read . . . It's a very sad account of the atrocities. It's a shameful account of how museums—some of the museums who were here today—actually competed with each other and hired people to rob graves of Native American people."[30]

Some other examples of the failure of "collectors" to respect the basic humanity of American Indians included the boiling of bodies of recently deceased Indians by Army physicians and others to secure "fresh" skulls for museums[31] and the retention of the bodies of four Inuit men and one Inuit girl who died in New York City in the early part of this century by the American Museum of Natural History. In the latter case, not only were the bodies not properly buried, but a mock funeral was held to convince the surviving son of one of the men that proper funeral rituals were being observed and that his father had been buried in accordance with Inuit custom.[32]

These activities continued well into the twentieth century. For example, in the late 1930s, scientists associated with the Smithsonian Institution descended upon Larsen Bay on Kodiak Island in Alaska and dug up a Native graveyard with more than 400 bodies and skeletons.[33]

In fact, beginning in 1906, federal law defined dead Indians interred on federal lands as "archaeological resources" and, contrary to long-standing common law principles, converted these dead persons into "federal property."[34] Over the years, thousands of Indian dead were classified as "archaeological resources" and exhumed as "federal property."[35] These excavations rarely, if ever, involved the descendant communities in the permit decisions. When tribes did protest, they found the courts were not available to them as a means to seek basic human rights or property rights.

An example of how the American court system failed to protect basic tribal property rights can be seen in the case of the Haudenosaunee (Iroquois) Wampum belts. Wampum belts served the function of a written language for the Iroquois. By means of belts of colored beads, different events and ideas could be communicated through the wampum belt. Elders familiar with the language of the wampum belts could read these belts and pass along the history, beliefs, and laws of the tribe from one generation to the next. In the late nineteenth century, some wampum belts were sold to a United States government official by an individual who had no right to transfer the belts under tribal law since they were the property of the tribe. A court case was brought in 1896; the tribe sought to have the wampum belts returned based upon conventional theories of property law, conversion, and removal without permission. The case was unsuccessful. The Haudenosaunee never gave up, however. The dispute was ultimately resolved in 1986, not by court action, but by the museum reviewing its own actions in receiving and holding the belts and coming to an agreement after consultation with the tribes.[36]

What led to NAGPRA: legislative history

In 1986, some Northern Cheyenne representatives discovered that almost 18,500 human remains were warehoused in the Smithsonian Institution.[37] This discovery helped serve as a catalyst for a national effort by Indian tribes and organizations to obtain legislation to repatriate human remains and cultural items to Indian tribes and descendants of the deceased.

Initial proposals provided for the creation of a Native American Museum Claims Commission, which was intended to provide a mechanism to resolve disputes between museums and Native Americans regarding the repatriation of "skeletal remains, cultural artifacts, and other items of religious or cultural significance."[38]

However, in the 101st Congress, this approach was abandoned in favor of legislation that would directly require the repatriation of human remains and cultural artifacts, as well as the protection of burial sites. This is the approach that was ultimately adopted by Congress when it enacted NAGPRA.

There were a few key events that preceded the enactment of NAGPRA. The first event was the enactment of the National Museum of the American Indian Act[39] (Museum Act) in November 1989. The Museum Act created a National Museum of the American Indian within the Smithsonian Institution.[40] The first draft of the Museum Act in 1987 had included an inventory and repatriation requirement.[41] However, in 1989 as the act was gaining momentum, the bill had been watered down to require only a study about repatriation.[42] At that time, there was a discussion within the Indian community about whether to insist upon stronger repatriation provisions in the Museum Act. Jerry Flute, then acting Director of the Association on American Indian Affairs, was a particularly strong advocate for this position. Based upon his discussion with traditional people, he believed that repatriation was of the utmost importance to Indian country, even more important than the creation of the museum.[43] His advocacy on this issue convinced those who were fearful that a push for a stronger repatriation provision might jeopardize the Museum Act. Indian organizations (including the three founding members of the AIRFA Coalition: AAIA, NARF, and NCAI) and Indian tribes spearheading the effort decided to take a strong position in favor of repatriation and were prepared to oppose the bill if it did not provide for repatriation. At a House hearing on the proposed Museum Act, Flute testified, "[W]here the Smithsonian takes a position that there are few and maybe a small group of people raising this issue, we feel that they are totally out of touch as to what Indian people are actually feeling and how they view the issue of skeletal remains."[44] Then-Executive Director of the National Congress of American Indians Suzan Harjo stated that while NCAI supported the establishment of the museum, "We are not here to be the instruments of our own oppression." She added, "The establishment of the National Museum of the American Indian is the stuff of dreams, but the existence of a beetle room [where flesh-eating beetles "clean" skeletons before they are stored in cardboard boxes] in box upon box of skeletal remains of our people is the stuff of nightmares."[45] In his written testimony, another witness on the same panel, NARF attorney Walter Echo-Hawk, stated, "There are many Trails of Tears and one of those trails leads directly to the doors of the Smithsonian Institution." [46]

Ultimately, the Smithsonian Institution came to an agreement with Indian leaders and a stronger repatriation provision was included.[47] The Museum Act required the Smithsonian, in consultation with Indian tribes and traditional Indian religious leaders, to inventory human remains and funerary objects in its possession or control. The goal of the inventory was to identify the origins of such remains based upon the best available scientific and historical documentation.[48] If the tribal origin of remains or objects were identified by a preponderance of the evidence, the Smithsonian was required to notify the Indian tribe,[49] and upon request of a lineal descendant or culturally affiliated tribe, human remains and funerary objects associated with those remains were required to be returned.[50]

The Museum Act was considered an "important first step" in "rectifying injustices done to Indian people over the years" and ensuring "that one day their ancestors will finally be given the final resting place that they so deserve."[51] In his statement during debate, Senator John McCain specifically noted that this bill "sends a clear signal to those in the museum community who have dismissed repatriation as a transitory issue that they would be wise to carefully consider the bills [pertaining to museums and federal agencies other than the Smithsonian] currently before the Congress."[52] The Museum Act was an important precedent for NAGPRA.[53]

The second key event that took place preceding the enactment of NAGPRA was a yearlong dialogue at the Heard Museum in Arizona, which included museum representatives, scientists and Native Americans. In early 1990, the *Report of the Panel for a National Dialogue on Museum/Native American Relations* ("Panel") was issued. The major conclusions of the Panel were as follows:

> The Panel found that the process for determining the appropriate disposition and treatment of Native American human remains, funerary objects, sacred objects and objects of cultural patrimony should be governed by respect for Native human rights . . . The Panel report indicated the need for federal legislation to implement the recommendations of the Panel. The Panel also recommended the development of judicially enforceable standards for repatriation of Native American remains and objects . . . Additional recommendations of the Panel included requiring regular consultation and dialogue between Indian tribes and museums; providing Indian tribes with access to information regarding remains and objects in museum collections; providing that Indian tribes should have the right to determine the appropriate disposition of remains and funerary objects and that reasonable accommodations should be made to allow valid and respectful scientific use of materials when it is compatible with tribal religious and cultural practices.[54]

The legislative history indicates clearly that the Panel report "provided a framework" for NAGPRA.[55]

NAGPRA legislative history: the process

NAGPRA was enacted after years of legislative efforts by tribal representatives and their supporters,[56] whose advocacy was based upon the widely held belief in tribal communities that the graves of tribal ancestors should not be disturbed and, in cases where they have been disturbed, the human remains and funerary objects should be returned to descendants for reburial or other culturally prescribed treatment. Thus, the basic purposes of the statute were to declare that tribes and individual lineal descendants have rights regarding the remains of their ancestors and certain kinds of cultural property, and to establish procedures for vindication of these rights. Achieving this goal was not easy. Many members of Congress started with the presumption that Native human remains and cultural items were collectibles and objects of study, and museums were the appropriate custodians for these objects. The right of scientists to possess and study these objects was often taken for granted.

Tribal people needed to reframe the debate. They had to educate Congress about their religious and cultural beliefs and their relationship with their ancestors. As part of this process, sympathetic articles were generated in the mainstream press, which highlighted the plunder of items from grave sites and sometimes asked readers how they would feel if their grandmother had been dug up for scientific study without their consent.[57]

The final legislative product went through many iterations, partly because of the refinement of the ideas and concepts that were incorporated into the legislation, and partly because of negotiations that took place between tribal representatives and those of the scientific and museum communities.

The bill that was ultimately enacted never lost its central focus: the need to provide redress to Native Americans whose human rights had been ignored. But it is also true that the enacted bill reflected a compromise forged by representatives of the museum, scientific, and Indian communities.[58] In negotiating, the primary objective of the tribal representatives was to ensure that the provisions dealing with human remains and associated funerary objects remained as strong as possible, since it was the possession of tribal ancestors by museums and federal agencies that was the primary catalyst for the tribal push for repatriation legislation. At the same time, those of us involved believed that compromises were necessary to get the legislation enacted. Indeed, the passage of NAGPRA was in doubt until the very end of the process.

Although by 1990 there was considerable momentum building in favor of a repatriation bill, there were some influential people in the museum and scientific communities who were very much opposed to a bill, and it is axiomatic that it is far easier to block a bill than to pass one. Two influential national museum and scientific organizations, the Society for American Archaeology (SAA) and American Association of Museums (AAM), were willing to negotiate with tribal representatives in response to the expressed intent of key senators to pass repatriation legislation.[59] In part, they were fearful of legislation that might pass without their input; but it was also the case that some of the individuals leading those organizations during this time period had modified their views about repatriation as a result of the "education" they had received from Native Americans. Thus, there was a narrow window of opportunity to negotiate modest changes to build consensus behind the bill and maximize its chances for passage. In order to obtain the support of the SAA, changes were made to the definition of "cultural affiliation" and to the provision addressing the ownership and control provisions dealing with grave sites. In order to gain the support of AAM, the definitions of "associated" and "unassociated funerary objects" and "sacred objects" were changed; the inventory requirement was modified and partially replaced by a summary requirement; the standard for repatriating unassociated funerary objects, sacred objects, and cultural patrimony was modified; and sections were added concerning competing claims and the federal-tribal trust relationship, as well as a museum "hold harmless" clause. (More details about some of these changes are included later in this chapter when specific NAGPRA sections are discussed.)

As it was, NAGPRA was passed on the last day of the 2nd Session of the 101st Congress. Adjournment had been scheduled two or three weeks earlier, but had been postponed due to an unrelated tax and budget dispute between President George H.W. Bush and Congress. If not for this unexpected extension of the legislative session, NAGPRA would not have passed in the 101st Congress.[60]

No one knows for sure what would have happened if the process had started over in the 102nd Congress, but the result may very well have been a weaker NAGPRA. In fact, shortly before NAGPRA passed, the American Museum of Natural History in New York and a few other museums suddenly mobilized and were working to defeat the bill, even though AAM had agreed to support NAGPRA. This is an indication that if Congress had not passed the bill in the 101st Congress, the opposition forces might have better organized themselves and pushed back more strongly against the bill in the next Congress. It is from this perspective that the legislative process that took place (as well as some of the compromises reflected in NAGPRA) should be understood.

It should also be noted that, for a number of years, the "preferred" approach by legislators was to establish a case-by-case process for negotiating the return of human remains and cultural items. Thus, the evolution of this earlier approach to legislation *mandating* repatriation under certain circumstances was a big step forward, even with the compromises that were made as part of the process.

NAGPRA legislative intent: an overview

On November 16, 1990, the Native American Graves Protection and Repatriation Act was signed into law.[61] NAGPRA provides various repatriation, ownership, and control rights over human remains and cultural items to descendants of a deceased Indian individual and to Indian tribes and Native Hawaiian organizations.

NAGPRA is, first and foremost, human rights legislation. It is designed to address the "flagrant violat[ion]" of the "civil rights of America's first citizens."[62] When NAGPRA was passed by the Senate, Senator Daniel Inouye stated that:

> When the Army Surgeon General ordered the collection of Indian osteological remains during the second half of the 19th century, his demands were met not only by Army medical personnel, but by collectors who made money from selling Indian skulls to the Army Medical Museum. The desires of Indians to bury their dead were ignored . . . When human remains are displayed in museums or historical societies, it is never the bones of white soldiers or the first European settlers that came to this continent that are lying in glass cases. It is Indian remains. The message that this sends to the world is that Indians are culturally

and physically different from and inferior to non-Indians. This is racism. In light of the important role that death and burial rites play in
native American cultures, it is all the more offensive that the civil rights
of America's first citizens have been so flagrantly violated for the past
century. Even today, when supposedly great strides have been made to
recognize the rights of Indians to recover the skeletal remains of their
ancestors and to repossess items of sacred value or cultural patrimony,
the wishes of native Americans are often ignored by the scientific community . . . [and] met with resistance from museums . . . [T]he bill
before us is not about the validity of museums or the value of scientific
inquiry. Rather, it is about human rights . . . For museums that have
dealt honestly and in good faith with native Americans, this legislation
will have little effect. For museums and institutions which have consistently ignored the requests of native Americans, this legislation will
give native Americans greater ability to negotiate.[63]

NAGPRA was designed to create a process that would reflect both the needs
of museums as repositories of the nation's cultural heritage and the rights of Indian
people. Congress believed that NAGPRA would "encourage a continuing dialogue
between museums and Indian tribes and Native Hawaiian organizations and . . .
promote greater understanding between the groups."[64]

Notwithstanding the accommodations made to scientific and museum interests,
however, it is clear that the central purpose of NAGPRA—in fact, in the end, the
only reason that it exists—was to rectify centuries of discrimination against Native
Americans. As Congress stated, NAGPRA was intended to "establish a process that
provides the dignity and respect that our Nation's first citizens deserve."[65] Congress
viewed NAGPRA as part of its trust responsibility to Indian tribes and people, specifically stating that it "reflects the unique relationship between the federal government and Indian tribes and Native Hawaiian organizations."[66] As such, the canons
of statutory construction applicable to Indian legislation apply here and warrant the
interpretation of any ambiguities in favor of Indian people,[67] a canon of construction
similar to that applicable to other types of remedial civil rights legislation.[68]

NAGPRA applies in three different contexts: repatriation of items from the
collections of federal agencies and museums to tribes and to lineal descendants
where known,[69] protection of burial sites and "cultural items" located on federal
lands and "tribal lands,"[70] and trafficking in Native American human remains and
cultural items.[71] The primary features of the Native American Graves Protection and
Repatriation Act of 1990 are summarized in the remainder of this article in order
to show the myriad issues that had to be resolved or defined for its creation and to

provide a fuller context for some of the chapters that follow. Of note, although there are many parts of NAGPRA whose interpretation is clear, there are still issues that arise, and it cannot be said that all of the issues surrounding NAGPRA's implementation have been settled.

The provisions of NAGPRA

Entities that have rights and responsibilities under NAGPRA. Lineal descendants of a deceased Native individual, Indian tribes, and Native Hawaiian organizations have rights under NAGPRA. "Lineal descendants" can be traced not only through the common law system used by federal and state courts, but "by means of the traditional kinship system of the appropriate Indian tribe or Native Hawaiian organization."[72] "Indian tribe" is defined to mean a tribe that is recognized by the federal government.[73] The Review Committee has approved voluntary repatriations to non-federally recognized tribes by federal agencies and museums, however.[74] Recently adopted regulations permit repatriations to be made to such groups, but do not require them.[75] These dispositions may take place only if, after consultation, no federally recognized tribe that could make a claim objects and the Secretary of the Interior or their designee so recommends.[76]

Although an overall reading of the law would suggest that any culturally distinct tribal entity with the authority to decide traditional cultural issues should be able to make a claim under NAGPRA, the commentary to the implementing regulations indicates that bands, tribes, and other sub-groups should make NAGPRA claims through an Indian tribe, rather than directly.[77] Tribes have banded together and established organizations to act collectively on their behalf.[78] Indeed, many of the claims that have been filed under NAGPRA have been joint tribal claims.[79]

"Native Hawaiian organization" is defined as an organization which (1) serves and represents the interests of Native Hawaiians; (2) has a primary purpose of providing services to Native Hawaiians; and (3) has expertise in Native Hawaiian affairs. The Office of Hawaiian Affairs and Hui Malama I Na Kupuna O Hawai'i Nei are specifically included as Native Hawaiian organizations.[80]

NAGPRA's repatriation, inventory and summary requirements are obligatory for federal agencies (except for the Smithsonian Institution, which is the subject of a separate law, the Museum Act, as previously discussed[81]) and all museums receiving federal funds, provided that they possess or control Native American cultural items.[82] This would include a museum that is part of a larger unit that has received federal funds, such as state and local governments, educational and other institutions.[83] Federal agencies and Indian tribes also have responsibilities in regard to sites that contain human remains and Native cultural items that are located on federal and tribal land.

Items covered by NAGPRA. NAGPRA covers Native cultural items. Cultural items are defined as human remains, funerary objects, sacred objects, and cultural patrimony.

Human remains are not defined in NAGPRA, but the term has been interpreted by the regulations to include bones, teeth, hair, ashes, and preserved soft tissue.[84] The regulations make clear that body items that were freely given or naturally shed by an individual (e.g., hair made into ropes) are not considered to be human remains.[85] To date, human remains that have been repatriated pursuant to NAGPRA include "complete and partial skeletons, isolated bones, teeth, scalps, and ashes."[86]

Funerary objects are "objects that, as part of the death rite or ceremony of a culture, are reasonably believed to have been placed with individual human remains either at the time of death or later . . . "[87] The regulations make clear that objects placed near human remains as part of a death rite or ceremony are covered by NAGPRA as funerary objects, in addition to those placed with human remains, which is the explicit statutory language. This provision reflects the variances in tribal funerary practices.

There are two categories of funerary objects: associated and unassociated. "Associated funerary objects" includes two categories of objects: (1) Objects "reasonably believed to have been placed with individual human remains either at the time of death or later . . . as part of a death rite or ceremony" where both the human remains and objects are presently in the possession or control of a federal agency or museum. The remains and objects need not be in the possession or control of the same agency or museum, only in the possession or control of a museum or agency so that a connection between the objects and remains is possible; and (2) Objects "exclusively made for burial purposes or to contain human remains."[88] The "possession or control" language indicates congressional intent to include objects consigned to individuals or museums not covered under NAGPRA, if a federal agency or museum covered by NAGPRA is responsible for the ultimate disposition of those objects.[89]

"Unassociated funerary objects" are those funerary objects which were found with human remains where (1) the objects can be related to specific individuals, families, or known human remains or to a specific burial site of a culturally affiliated individual; and (2) the human remains are not presently in the possession or control of a federal agency or museum.[90]

Funerary objects that have been repatriated to date include beads, pottery, tools, trade silver, weapons, and clothing.[91]

"Sacred objects" are those objects that are (1) ceremonial in nature, and (2) needed by traditional Native American religious leaders for the present day practice of traditional Native American religions.[92] This includes both the use of the objects in ceremonies currently conducted by traditional practitioners and instances where the objects are needed to renew ceremonies that are part of a traditional religion.[93] The operative part of the definition is that there must be "present day adherents" that need the items.[94] Congress recognized that "the practice of some ceremonies has been interrupted because of government coercion, adverse societal conditions, or the loss of objects through means beyond the control of the tribe at the time."[95] Although part of the purpose of the definition was to reassure museums that not everything in their collections would be considered "sacred," at the same time the definition was a groundbreaking definition from a tribal perspective. It recognized that the ultimate determination of continuing sacredness must be made by the Native American religious leaders themselves; they must determine the current ceremonial need for the object. Thus, the term "sacred" is not defined explicitly in the legislative definition. Rather the definition will vary in accordance with the traditions of the tribe or community.[96] The regulations define "traditional religious leader" as a person "recognized by members of an Indian tribe or Native Hawaiian organization," as an individual who is "responsible for performing cultural duties relating to the ceremonial or religious traditions of that Indian tribe or Native Hawaiian organization," or who exercises "a leadership role in an Indian tribe or Native Hawaiian organization based on the tribe or organization's cultural, ceremonial, or religious practices."[97] Sacred objects that have been repatriated to date include "medicine bundles, prayer sticks, pipes, effigies and fetishes, basketry, rattles, and a birch bark scroll."[98]

"Cultural patrimony" are those objects that have "ongoing historical, traditional, or cultural importance central to the Native American group or culture itself," and were owned by the tribe, or a subgroup thereof such as a clan or band, and could not be sold or given away by an individual.[99] The object must have been considered inalienable by the Native American group when the object was separated from such group; thus, tribal law or custom would be determinative of the legal question of alienability at the time that the item was transferred.[100] Examples given by Congress of "cultural patrimony" were the Zuni war gods and the Wampum belts of the Haudenosaunee.[101] Items of cultural patrimony repatriated under NAGPRA to date include "a wolf head headdress, clan hat, several medicine bundles, and ceremonial masks."[102]

Responsibilities of museums and federal agencies for items in their possession or control. When NAGPRA was enacted in 1990, it required museums and federal agencies to complete an item-by-item inventory of human remains and associated funerary objects[103] in consultation with Native American governmental and traditional leaders.[104] As part of the inventory, the museum or agency was required to identify the geographical and cultural affiliation of each item, to the extent possible, based upon information within its possession.[105] This provision did not require museums to conduct "exhaustive studies and additional scientific research to conclusively determine" cultural affiliation.[106] NAGPRA was not to "be construed to be an authorization for the initiation of new scientific studies of such remains and associated funerary objects or other means of acquiring or preserving additional scientific information from such remains and objects."[107] Rather, NAGPRA's intent was merely to require a good faith effort to identify cultural affiliation based upon presently available evidence.[108]

Final notice was required within six months after the completion of the inventory to all tribes that were reasonably believed to be culturally affiliated with human remains or associated funerary objects in the possession or control of the museum or agency.[109] The notice had to include information about the circumstances surrounding the acquisition of each identified item and information about cultural affiliation.[110] NAGPRA broadly intended that all potential tribal claimants, including Native Hawaiian organizations, receive notice. A tribe or Native Hawaiian organization that received, or should have received, notice could request additional background information from the museum or agency relevant to the "geographical origin, cultural affiliation, and basic facts surrounding [the item's] acquisition and accession."[111] In addition, museums were required to make the inventory and identification process available to the NAGPRA Review Committee for monitoring and review.[112]

Inventories have been prepared pursuant to the statutory mandate, but even though the deadline for completing inventories has long passed, there has not yet been full compliance with the inventory requirement.[113]

NAGPRA also required that federal agencies and museums summarize their collections of unassociated funerary objects, sacred objects and items of cultural patrimony. The summary was in lieu of an object-by-object inventory and required the museum or agency to "describe the scope of the collection, kinds of objects included, reference to geographical location, means and period of acquisition and cultural affiliation, where readily ascertainable."[114] A consultation process with Native American governmental and traditional leaders was required.[115] Upon request, all tribes and Native Hawaiian organizations were entitled to obtain data pertaining to geographical origin, cultural affiliation and acquisition and accession of these objects.[116]

This was one of the major concessions made to museum interests during negotiations. The museums believed that the costs of an item-by-item inventory of all objects defined under the act would be exorbitant. Tribal representatives agreed to limit the inventory requirement to human remains and associated funerary objects, and replace it with preparation of a summary for other items covered by NAGPRA.

Repatriation of human remains and associated funerary objects. NAGPRA requires federal agencies and museums to return human remains and associated funerary objects as quickly as possible (1) upon request of a direct descendant of the deceased, or (2) upon request of an Indian tribe or Native Hawaiian organization where the tribe or organization has a "cultural affiliation" with the human remains and associated funerary objects.[117]

"Cultural affiliation" is a key term in NAGPRA. It is defined as "a relationship of shared group identity which can be reasonably traced historically or prehistorically between a present day Indian tribe or Native Hawaiian organization and an identifiable earlier group."[118] The House committee explained that this requirement "is intended to ensure that the claimant has a reasonable connection with the materials."[119] Congress recognized, however, that "it may be extremely difficult, in many instances, for claimants to trace an item from modern Indian tribes to prehistoric remains without some reasonable gaps in the historic or prehistoric record. In such instances, a finding of cultural affiliation should be based upon an overall evaluation of the totality of the circumstances and evidence pertaining to the connection between the claimant and the material being claimed and should not be precluded solely because of some gaps in the record."[120]

Thus, in order for "cultural affiliation" to be established, it must be determined that (1) it is likely that the remains are those of a member of a particular tribe or group which existed at the time the deceased lived; and (2) there is a reasonable connection ("shared group identity") between the present-day tribe or organization making the request and the earlier tribe or group based upon the totality of the circumstances and evidence.[121] A finding of cultural affiliation is appropriate when the evidence shows it is more likely than not that there is an affiliation.[122] Cultural affiliation need not be established with scientific certainty.[123]

Cultural affiliation can be determined by a museum or federal agency through the inventory process; the determination of cultural affiliation in an inventory should be based upon information within the current possession of the museum or agency.[124] Cultural affiliation may also be proven by a tribe or Native Hawaiian organization. Many types of evidence can be used to prove cultural affiliation, including "geographical, kinship, biological, archaeological, anthropological, linguistic, folkloric, oral traditional, historical, or other relevant information or expert opinion."[125] Thus, traditional knowledge is considered as relevant to this determination as scientific knowledge. Factors that may be relevant to a determination of cultural affiliation include the cultural characteristics and biological distinctiveness of, and the production and distribution of, material items by the earlier group and current day tribe.[126]

The concept of a "shared group identity" was developed in negotiations with the Society for American Archaeology (SAA). It was a middle course between the Senate bill (S. 1980), which would have required a showing of a "continuity" of group identity, and the House bill (H.R. 5237), which would have created a presumption of cultural affiliation for all items that had been collected from tribal land or aboriginal territory.

In general, repatriation is not to be delayed pending additional scientific re-search.[127] The only exception is in those circumstances where the item is "indispens-able for completion of a specific scientific study, the outcome of which would be of major benefit to the United States."[128] If this exception applies, the items must be returned within ninety days after the completion of the study.[129] There is no prohi-bition, however, against voluntary agreements between claimants and agencies or museums that would permit additional studies or other arrangements in regard to cultural items.[130]

The other exception to the requirement that human remains and associated funerary objects be "expeditiously returned" after cultural affiliation has been deter-mined is a situation where multiple requests for a cultural item are made and the federal agency or museum "cannot clearly determine which requesting party is the most appropriate claimant."[131] In such a case, the federal agency or museum may retain the item until the parties agree upon disposition (with the Review Committee available for a mediating role) or the dispute is resolved by a court of competent jurisdiction.[132]

As for human remains and associated funerary objects whose cultural affilia-tion cannot be determined, NAGPRA provides that the statutorily created Review Committee[133] compile an inventory of culturally unidentifiable human remains and recommend "specific actions for developing a process for disposition of such remains."[134] The Review Committee's recommendations are to be made "in consulta-tion with Indian tribes and Native Hawaiian organizations and appropriate scientific and museum groups."[135] This issue was referred to the Review Committee because there was "general disagreement on the proper disposition of such unidentifiable remains. Some believe that they should be left solely to science while others contend that, since they are unidentifiable, they would be of little use to science and should be buried and laid to rest."[136]

The Secretary of the Interior recently issued regulations based upon the recom-mendations of the Review Committee.[137] A museum or federal agency must offer to return any culturally unidentifiable human remains in its possession that were originally removed from land that is currently tribal land or the aboriginal land of a particular tribe.[138] Before these remains are returned, there must be a consultation process involving all such tribes, which must start within ninety days of a request for repatriation by a tribe or an offer by the museum or agency to return culturally un-identifiable human remains.[139] Aboriginal land includes lands recognized by a final judgment of the Indian Claims Commission or the United States Court of Claims, a treaty, act of Congress, or executive order.[140] (Most land in the United States has been recognized as aboriginal land through one of these legal mechanisms.) In some cases, the consultation may result in a finding of cultural affiliation. Where this does not happen, it is anticipated that tribes will agree upon a disposition in most cases. If tribes cannot agree, the regulations provide that claims from a tribe from whose tribal land the remains were removed would have the first priority, followed by claims from tribes that are aboriginal to the area.[141] This is similar to the way in which the statute treats human remains discovered and unearthed on tribal or federal land after 1990.

The regulations acknowledge that some of the so-called "culturally unidentifiable remains" may be culturally affiliated with tribes not recognized by the federal government. The regulations permit repatriations to be made to such groups, but do not require them.[142] The regulations also permit museum and federal agencies to rebury the human remains under state or other law if no tribe agrees to accept control.[143] Both of these dispositions may take place only if, after consultation, no federally recognized tribe that could make a claim objects and the Secretary of the Interior or his designee so recommends.[144] The regulations also recommend, but do not require, repatriation of culturally unidentifiable associated funerary objects on the same basis as human remains.[145]

Repatriation of unassociated funerary objects, sacred objects, and cultural patrimony. The act requires museums and federal agencies to repatriate unassociated funerary objects, sacred objects, and cultural patrimony pursuant to a four-step process.

First, the claimant must show that the item claimed is an unassociated funerary object, sacred object, or item of cultural patrimony.[146] Once it has been shown that the item meets one of these definitions, either the cultural affiliation must be determined[147] or, in the case of sacred objects and items of cultural patrimony, the requesting tribe or Native Hawaiian organization must show that the object was previously owned or controlled by the tribe, organization, or a member thereof.[148] A direct lineal descendant may also request repatriation of a sacred object.[149] If a tribe or Native Hawaiian organization is making a claim to a sacred object based upon prior ownership or control by a tribal member, as opposed to the tribe, the claimant must show that no identifiable lineal descendants exist or that the lineal descendants have been notified and have failed to make a claim.[150]

The third step in the process requires a claimant to present "evidence which, if standing alone before the introduction of evidence to the contrary, would support a finding that the federal agency or museum did not have the right of possession" of the items.[151] Since the original "transfer" of many of these objects occurred when recordkeeping of such transactions was virtually nonexistent, and because of the near impossibility of proving that a legal document does not exist, evidence, by necessity, may include oral traditional and historical evidence, as well as documentary evidence. In making its *prima facie* case, the claimant is entitled to "records, catalogues, relevant studies or other pertinent data" possessed by the federal agency or museum that relate to "basic facts surrounding acquisition and accession" of the items being claimed.[152]

"Right of possession" means "possession obtained with the voluntary consent of an individual or group that had authority of alienation."[153] This term was intended "to provide a legal framework in which to determine the circumstances by which a museum or agency came into possession of these . . . objects,"[154] and is designed to ensure that the object did not pass out of tribal, or individual Native American, possession without appropriate consent.[155]

Right of possession is based upon the general property law principle that "an individual may only acquire the title to property that is held by the transferor."[156] Authority to alienate would be determined by the law of the governmental entity having jurisdiction over a transaction.[157] In most cases, the initial transfer of the item out of tribal control would most likely be governed by tribal law or custom.[158] The definition does not apply only in the rare instance where its application would result in a Fifth Amendment taking of private property for a public purpose without just compensation.[159] Where there would be a taking within the meaning of the constitutional provision, applicable federal, state, or tribal law would apply.[160] In this rare instance, however, the party asserting a Fifth Amendment taking would first be required to obtain a ruling from the Court of Claims upholding such an assertion, before federal, state, or tribal laws would be used to replace the statutory standard.[161]

If the claimant surmounts these three hurdles, the fourth step places a burden upon the museum or agency to prove that it has a right of possession in regard to the items in question.[162] If the museum or agency cannot prove right of possession, the unassociated funerary object, sacred object, or item of cultural patrimony must be returned unless the scientific study or competing claims exceptions apply.

An example of how the right of possession provisions work in practice was a case involving a sacred Hawaiian spear rest in the possession of a museum owned by the city of Providence, Rhode Island. I represented Hui Malama I Na Kupuna O Hawai'i Nei and the Office of Hawaiian Affairs in this case. Whether the item in question had been obtained with the consent of the Native Hawaiians was an important issue. To meet the initial *prima facie* burden, the Native Hawaiians introduced evidence before the NAGPRA Review Committee about Hawaiian history, specifically information that prior to 1819 it would have been extremely unlikely that an item such as this would have been freely given away. This information was combined with information about the ship captain that was the likely source of the "gift" to the museum's predecessor in interest (the Franklin Society), including the fact that the two ships that he had commissioned were in Hawaii in 1815 and 1818. The Native Hawaiians asserted that this testimony constituted a *prima facie* case that the museum did not have right of possession and that the burden should be shifted to the museum to prove right of possession. The case was ultimately settled and legal findings on right of possession were never made. Nonetheless, this is an instructive example of how these legal provisions can play out in the context of an actual repatriation.

Protection of embedded human remains and cultural items. Burial sites located on federal land and tribal lands are covered by NAGPRA.[163] "Burial site" as defined in the statute includes "any natural or prepared location, whether below, on, or above the surface of the earth, into which as a part of the death rite or ceremony of a culture, individual human remains are deposited."[164] In addition, the regulations clearly recognize rock cairns, funeral pyres, and other customary depositories for human remains which may not fall within the ordinary definition of a grave site.[165]

"Federal land" is defined as non-tribal land controlled or owned by the United States, including lands selected by, but not yet conveyed to, Alaska Native corporations and groups pursuant to the Alaska Native Claims Settlement Act of 1971.[166]

"Tribal land" is defined to include (1) all lands within the exterior boundaries of a reservation, whether or not the land is owned by the tribe, Indian individuals, or non-Indians, (2) all dependent Indian communities, and (3) any lands administered for Native Hawaiians pursuant to the Hawaiian Homes Commission Act of 1920, as amended, and the Hawaii Statehood Bill.[167]

Of note, the commentary to the regulations clarifies that lands held in trust by the United States for an Indian tribe that are not within a reservation boundary or an Indian community are considered to be federal lands.[168] The regulations exclude non-tribal land within reservation boundaries if application of the statute to that land would constitute the unconstitutional taking of land without just compensation.[169]

Whenever a party intends to intentionally excavate a burial site on federal or tribal land, that party must obtain a permit pursuant to the Archaeological Resources Protection Act (ARPA).[170] An ARPA permit may be issued by the agency managing the land upon which a burial site is located or, in the case of tribal lands, by the Bureau of Indian Affairs.[171] In order for a permit to be issued, the applicant must be "qualified" and the undertaking must be designed to advance archaeological knowledge in the public interest. The "resources" remain the property of the United States and the permittee must agree to preserve them in an appropriate institution (except where NAGPRA provides for ownership or control by tribes, Native Hawaiian organization, or lineal descendants). Finally, the activity must not be inconsistent with the applicable land management plan.[172]

If tribal lands are involved, the items may be excavated only after notice to, and consent of, the tribe or Native Hawaiian organization.[173] If federal lands are involved, the items may be excavated only after notice and consultation with the appropriate tribe or Native Hawaiian organization.[174]

Where buried cultural items are inadvertently discovered as part of another activity, such as construction, mining, logging, or agriculture, the person who has discovered the items must temporarily cease activity and notify the responsible federal agency in the case of federal land, or the tribe on whose land the site is located in the case of tribal land.[175] In the case of Alaska Native Claims Settlement Act lands (still owned by the federal government and considered federal land) selected by, but not conveyed to, the Alaska Native corporation or group,[176] that corporation or group is the appropriate organization to be notified.[177] When notice is provided to the federal agency, that agency has the responsibility to promptly notify the appropriate tribe or Native Hawaiian organization.[178] Activity may resume thirty days after the secretary of the appropriate federal department (the Secretary of the Interior if authority has been so delegated) or the Indian tribe or Native Hawaiian organization certifies that notice has been received.[179] The activity that resulted in the inadvertent discovery may also resume prior to the thirty-day period specified in the statute, if a written agreement on a recovery plan is executed by the Indian tribe or Native Hawaiian organization and the federal agency prior to the expiration of the thirty-day period.[180] This requirement must be included in federal leases and permits.[181] Other federal agencies may delegate their responsibilities under this provision to the Secretary of the Interior.[182]

The intent of this provision is to "provide for a process whereby Indian tribes . . . have an opportunity to intervene in development activity on federal or tribal lands in order to safeguard Native American human remains, funerary objects, sacred objects, or objects of cultural patrimony . . . [and to afford] Indian tribes . . . thirty days in which to make a determination as to appropriate disposition for these human remains and objects."[183]

The commentary to the regulations indicates that one goal of NAGPRA is "in situ" preservation, and that this should be considered whenever possible.[184] However, "in situ" preservation of sites is not required by NAGPRA or the regulations, except in the case of intentional excavations on tribal lands where the required tribal consent has not been obtained.[185] This is a significant limitation of NAGPRA, particularly where a site is considered to be an "obstacle" to completion of an unrelated development project. Nonetheless, the ownership and control rules established by the statute, laid out in the following summary, diminish the incentive to excavate such sites simply for the purpose of excavation.

The regulations spell out in detail the notice and consultation that is required in the case of excavations on federal lands. Consultation is meant to be a process involving open discussion and joint deliberation.[186] Written notice must be sent prior to the issuance of any approval or permit, proposing a time and a place for meetings and consultation, and describing the planned activity, its location, the basis for believing that excavation may occur, the government's proposed treatment, and disposition of the objects which are to be excavated.

This notice must be sent to any known lineal descendants, Indian tribes, and Native Hawaiian organizations that are likely to be culturally affiliated with the items at the site, any Indian tribe which aboriginally occupied the area where the activity is taking place, and any Indian tribe or Native Hawaiian organization that may have a cultural relationship with the embedded items.[187] Written notification should be followed by telephone contact if there is no response within fifteen days of the notice.[188]

At the consultation, the federal officials must (1) provide a list of all lineal descendants, Indian tribes, and Native Hawaiian organizations that have been consulted, and information stating that additional documentation on cultural affiliation is available if requested;[189] (2) seek to identify traditional religious leaders (although tribal officials are under no obligation to identify such leaders), lineal descendants, and culturally affiliated Indian tribes and Native Hawaiian organizations, as well as methods for contacting lineal descendants; (3) obtain the name and address of the tribal contact person; (4) obtain recommendations on how the consultation process should be conducted; and (5) identify the kinds of objects that may be considered unassociated funerary objects, sacred objects, and cultural patrimony.[190]

Federal agencies are required to develop written action plans following consultation which include the following information: (1) the kinds of objects considered cultural items, (2) the information that will be used to determine custody and how items will be disposed of in accordance with that determination, (3) the planned care, handling, and treatment (including traditional treatment) of cultural items, (4) the planned archaeological recording and analysis of items and reports to be prepared, and how tribes will be consulted at the time of excavation.[191]

The regulations also encourage the development of comprehensive agreements between Indian tribes, Native Hawaiian organizations, and federal agencies which would "address all federal agency land management activities that could result in the intentional excavation or inadvertent discovery" of NAGPRA items, and establish processes for consultation and determination of custody, treatment, and disposition of such items.[192]

In the case of inadvertent discoveries, the responsible federal official must be immediately notified by telephone in the case of federal land, or the tribal official in the case of tribal land. Telephone notification must be followed by written confirmation.[193] In the case of federal lands, the federal official has three working days to certify receipt of the notification, take steps to secure and protect the items, and provide notice to the same categories of tribes and Native Hawaiian organizations specified in the intentional excavation section.[194] The regulations governing consultation are similar to those pertaining to intentional excavations, and specifically encourage tribal-federal agency agreements in terms of specific discoveries and more generally in advance of a project that involves an area that could include such sites[195] and require the agency to develop a written plan for excavation within a thirty-day period in the case where excavation is necessary.[196]

Ownership and control rights. Under NAGPRA, Indian tribes, Native Hawaiian organizations, or descendants of the deceased will usually have ownership and control over human remains and cultural items which may be discovered or excavated on federal and tribal lands in the future, regardless of whether such discovery or excavation is intentional or inadvertent.[197]

In the case of human remains and associated funerary objects, any lineal descendant of the buried person has the initial right of ownership or control of that person's remains and funerary objects associated with the remains.[198] Where descendants of the human remains and associated funerary objects cannot be determined and in the case of unassociated funerary objects, sacred objects and items of cultural patrimony, NAGPRA establishes the following rules. (1) The tribe or Native Hawaiian organization owns or controls all cultural items discovered on tribal land.[199] (2) In the case of federal land, the tribe or Native Hawaiian organization with the closest cultural affiliation to the items has ownership or control.[200] Agreements between tribes regarding disputed items are possible and the NAGPRA Review Committee may serve as a mediator if there is an intertribal dispute.[201] (3) Where cultural affiliation of the items cannot be established, but the objects are discovered on federal land which the Indian Claims Commission (ICC)[202] or United States Court of Claims (now known as the United States Court of Federal Claims) has determined to be the aboriginal land of a particular tribe, the tribe which obtained the judgment has the right of ownership and control over the items unless another tribe can show a stronger cultural relationship.[203]

The limitation of aboriginal land to land that has been recognized by an ICC or Court of Claims judgment was the result of negotiations with the SAA. Their concern about aboriginal land as a concept was that it would be so broad that continual disputes would arise regarding which tribes might make a claim. Tying an aboriginal land claim to specific legal determinations was meant to provide more certainty to the process. At the same time, the provision allowing a tribe with a "closer cultural connection" to make a claim was added in recognition that ICC and court judgments are linked to particular time periods, and that grave sites discovered from different time periods might have a closer connection to a tribe other than the one with the ICC or court judgment. Thus, the provision on "closer cultural connection" was meant to increase the chance that the most appropriate tribe would ultimately have ownership of, or control over, the item and/or human remains.

Prior to transferring ownership or control of embedded cultural items to lineal descendants, tribes, or Native Hawaiian organizations, the federal agency must publish at least two general notices of the proposed disposition, a week apart, in a newspaper circulated in the area of removal and, if applicable, the area where the members of the tribe or organization reside. Transfer may not take place until thirty days after the second notice. If competing claimants come forward, the proper recipient must be determined in accordance with the statutory preferences.[204] The transfer of items must take place using appropriate procedures that respect traditional customs and practices.[205]

Unlike the regulations dealing with repatriation from museum and federal agency collections, there are no time limits placed upon the transfer of excavated items to the appropriate claimant. Indeed, the notice provisions and the written plan requirements build a significant delay into the process beyond the thirty days contemplated by the NAGPRA statute itself, during which various types of recording and analysis can occur.[206] For that reason, these regulations have been viewed by some as a questionable interpretation of the statute, which unduly delays the transfer of items to tribes.

There is no time limit for submitting a repatriation claim.[207] However, a claim is waived if it is made after a valid repatriation of human remains or cultural items has already taken place.[208] If more than one tribe makes a claim and the federal agency cannot clearly determine which party is the appropriate claimant, the agency may retain the item until the parties agree or a court decides who should receive the items.[209]

The statute provides that Native American cultural items not claimed pursuant to these provisions will be disposed of in accordance with regulations adopted by the Secretary of the Interior, in consultation with the Review Committee established by the act.[210] These regulations have not yet been promulgated. (See Chapter 2 for a further explanation of the process followed to promulgate NAGPRA regulations.)

Trafficking. NAGPRA prohibits trafficking in Native American human remains for sale or profit unless the remains have been "excavated, exhumed, or otherwise obtained with full knowledge and consent of the next of kin or the official governing body of the appropriate culturally affiliated Indian tribe or Native Hawaiian organization."[211] This prohibition applies to human remains wrongfully acquired at any time, whether before or after the enactment of NAGPRA. It also prohibits trafficking in funerary objects, sacred objects, and items of cultural patrimony obtained in violation of the act.[212] This section may be violated by removing cultural items from federal or Indian lands without a permit or in a manner inconsistent with the ownership provisions in NAGPRA.[213] This provision in NAGPRA applies only to wrongful acquisitions after the date that NAGPRA was enacted (November 16, 1990). Of course, existing state or federal law involving theft or stolen property would be available should an individual have obtained possession of a cultural item by such means before or after the enactment of NAGPRA.[214] Violators are subject to a fine of up to $100,000 and face up to a one-year jail sentence for a first offense; subsequent violations subject the offender to a fine of up to $250,000 and a maximum of five years in jail.[215]

NAGPRA Review Committee. NAGPRA provides for the appointment of a Review Committee to monitor and review the implementation of the act.[216] The Review Committee consists of seven members: three are appointed by the Secretary of the Interior from nominations submitted by Indian tribes, Native Hawaiian organizations, and traditional Native American religious leaders (at least two of the three must be traditional Native American religious leaders); three are appointed by the Secretary of the Interior from nominations submitted by national museum organizations and scientific organizations; and one person is chosen from a list compiled by the other six members.[217] Federal officers and employees may not serve on the committee.[218]

The Review Committee's functions are to monitor the inventory and identification process,[219] upon request, make findings relating to the cultural affiliation and return of cultural items and to help resolve disputes between interested parties,[220] compile an inventory of culturally unidentifiable human remains and make recommendations as to an appropriate process for their disposition,[221] consult with the Secretary of the Interior in the development of regulations to implement NAGPRA,[222] make recommendations as to the future care of repatriated cultural items,[223] and submit an annual report to Congress.[224]

Other provisions. An Indian tribe, Native Hawaiian organization or individual, or other entity with protected rights under NAGPRA can file a lawsuit to enforce the provisions of NAGPRA if there is a violation of the act.[225] Once a written claim has been submitted and denied, this constitutes "exhaustion of remedies," and a claiming party may seek review of the determination by a federal court.[226] Federal courts have authority to issue any necessary orders.[227] The claiming party also has the option to seek review of the denial by the NAGPRA Review Committee before pursuing a court remedy. The Review Committee's findings are non-binding, but may be used as evidence (similar to an independent expert's opinion) in any subsequent court proceeding.[228] If a museum repatriates an item in good faith, however, it is not liable for claims against it predicated upon a claim of wrongful repatriation, breach of fiduciary duty or public trust, or violations of state law.[229]

Tribes and Native Hawaiian organizations also retain any pre-existing procedural or substantive legal rights which they may have possessed before NAGPRA.[230] NAGPRA is not meant to limit the general repatriation authority of federal agencies and museums.[231] Further, NAGPRA does not preclude agencies or museums from entering into agreements with tribes and organizations regarding any Native American objects owned or controlled by the museums or agencies.[232]

NAGPRA provides for the Secretary of the Interior to assess civil penalties against museums that do not comply with the act.[233] The amount of the penalties are determined by (1) the archaeological, historical, or commercial value of the item involved; (2) economic and noneconomic damages suffered by an aggrieved party; and (3) the number of violations.[234]

To facilitate implementation, NAGPRA authorizes the Secretary of the Interior to make grants to museums to undertake the inventory and summary, and to tribes and Native Hawaiian organizations to assist them in repatriating cultural items.[235]

Conclusion

After centuries of discriminatory treatment, the Native American Graves Protection and Repatriation Act finally recognizes that Native American human remains and cultural items are the remnants and product of living people, and that descendants have a cultural and spiritual relationship with the deceased. Human remains and cultural items can no longer be thought of as merely "scientific specimens" or "collectibles."

NAGPRA is a part of a larger historical tragedy: the failure of the United States government, and other institutions, to understand and respect the spiritual and cultural beliefs and practices of Native peoples. Governmental policies that threaten Native American religions are not merely historical anachronisms, but continue to have an impact upon contemporary Native Americans. While much progress has been made in the twenty years since NAGPRA was enacted, sites sacred to traditional Indian religious practitioners are still threatened with destructive development and craftsman producing items for ceremonial use sometimes still have eagle feathers seized from them by federal law enforcement officials. It is important that the policies of the United States continue to move in the direction of protecting the practice of traditional Native American cultures.

The law provides the legal standards, framework, and the process, but the actual results rely largely upon those with the actual knowledge: the tribes and Native Hawaiian organizations. NAGPRA was human rights legislation at its core, but its goal was also to foster cooperation and understanding. Where it has worked well, museums and federal agencies have begun to work with tribes in all areas of their domain that should or could involve tribes.

NAGPRA was unique legislation because it was the first time the federal government and non-Indian institutions were required to consider what is sacred from an Indian perspective. NAGPRA is a law that has served as an example to the world and as a catalyst for other countries to address these fundamental issues of human dignity. In fact, article 12 of the United Nations Declaration on the Rights of Indigenous Peoples (UNDRIP), which has been unanimously endorsed by all of the nations of the world that have considered it, provides that "Indigenous peoples have . . . the right to the use and control of their ceremonial objects; and the right to the repatriation of their human remains . . . States shall seek to enable the access and/or repatriation of ceremonial objects and human remains in their possession through fair, transparent and effective mechanisms developed in conjunction with indigenous peoples concerned." If not for NAGPRA, it is very unlikely this concept would have been embraced by the international community. Thus, NAGPRA has had a profound impact not only in the United States, but in the area of international indigenous human rights, as well.

Notes

1   This chapter was adapted in part from Jack F. Trope and Walter R. Echo-Hawk, "The Native American Graves Protection and Repatriation Act: Background and Legislative History," 24 *Arizona State Law Journal*, 35, 42 (1992), and Section 1, Chapter 1 and Supplement 1 (authored by Jack F. Trope) in *Mending the Circle: A Native American Repatriation Guide* (New York: American Indian Ritual Object Repatriation Foundation, 1996-1997). (Articles used with the permission of the publishers and authors.)

2   Jack F. Trope, "Protecting Native American Religious Freedom: The Legal, Historical, and Constitutional Basis for the Proposed Native American Free Exercise of Religion Act," *N.Y.U. Review of Law and Social Change* 373, 374 (1993).

3   Public Law 95–341, 92 Stat. 469 (1978) (codified at 42 U.S.C. 1996).

4   Ibid.

5   485 U.S. 439 (1988).

6   Trope, "Protecting Native American Religious Freedom: The Legal, Historical, and Constitutional Basis for the Proposed Native American Free Exercise of Religion Act," 384–385.

7   20 U.S.C. 80q-1 et seq.

8   Another significant accomplishment of the coalition was the passage in 1992 of a federal law protecting the ceremonial use of peyote, 42 U.S.C. 1996a. At about the same time, the National Historic Preservation Act (NHPA) was amended to recognize properties of traditional religious and cultural importance as eligible for the National Register of Historic Places, to mandate tribal consultation pertaining to these places, and to authorize tribes to assume the responsibilities of a SHPO on tribal lands. 16 U.S.C. 470a(d)(6). The AIRFA Coalition was supportive of this effort, but did not take the lead. Instead, a loose coalition of tribal and federal historic preservation staff, working closely with Indian law advocates and attorneys in Washington, DC (some of whom had previously worked with the NCAI), spearheaded

the effort to obtain these amendments. Senator Wyche Fowler (D-GA) was instrumental in including tribal concerns in this legislation. The effort by the AIRFA Coalition to enact broader legislation providing specific and judicially enforceable substantive protections for sacred lands located on federal lands was unsuccessful, however. See Trope, supra note 2, 386–388, for an analysis of the proposed Native American Free Exercise of Religion Act (only the peyote provisions in that bill were ultimately enacted). A non-binding executive order on sacred sites was issued by President Bill Clinton, which still remains in force. Executive Order 13,007 (1996).

9   R. F. Martin, "Annotation, Removal and Reinterment of Remains," 21 *American Law Reports* 2d 472, 475–76 (citations omitted).

10   See generally Catherine Bergin Yalung and Laurel I. Wala, Comment, "Survey of State Repatriation and Burial Protection Statutes," 24 *Arizona State Law Journal* 419 (1992); see also *Hearings Before the Senate Select Committee on Indian Affairs on S. 1021 and S. 1980*, 101st Cong., 2d Sess. (May 14, 1990), 248–266 (Exhibit 5 to Statement of Walter R. Echo-Hawk entitled "State-to-State Survey on Laws to Protect Dead Bodies and to Guarantee Decent Burials") (hereinafter *Senate Hearing on S. 1021 & S. 1980*).

11   See generally Percival Jackson, *The Law of Cadavers and of Burials and Burial Places* (2d. Ed. New York: 1950).

12   See, e.g., Stastny v. Tachovsky, 132 N.W. 2d 317 (Neb. 1964); Neb. Rev. Stat. 71-605 (5)-(6) (specifying that disinterment may only be done by a licensed funeral director under a permit from the Bureau of Vital Statistics requested by next of kin; if more than one human body is concerned then the applicant must also obtain a court order which must specify the place for reinterment).

13   See generally Yalung and Wala, "Survey of State Repatriation and Burial Protection Statutes."

14   See generally David Bushnell, "Burials of the Alqonoquian, Siouan, and Caddoan Tribes West of the Mississippi, Smithsonian Institution," *Bureau of American Ethnology Bulletin* 83 (1927); H.C. Yarrow, *North American Indian Burial Customs* (Ogden, UT: Eagle's View Publishing,1988).

15   128 Cal.App. 3d 536, 180 Cal.Rptr. 423, 425–427 (1982).

16   273 N.E.2d 893, 896–898 (Ohio Ct. App. 1971).

17   52 N.E. 126, 127 (Ohio 1898).

18   This information can be found on the National Park Service, National NAGPRA website at http://www.nps.gov/history/nagpra/ONLINEDB/INDEX.HTM#SumDB.

19   This information can be found on the Smithsonian National Museum of Natural History website at http://anthropology.si.edu/repatriation/collections/index.htm.

20   Douglas Cole, *Captured Heritage: The Scramble for Northwest Coast Artifacts* (Norman, OK: University of Oklahoma Press,1995), 286–310.

21   Robert Bieder, *A Brief Historical Survey of the Expropriation of American Indian Remains* (Boulder, CO: Native Amercian Rights Fund, 1990) (hereinafter *Bieder Report*), reprinted in *Senate Hearing on S. 1021 & S. 1980*, 278–363. See also Robert Bieder, *Science Encounters the Indian, 1820-1880* (Norman, OK: University of Oklahoma Press, 1986); Douglas Cole, *Captured Heritage: The Scramble for Northwest Coast Artifacts*; Stephen J. Gould, *The Mismeasure of Man* (New York: W.H. Norton & Company,1981); Orlan J. Svingen, *History of the Expropriation of Pawnee Indian Graves in the Control of the Nebraska State Historical Society* (Boulder, CO: Native American Rights Fund, 1989); James T. Riding In, "Report Verifying the Identity of Six Pawnee Scout Crania at the Smithsonian and the National Museum of Health and Medicine" (1990), reprinted in *Senate Hearing on S. 1021 & S. 1980*, Cole, *Captured Heritage: The Scramble for Northwest Coast Artifacts*, 211–229.

22 *Senate Hearing on S. 1021 & S. 1980,* Cole, *Captured Heritage: The Scramble for Northwest Coast Artifacts,* 290–318.

23 Ibid., 294.

24 Ibid., 290–293.

25 Ibid., 319–320. The Surgeon General's Order is reproduced in full in the *Bieder Report.*

26 Ibid., 306–318.

27 Ibid., 292–295, 301–303.

28 Ibid., 329.

29 Ibid., 313.

30 Ibid., 76.

31 Ibid., 321–322.

32 Kenn Harper, *Give Me My Father's Body: The Life of Minik, The New York Eskimo* (New York: Simon and Schuster, 1986), 89–95.

33 See generally, Tamara L. Bray and Thomas W. Killion, eds., *Reckoning with the Dead: The Larsen Bay Repatriation and the Smithsonian Institution* (Washington DC: Smithsonian,1994).

34 American common law has always held that a dead body is not "property". See 22 *American Jurisprudence* 2d. *Dead Bodies,* Sec. 4; 25A C.J.S. *Dead Bodies,* Sec. 2; *Annotation: Corpse— Removal and Reinterment,* 21 *American Law Reports* 2d. 472, 480, 486; Jackson, *The Law of Cadavers and of Burials and Burial Places,* 129–31, 133–34; 88-73 Kan. Op. Atty. Gen. (1988).

35 Trope and Echo-Hawk, "The Native American Graves Protection and Repatriation Act," 42.

36 Martin Sullivan, "A Museum Perspective on Repatriation: Issues and Opportunities," *Arizona State Law Journal* 283, 284–290 (1992); see also Onondaga Nation v. Thatcher, at 61 N.Y.S. 1027 (Sup. Ct. Onondaga Co. 1899), 65 N.Y.S. 1014 (App. Div. 1900), and 62 N.E. 1098 (N.Y. 1901).

37 Douglas J. Preston, "Skeletons in our museums' closets: Native Americans want their ancestors' bones back," *Harper's,* Feb. 1989, 68.

38 *Hearing on S. 187 Before the Senate Select Committee on Indian Affairs on Native American Museum Claims Commission Act,* 1 (Statement of Senator Daniel K. Inouye).

39 20 U.S.C. 80q-1-80q-15.

40 20 U.S.C. 80q-1.

41 S. 1722, 100th Cong., 1st Session, sections 202–206 (1987).

42 S. 978, 101st Cong., 1st Session, section 9 (1989).

43 See e.g, May 18, 1989, Memo from Jerry Flute and Jack Trope to AAIA Board of Directors which can be found in the Association on American Indian Affairs Archives housed in the Seeley G. Mudd Manuscript Library at Princeton University, Princeton, New Jersey.

44 *Joint Hearing Before the House Committee on Interior and Insular Affairs, House Committee on House Administration, Subcommittee on Libraries and Memorials, and the House Committee on Public Works and Transportation, Subcommittee on Public Works and Grounds, on H.R. 2668,* 101th Cong., 1st Sess. (July 20, 1989) at 183.

45 Ibid., 225.

46 Ibid., 157–158.

47 135 Cong. Rec. S12388 (Oct. 3, 1989) (Statement of Senator Daniel Inouye during debate on passage of the bill by the Senate).

48 20 U.S.C. 80q-9(a)(1), (2).

49 20 U.S.C. 80q-9(b).

50 20 U.S.C. 80q-9(c).

51   Ibid.; 135 Cong.Rec. H8448 (daily ed., Nov. 13, 1989) (Statement of Rep. Nick J. Rahall, II, during the debate preceding passage of the bill by the House of Representatives); 135 Cong. Rec. S12397 (daily ed., Oct. 3, 1989) (Statement of Senator John McCain).

52   135 Cong. Rec. S12397 (daily ed. Oct. 3, 1989) (Statement of Senator John McCain).

53   136 Cong. Rec. H 10988-10989 (daily ed., Oct. 22, 1990) (Statements of Representative Ben Nighthorse Campbell and Representative John J. Rhodes III); 136 Cong. Rec. S 17174-17175 (daily ed., Oct. 26, 1990) (statements of Senators Daniel K. Inouye and Daniel K. Akaka).

54   S. Rep. No. 473, 101st Cong. 2d. Sess. (1990) (hereinafter *Senate Report 101-473*), 2–3. The House Report pertaining to NAGPRA noted further that the "majority [of the Panel] believed that 'Respect for Native human rights is the paramount principle that should govern resolution of the issue when a claim is made . . .'" H.R. Rep. No. 877, 101st Cong., 2d Sess. (1990) (hereinafter *House Report 101-877*), 10–11.

55   136 Cong. Rec. S 17173 (daily ed., Oct. 26, 1990) (Statement of Senator John McCain, one of the sponsors of NAGPRA in the Senate); See also 136 Cong. Rec. H10989 (daily ed., Oct. 22, 1990) (Statement of Representative John J. Rhodes III) (report "helped immensely to shape the policies in this bill"); 136 Cong. Rec. S17174 (daily ed., Oct. 26, 1990) (Statement of Senator Daniel K. Inouye); *Senate Report 101-473*; Martin, "Annotation, Removal and Reinterment of Remains," 6 ("The Committee agrees with the findings and recommendations of the Panel for a National Dialogue on Museum/Native American Relations.").

56   Trope and Echo-Hawk, "The Native American Graves Protection and Repatriation Act."

57   Preston, "Skeletons in our museums' closets," 66–76.

58   136 Cong. Rec. S17173 (daily ed. Oct 26, 1990) (Statement of Senator John McCain).

59   135 Cong. Rec. S12397 (daily ed. Oct. 3, 1989) (Statement of Senator John McCain).

60   In addition, we also knew that some elements in the Bush Administration were against the bill and we concluded that it was more likely that President Bush would sign a "consensus" bill. In the end, a joint letter urging President Bush to sign the bill was sent by the American Anthropological Association, American Association of Physical Anthropologists, Archaeological Institute of America, Association on American Indian Affairs, Native American Rights Fund, National Conference of State Historic Preservation Officers, National Congress of American Indians, National Trust for Historic Places, Preservation Action, Society for American Archaeology, Society for Historical Archaeology, and Society for Professional Archaeology. Trope and Echo-Hawk, "The Native American Graves Protection and Repatriation Act: Background and Legislative History."

61   25 U.S.C. 3001-3013 (Supp. 1991).

62   136 Cong. Rec. S17174 (daily ed., Oct. 26, 1990). (Statement of Senator Daniel K. Inouye at the time of the enactment of the bill by the Senate).

63   Ibid. Other parts of the legislative history also emphasize the "human rights" genesis of NAGPRA, the *Panel Report*, which is reprinted in 24 *Arizona State Law Journal* 487 (1992), expresses the belief that "human rights should be the paramount principle where claims are made by Native American groups that have a cultural affiliation with remains and other materials."

64   *Senate Report 101-473*, 6.

65   136 Cong. Rec. S 17173 (daily ed., Oct. 26, 1990) (statement of Senator John McCain). Both Senators McCain and Inouye recognized the importance of museums in maintaining our cultural heritage, as well as the interest of Native Americans in the return of ancestral human remains and funerary objects, sacred objects and cultural patrimony. 136 Cong. Rec. S17173-17175 (daily ed., Oct. 26, 1990).

66   25 U.S.C. 3010. The trust responsibility of the federal government to Indian tribes and people is a judicially created concept that requires the United States to "adhere to fiduciary standards in its dealings with Indians." Felix S. Cohen, *Felix S. Cohen's Handbook of Federal Indian Law* (Dayton, OH: Lexix Law Publishing, 1982), 207. Ironically, the museum community strongly supported this section for another reason. They believed that it would limit the precedential value of this legislation in terms of international claims of repatriation that might be made to their institutions in the future.

67   See e.g., Yankton Sioux Tribe v. U.S. Army Corps of Engineers, 83 F.Supp.2d 1047 (D.S.D. 2000).

68   See e.g., Green v. Dumke, 480 F.2d 624, 628 n.7 (9th Cir. 1973); Schorle v. City of Greenhills, 524 F. Supp. 821, 825 (S.D. Ohio 1981).

69   The statutory provisions relating to repatriation are set out, for the most part, in 25 U.S.C. 3003, 3004, and 3005.

70   The statutory provisions relating to graves protection are set out, for the most part, in 25 U.S.C. 3002.

71   The statutory provisions relating to illegal trafficking, enacted as section 4 of NAGPRA, are set out in 18 U.S.C. 1170.

72   43 C.F.R. 10.2(b)(1); 43 C.F.R. 10.14(b).

73   25 U.S.C. 3001(7). A Federal District Court found that the definition of Indian tribe includes both tribes recognized by the Secretary of the Interior and other "aggregations" of Indians that have been receiving funds and assistance from other departments of the Federal government. Abenaki Nation of Missiquoi Indians v. Hughes, 805 F.Supp. 234 (D.Vt. 1992), aff'd 990 F.2d 729 (2nd Cir. 1993). However, the Department of Interior, in regulations adopted after this court case, included only those tribes commonly thought of as "federally recognized." 43 C.F.R. 10.2(b)(2).

74   Timothy McKeown and Sherry Hutt, "In the Smaller Scope of Conscience: The Native American Graves Protection and Repatriation Act Twelve Years After," 21 *UCLA Journal of Environmental Law and Policy* (2003): 155, 178 .

75   43 C.F.R. 10.11(c)(2)(ii)(A).

76   43 C.F.R. 10.11(c)(2).

77   60 *Fed. Reg.* 62139 (December 4, 1995).

78   McKeown and Hutt, "In the Smaller Scope of Conscience," 185–186.

79   Jason C. Roberts, "Native American Graves Protection and Repatriation Act Census: Examining the Status and Trends of Culturally Affiliating Native American Human Remains and Associated Funerary Objects Between 1990 and 1999," *Topics in Cultural Resource Law* (2000): 79, 84–85 .

80   25 U.S.C. 3001(11).

81   20 U.S.C. 80q-9.

82   25 U.S.C. 3001(8).

83   Ibid; 43 C.F.R. 10.2(a)(3)(iii).

84   43 C.F.R. 10.2(d)(1).

85   43 C.F.R. 10.2(d)(1).

86   McKeown and Hutt, "In the Smaller Scope of Conscience," 164–165.

87   25 U.S.C. 3001(3)(A) and (B).

88   25 U.S.C. 3001(3)(A).

89   25 U.S.C. 3001(3)(A),(B), 3001(8), 3003(a), 3004(a).

90   25 U.S.C. 3001(3)(B).

91   McKeown and Hutt, "In the Smaller Scope of Conscience," 165.

92   25 U.S.C. 3001(3)(C).

93   43 C.F.R. 10.2(d)(3); House Report 101-877.

94   Ibid.

95   Ibid.

96   *Senate Report 101-473.*

97   43 C.F.R. 10.2(d)(3).

98   McKeown and Hutt, "In the Smaller Scope of Conscience," 165–166.

99   25 U.S.C. 3001(3)(D).

100 25 U.S.C. 3001(3)(C)(D), see Trope and Echo-Hawk, "The Native American Graves Protection and Repatriation Act: Background and Legislative History."

101 *Senate Report 101-473.*

102 McKeown and Hutt, "In the Smaller Scope of Conscience," 166.

103 25 U.S.C. 3003(a).

104 25 U.S.C. 3003(b)(1)(A), (C).

105 Ibid.

106 *Senate Report 101-473.*

107 25 U.S.C. 3003(b)(2).

108 *Senate Report 101-473.*

109 25 U.S.C. 3003(d)(1), (2).

110 25 U.S.C. 3003(d)(2).

111 25 U.S.C. 3003(b)(2).

112 25 U.S.C. 3006(a)

113 *Native American Graves Protection and Repatriation Act: After Almost 20 Years, Key Federal Agencies Still Have Not Fully Complied with the Act.* (Washington DC: GAO-10-768, July 28, 2010), 26.

114 25 U.S.C. 3004(a), (b)(1)(A).

115 25 U.S.C. 3004(b)(1)(B), (C).

116 25 U.S.C. 3004(b)(2).

117 25 U.S.C. 3005(a)(1) and (4).

118 25 U.S.C. 3001(2).

119 *House Report 101-877.*

120 Ibid.

121 25 U.S.C. 3001(2); 43 C.F.R. 10.14(d).

122 43 C.F.R. 10.14(d) and (f).

123 *Senate Report 101-473.*

124 43 C.F.R. 10.14(d) and (f); 60 Fed.Reg. 62156 (1995).

125 25 U.S.C. 3005(a)(4).

126 43 C.F.R. 10.14(c).

127 See 25 U.S.C. 3003(b)(2); 25 U.S.C. 3005(a).

128 25 U.S.C. 3005(b).

129 Ibid.

130 25 U.S.C. 3009(1)(B).

131 25 U.S.C. 3005(e). 25 U.S.C. 3005(a)(1) and the portion of 25 U.S.C. 3005(a)(4) applicable to human remains and associated funerary objects refer only to subsections (b) and (e) of 25 U.S.C. 3005 as exceptions to the repatriation requirement.

132   Ibid. Section 3005(e) also provides that the dispute may be settled "pursuant to the provisions of this Act". Ibid. This refers to the authority of the Review Committee created by 25 U.S.C. 3006 to "facilitat[e] the resolution of any disputes among Indian tribes, Native Hawaiian organizations, or lineal descendants and Federal agencies or museums relating to the return of such items including convening the parties to the dispute if deemed desirable." 25 U.S.C. 3006(c)(4). Although any findings of the committee are admissible in a court proceeding, the committee has no binding authority upon any of the parties. 25 U.S.C. 3006(d). Thus, while the committee can certainly play an important role in resolving these disputes, ultimately the disputes must be resolved by agreement or judicial determination.

133   25 U.S.C. 3006.

134   25 U.S.C. 3006(c)(5).

135   25 U.S.C. 3006(e).

136   *House Report 101-877*. The House Interior Committee indicated that it "look[ed] forward" to the committee's recommendations. Ibid. The Report of the Panel for a National Dialogue on Museum/Native American Relations also reflected a division on this issue. Ibid, 11.

137   43 C.F.R. 10.11.

138   43 C.F.R. 10.11(c)(1)(i), (ii).

139   43 C.F.R. 10.11(b).

140   43 C.F.R. 10.11(b)(2)(ii).

141   43 C.F.R. 10.11(c)(1)(i), (ii).

142   43 C.F.R. 10.11(c)(2)(ii)(A).

143   43 C.F.R. 10.11(c)(2)(ii)(B).

144   43 C.F.R. 10.11(c)(2), (3).

145   43 C.F.R. 10.11(c)(4).

146   See generally 25 U.S.C. 3005, 3001(3).

147   Cultural affiliation can be determined by the summary process, 25 U.S.C. 3005(a)(2), or, in the case of unassociated funerary objects, by the claimant making a showing by a preponderance of the evidence, 25 U.S.C. 3005(a)(4).

148   25 U.S.C. 3005(a)(5).

149   25 U.S.C. 3005(a)(5)(A). An object of cultural patrimony cannot be owned by an individual.

150   25 U.S.C. 3005(a)(5)(C).

151   25 U.S.C. 3005(c).

152   25 U.S.C. 3004(b)(2).

153   25 U.S.C. 3001(13).

154   *Senate Report 101-473*.

155   *Senate Report 101-473*.

156   136 Cong. Rec. S17176 (daily ed., Oct. 26, 1990) (Statement by Senator McCain during debate at time of the passage of the bill by the Senate).

157   See generally 16 *American Jurisprudence 2d, Conflict of Laws*, secs. 43, 44.

158   Trope and Echo-Hawk, "The Native American Graves Protection and Repatriation Act," 68.

159   25 U.S.C. 3001(13).

160   Ibid.; see also *House Report 101-877*.

161   25 U.S.C. 3001(13).

162   25 U.S.C. 3005(c).

163   In one instance, subsequent legislation has made NAGPRA applicable to state land. The one circumstance in which burial sites on state-owned lands are covered is found in the Water

Resources Development Act of 1999, P.L. 106-53, which transferred certain federal land to the State of South Dakota, but requires the federal government to comply with NAGPRA if any covered sites are located on the transferred land. Ibid., section 605(h)(3).

164   25 U.S.C. 3001(1). It had been understood that NAGPRA provisions automatically applied to any grave site on federal or tribal land (except for those that are clearly non-indigenous in nature, e.g., Euro-American). However, the Ninth Circuit Court of Appeals issued a decision in the case of Bonnichsen v. United States. 367 F. 3d 864 (9th Cir. 2004), where it held that the term "Native American" in NAGPRA, which modifies the terms "human remains, objects and cultural items" in the grave sites section of the act, refers only to aboriginal tribes, peoples, and cultures that exist in modern times. Thus, according to the court in *Bonnischen,* in order for NAGPRA to apply to human remains and cultural items found on federal and tribal lands, there must be an initial showing that the remains or items "bear a significant relationship to a *presently existing* tribe, people or culture." Ibid., 874–876. The *Bonnischen* decision is highly suspect as a matter of law, given that it would render numerous sections of the act virtually superfluous, e.g., 25 U.S.C. 3002(a)(2)(C) (claims based solely upon aboriginal occupation), 25 U.S.C. 3006(c)(5) (disposition of culturally unaffiliated remains). Thus far, no regulations have been altered by the Department of Interior as a result of this decision.

165   43 C.F.R. 10.2(d)(2).

166   25 U.S.C. 3001(5).

167   25 U.S.C. 3001(15).

168   60 Fed.Reg. 62142 (December 4, 1995). The commentary also expresses the secretary's interpretation that allotted Indian lands that are not located within the boundaries of a reservation or dependent Indian community are not "tribal lands." Ibid., 62140. Presumably they would be federal lands, although the commentary is not explicit about this. The commentary also suggests that lands held in fee simple by an Indian tribe that are not within the reservation or part of a dependent Indian community are not covered by NAGPRA. Ibid., 62142.

169   43 C.F.R. 10.2(f)(2)(iv). This is a questionable interpretation of the law. The "Fifth Amendment takings" exception in NAGPRA is found in the "right of possession" definition, 25 U.S.C. 3001(13), which applies only to repatriation of remains and objects which are in the possession of museums or federal agencies and not to the issue of the excavation of cultural items that are still embedded on tribal lands.

170   25 U.S.C. 3002(c)(1).

171   43 C.F.R. 10.3(b)(1).

172   16 U.S.C. 470cc(b).

173   25 U.S.C. 3002(c)(2).

174   25 U.S.C. 3002(c)(2).

175   25 U.S.C. 3002(d)(1).

176   Although the regulations provide for notice to the Alaska Native corporations, the Interior Solicitor's Office has also indicated that Alaska Native corporations are not to be considered tribes within the meaning of NAGPRA. See memo dated March 18, 2011 from Associate Solicitor Blackwell to National NAGPRA Program Manager Hutt, which can be found at http://www.nps.gov/nagpra/DOCUMENTS/Solicitors_Memo_ANCSA_03182011.pdf. Thus, in this case, there is a bit of disconnect between the entity that receives notice (the corporation) and the entity (the Alaska Native village) that has the right to file a repatriation claim.

177   43 C.F.R. 10.4(d)(1)(iv).

178   43 C.F.R. 10.4(d)(1)(iii).

179   25 U.S.C. 3002(d)(1) and (3).

180 43 C.F.R. 10.4(d)(2).

181 43 C.F.R. 10.4(g).

182 25 U.S.C. 3002(d)(3).

183 *Senate Report 101-473*. (Of note, there are special provisions dealing with Native Hawaiian land and organizations, as well as land owned by Alaska Native corporations.) 25 U.S.C. 3001(15)(c); 25 U.S.C. 3002(d)(1).

184 60 Fed.Reg. 62141, 62146 (December 4, 1995).

185 25 U.S.C. 3002(c) and (d); 43 C.F.R. 10.4.

186 *House Report 101-877*.

187 43 C.F.R. 10.3(c)(1), 43 C.F.R. 10.5(b)(1) and (2).

188 43 C.F.R. 10.3(c)(1).

189 43 C.F.R. 10.5(c).

190 43 C.F.R. 10.5(b)(3), (d) and (g).

191 43 C.F.R. 10.5(e).

192 43 C.F.R. 10.5(f).

193 43 C.F.R. 10.4(b).

194 43 C.F.R. 10.4(d). In the case of tribal lands, the tribe may (but is not required to) certify receipt of the notice, take steps to secure and protect the items and ensure proper distribution of the items if excavated. 43 C.F.R. 10.4(e).

195 43 C.F.R. 10.4(d)(iv); 43 C.F.R. 10.5(f).

196 43 C.F.R. 10.4(d)(v); 43 C.F.R. 10.3(c)(2).

197 However, the case of Bonnischen v. United States, discussed in footnote 164, raises some problematic questions about whether this intent of the legislation will be fully fulfilled.

198 25 U.S.C. 3002(a)(1).

199 25 U.S.C. 3002(a)(2)(A).

200 25 U.S.C. 3002(a)(2)(B).

201 25 U.S.C. 3006(c)(4); 43 C.F.R. 10.17.

202 The Indian Claims Commission was established in 1946 to hear claims by tribes seeking compensation for territory lost as a result of broken federal treaties. Judicial findings about tribal aboriginal territories were an integral part of the process. In 1978, its pending docket of 170 cases was transferred to the United States Court of Claims.

203 25 U.S.C. 3002(a)(2)(C). This clause has been interpreted by the Department of the Interior to include preliminary findings of fact, and not just final judgments, and the department ruled that joint aboriginal use is sufficient to meet the criteria of this section; a finding of exclusive use and occupancy is not required. This interpretation was rejected by the federal magistrate judge in Bonnichsen v. United States, 217 F.Supp.2d 1116 (D.Or. 2002), affd. 357 F.3d 962 (9th Cir. 2004), modified and rehearing en banc denied, 367 F.3d 864 (9th Cir. 2004). That part of the magistrate's decision was not addressed in the Ninth Circuit opinion.

204 43 C.F.R. 10.6(c).

205 43 C.F.R. 10.6(c).

206 It is conceivable that this will give rise to a legal dispute in a case where the ownership or control of the items to be excavated is clear and the claimant wants immediate return of the items without analysis.

207 60 Fed.Reg. 62154 (December 4, 1995).

208 43 C.F.R. 10.15(a)(1).

209 43 C.F.R. 10.10(c)(2); 43 C.F.R. 10.15(a)(2).

210 25 U.S.C. 3002(b).

211 18 U.S.C. 1170(a), as amended by section 4(a) of P.L. 101-601; 25 U.S.C. 3001(13).

212 18 U.S.C. 1170(b), as amended by section 4(a) of P.L. 101-601.

213 McKeown and Hutt, "In the Smaller Scope of Conscience: The Native American Graves Protection and Repatriation Act Twelve Years After," 208.

214 25 U.S.C. 3009(5).

215 18 U.S.C. 1170(a), as amended by section 4(a) of P.L. 101-601.

216 25 U.S.C. 3006.

217 25 U.S.C. 3006(b)(1).

218 25 U.S.C. 3006(2).

219 25 U.S.C. 3006(c)(2).

220 25 U.S.C. 3006(c)(3), (4) and 25 U.S.C. 3006(d).

221 25 U.S.C. 3006(c)(5).

222 25 U.S.C. 3006(c)(7).

223 25 U.S.C. 3006(c)(9).

224 25 U.S.C. 3006(h).

225 25 U.S.C. 3013.

226 43 C.F.R. 10.15(c).

227 25 U.S.C. 3013. The language in NAGPRA is that "any person" may bring an action to enforce the law's provisions. The senate report explains this provision as meaning that "any party, including an Indian tribe, Native Hawaiian organization, museum or agency" may bring a cause of action. *Senate Report 101-473.*

228 43 C.F.R. 10.16(b); 25 U.S.C. 3006(d).

229 25 U.S.C. 3005(f).

230 25 U.S.C. 3009(3), (4).

231 25 U.S.C. 3009(1)(A).

232 25 U.S.C. 3009(1)(B).

233 25 U.S.C. 3007.

234 25 U.S.C. 3007(g).

235 25 U.S.C. 3008(a). As the summaries and inventories have been completed, the grant program has evolved and grants are currently focused on consultation and documentation, as well as repatriation.

Chapter 2
"The Secretary Shall":
Actual and Apparent Delegation of
NAGPRA's Implementation Responsibilities

C. TIMOTHY McKEOWN

When the Native American Graves Protection and Repatriation Act (NAGPRA) was signed into law on November 16, 1990, it contained provisions requiring the Secretary of the Interior to carry out certain administrative duties and authorizing the secretary to carry out others.

Required duties relate to the Review Committee, regulations, and notices. The secretary was directed to establish a committee to monitor and review the implementation of the summary, inventory, and repatriation provisions of the act by February 16, 1991, and to promulgate implementing regulations by November 16, 1991. The secretary was also required to publish in the *Federal Register* a copy of the notification prepared by each federal agency or museum regarding the identity, acquisition, and cultural affiliation of Native American human remains and associated funerary objects in its possession or control.

The secretary was authorized to carry out certain discretionary duties related to inventory deadlines, grants, civil penalties, and disposition of certain excavated or discovered cultural items. The secretary could extend the November 16, 1995, deadline for any museum that made a good faith effort to complete its inventory of Native American human remains and associated funerary objects. The secretary was authorized to make grants to assist museums, Indian tribes, and Native Hawaiian organizations in conducting summary, inventory, and repatriation activities, and to assess a civil penalty on any museum that failed to comply with the requirements of the act. Lastly, upon the request of the secretary of any other U.S. department or the head of any other agency or instrumentality, the Secretary of the Interior was authorized to accept responsibility for the certification and disposition duties related to inadvertent discovery of Native American cultural items on lands controlled by another department or agency.

The Secretary of the Interior was in many ways a logical choice to carry out NAGPRA's assigned administrative duties. The secretary serves as the head of the Department of the Interior, the nation's principal conservation agency, which manages 500 million acres of surface land (about one-fifth of the land of the United States); curates 140 million historical and cultural objects and documents (second in size only to the Smithsonian Institution); and honors the nation's trust responsibilities to American Indians and Alaska Natives. Since 1990, six individuals have served as Secretary of the Interior and been responsible for carrying out these duties: Manuel Lujan Jr. (February 3, 1989–January 20, 1993), Bruce Babbitt (January 22, 1993–January 2, 2001), Gale Ann Norton (January 31, 2001–March 30, 2006), Dirk Kempthorne (May 29, 2006–January 19, 2009), Ken Salazar (January 21, 2009–April 12, 2013), and Sally Jewell (April 12, 2013–present).

Each Secretary of the Interior appoints a number of assistant secretaries to carry out duties in particular areas. The Assistant Secretary for Fish and Wildlife and Parks is responsible for the development, conservation, and utilization of fish, wildlife, recreation, historical, and national park system resources of the nation. The Assistant Secretary for Policy, Management and Budget is responsible for management, budget, and other administrative activities, including overseeing how the department's museum property is managed. The Assistant Secretary for Indian Affairs exercises the authorities and responsibilities of the secretary relating to Indian tribes, individual Indian tribal members, and Indian affairs in general.

Taken together, the department's expertise and infrastructure seemed custom-made for implementing the act. The reality was somewhat more complex. While the department had testified before Congress on other repatriation bills, represented by a senior official from the National Park Service, it declined to provide a witness for the hearing on H.R. 5237, the bill that would become NAGPRA (U.S. House of Representatives 1990b: 2). Executive correspondence to the House of Representatives made it clear that the department opposed passage of H.R. 5237 without extensive amendments, including removal of provisions applying to sacred objects and objects of cultural patrimony, disposition of discovered cultural items based on the "closest" cultural affiliation, or discovery on aboriginal lands. This required the Review Committee to compile a list of culturally unidentifiable human remains and make recommendations regarding their disposition. It also authorized open-ended and unlimited grants to tribes and museums involved in the repatriation process (U.S. Department of the Interior 1990). Congress ignored the department's objections in the final legislation, but nevertheless retained the provisions entrusting implementation of the act to the secretary.

Any vestigial ambivalence on being charged with implementing the provisions of the act was exacerbated by a lack of funding. The federal fiscal year covers the twelve-month period from October 1 through September 30. When NAGPRA was enacted on November 16, 1990, the Department of the Interior's budget for fiscal year 1991 was awaiting passage by Congress, and funding was being provided under a continuing resolution based on the previous year's funding level. Even when the FY1991 budget was eventually enacted on November 5, 1991, no funding was included to implement any of the NAGPRA requirements. The February 13, 1991, deadline for establishing the Review Committee passed with no visible activity by the Secretary. In August 1991, thirteen national Indian, scientific, museum, and preservation groups that had worked together to pass NAGPRA wrote to Secretary Manuel Lujan to urge him to take prompt and positive action to establish the Review Committee, start drafting of implementing regulations, and to include grants funding in the department's funding request for fiscal year 1993 (American Association of Museums 1991). "It's taken them forever," commented the director of one museum. "Interior has not been taking a leadership role, and we need them to." (Associated Press 1991). In response to a related congressional inquiry, an Interior Department official indicated that the budget request for fiscal year 1992 included new resources to develop draft regulations and support the Review Committee, and that inclusion of grant funding in the fiscal year 1993 request was under consideration (U.S. Department of the Interior 1991c).

One of the first administrative decisions facing the secretary was who within the department should be delegated authority to carry out certain provisions of the act. The secretary has several methods for delegating authority to subordinate employees. The quickest method is by means of a secretarial order. Such orders are by definition temporary in nature and must include a statement addressing the effective and expiration dates of the delegation. Secretarial orders that are not converted to the Departmental Manual by the expiration date are revoked automatically. The Departmental Manual is the authorized way of documenting delegations of authority of general and continuing applicability, and orders within remain in force until they are revised or revoked. A third method of delegation for certain responsibilities related to the administration of advisory committees is by means of the committee charter. Issued for a period not to exceed two years, the charter can include a delegation to serve as the committee's designated federal officer who is responsible for calling, attending, and adjourning committee meetings, approving meeting agendas, and ensuring the committee's efficient operation. Carrying out activities without actual delegation of authority under a secretarial order, Departmental Manual section, or Review Committee charter can have a serious adverse impact on the government, the department, and the official who acts without legal authority.

In August 1991, Secretary of the Interior Manuel Lujan took an initial administrative step toward implementation by signing and filing the charter for the Native

American Graves Protection and Repatriation Review Committee (U.S. Department of the Interior 1991a). The Review Committee reported to the the departmental consulting archaeologist, a position within the National Park Service delegated with providing oversight for archaeological work conducted by the various Interior Department bureaus. The secretary took another administrative step forward in October 1991 by signing a secretarial order delegating other implementation responsibilities to the departmental consulting archaeologist, in consultation with the Bureau of Indian Affairs (U.S. Department of the Interior 1991b). The delegated duties included assisting in seeking nominations and providing recommendations for members of the Review Committee, as well as providing the Review Committee's staff administrative support; providing regulations to implement the statute; administering the as-yet unfunded grants-in-aid program; reviewing requests from museums for extensions of time to complete inventories; and developing and providing guidelines, technical information, and training. The secretary reserved exclusive authority to establish the Review Committee, select its members, make final decisions regarding its recommendations, and to assess civil penalties against any museum that failed to comply with statutory requirements. These delegations were eventually codified in the Departmental Manual (U.S. Department of the Interior 1994). Responsibilities not mentioned in the secretarial order or the Departmental Manual, and thus apparently retained by the secretary, were the statutory duties to publish notices in the *Federal Register* and accept responsibility for the certification and disposition duties for cultural items discovered on lands controlled by another department or agency. With these initial delegations in place, the secretary and his team were ready to proceed with implementation of his duties related to the Review Committee, regulations, notices, inventory deadlines, grants, civil penalties, and disposition of excavated or discovered cultural items. These delegations would shift over the next two decades as successive secretaries responded to criticism from the Review Committee and Congress.

Review Committee

The secretary's specific responsibilities to the seven-member committee are narrowly defined to include establishing the committee itself, appointing committee members, providing administrative and staff support and establishing necessary committee rules and regulations, ensuring committee access to cultural items and associated scientific and historical documents, and consulting with the committee in promulgating regulations for the disposition of unclaimed cultural items that are excavated or discovered on federal or tribal lands.[1]

Under provisions of the Federal Advisory Committee Act, a federal advisory committee may not meet or take any action until a charter is filed with the head of the agency to whom the committee reports and with the Senate and House of Representatives standing committees with legislative jurisdiction over the agency.[2] The committee's first charter, signed by Secretary of the Interior Manual Lujan, was filed with the appropriate Congressional committees on August 2, 1991 (U.S. Department of the Interior 1991a). The Review Committee's official designation was the Native American Graves Protection and Repatriation Review Committee. The purpose of the Review Committee was to monitor and review the implementation of the repatriation provisions of the statute, including designating one of the members of the committee as chairman; monitoring the inventory and identification process to ensure a fair and objective consideration of all available relevant information and evidence; reviewing and making findings regarding the identity or cultural affiliation and return of cultural items; facilitating the resolution of disputes; compiling an inventory of culturally unidentifiable Native American human remains and recommending specific actions for developing a process for their disposition; consulting with affected parties regarding implementation of the statute; consulting with the Secretary of the Interior regarding the development of regulations; performing other functions as assigned by the secretary; making recommendations regarding future care of repatriated cultural items; and submitting an annual report to Congress. According to the charter, the Review Committee would hold two meetings per year and its activities would continue into the foreseeable future. Staff support to the Review Committee would amount to .25 full-time equivalent (FTE). Members were appointed to five-year terms.

The Federal Advisory Committee Act also requires that each committee has a designated federal officer responsible for calling, attending, and adjourning committee and subcommittee meetings. The August 2, 1991, charter named the departmental consulting archaeologist as the committee's designated federal officer, and that person retained the delegation in successive charters through November 15, 2000. The designated federal officer was changed in the charter filed on November 22, 2000, to the National Park Service's Assistant Director for Cultural Resources Stewardship and Partnership, and changed again in the charter filed on May 2, 2003, to the manager of the National NAGPRA Program. Each charter included a specific authorization to further delegate the designated federal officer duties under certain circumstances except the charter filed on November 24, 2010, in which this authorization was stricken. Concerns that a National Park Service employee might not be impartial during disputes involving National Park System units led to delegation of an alternate designated federal officer for specific disputes (see Chapter 6: Federal Agency Perspective).

The secretary's duty to appoint committee members was not delegated and was constrained by statutory provisions regarding the source of nominations.[3] Three members are appointed from nominations submitted by Indian tribes, Native Hawaiian organizations, and traditional Native American religious leaders, with at least two of these three being traditional religious leaders. Three members are appointed from nominations submitted by national museum organizations and scientific organizations. The seventh member is appointed from a list of persons developed and consented to by the other members. Secretary Lujan appointed the first six members to five-year terms on March 3, 1992, and from then through 2010, eighteen men and six women have served cumulative terms ranging from 2 to 10 years. The appointment process was not without controversy. In 2010, the Government Accountability Office identified a number of situations in which the process for recruitment and screening of nominees damaged the credibility of the Review Committee and the department (Government Accountability Office 2010: 44).

In the nineteen years since its first meeting in Washington, DC, the Review Committee met forty-two times at various locations around the country. Figure 1 provides a breakdown of the amount of time the Review Committee spent on its various responsibilities for each fiscal year. The committee's greatest amount of activity was in fiscal year 1993 when it initiated consultation on the development of implementing regulations, deliberated on its first disputes, and actively consulted with tribal, museum, and federal representatives. The amount of Review Committee activity dipped dramatically in fiscal years 2004 and 2005 when it did not meet for fourteen months, six months of which it did not have a valid charter and was considered moribund by the General Services Administration. Yearly expenditures for Review Committee activities, including member and staff compensation and meeting costs, ranged between $90,000 and $208,000. Staff support for the Review Committee ranged from .25 to 1.75 full-time equivalents (FTE). The Government Accountability Office reported some dissatisfaction from Review Committee members concerning the level of administrative support provided to the Review Committee by the Department of the Interior (Government Accountability Office 2010: 37). In addition, the Review Committee's meeting of November 17–19, 2010, appears to have been held in a hiatus between the expiration of the committee's charter on the biannual anniversary of NAGPRA's November 16 enactment, and the filing of a new charter on November 24, raising questions about the validity of the committee's actions at that meeting.[4]

Regulations

While section 13 provides the secretary with broad authority to promulgate regulations needed to carry out the act,[5] only two regulatory provisions are specifically required by Congress. Native American cultural items which are excavated or discovered on federal or tribal lands after November 16, 1990, and which are not

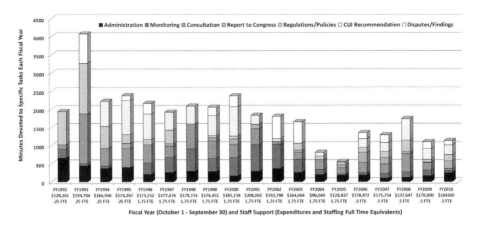

Fig 1. Time & Funds Devoted to Review Committee Functions

claimed by a lineal descendant, Indian tribe, or Native Hawaiian organization are to be disposed of according to regulations developed in consultation with the Review Committee, Native American groups, representatives of museums, and the scientific community.[6] Similarly, the amount of a civil penalty may only be assessed pursuant to regulations.[7] Promulgation of regulations related to other sections of the act is at the discretion of the secretary. Like all legislation, NAGPRA could not include all of the details needed to ensure effective implementation. Some of these omissions were intentional, such as the provisions for disposition of unclaimed cultural items or assessment of civil penalties that Congress considered to be in need of additional deliberation prior to full implementation. Similarly, Congress was unable to resolve the disposition of culturally unidentifiable human remains, so it tasked the Review Committee with recommending specific actions for developing a disposition process. Other omissions were apparently unintentional. For example, while Congress included a requirement to publish a notice in the *Federal Register* prior to the repatriation of Native American human remains or associated funerary objects, it neglected to include a similar due process notification for unassociated funerary objects, sacred objects, or objects of cultural patrimony. In addition, certain critical terms, such as "human remains," "lineal descendant," "consultation," "possession," and "control," are not defined in the act.

General procedures for rule-making are established by the Administrative Procedure Act,[8] and include publication of a notice of proposed rule-making in the *Federal Register,* soliciting from the public written data, views, or arguments. Received comments must be addressed concisely in a preamble when the final rule is published. Notice and comment rule-making is not required if the agency finds that it is impracticable, unnecessary, or contrary to the public interest. In addition to the general procedures for rule-making, NAGPRA specifically requires the Review Committee to consult with the secretary in the development of regulations. Taken together with the funding delays, the various procedural requirements made it impossible to meet the statutory requirement that regulations be promulgated by November 16, 1991.

Initially, the secretary's authority to promulgate regulations to carry out the act was not specifically delegated. The proposed rule, which was developed by a working group drawn from several federal agencies and then reviewed several times by the Review Committee, was published in 1993 by the Assistant Secretary for Fish and Wildlife and Parks under a general authority to issue additions to the Code of Federal Regulations (U.S. Department of the Interior 1993). The proposed rule drew eighty-two written comments representing thirteen Indian tribes, ten Indian organizations, twenty-seven museums, three national scientific and museum organizations, nineteen federal agencies, nine other organizations, and nine individuals. After review of all the comments, the Assistant Secretary issued a thirteen-section final rule which went into effect on January 3, 1996, over four years after the statutory deadline for regulation promulgation, two years after the summary deadline, and nearly two months after the inventory deadline. Four regulatory sections were reserved for future consideration, including the required provisions for disposition of unclaimed cultural items and assessment of civil penalties (U.S. Department of the Interior 1995).

The civil penalty rule was the first reserved section to be promulgated, the Assistant Secretary deciding to issue it as an interim rule, since delay would likely result in further loss of cultural items or in an inability to remedy losses that had already occurred (U.S. Department of the Interior 1997). The interim rule drew only twenty-four written comments and was issued as a final rule in 2003 (U.S. Department of the Interior 2003).

In 2004, a notice of proposed rulemaking was published for the second reserved section, establishing future deadlines for summary and inventory completion (U.S. Department of the Interior 2004). The proposed rule drew only ten written comments and was issued as a final rule in 2007 (U.S. Department of the Interior 2007a).

The third reserved section dealing with the disposition of culturally unidentifiable human remains underwent an extended development process. The Review Committee circulated three separate drafts for public comment before fulfilling its statutory responsibility to recommend specific actions for developing a process for disposition of culturally unidentifiable Native American human remains in 2000 (Native American Graves Protection and Repatriation Review Committee 2000). One of the Review Committee's recommendations was for the secretary to develop proposed regulations. When a notice of proposed rule-making was finally published in 2007, it drew 151 written comments, almost twice the number submitted when the main body of the regulations was published for comment in 1993 (U.S. Department of the Interior 2007b). The final regulations, issued in 2010, also included a request for comment, which drew an additional seventy-two written comments (U.S. Department of the Interior 2010). Taking the two solicitations together, written comments on the culturally unidentifiable rule were received from fifty-nine Indian tribes, twenty Indian organizations, thirty-seven museums, fifteen national scientific and museum organizations, two federal agencies, forty-five individuals, the Review Committee, the Smithsonian Institution, and one member of Congress.

Two provisions of the secretary's regulations have been challenged. The act applies to certain types of "Native American" cultural items, and defines the term as "of, or relating to, a tribe, people, or culture that is indigenous to the United States".[9] The regulations published in 1995 reiterated the statutory definition, with the exception that the phrase "that is" was omitted.[10]. In *Bonnichsen v. United States*, the Ninth Circuit Court of Appeals ruled that the statutory definition unambiguously requires that human remains bear some relationship to a presently existing tribe, people, or culture to be considered Native American, and that the secretary's alternative regulatory definition is invalid (*Bonnichsen v. United States*, 357 F.3d 962 [9th Cir. 2004]). However, to date, the regulatory definition has not been changed, meaning that the more restricted interpretation of the Ninth Circuit applies in Alaska, Washington, Oregon, Idaho, Montana, Nevada, California, Arizona, and Hawaii, while the rest of the country is bound by the regulatory definition.

The second challenge also relates to one of the regulatory definitions. The act establishes procedures to claim Native American cultural items by certain individuals and groups, including "Indian tribes" defined as "any tribe, band, nation, or other organized group or community of Indians, including any Alaska Native village (as defined in, or established pursuant to, the Alaska Native Claims Settlement Act), which is recognized as eligible for the special programs and services provided by the United States to Indians because of their status as Indians."[11] The regulations published in 1995 amended the statutory definition to also include the over 200 Alaska Native village corporations and thirteen Alaska Native regional corporations established pursuant to the Alaska Native Claims Settlement Act. In 2010, the Government Accountability Office pointed out that inclusion of Alaska Native corporations within NAGPRA's definition of Indian tribe was at odds with the department's current legal position regarding the status of Alaska Native corporations (Government Accountability Office 2010: 42). In 2011, the department's Office of the Solicitor found that the statutory definition "clearly does not include Alaska regional and village corporations within its definition of Indian tribes" and that this was an intentional omission on the part of Congress (Department of the Interior

2011a). The regulatory definition of "Indian tribe" was subsequently removed and reserved (Department of the Interior 2011b). The regulatory revision did not address the Department's potential liability regarding museums that repatriated Native American human remains, funerary objects, sacred objects, or objects of cultural patrimony to an Alaska Native regional or village corporation between 1996 and 2010, as required by the then-current regulations, and subject to civil penalty for failure to comply.

Notices

One of the Secretary's major responsibilities is to publish copies of notices prepared by museums and federal agencies in the *Federal Register*. The act requires each museum and federal agency to compile an inventory of Native American human remains and associated funerary objects by November 16, 1995, and, within six months, notify all culturally affiliated Indian tribes or Native Hawaiian organizations.[12] The notice must identify each Native American human remain or associated funerary object and the circumstances surrounding its acquisition, and distinguish between those that are clearly identifiable as to tribal origin, and those that are not clearly identifiable but, given the totality of circumstances surrounding their acquisition, are reasonably believed to be remains or objects culturally affiliated with an Indian tribe or Native Hawaiian organization.[13] A copy of the notice must be sent to the secretary who is required to publish it in the *Federal Register*.[14] This deceptively simple requirement of receiving a notice from a museum or federal agency and publishing it in the *Federal Register* has proved to be the focus of considerable criticism of the Department of the Interior.

The first layer of complexity derives from the *Federal Register* itself. Established in 1935 as the official daily journal of the federal government, the *Federal Register* publishes regulations and legal notices issued by all federal agencies and the president. Rudimentary format requirements ensure consistency in the various submissions. Notices must include a signature block, an authority citation, standardized headings, text, and a billing code. The signature block is generally signed by an official from the submitting federal agency which, under NAGPRA, was designated to the Secretary of the Interior. NAGPRA's statutory notice requirement is unusual by *Federal Register* standards, in that the majority of notices are actually submitted by non-federal museums. The text of a notice may be presented in any organized and logical format; one *Federal Register* employee once explaining that a notice written in iambic pentameter would still be published, but should generally conform to the U.S. Government Printing Office Style Manual. Unfortunately, museums and federal agencies were not informed of *Federal Register* format requirements prior to the 1996 notification deadline, so notices arrived in a variety of formats, though none actually emulated the verse of the Bard of Avon.

The first Notice of Inventory Completion was published in the *Federal Register* on June 18, 1992, and became a model for subsequent notices (National Park Service 1992). The notice reported the cultural affiliation of the remains of eleven Native American individuals and approximately 12,225 associated funerary objects in the possession of Joshua Tree National Monument in California. The notice did not identify specific Indian tribes as culturally affiliated with the remains and objects, instead identifying broader cultural groups, and requested that any other Indian tribes believed to be culturally affiliated with the human remains and associated funerary objects contact the park superintendent within thirty days. The notice was signed by the departmental consulting archaeologist, although the then current secretarial order did not delegate the secretary's responsibility to publish notices to anyone. When proposed regulations were published on May 28, 1993, the Joshua Tree notice was included as a non-binding example.

Final NAGPRA regulations, which went into effect on January 3, 1996, nearly two months after the inventory deadline, but before the deadline for notifying culturally affiliated Indian tribes and Native Hawaiian organizations, elaborated and formalized the notice process. Notices of Inventory Completion must summarize the contents of the inventory in sufficient detail so as to enable the recipients to determine their interest in claiming the inventoried items, including identifying each particular set of human remains or each associated funerary object and the circumstances surrounding its acquisition.[15] A museum or federal agency must also submit a copy of the inventory of human remains and associated funerary objects upon which the notice was based to the departmental consulting archaeologist.[16] The Joshua Tree notice was replaced in the final regulations by another nonbinding example published by Acadia National Park in Maine, again signed by the departmental consulting archaeologist.[17] (The final regulations also directed museums and federal agencies to submit a second type of notice, called a notice of intent to repatriate, to ensure due process in the repatriation of unassociated funerary objects, sacred objects, and objects of cultural patrimony.[18]) Museums and federal agencies were precluded from repatriating any cultural item until at least thirty days after the appropriate notice was published in the *Federal Register*.[19]

Publication generally kept pace with submissions through the 1995 inventory completion deadline, after which the number of submissions increased dramatically (Figure 2). By the end of fiscal year 1999, 1,002 notices had been submitted while only 546 had been published in the *Federal Register*. There are several reasons behind the backlog. One is that the number of federal staff devoted to publishing notices remained relatively constant despite the increased number of submissions. Second, submitted notices were subjected to review beyond the rudimentary *Federal Register* formatting requirements, including reconciling the notice content with the underlying

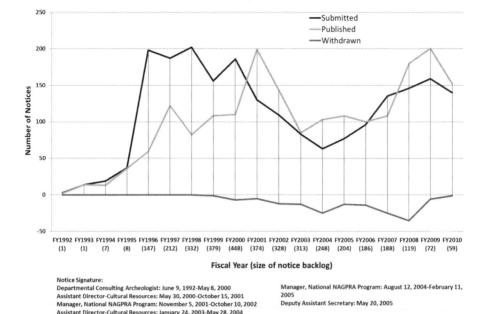

Fig. 2. Status of Submitted Federal Register Notices

inventories of human remains and associated funerary objects, a process that could take several days for a particularly lengthy notice. The third factor contributing to the backlog was that senior federal officials occasionally refused to publish submitted notices with which they did not agree, such as a notice submitted by Bandelier National Monument for fifty-three projectile points claimed as sacred objects by the Pueblo of Cochiti (Native American Graves Protection and Repatriation Review Committee 1999a: 16); a notice submitted by Wyoming State Museum for a bow, two arrows, and a pipe stem claimed as sacred objects by the Cheyenne River Sioux Tribe (Native American Graves Protection and Repatriation Review Committee 1999a: 31); a notice submitted by the Peabody and Essex Museum that contained a paragraph allegedly misinterpreting a letter from the National Park Service (U.S. Senate 2000: 54); and a notice submitted by the University of Nebraska for the remains of 491 individuals culturally affiliated with sixteen Indian tribes (U.S. Senate 2000: 207). The notice backlog became an ongoing concern of the Review Committee (Native American Graves Protection and Repatriation Review Committee 1998: 3; 1999b: 5; 2003: 7; 2005: 3) and of Congress (U.S. Senate 1999: 39, 166, 171, 181; 2000: 5, 24, 28, 49, 54, 207).

The National Park Service's February 2000 decision to reorganize the NAGPRA function was in part a reaction to controversy over the growing notice backlog.

Additional staff was hired and nearly 200 notices were published during fiscal year 2001. Thereafter, the number of notices published each fiscal year exceeded the number received except during fiscal year 2007. Simultaneously, the National Park Service began contacting museums and federal agencies that had placed a publication "hold" on previously submitted notices, asking them to authorize publication within thirty days or consider the notice withdrawn. Between 1999 and 2010, 157 notices were withdrawn from publication and most, though not all, of them were notices that had previously been on "hold." On the twentieth anniversary of the act's enactment, the remains of 16,575 individuals and 125,052 associated funerary objects were "off the radar," having neither been reported in a published notice nor posted on the culturally unidentifiable database (National Park Service 2011).

The secretary's authority to publish notices in the *Federal Register* was not delegated initially. From 1992 to 2005, notices were signed by various National Park Service officials, including the departmental consulting archaeologist, the associate director–cultural resources, and the manager of the National NAGPRA Program. While reviewing the proposed secretarial order to realign the functions related to implementation of the act, the Office of the Solicitor realized that authority for publishing notices had never been delegated specifically and for a short period all notices were signed by the deputy assistant secretary. The secretarial order delegating authority to publish notices in the *Federal Register* to the manager of the National NAGPRA Program was signed in 2005 and was converted to the Departmental Manual in 2007.

Extensions

Each federal agency and museum was required to compile an inventory of Native American human remains and associated funerary objects in its possession or control by November 16, 1995. Section 5(c) of the act authorizes the secretary to extend the inventory deadline for any museum that makes a good faith effort but is unable to complete the inventory process. The act does not authorize extensions of the inventory deadline for federal agencies. Secretarial authority to grant extensions was not delegated.

As the inventory deadline approached, extension criteria were developed and included in the fiscal year 1996 grant materials (National Park Service 1995). Appeals for extensions were required to include a letter from the museum's governing body describing the reason for the expected failure to comply; a description of all human remains and associated funerary objects in the museum's control; a list of all Indian tribes, Native Hawaiian organizations, and traditional religious leaders who have been consulted; and a detailed plan to complete the inventory by a specific date. Eighty-four extension appeals were eventually received, several of which were from museums that did not have human remains or associated funerary objects in their collections or had already submitted inventories. Extensions ranging from four and a half months to three years were awarded to the remaining fifty-eight museums on July 12, 1996. The notice was signed by the departmental consulting archaeologist (National Park Service 1996).

In November 1999, when six museums that had still not completed their inventories asked the departmental consulting archaeologist for extensions, the secretary's chief of staff intervened. The Assistant Secretary for Fish and Wildlife and Parks met personally with representatives of the American Museum of Natural History, Hearst Museum, New York State Museum, Ohio Historical Center, the Peabody Museum at Harvard, and Texas Archaeological Research Lab. While all of the requested extensions were denied, the assistant secretary agreed to exercise forbearance in the assessment of civil penalties, provided that the museum complete its inventory by a specified date (U.S. Department of the Interior 1999). All six museums completed their inventories by the deadlines and no penalties were assessed.

In 2005, the secretary signed an order formally delegating authority to grant extensions of the inventory deadlines to the Assistant Secretary for Fish and Wildlife and Parks (U.S. Department of the Interior 2005).

Grants

Section 10 of the act authorizes the Secretary of the Interior to make grants to assist museums in conducting summaries and inventories and to assist Indian tribes and Native Hawaiian organizations in repatriating cultural items.[20] Funding for inventories is limited to the compilation of existing museum records and consultation, since a separate statutory provision stipulates that the act may not be construed to authorize the initiation of new scientific studies or other means of acquiring or preserving additional scientific information from human remains and associated funerary objects.[21] Assistance to museums was estimated at the time of enactment to require about $10 million over five years and assistance to Indian tribes and Native Hawaiian organizations was estimated to require between $5 million to $10 million over five years (U.S. House of Representatives 1990b: 22).

Congressional appropriation of grants funding lagged behind both the summary deadline and the amounts needed by museums, Indian tribes, and Native Hawaiian organizations. When Congress finally appropriated $2.3 million for grants in fiscal year 1994, applications totaled $12.7 million and funds were not made available until after the November 16, 1993, summary deadline. Thirty-six museums received $1.9 million in grants prior to the November 16, 1995, inventory deadline. The National Park Service granted extensions of up to three years to the inventory deadline to fifty-eight museums due in part to the delay in grants funding (National Park Service

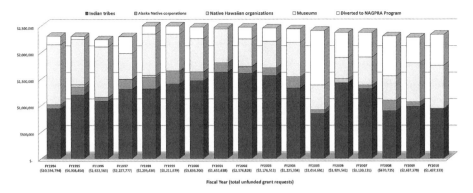

Fig. 3 Disbursement of NAGPRA Grant Funding, 1994-2010

1996). Congress increased the grants appropriation from $2.3 million to nearly $2.5 million in fiscal year 1998. When the last museum inventories were finally completed in 2001, sixty-eight museums had received slightly over $6 million in grants and 102 Indian tribes, seven Alaska Native corporations, and two Native Hawaiian organizations had received $11.6 million.

Grant applications evolved over time (National Park Service 2008, Chari 2010). Grants were initially administered as two separate programs, one for museums and the other for Indian tribes and Native Hawaiian organizations. Museums typically requested funding to complete their inventories of Native American human remains and associated funerary objects, coordinate consultation with Indian tribes and Native Hawaiian organizations, and train staff in techniques for consultation and documenting cultural affiliation. Indian tribes and Native Hawaiian organizations typically used grant funds for assessing and evaluating summaries, inventories, and documentation; training staff members in techniques for consultation and documenting the cultural affiliation of Native American human remains and cultural items; consulting with museum officials regarding culturally affiliated human remains and cultural items; and planning for the care or treatment of repatriated human remains or cultural items. Starting in 2002, a single application has been used with a typical project involving museums, Indian tribes, and Native Hawaiian organizations.

Congress has appropriated slightly over $40 million in grants over seventeen years, with Indian tribes and Native Hawaiian organizations receiving 58 percent and museums receiving 28 percent (see Figure 3). The remaining funds were diverted to other purposes, particularly from fiscal year 2002 onward, when the amount diverted averaged 23 percent per year. In fiscal year 2005, $667,800 of grant funding was used to pay a portion of the plaintiffs' legal fees in the case of *Bonnichsen v. United States*, and another $355,011 was diverted for administrative expenses. From 20 percent to 33 percent of grant funds have been diverted for administrative costs each fiscal year since 2006. The diversion was institutionalized in the fiscal year 2011 budget, with $581,000 being transferred to fund National Park Service "National Register Programs" (National Park Service 2010a: Overview-29).

Civil penalties

NAGPRA's civil penalty provisions were forged in the days immediately before enactment, during marathon negotiations between representatives of the American Association of Museums, Native American Rights Fund, Association on American Indian Affairs, and the Morning Star Foundation. The initial version of H.R. 5237 stipulated that any museum that failed to expeditiously repatriate human remains, funerary objects, sacred objects, or objects of inalienable communal property to a lineal descendant or culturally affiliated Indian tribe or Native Hawaiian organization would be ineligible for federal grants or other assistance during any period of noncompliance (U.S. House of Representatives 1990a). The museum and tribal negotiators recommended replacing this simple provision with a more complex compromise (American Association of Museums 1990). The Secretary of the Interior would be authorized to assess a civil penalty on any museum that failed to comply with any provision of the act. Instead of the broad ban on receiving federal funds, the compromise outlined several factors to be included in calculating a penalty amount, including the archaeological, historical, or commercial value of the item involved; economic and noneconomic damages to any aggrieved party; and the number of violations that had occurred. Lastly, civil penalties could only be assessed after promulgation of implementing regulations. The compromise language was added verbatim to the bill and enacted.[22]

Draft regulations implementing the civil penalty provisions were initially considered by the Review Committee in 1992. The draft provisions were based in part on similar regulations implementing civil penalties for the Archaeological Resources Protection Act. Committee members, including two who represented the American Association of Museums in the 1990 negotiations, were critical of the draft (Native American Graves Protection and Repatriation Review Committee 1992). The Department of the Interior ultimately decided to reserve the civil penalty regulations for later consideration (U.S. Department of the Interior 1993). Civil penalty regulations finally went into effect in 1997 (U.S. Department of the Interior 1997). The interim rule identified six specific situations as constituting a failure to comply, including not completing a summary, inventory, notification, or notice publication by the appropriate deadlines; refusing to repatriate cultural items to a lineal descendant or cultural affiliated Indian tribe or Native Hawaiian organization; or selling or transferring cultural items in violation of the act. The interim rule also established a two-stage penalty process. The initial penalty amount was based on a percentage of the museum's annual budget; archaeological, historical, or commercial value of the cultural item; economic and non-economic damages; and previous violations. An additional penalty of $100 per day could be assessed if the museum's violation continued after the date of the final administrative decision.

The Secretary of the Interior steadily received allegations of failure to comply: one in fiscal year 1996, five in 1997, and three more in 1998 (National Park Service 2010b: 17). In November 1998, when the six museums contacted the Department of the Interior to admit that they still had not completed their inventories of human remains and associated funerary objects, the museums' requests for additional extensions were denied. Although each of the six museums failed to comply with the inventory requirement, the Department of the Interior agreed to grant a specific period of forbearance from civil penalty as long as the inventory was completed by a certain date (U.S. Department of the Interior 1999).

At separate hearings before the Senate Indian Affairs Committee in 1999 and 2000, a growing number of witnesses expressed frustration with the lack of civil penalties. One witness complained that there had been no action on an allegation against a museum in Colorado referred to the Department of the Interior by the Department of Justice (U.S. Senate 2000: 27). Another witness testified that there had likewise been no action on an allegation filed by the Rosebud Sioux Tribe and the estate of Crazy Horse against a Maryland museum, and suggested that "the National Park Service is ill-equipped or ill-disposed to properly carry out the enforcement functions of NAGPRA" (U.S. Senate 1999: 32). Another witness testified that the National Park Service had been uncharacteristically aggressive regarding an allegation submitted against his museum when it loaned funerary objects to a Native Hawaiian organization (U.S. Senate 2000: 40). He characterized some of the National Park Service correspondence on the matter as inappropriate and suggested that his museum had been singled out for such keen scrutiny because funerary objects from the same site as the loaned items were in the National Park Service collections. He was also concerned that the correspondence had been leaked to the local press by a National Park Service employee, creating an atmosphere of suspicion and ill will within his museum and the outside community. In response, NPS Associate Director Katherine Stevenson reported that seven allegations were "under investigation," another three "under review," and final civil penalty regulations were being prepared (U.S. Senate 2000: 49).

By the time final civil penalty regulations went into effect in 2003, the Secretary of the Interior had received twenty-three allegations of failure to comply, but still no civil penalties had been assessed (National Park Service 2010b: 17). The final regulations added two additional situations to the six listed in the 1997 interim rule as constituting failures to comply: not consulting with lineal descendants, Indian tribe officials, and traditional religious leaders as required; and not informing the recipients of repatriations of any presently known treatment with pesticides, preservatives, or other substances that represent a potential hazard to the objects or to persons handling the objects. The final rule also raised the amount of the per-day penalty that could be assessed for a continued violation from a flat $100 to a range not to exceed $1,000. Shortly after publication of the final rule, the National Park Service named a civil penalty officer to coordinate the investigatory process.

A major change in the department's approach was signaled by the 2005 delegation of responsibility for investigating allegations of failure to comply and assessing civil penalties to the Assistant Secretary for Fish and Wildlife and Parks (U.S. Department of the Interior 2005). An NPS law enforcement officer was assigned to investigate the allegations and the first civil penalty was finally assessed the following year. Through the end of fiscal year 2010, the Secretary of the Interior received a total of sixty-nine separate allegations of failure to comply, of which thirty-one had been investigated (National Park Service 2010b). Sixteen of the investigated allegations were shown to be without merit. In each of the other fifteen allegations, the museum was shown to have failed to comply with one or more of NAGPRA's requirements. Museums found to have failed to comply with one or more provisions include the Bishop Museum; City of Harrisburg, Pennsylvania; East Carolina University; the Peabody Museum at Harvard; Nelson-Atkins Museum; Northern Illinois University; Oregon State University; Pacific Lutheran College; Pierce College; Safety Harbor Museum; St. Joseph Museum; Texas Parks and Wildlife Department; University of Massachusetts-Amherst; and the University of Puget Sound. The fifteen allegations yielded a total of twenty-one confirmed failures to comply, including one count of sale or transfer of cultural items contrary to the provisions of the act, two counts of failure to complete a summary, nine counts of failure to complete an inventory, six counts of refusal to repatriate, and three counts of failure to consult. Fourteen of the fifteen confirmed allegations were filed after publication of the final civil penalty rule in 2003, indicating that the Department of the Interior has generally declined to take action on allegations filed under the interim civil penalty rule from 1997 through 2003.

Civil penalties were assessed against nine museums, including the City of Harrisburg, East Carolina University; Northern Illinois University; Pierce College; Safety Harbor Museum; St. Joseph Museum; Texas Parks and Wildlife Department; and the University of Puget Sound. In most cases, the penalty consisted of an initial amount of $5,000 or less, based on the museum's annual budget, and was reduced by 25 percent or 50 percent, depending on whether the museum's failure to comply was willful or if, upon notification of the allegation, the museum took steps to mitigate the failure to comply. In the case of the City of Harrisburg, an additional penalty was included based on documented expenditures by the aggrieved party to compel the museum to comply with the act. Penalty amounts ranged from $439.34 (Safety Harbor Museum) to $9,820 (City of Harrisburg). In addition to the eight formally assessed penalties, the Bishop Museum paid $13,500 as part of a settlement following a hearing before the Office of Hearings and Appeals. All civil penalties paid to the U.S. were sent directly to the U.S. Treasurer. The Department determined civil penalties to be inappropriate for five museums, including the Bishop Museum, the Peabody Museum at Harvard, Oregon State University, and Pacific Lutheran College.

Assuming responsibility for inadvertent discoveries

Section 3 (d)(3) of the act authorizes the Secretary of the Interior to assume certain responsibilities for Native American cultural items discovered inadvertently on federal land managed by another department. These duties include certifying receipt of notification of the discovery and determining the disposition of the discovered cultural items.[23] The idea for the Secretary of the Interior to assume certain responsibilities is based on a fundamental canon of judicial interpretation: when a statute is ambiguous and falls within the subject-matter jurisdiction of a federal agency, the agency's official interpretation of the statute, if reasonable, is given deference by the court.[24] The Secretary of the Interior's reasonable interpretation of ambiguous provisions of NAGPRA should be given deference by the court, particularly if the interpretation is developed as part of notice and comment rulemaking. A similar interpretation by another agency might not be accorded such deference.

Assumption of the inadvertent discovery responsibilities has occurred only once, related to human remains found on land controlled by the U.S.. Army Corps of Engineers near Kennewick, Washington. The corps initially determined that the human remains were Native American and were culturally affiliated with five Columbia River Basin tribes. On June 27, 1997, a federal district court vacated the corps's determination and remanded the matter back to the agency for further consideration. The Department of the Army contacted the Department of the Interior and in March 1998 the two departments signed an interagency agreement transferring responsibility for determining whether the human remains were Native American within the meaning of NAGPRA, and, if it was determined that they were, to provide for their disposition (U.S. Department of the Interior 1998). The acting Assistant Secretary for Fish and Wildlife and Parks signed the interagency agreement for the Secretary of the Interior. Two years later, a memorandum of decision signed by the Assistant Secretary for Fish and Wildlife and Parks summarized the archaeology, geomorphology, physical anthropology, sedimentology, and other scientific evidence and determined that the human remains were "Native American" as defined by the act (U.S. Department of the Interior 2000a). This was followed by a letter from Secretary of the Interior Bruce Babbitt to Secretary of the Army Louis Caldera determining that evidence of cultural continuity was sufficient to show that the human remains were culturally affiliated with the present-day Indian tribe claimants. The letter also substantiated the claim based on aboriginal occupation (U.S. Department of the Interior 2000b).

On August 30, 2002, the federal district court set aside the Secretary of the Interior's determination, finding that the record did not support the finding that the human remains were "Native American" or that the human remains were culturally affiliated with the tribal claimants. The court also concluded that the secretary's determination that aboriginal lands furnished a valid alternative basis for awarding the human remains to the tribal claimants was arbitrary and capricious, contrary to law, and in excess of the secretary's authority (*Bonnichsen v. United States*, 217 F. Supp. 2d 1116 (D. OR. 2002)). The U.S. Court of Appeals for the Ninth Circuit affirmed the district court opinion, taking the additional step of identifying the regulatory definition of "Native American" as conflicting with the plain language of the act and thus being invalid (*Bonnichsen v. United States*, 357 F.3d 962 [9th Cir. 2004]). In fiscal year 2005, the United States paid the plaintiff's legal fees of approximately $3 million, $667,800 from NAGPRA grant funding and the remaining balance from funding to the Bureau of Indian Affairs and the U.S. Army Corps of Engineers.

Delegation

Criticism of the secretary's delegation of certain NAGPRA implementation duties to the departmental consulting archaeologist circulated for several years, particularly after oversight for National Park Service compliance was assigned to the same office as part of a 1995 reorganization (see Figure 4). These concerns crystallized at the April 20, 1999, oversight hearing held by the Senate Indian Affairs Committee (U.S. Senate 1999). The committee heard from eight witnesses, including representatives of the American Association of Museums, Society for American Archaeology, National Congress of American Indians, three Indian tribes, and two private citizens. Witnesses were concerned that the departmental consulting archaeologist may have abused his discretion in granting inventory extensions in 1995, had refused to publish several submitted notices in the *Federal Register*, and that allegations of failure to comply were not being investigated and civil penalties assessed. A number of witnesses strongly urged the secretary to redelegate NAGPRA's administrative duties to a more neutral location within the department, while only one witness opposed redelegation.

Shortly after the Senate hearing, the Assistant Secretary for Policy, Management and Budget submitted an options paper to the secretary's chief of staff outlining seven possible administrative locations for the department's NAGPRA responsibilities

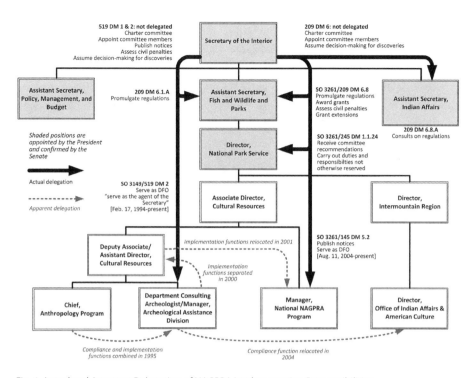

Fig. 4. Actual and Apparent Delegation of NAGPRA Implementation Responsibilities

(U.S. Department of the Interior 1999b). One option was to retain the current delegation to the departmental consulting archaeologist, although the options paper acknowledged that there was a perceived conflict of interest related to the position's science responsibilities and strong identification with the archaeological constituency. A second option was to move the program functions to another program within the National Park Service. Both the first and second options were thought to be burdened by perceived land management and collection management biases, as well as the National Park Service having been unresponsive to perceived conflicts of interest. The remaining five options were to create a new program reporting directly or indirectly to the Assistant Secretary for Fish, Wildlife and Parks; Indian Affairs; or Policy, Management and Budget. Each of these options was thought to signal heightened concern, by elevating the program to the department level, although each would also include a brief disruption of program activity due to office relocation.

The Director of the National Park Service submitted a counter-proposal to the secretary's chief of staff on August 5, 1999 (National Park Service 1999). All three of the director's options were located within the National Park Service, which he believed to be the most appropriate bureau because of its lead role in providing guidance and expertise in the preservation of cultural resources. Option one was to separate national implementation duties from those related to National Park Service compliance with the act, but to retain both functions within the Archeology and Ethnography Program. Option two would retain compliance duties within the Archeology and Ethnography Program and reorganize the supervision of government-wide implementation under the Assistant Director for Cultural Resources. In the third option, the compliance function would again be retained by the Archeology and Ethnography Program and national implementation would relocate under the Associate Director for Cultural Resources. The director recommended option one. In the fall issue of *Common Ground*, the National Park Service's journal on public archaeology and ethnography, the departmental consulting archaeologist underlined the status quo recommendation when he cautioned archaeologists, particularly those working for Indian tribes, to "take care to distinguish between advocating for tribal positions and providing professional advice" (McManamon 1999). The secretary's chief of staff finally made a decision on November 23, 1999, selecting the NPS director's second option. While the secretary named the Assistant Director for Cultural Resources as the Review Committee's designated federal officer in the 2000 charter, none of the other duties were formally redelegated.

Redelegation of NAGPRA duties was again a central topic of the July 25, 2000, oversight hearing before the Senate Indian Affairs Committee. The committee heard from fourteen witnesses, including two members of the Review Committee, representatives of the American Association of Museums, Society for American Archaeology, four Indian tribes, one museum, three private citizens, and, from the National Park Service, the Associate Director for Cultural Resources and the departmental consulting archaeologist. Committee Vice-Chairman Senator Daniel Inouye described recent administrative changes as a "reorganization of sorts" (U.S. Senate 2000: 1). The Review Committee members presented the committee's unanimous recommendation that the secretary move the NAGPRA administrative structure from the National Park Service to the department's secretariat, and the majority of other witnesses agreed. The NPS associate director later reported that in all her years of testifying before Congress she had never been attacked the way she was at the July 25th hearing. When the redelegation issue was again brought up to the secretary's chief of staff the following September, however, she refused, reportedly describing the current situation a National Park Service problem that would need to be fixed by the National Park Service.

Assignment of implementation duties to the NPS assistant director did not last for long. In 2001, a separate general NAGPRA program was informally established under the direction of a separate program manager. The new administrative structure was not formally acknowledged until 2003 when the National NAGPRA Program manager was delegated as the Review Committee's designated federal officer. Finally, in 2005, Secretary Gale Norton issued Secretarial Order 3261 to realign functions related to implementation of NAGPRA (U.S. Department of the Interior 2005). The secretary retained authority to charter and appoint members to the Review Committee. The Assistant Secretary for Fish and Wildlife and Parks was explicitly delegated authority to issue regulations, in consultation with the Assistant Secretary–Indian Affairs; grant extensions of inventory deadlines; award grants; and investigate allegations of failure to comply and assess civil penalties. Duties other than those reserved to the Assistant Secretary for Fish and Wildlife and Parks were delegated to the Director of the National Park Service, supported by the National NAGPRA Program manager. The latter position was specifically delegated to publish notices in the *Federal Register* and serve as the Review Committee's designated federal officer. The secretarial order also authorized the manager of a separate National Park Service NAGPRA program to ensure compliance by the National Park system with statutory requirements. These delegations were converted to the Departmental Manual in 2007.

Concerns over NAGPRA implementation were again voiced at the October 9, 2009, oversight hearing held by the House Natural Resources Committee (U.S. House of Representatives 2009). The committee heard from six witnesses, including representatives of the Society for American Archaeology, two Indian tribes, one Native American organization, a former chair of the Review Committee, and the acting Director of the National Park Service. The witnesses expressed concerns that notices were withdrawn from publication in the *Federal Register* without prior consultation with Indian tribes, that the online databases were not accurate, that a substantial amount of grant funding was diverted to other purposes, and that there was a lack of transparency in how program decisions were made.

In the twenty years since NAGPRA was enacted, the secretary has changed the delegation of specific duties several times. Generally, the shift has been from lower to higher levels, from the departmental consulting archaeologist or National NAGPRA Program manager to the Director of the National Park Service or to the Assistant Secretary for Fish and Wildlife and Parks, in recognition of the inherent conflict in having any administrative unit being responsible for complying with a law it also implements. While most delegations were made explicitly by means of secretarial orders, Departmental Manual revisions, and Review Committee charters, some were only apparent delegations, particularly during the period from 2000–2004 when the Assistant Director for Cultural Resources or the National NAGPRA Program manager began signing *Federal Register* notices and other implementation documents without an actual change in the delegation. Review of the current Departmental Manual reveals a tangle of conflicting delegations with the departmental consulting archaeologist and the manager of the National NAGPRA Program both delegated to serve as the Review Committee's designated federal officer (see 519 DM 2 and 145 DM 5.2), and general delegations to both the departmental consulting archaeologist and the Director of the National Park Service (519 DM 2 and 245 DM 1.1.24).

Regardless of previous delegations, the ultimate authority and responsibility for implementation of the act remains with the Secretary of the Interior. The twentieth anniversary of the act provides an opportunity for the secretary to reconsider how these duties can best be carried forward.

NAGPRA reconciles four major areas of federal law (McKeown and Hutt 2002). As civil rights law, the act acknowledges that Native American human remains and funerary objects suffered disparate treatment as compared with the human remains and funerary objects of other groups and provides a procedural system for lineal descendants, Indian tribes, and Native Hawaiian organizations to obtain redress. The department's Office of Civil Rights, which provides the focal point for all civil rights functions within the department, reports to the Assistant Secretary for Policy, Management and Budget.

As Indian law, the act explicitly acknowledges tribal sovereignty and the government-to-government relationship between the United States and Indian tribes, and implicitly recognizes that ambiguous statutory provisions must be interpreted liberally in favor of the Indians. The Assistant Secretary for Indian Affairs exercises the authorities and responsibilities of the secretary relating to Indian tribes, individual Indian tribal members, and Indian affairs.

As property law, the act clarifies the unique status of the dead as well as highlighting the failure of American law to adequately recognize traditional concepts of communal property in use by some Indian tribes. The department's Office of Acquisition and Property Management, which is responsible for developing policy on museum property, reports to the Assistant Secretary for Policy, Management and Budget.

As administrative law, the act directs the Secretary of the Interior to implement Congress's mandate, including establishing the Review Committee, promulgating regulations, publishing inventory notices, granting inventory extensions, awarding grants, assessing civil penalties, and assuming the decision-making role in determining the disposition of certain discovered cultural items. The offices responsible for many of these duties report either to the Assistant Secretary for Policy, Management and Budget, or to the deputy secretary.

NAGPRA runs counter to much of preservation law. Instead of placing federal restrictions on the use of objects of antiquity;[25] historic objects;[26] significant districts, sites, buildings, structures, and objects;[27] or archaeological resources;[28] the act transfers complete control of certain Native American cultural items to lineal descendants, Indian tribes, or Native Hawaiian to do with as they see fit.

In light of the past twenty years of implementation history, the secretary might consider delegation of NAGPRA responsibilities to one of the other assistant secretaries, particularly the Assistant Secretary for Policy, Management and Budget, or the Assistant Secretary for Indian Affairs, or, as has been done for other cross-cutting functions like the Federal Subsistence Board or the Special Trustee for American Indians, establishing a new office reporting directly to the Secretary of the Interior.

Notes

1   25 U.S.C. § 3002(b) and § 3006. See McKeown 2010 for an overview of the Review Committee's responsibilities.
2   5 U.S.C. Appendix § 9(c).
3   25 U.S.C. § 3006(b)(1).
4   5 U.S.C. App. 2, § 14(b).
5   25 U.S.C. § 3011.
6   25 U.S.C. § 3002(b).
7   25 U.S.C. § 3007(b).
8   5 U.S.C. § 553.
9   25 U.S.C. § 3001(9).
10   43 C.F.R. 10.2(d).
11   25 U.S.C. 3001(7).
12   25 U.S.C. § 3003(d)(1).
13   25 U.S.C. § 3003(d)(2).
14   25 U.S.C. § 3003(d)(3).
15   43 C.F.R. § 10.9(e)(2).
16   43 C.F.R. § 10.9(e)(4).
17   43 C.F.R. § 10, App. B.
18   43 C.F.R. § 10.8(f).
19   43 C.F.R. § 10.10(a)(3) and (b)(2).
20   25 U.S.C. § 3008.
21   25 U.S.C. § 3003(b).
22   25 U.S.C. § 3007.
23   25 U.S.C. § 3002(d).
24   Chevron U.S.A. v. Natural Resources Defense Council, 467 U.S. 837 (1984).
25   16 U.S.C. § 431 et seq.
26   16 U.S.C. § 1.
27   16 U.S.C. § 470 et seq.
28   16 U.S.C. § 470aa et seq.

Bibliography

American Association of Museums
1990   Final Agreement: Proposed Amendments to H.R. 5237 in order to meet AAM Concerns (Oct. 5, 1990).
1991   Letter from Geoffrey Platt Jr., Director of Government Affairs, American Association of Museums to Secretary of the Interior Manuel Lujan. Co-signed by representatives

of the American Anthropological Association, American Association of Physical Anthropologists, American Association of Universities, Archaeological Association of America, Association of American Indian Affairs, National Conference of State Historic Preservation Officers, National Congress of American Indians, National Trust for Historic Preservation, Native American Rights Fund, Preservation Action, Society for American Archaeology, and Society for Professional Archaeology (Aug. 27, 1991).

Associated Press

1991   "Return of Indian Remains a Slow Process. Implementation of Law Frustrating to Tribal Advocates, Scientists." *Rocky Mountain News*, 36 (Sept. 8, 1991).

Chari, Sangita

2010   "Journeys to Repatriation: 15 Years of NAGPRA Grants, 1994–2008." *Museum Anthropology*, Vol. 33, No. 2, 210–217.

Government Accountability Office

2010   Native American Graves Protection and Repatriation Act: After Almost 20 Years, Key Federal Agencies Still Have Not Fully Complied with the Act. GAO-10-768 (July 28, 2010).

McKeown, C. Timothy

2010   "A Willingness to Listen to Each Side": The Native American Graves Protection and Repatriation Review Committee, 1991–2010. *Museum Anthropology*, Vol. 33, No 2, 218–233.

McKeown, C. Timothy and Sherry Hutt

2002   "In the Smaller Scope of Conscience: The Native American Graves Protection and Repatriation Act Twelve Years After." *UCLA Journal of Environmental Law and Policy*, Vol. 21, 153–212.

McManamon, Francis P.

1999   "Working for 'the Other'," in *Common Ground, Archeology and Ethnography in the Public Interest* (Fall 1999).

National Park Service

1992   Notice of Completion of Inventory of Native American Human Remains and Associated Funerary Objects within the Campbell Collection, Joshua Tree National Monument, Twentynine Palms, CA. 57 *Fed. Reg.* 27269 (June 18, 1992).

1995   1995 NAGPRA Grants for Museums.

1996   Extension of Time for Inventory. 61 *Fed. Reg.* 36756-36757 (July 12, 1996).

1999   Memorandum from Director Bob Stanton to the Secretary's Chief of Staff Ann Shields, Recommended Alternatives for Implementation of Secretary's Responsibilities Under the Native American Graves Protection and Repatriation Act (NAGPRA) (Aug. 5, 1999).

2009   *Journeys to Repatriation: 15 Years of NAGPRA Grants (1994–2008).*

2010a   Budget Justifications and Performance Information: Fiscal Year 2011.

2010b   National NAGPRA Program FY 2010 Final Report For the Period October 1, 2009– September 30, 2010. http://www.nps.gov/nagpra/DOCUMENTS/NAGPRA_FY10_ Program_Report.pdf (accessed October 9, 2011).

2011   Culturally Affiliated Native American Inventories Database. http://grants.cr.nps.gov/ CAI/index.cfm (accessed November 3, 2011).

Native American Graves Protection and Repatriation Review Committee

1992   Minutes, Second Meeting: Aug. 26–28, 1992, Lakewood, CO.

1998   Report to Congress: 1995–1997.

1999a   Minutes of the Sixteenth Meeting: December 10–12, 1998, Santa Fe, NM.

1999b   Report to Congress: 1998.

2000   Recommendations Regarding the Disposition of Culturally Unidentifiable Native American Human Remains. 65 *Fed. Reg.* 36462–36464 (June 8, 2000).

2003   Report to Congress: 1999–2001.

2005   Report to Congress: 2002–2004.

U.S. Department of the Interior

1990   Letter from Deputy Assistant Secretary for Fish and Wildlife and Parks Scott Sewell to Representative Morris Udall (Oct. 2, 1990).

1991a   Charter: Native American Graves Protection and Repatriation Review Committee (signed and filed August 2, 1991).

1991b   Secretarial Order 3149: Delegation of Authority—Native American Graves Protection and Repatriation Act (P.L. 101-601) Responsibilities (Oct. 16, 1991).

1991c   Letter from Assistant Secretary of the Interior for Fish and Wildlife and Parks Mike Hayden to Senator Daniel K. Inouye (Nov. 6, 1991).

1993   Notice of Proposed Rulemaking: Native American Graves Protection and Repatriation Act Regulations, 43 C.F.R. 10. 58 *Fed. Reg.* 31123-31134 (May 28, 1993).

1994   Preservation of Historical Property, 519 DM 1 (Feb. 17, 1994) and Preservation of American Antiquities and Treatment and Disposition of Native American Cultural Items, 519 DM 2 (Feb. 17, 1994).

1995   Native American Graves Protection and Repatriation Act Regulations, Final Rule, 43 C.F.R. 10. 60 *Fed. Reg.* 62134-62169 (Dec. 4, 1995).

1997   Native American Graves Protection and Repatriation Act Regulations—Civil Penalties, Interim Rule, 43 C.F.R. 10.12. 62 *Fed. Reg.* 1820-1823 (Jan. 13, 1997).

1998   Interagency Agreement Between the Department of the Army and the Department of the Interior on the Delegation of Responsibilities Under Section 3 of the Native American Graves Protection and Repatriation Act Pertaining to Human Remains Discovered Near the City of Kennewick, Washington (Mar. 24, 1998).

1999a   Letters from Donald J. Barry, Assistant Secretary for Fish and Wildlife and Parks, to the American Museum of Natural History, Hearst Museum, New York State Museum, Ohio Historical Society, the Peabody Museum at Harvard, and Texas Archaeological Research Lab (May, 1999).

2000a   Determination That the Kennewick Human Skeletal Remains are "Native American" for the Purposes of the Native American Graves Protection and Repatriation Act (NAGPRA), signed by Assistant Secretary for Fish and Wildlife and Parks Donald J. Barry (Jan. 11, 2000).

2000b   Letter from Secretary of the Interior Bruce Babbitt to Secretary of the Army Louis Caldera (Sept. 21, 2000).

2003   Native American Graves Protection and Repatriation Act Regulations—Civil Penalties, Final Rule, 43 C.F.R. 10.12. 68 *Fed. Reg.* 16354-16364 (April 3, 2003).

2004   Native American Graves Protection and Repatriation Act Regulations—Future Applicability, Proposed Rule, 43 C.F.R. 10.13, 69 *Fed. Reg.* 61613 (Oct. 20, 2004).

2005   Secretarial Order 3261: Realignment of Functions Relating to the Native American Graves Protection and Repatriation Act (May 23, 2005).

2007   145 DM 5.2: National Park Service, Associate Director for Cultural Resources, National NAGPRA Program (May 31, 2007); and 245 DM 1.1.24: Delegation, National Park Service, General Program Delegation, Director (May 31, 2007).

2007a Native American Graves Protection and Repatriation Act Regulations—Future Applicability, Final Rule, 43 C.F.R. 10.13, 72 *Fed. Reg.* 13184-13189 (Mar. 21, 2007).

2007b Native American Graves Protection and Repatriation Act Regulations—Disposition of Culturally Unidentifiable Human Remains, Proposed Rule, 43 C.F.R. 10.11. 72 *Fed. Reg.* 58582-58590 (Oct. 16, 2007).

2010 Native American Graves Protection and Repatriation Act Regulations—Disposition of Culturally Unidentifiable Human Remains, Final Rule, 43 C.F.R. 10.11, Final rule with request for comments. 75 *Fed. Reg.* 12377-12405 (Mar. 15, 2010).

2011a Memorandum from Associate Solicitor Edith R. Blackwell and Associate Solicitor Barry N. Roth to Sherry Hutt, List of Indian tribes for the purposes of carrying out the Native American Graves Protection and Repatriation Act (NAGPRA) (Mar. 18, 2011).

2011b Native American Graves Protection and Repatriation Act Regulations—Definition of "Indian Tribe," Interim final rule with request for comments. 76 *Fed. Reg.* 39007-39009 (July 5, 2011).

U.S. House of Representatives

1990a Native American Graves Protection and Repatriation Act, H.R. 5237, 101st Congress (July 10, 1990).

1990b Protection of Native American Graves and the Repatriation of Human Remains and Sacred Objects: Hearing on H.R. 1381—Native American Burial Site Preservation Act of 1989; H.R. 1646—Native American Grave and Burial Protection Act; and H.R. 5237—Native American Graves Protection and Repatriation Act. H.R. Hearing 101-62 (July 17, 1990).

2009 Native American Graves Protection and Repatriation Act (NAGPRA). Oversight Hearing before the House Committee on Natural Resources. H.R. Hearing 111-38 (Oct. 7, 2009).

U.S. Senate

1999 Hearing before the Committee on Indian Affairs, United States Senate on the Native American Graves Protection and Repatriation Act. S. Hrg. 106-57 (April 20, 1999).

2000 Hearing before the Committee on Indian Affairs, United States Senate on the Native American Graves Protection and Repatriation Act. S. Hrg. 106–708 (July 25, 2000).

Chapter 3
Finding Our Way Home

ERIC HEMENWAY

Introduction

Throughout Indian Country,[1] introductions are very important. You are expected to announce yourself by providing information including who you are, where you come from, and what tribe you are from. Therefore, before the purpose of this chapter is presented, I feel obligated to state some personal facts. My name is Eric Hemenway. I am an Odawa/Anishnaabek[2] from Cross Village, Michigan. I work for the Little Traverse Bay Bands of Odawa Indians (LTBB Odawa) in northern Michigan in their NAGPRA program. I have been with this program for over five years and have worked with over twenty museums across the country, as well as with Michigan tribes and tribes from other states on multiple repatriations of human remains and cultural objects.

LTBB Odawa was awarded a 2009 NAGPRA consultation/documentation grant to create a repatriation manual for tribes that guides them through the various components of running a NAGPRA program. A large part of this manual requires gathering advice and expertise from tribes across the country that have active NAGPRA programs. Interviewing these tribes has been a very educational experience. It has given me a greater perspective of NAGPRA and how tribes implement it. Additionally, I am currently serving a four-year term (2010–2013) on the NAGPRA Review Committee[3] where I have the opportunity to further the work of NAGPRA on a national level. The purpose of this chapter is to provide a better understanding of what NAGPRA means to tribes, the impact repatriation has on Native communities, and the reasons tribes go through the struggle of having remains and items returned to their communities. I write this chapter from the viewpoint of a tribal person; a perspective, I feel, that is often forgotten in the realm of legal and scholarly opinions. My experience as an Odawa who works on NAGPRA, locally and nationally, provides the foundational work of this chapter.

Repatriation is such a unique line of work; it encompasses vastly different issues: religion, history, law, human rights, tribal identity, tribal lands, graves/burial sites, and the dead. I feel that the legal aspects of NAGPRA and the effect of NAGPRA on museums and federal agencies tend to receive the most attention. But the real issue, from mine and many others' perspectives, both Indian and non-Indian, is that NAGPRA is about human rights. Part of recognizing a group's human rights is the need to recognize their belief systems and one of the core elements of those beliefs is the right to retain a group's identity. By identity, I mean their worldview, sacred and religious beliefs, and cultural practices. To me, identity is at the core of NAGPRA. Every person, every ethnic group, has an inalienable right to worship and practice their beliefs as they see fit. For tribes, our traditions and beliefs are a few of the only aspects of our identities that are still within the ownership of the tribes. For centuries, our beliefs were under attack, under persecution, and even deemed illegal. Land, language, people, and items were all stolen from every tribe in the United States. The very core of tribal identities was challenged. But our beliefs carried us through these dark times, solidified who we were, and promoted the continuation of age-old rites and customs. While the world changed drastically from generation to generation for the tribes of the United States, those tribes still held onto their beliefs and honored their dead as best they could. Without the traditional knowledge, customs, ceremonies, and sacred items to help perpetuate identity, the very essence of who we are as a people would have died out.

People (both living and dead), ceremonies, beliefs, and communities are all elements influenced by NAGPRA. Native American tribes across the country, as well as Native Hawaiians and Alaska Natives,[4] have different beliefs and ceremonies, and use different items. One common characteristic we all share is a fundamental belief in the importance of respecting the dead, and the need for certain sacred objects to be returned for the revival and continuation of ceremonies that are important to our tribes' prosperity and overall well-being. Tribes develop NAGPRA programs because they know it is their responsibility to take care of their dead and their sacred items; nobody will or should do it for them. This was true before the arrival of Europeans and is still true today.

As Native Americans, our culture has been fragmented; in some cases, literally stolen from the ground in which our ancestors were laid to rest. Sacred items vital to age-old ceremonies were taken without the consent of the tribe. Some of these grievances are sacrilegious in the eyes of the tribe; for example, systematically digging up the dead, taking them and their sacred funerary objects and transporting them to museums to be studied and placed in boxes on shelves. I have personally performed numerous reburials, and never has an individual been complete, the remains are fragments of that person. More often than not, it is only the skull. Why only the skull? Because it was very common during the early twentieth century for people to find Indian graves, sever the head from the deceased Indian and sell the skull to whoever would buy it. It is appalling and mortifying to learn this happened, not only to my tribe but to tribes all across the country, and not in the too-distant past. This is a direct violation of our beliefs as Odawa; we feel strongly that the dead should never be disturbed. Having our beliefs and knowing the true history of how museums acquired certain items from tribes brings a certain responsibility to do something to correct these historical injustices. NAGPRA provides an avenue for tribes to do just that.

Working on NAGPRA is more than just a job. I reaffirm the identity of my tribe in one way or another every day. When requesting an inventory from a museum, I look to where my tribe has had historical and aboriginal occupation to understand the importance of certain geographic locations to the tribe. When pursuing remains, I rely on the beliefs of the Odawa people and how we care for the dead. The many sacred objects we submit claims for are directly related to our identity. A certain object may have a design that identifies it as an Odawa item; without knowledge of our culture and way of life, I would not know if this item was originally in our tribe or not. As one Anishnaabe elder told me when I was growing up, "Everybody has a job, for the betterment of the tribe." I think about that statement now and I see what I am doing as "my job for the tribe." What is being done through repatriation helps to heal past wrongs and uphold my tribe's beliefs and identity as Odawa. The elder who told me this when I was younger was somebody I greatly respected. He has long since passed, but I know he is watching in approval.

Little Traverse Bay Bands of Odawa Indians repatriation program

The LTBB Odawa recognized the need to have a NAGPRA program as soon as its federal recognition was reestablished. In 1994, against all odds, the Little Traverse Bay Bands of Odawa Indians won a legal battle that spanned 150 years before the reaffirmation of its federal recognition was officially recognized by the United States government.[5] Strong historical records were critical in the process, but just as important was a vibrant, continued cultural presence in our community at Little Traverse. Knowledge was kept in many books, letters, and photos, but the thriving cultural activity passed on from generation to generation was the foundation for all these records being retained. Our history and our culture define who we are as a tribe, a group distinct from others. The values that shape our culture and the strong commitment to knowing our history transcend all aspects of our community, ranging from economics to language acquisition. This appreciation and respect for history and culture has resulted in many wonderful developments at LTBB Odawa, including the decision to make NAGPRA and repatriation a priority. The Gijigowi Bipskaabiimi[6] Department for LTBB Odawa is where the current NAGPRA work occurs.

As mentioned, LTBB Odawa has had a NAGPRA officer since 1994. In 2006, I was hired to be the NAGPRA specialist for the Little Traverse Bay Bands of Odawa

Indians because of my background in research and active involvement in the ceremonies and the culture of my tribe. Even though this position had changed hands several times before I came on, I was fortunate to have well-documented records to utilize and the ability to draw on the experiences of earlier repatriations. From the previous records, I could see all contacts made, inventories[7] and summaries[8] filed, where consultations stopped and where they never started, completed repatriations, and notes from trips to museums. It was as if I was watching this long journey unfold and my job began where my predecessors left off. These records were a testament to the persistence needed to complete work under NAGPRA. I discovered a summary that we received in 1997 along with records of multiple phone calls, emails, and visits paid to this museum. Despite all this work, a claim to return ceremonial bags identified as sacred objects to LTBB Odawa was never submitted to this museum. I immediately began working to have the ceremonial bags returned. I was very excited, as this was my first claim. To my dismay, the claim was sent back with a letter stating that it was denied. It was tough seeing my tribe's views rejected; after all, I thought we knew best if an object was sacred or not! We regrouped, revamped our claim, and sent it back. The resubmitted claim was accepted. It took over ten years for the ceremonial bags to come back home, but they finally did in 2009.

NAGPRA affords our tribe the opportunity to reclaim vital aspects of our culture, things that define who we are as a people, as Anishnaabek, legally as well as in a cultural and spiritual sense. Since that first repatriation, I have learned that implementing NAGPRA on a tribal level comes down to patience, persistence, and knowledge of the process. I have learned that you must possess the emotional and mental fortitude to deal with not having your beliefs taken seriously—with rejection, narrow ideas, and difficult personalities, all the while knowing that the spirits of the dead languish while their remains await reburial. This is why I believe it is so important to have a ceremonial element present throughout all phases of NAGPRA work. One of the cornerstones of being Anishnaabek is caring for our dead. These ceremonies have been with the Anishnaabek since time immemorial and continue to be a vital part of our existence. Reclaiming our ancestors and reburying is a new development, but is in keeping with our traditional beliefs that we honor and respect the ones who walked on before us. Cultures and traditions do change, and repatriation of our ancestors is one means of adapting to these changes. Without our ancestors, we would not be who we are today. The ancestors overcame tremendous difficulties to provide the living the opportunity to be in our homelands and to be Anishnaabek. It is the duty of the living to honor that and care for our ancestors, and we do so today in this new way.

I have been blessed with having success working under NAGPRA. Since I first started this work in 2006, I have engineered over fifteen separate repatriations for human remains, totaling approximately 400 individuals. In addition to the repatriations for remains, I have written successful repatriation claims for sacred items, funerary objects, and objects of cultural patrimony, resulting in a dozen items coming back home. Some of the claims for remains have been joint collaborations with other tribes, and some have been strictly affiliation claims for LTBB Odawa. By far, the return of remains has been the most important element of my NAGPRA work and has had the most profound impact on my personal life. Going from the uncertainty of the first phone call to a museum about remains in their collection, to digging the grave to rebury the remains years later is an incredible experience. The immense feeling of accomplishment and sense of duty to your beliefs is hard to describe in words. Performing the reburial ceremony is always bittersweet. I feel happy to have made a difference in helping my Anishnaabek relations that have passed on but at the same time, it is extremely sad and incomprehensible to me that such work needs to be carried out, that my people were disrespected in such a horrible manner by being dug out of their final resting places, studied, put in boxes, and dehumanized. I have done dozens of reburials. Each one is very difficult, especially when I must rebury small children. I am no expert in identifying remains, but the remains of kids are obvious. Putting these individuals back to rest really emphasizes the humanity of repatriation and the sacred importance of this work.

First and foremost, I rely on my Anishnaabek teachings and beliefs to lead my work. In fact, I first had to get permission from my elders to handle remains before I could accept the job. Even when items are returned, there is a cultural protocol that must be met. Some of these items have been out of our community for over a hundred years! Reintroducing the items helps revitalize traditions that have waned or been forgotten to the majority of the community. But, we find that bringing certain items back sparks the memories of a few individuals, which in turn leads to the sharing of knowledge that helps reconstruct our beliefs. I continually seek guidance from the spirits in my endeavors under NAGPRA. I believe the spirits are the real foundation of my work, and everything in NAGPRA is infused with them, including remains, cultural objects, sacred areas, and burial grounds.

Although I am led by my traditional beliefs, I rely on my knowledge of the law, sound research, and a good work ethic to get the work done. I have found the best claims are those that combine academic research with traditional knowledge. I do not agree that claims need to be heavy on research, but if having more written sources results in a successful repatriation claim, I submit as many credible sources as possible. This has been a successful formula thus far and gathering information is one of the perks of my job. Not only am I reading about my tribe, I am interviewing elders and getting the information first hand—and, sometimes, implementing it on a personal level. It is one thing to read about how pipes are sacred, but it is another to actually use them and know from personal experience the sacredness they possess. Research comes in all forms: newspaper articles, books, reports, dissertations, interviews, and traditional knowledge. What has helped me is the ability to use all of the above together, as equally as possible, to make the strongest argument on why something, or someone, needs to be returned. How you present the information has proven to be as important as the information itself. Nobody wants to get yelled at, nobody wants an ethics speech, and shaming does not work well. What works is patience, persistence, conviction in your beliefs, knowledge of the law, and the ability to see the bigger picture of what repatriation means to your people. But at the end of the day, it is the feeling that this work needs to get done that creates the extra effort. These are our ancestors, our sacred items; nobody but us is going to get them back for us.

Working with museums

NAGPRA gives tribes the unique opportunity to reestablish their identity by having certain items recognized as sacred or cultural patrimony, and necessary to a tribe. It is a tremendous change in thinking to go from having museums control a tribe's cultural objects and how the story of a tribe is interpreted, to having the tribe not only tell the museum they were wrong, but that, in fact, they need to return the objects in their collection to the tribe. Years of academic dogma have created many misconceptions of who and what Indians are as a people. NAGPRA creates an opportunity for tribes and museums to interact on a completely different level, through consultation and repatriation, and begin to clear up misconceptions. Honest efforts of communication are at the core of making progress under NAGPRA.

From the beginning, a lack of communication has hindered repatriation efforts. Part of the problem was the overwhelming nature of NAGPRA in the initial years. When NAGPRA was first introduced on November 16, 1990, everybody was scrambling to understand the law and how it would affect their respective groups. Museums were afraid tribes would empty out entire collections and indeed, many tribes wanted everything back, and back right now! Both sides were unrealistic, and coming to understand how NAGPRA actually works took some time. Tribes were being swamped with inventories and requests for consultation in the early years. Unfortunately, the norm was that a tribe would charge one individual with this new NAGPRA role, in addition to their other duties. Many tribes could not keep up with all the information coming to them, and many times responses were not given to museums in a timely manner. Because of these delays, many museums assumed that tribes were not interested or not capable of dealing with NAGPRA. In fact, the opposite was true, tribes did know the importance of repatriation and would eventually make the essential contact with museums, even if it took years and a few personnel changes.

Many museums had never worked with tribes and were unprepared to manage the consultation process. A lack of understanding about tribal structures and ways of working with tribes continues to be a problem. I believe that poor consultation and a lack of respect for tribal knowledge are some of the main reasons for a lack of progress. Tribes continue to encounter age-old stereotypes and assumptions. The stereotype that all Indians are the same is slowly being removed from American society but it is not entirely gone, by any means.

Having people that are not part of your tribe tell you they know more about your tribe than you do is a problem that has plagued Indian people for hundreds of years, and it is a daily occurrence in the world of NAGPRA. During one consultation, I had a museum tell me that from their discussions with other tribes, an object we requested in a repatriation claim was not a sacred object. The item clearly came from within our tribe's reservation boundaries during the 1800s and our information provided enough evidence to meet the mandatory requirements for any repatriation claim.[9] However, basing their decision on conversations with tribes not in any way affiliated with our tribe, this museum came to the conclusion that the object was not sacred. This was quite disappointing coming from professionals in the museum field, but I was not altogether surprised. Indians share a long history of having other groups define who they are as a culture and a people. In fact, the opinions of churches, federal and state governments, and educational institutions about who we are as Indians permanently altered life for tribes across the country. We hear the opinions of outsiders and are impacted by their power to interfere with our communities and ways of life on a daily basis. Hearing the stories of kids being forced into boarding schools, living with the results of what broken treaties did to tribes, and continuing to have our young people be forced to learn how all Indians came from Asia in schools, are just some of the results of others' opinions that Indians must face on a daily basis. We are accustomed to others telling us that we are wrong and that what they believe is better for us. I have personally been told by both education professionals and average citizens that I do not "look Indian enough" and my name "doesn't sound Indian." So when a museum says an item is not sacred in their opinion, I am not surprised. At this time we are trying to work out a solution and avoid bringing a dispute against this museum before the NAGPRA Review Committee.

Another common frustration has been the failure of many museums to recognize a tribe's oral history as a line of evidence that is as relevant and valid as written documentation. A museum not seeing oral history as a legitimate line of evidence is not only a violation of the law, but is also highly disrespectful, and limits determining affiliation. NAGPRA clearly states that a tribe's oral tradition is a viable line of evidence, yet when it comes time to consult, oral history is not given the merit it deserves. It is a one-sided argument (with tribes many times on the losing end), because the decision to honor a repatriation claim ultimately resides with the museum. Time and again, claims are denied because the written documentation is thin and the oral tradition is not given a chance. The fact is, not everything is written down. On the contrary, the majority of information and traditions of a tribe, prior to European contact, were passed down orally from generation to generation enabling tribes to retain their traditions within their community. Not everything has been kept, but given the ordeals Indian people have faced since 1492, a lot of cultural knowledge has been retained. I am sure that there would be many more thousands of ancestors returned back to the earth if oral history was given serious consideration and the same respect as written records.

Sometimes the fight to have remains and items returned will span decades and NAGPRA positions will change hands multiple times within a tribe during that time. If full consultation (that included using oral history as credible evidence) was undertaken from the onset of repatriation negotiations, a great deal of stress and anxiety would be alleviated from both tribes and museums, and results would happen quickly. The tribe has reasons for pursuing remains and items, while museums have reasons for keeping them. I recognize that years of research have been invested in certain museum collections, and entire careers are built upon certain archaeological digs. When individuals have put their reputations and careers into digs and interpretation of the sites, I can see why museum staff may feel their own connectedness to the remains and items. Do I agree with it? Absolutely not, but it helps me to understand where they may be coming from when consulting with a museum that may be less than willing to repatriate. When two vastly different groups who feel strongly about the same thing come together, it can be quite dynamic.

I recognize that some tribes and museums would come to an agreement to return certain items even if NAGPRA was not in place. Stories of museums voluntarily returning remains and items years before NAGPRA are not unheard of, but these stories are the exception, not the norm. The vast majority of museums needed NAGPRA to make them willing to return items not rightfully theirs. It can be very frustrating and emotional for tribes to deal with a museum that has such a radical, opposite train of thought. This is why NAGPRA is needed; sometimes it takes a forceful hand to do what is right. Thankfully, most of the museums I have contacted see the importance of having the dead returned, and believe that a tribe's rights under NAGPRA trump an individual's chosen profession. However, when I encounter museum staff who have made it their life's work to conduct archaeological digs and research the "material" from those digs, just the opposite occurs. The tribe's identity is not recognized, their beliefs are given marginal credibility, and the museum's work actually trumps the tribe's request because the museum feels it knows more about the remains and items than anyone else. As stated before, this is why NAGPRA is needed. Many museums would absolutely not return anything if NAGPRA was not in place. Certainly even with the passage of NAGPRA, it can be difficult to achieve repatriation. It is sad and difficult to come to this realization, but it is true.

Over time, I have noted that the size of the museum and their collections has a significant impact on their relationship to a tribe as well. Larger museums like the Field Museum, American Museum of Natural History, and larger universities have staff dedicated to NAGPRA. But the smaller museums, county museums, historical societies, and smaller universities generally do not have staff or faculty who focus on NAGPRA. The smaller museums usually inherit small, sometimes obscure collections of Native American artifacts and remains. These collections will sit for years, with little attention given to them by the museum, usually because these items will never be on display. If such a small collection resides in the museum, NAGPRA is rarely given much thought and the sensitive issue of remains is often handled by not addressing the issue at all. In many cases, collections of remains will be dormant for years, sometimes over a century. Then the tribe makes contact with the museum and everything changes with one phone call. Boxes of remains that have been dormant suddenly have life again. They are given attention and energy surrounds them, as museum and tribal staffs work toward repatriation.

Tribes can be equally guilty of harboring assumptions regarding the intent of museums, many times assuming that if somebody works at a museum they are anti-repatriation; therefore, it's useless to contact them. This attitude usually comes from tribes being treated poorly by museum staff at a prior consultation. From my experience, I have noticed that museum staff can be gun-shy to contact tribes, partially because they do not have a strong grasp of NAGPRA, and in some cases because the museum staff had a bad experience working with tribes when they made prior attempts to initiate consultation. Although NAGPRA is a national issue, it is a small field of people that work in it. So when an individual is treated in a disrespectful manner, either by a museum or a tribe, it can result in less-than-productive working relationships. Emotions often run high with this work, and it's vital to keep them in check. One bad phone call or soured meeting could spell disaster for the immediate future. If both the museum and tribe are treated with respect and openness, productivity will ensue in one form or another. But if one group acts in the opposite manner, nothing results except more ill will.

The long road to repatriation

I have spoken with other tribal NAGPRA departments,[10] and it is normal for years to pass before items and remains finally make it back home to the tribe. I wish the consultation process did not take so long, but the reality of the matter is that it can be a terribly complicated process. Being told no so many times can wear an individual down. It is frustrating and demoralizing when claims are denied and requests for dispositions are rejected. There have even been times when a museum has refused to consult. A total lack of communication can be the most difficult thing to handle. For us and many other tribes, the only way to combat this is to keep pursuing what we feel rightfully belongs with our tribe. Many times I have been very angry at museums and I am sure some museums have been angry at me, but the key is to get past that anger and move forward. The tribes feel that remains and items are alive and should be returned because the museum never had the right to own them. These remains, these people, were not intended to be unearthed. Individuals did not have the right to alienate items without the consent of the tribe as a whole. The individual and the items are part of the tribe and we are connected to them still to this day.

Mutual respect has been one of the greatest attributes for our work getting accomplished. Tribes also recognize, for the most part, that the current staff at these museums did not do the actual digging of remains. They inherited the remains and are trying to do what they can, but without the information and knowledge of how NAGPRA works, the next steps to repatriation cannot be taken. It is a fine line between being too pushy and being a pushover. Either one may hinder a repatriation. If a museum is making a good faith effort to honor a claim but is taking longer than anticipated, the requesting tribe must decide whether to push harder or not. Many times a museum will not know the ins and outs of NAGPRA and will need time to acclimate themselves to the law. If the museum is readily consulting and working towards affiliation and repatriation, it is reasonable to allow more time. Face-to-face consultation and phone conversations will play a big part in determining this progress. If a museum is not responding and does not appear to be taking the tribe's request seriously, the tribe must decide whether or not to pursue the possibility of filing an official complaint with the National NAGPRA Program, citing that the museum is out of compliance. It's a long and sometimes difficult route, but at least the option is there for tribes to explore. In my experience, once a museum sees our efforts are persistent; the museum will work to match our efforts. They see how important the issue of repatriation is by the multiple phone calls, emails, research put into the claim, and the repeated message delivered by us, that we need the human remains or cultural objects returned. A tribe could simply submit a claim and leave it at that, waiting for the museum to respond. But when a tribe makes the process fluid and dynamic, with constant interaction, the repatriation process takes on another form. The life of the objects is realized or the remains are seen as people and not merely material or collections.

The tribes in Michigan all work together on NAGPRA issues, forming a coalition to strengthen our efforts.[11] Other tribes in different parts of the country have formed similar coalitions and have had similar success. One of the main reasons we work together is to counter the argument presented by some museums that affiliation cannot be established for a specific tribe. The Odawa/Ottawa, Ojibwa/Chippewa, and Potawatomi all form the Anishnaabek and are represented by twelve federally recognized tribes in Michigan. A museum may present the argument that older remains are Anishnaabek and therefore could be any of the twelve tribes, so affiliation cannot be established. On the contrary, specific affiliation to a single tribe is not necessary if we are all in agreement on the repatriation to the twelve tribes because we all are descendants of the individuals. Working together amongst tribes is critical. Traditional tribal territories are still recognized from tribe to tribe to this day, and respecting each other's territory has always been a cornerstone of good relationships. If tribes bicker amongst themselves about repatriation issues, it only makes it that much easier for the museums to not return anything. Unity by the tribes is a powerful force.

Our sacred duty: reburying the dead

It has always been expected that we take care of the ones who have walked on. I personally feel very fortunate to be able to help my tribe in such a unique way; to help people who cannot help themselves—the dead. As a young boy, my family would go all over our community to Ghost Suppers or Feasts of the Dead. This is a time-honored ceremony practiced by my tribe and one of the cornerstones of our community. Ghost Suppers are when families host a feast that is open to the community. During this feast, the spirits of those who have passed on come and eat with the living. My earliest memories include such meals and I have always made it a priority to participate in my family's Ghost Suppers.

Every tribe that I have spoken with has some type of ceremony or means of honoring their dead. The ceremonies have endured, and these have helped keep tribal communities intact. For us at LTBB Odawa, the basis for all of our work is rooted in our beliefs as Anishnaabek. Our ceremonial beliefs permeate everything we do. I have put down countless hands of tobacco, asking for help and guidance to get our ancestors and sacred items back home. When talking with elders, they always point out the spiritual help that we receive, even if we do not see it. I credit much of our success to the spirits being the backbone of our efforts and making things happen, in ways we do not always understand or see.

I feel like the most overlooked aspect of tribal repatriation programs is the ceremonial duty tribes are charged with in having remains and items returned. Reburials are a new occurrence in Indian country, and tribes, Alaska Natives, and Native Hawaiians are adjusting to this new and strange dilemma of reburying the dead that were unearthed and disrespected. It is a drastic change from remains being seen as merely specimens, to being treated as people whose death rights are finally being honored. Having the dead returned and reburied affects the tribe in unexplainable, positive ways that cannot be tangibly measured, but it is part of our faith, beliefs, religion, and spirituality.

Land is a significant issue. Not all tribes have the luxury of a safe, secure area that they can use for reburials. The ultimate goal is to rebury remains in a location with no possibility of being disturbed again, and I believe that tribal land is the safest bet. My tribe had the good fortune to not be displaced while so many other tribes have been moved. Not having the physical space hinders some tribes in their NAGPRA efforts. What if a tribe has had their land base significantly diminished? What if they have been relocated from their original homeland? A dilemma faces these tribes whose ancestral homelands are hundreds, sometimes thousands, of miles from their present-day location. Does a displaced tribe repatriate remains and rebury them at a location the remains are not originally from? Or does the tribe wait and see if they can secure land back in their original homelands? These are questions only the tribe themselves can answer.

So what does a tribe do to prepare for remains and items actually being returned? It is one thing to know how to implement NAGPRA, to understand the law and write claims, but preparation for the return must be undertaken before any research, writing, or phone calls are ever made. This preparation is completely internal to the tribe and involves having the mental, emotional, spiritual, and physical readiness to have these items back. From my own personal experience, performing reburials is one of the most difficult tasks I have ever had to perform; at the same time, it is also one of the most rewarding. Speaking with other Indians who do the same work, it seems the sentiment is shared.

In the end, it's always about the spiritual work. During the entire repatriation process, ceremony is involved. Each tribe may have different protocols for reburials, but the end result is the same: the return of ancestors back to the earth.[12] When remains were originally dug out of the ground, their original ceremony was disturbed in manners none of us will fully understand. With the remains being returned so many years later, the ceremony of reburying them is the closure needed by both the remains and their descendants. The tribe is then solely responsible for the final step in this long and difficult journey, one that sometimes spans over a century. Each tribe is charged with the reburial, hopefully the last stop on the journey of these remains. Repatriation is something needed by all. The healing that occurs within tribes when remains and items are returned is a wonderful feeling, but the healing is not limited to tribes. Many of the museums I have worked with on repatriation have also expressed a sense of healing in their own institution and lives as well. After each repatriation of human remains, there is a sense of accomplishment shared by both the tribe and museum. The museum and tribal staff know they have done something fundamentally, morally, and spiritually right, together. It is a once-in-a-lifetime experience to have this feeling. In the future, when I run into the various museum people I have worked with, we will both know we participated in something very special.

Personal experiences

Working with NAGPRA has been one of the most rewarding events of my life. It has increased my ability to help my tribe and that has been a wonderful experience. But the rewards do not come without struggles and these struggles have been great at times. I share the following experiences as a way to highlight what it is like to work on NAGPRA issues within a tribe—one experience where it was difficult to work with a museum, one where it went well, and two that show the creativity that can occur to make repatriations happen.

The first experience begins with a repatriation request that was submitted in 2008 to a large museum in Michigan, for human remains. The remains were removed from within our reservation boundaries and had historic material associated with them that placed them within the post-Contact era. I had found in my experience that these were often straightforward cases where making cultural affiliation was fairly uncomplicated. However, the NAGPRA designee for the museum never consulted with my tribe and simply lumped the human remains into the culturally unidentifiable (CUI) category,[13] resulting in the individuals sitting in the museum for years before they were discovered. Upon reviewing the inventory for this museum, I immediately saw this as an affiliation to LTBB Odawa. I submitted a claim and began calling the museum. The museum sent back notes saying the remains were of both European and Indian lineage and NAGPRA did not apply. I was shocked and very angry. This individual was going to deny affiliation, thus deny returning the remains, on the ground that because they were mixed lineage they were not really Indian. This argument did not hold up and our claim was eventually honored. In August 2009, I made the trek to pick-up these individuals' remains and for some odd reason, the NAGPRA designee I worked with did not show up to meet me. I drove five hours and this person could not be physically present to make the transfer. From the onset of this repatriation, I had felt disrespected by him and this seemed to be yet another frustrating incident, but upon actually taking control of the remains, I set that aside and focused on getting them back to LTBB. I drove home and reburied the remains the next day. Putting up with this museum's antics was tough, but was well worth it once the reburial happened. I had finally brought part of me and my tribe home.

In 2008, I went to gather remains from a local museum from a disposition. This museum, in contrast to the previous museum, was great to work with. Unfortunately, after all the legal requirements were met, it was January before I could get the remains. January in northern Michigan can be a very cold, snowy affair and my main concern was frozen ground. I did not want to have these remains waiting to be reburied until spring. When I got back to the office, I grabbed my shovel and snowshoes, and carried the remains to our burial grounds. For security reasons, this area is in a remote location. Upon arriving there, I had to snowshoe into the woods. It was cold, snowing and windy, but I was determined to rebury that day even if it meant starting a fire to thaw out the ground. After digging through four feet of snow, I found the ground was amazingly unfrozen! I was so happy, but my happiness quickly turned to sadness, as I now had to rebury. The remains were of children, six of them, fragments of sons and daughters. With the wind howling and snow falling, six Anishnaabek children were put back to rest. I thought about my youth, how I enjoyed living in Northern Michigan and how without a doubt these kids enjoyed the same things. But they never got a chance to grow up and enjoy life like I had. I thought about how their resting place had been disrupted in such a horrible manner. Not only had these Anishnaabek children had a short time on this earth with loved ones, but their journey and beings were disturbed when they were dug out of the ground. I was grateful to be able to do something to benefit my fellow Anishnaabek, even though they were long since passed. I could only ask for forgiveness from them as I completed the reburial ceremony and pray that they would accept that what I was doing was for their benefit.

Two creative repatriations occurred in 2007 and 2009. In 2007, we at LTBB submitted a repatriation claim for an unassociated funerary object, a small copper kettle. The claim was pretty straightforward. The summary information provided by the museum, which was in New York, stated the kettle came from an Ottawa grave in Emmet County, Michigan. The claim was honored, the *Federal Register* notice was published, and the day came when we could take possession of the kettle. It was a long way to the museum from Michigan, but we would rather have such items be retrieved in person. The museum staff we worked with on this repatriation happened to be going to the fall 2008 NAGPRA Review Committee meeting in San Diego, California. I was going to the same meeting and it was arranged that they would bring the kettle and give it to me at the meeting. This worked out well and the kettle made it back home safe and sound.

A similar situation happened the next year, in 2009. After consulting with two museums in Michigan on the repatriation of human remains, it came time to bring these ancestors home. Both museums were in southern Michigan, a three- to four-hour drive. As I was planning my repatriation tour, one of the museums we worked with, the Grand Rapids Public Museum, informed me that the Michigan Museum Association was having its annual meeting in Traverse City, Michigan. The other museum from which we were getting remains was going to be at this meeting as well. It was arranged that both museums would bring the remains to the meeting and I would receive them. Traverse City is only an hour and a half drive from LTBB Odawa headquarters. The timing of the meeting was perfect and saved me days on the road. I met the museum staff in the lobby of the hotel that was hosting the meeting. They were each holding boxes for me. I quietly thanked them and took the remains to my car. I had a meeting the next morning, so I was staying the night in Traverse City. One of the women I worked with on one of the repatriations asked, "You aren't keeping those in your car, alone, overnight are you?" She caught me off guard and I replied, "No, they will stay with me." I brought them into my room for the night, out of respect. It was a little unnerving, having them in the room, but the night was quiet and the next day, they were put back to rest.

Conclusion

Working under NAGPRA has been a journey with the greatest sensation of fulfillment one moment, and in the next, the worst feelings of frustration and helplessness. NAGPRA is the ultimate test of perseverance, but with each item returned, traditions as old as the Anishnaabek people themselves are given a chance to be practiced again. Tribal communities have the opportunity to heal, with each set of remains laid back to rest. NAGPRA is so much more than a law. It is about how a group of people interact with Creation and the powers that govern their universe, as they know it. Not every tribe, Alaska Native or Native Hawaiian practices the same beliefs regarding the dead, burial grounds, and sacred items. However, in Indian Country, these differences are accepted and paid a certain amount of respect. NAGPRA creates a unique opportunity for museums to honor that respect and truly make a positive difference in not just the tribal communities, but for the museums as well.

In the end, NAGPRA is about people, living and dead. It is about how the living practice their religious and spiritual beliefs, rights every person should enjoy, regardless of race or origin. It is about how every person has the right to rest in peace, regardless of when they were laid to rest. I hope this chapter provides a different insight into why NAGPRA is needed, and just as importantly, shows that the people for whom NAGPRA was created—the tribes, Alaska Natives and Native Hawaiians of the United States—are distinct people whose beliefs and customs are equal to any on the planet. Like all cultures, they have the right to have their ways honored.

Notes

1   This is not the "Indian Country" that has a specific legal definition under 18 U.S.C. 1151, I mean it more generally as the places where Indians work and live.

2   *Anishnaabek* is the plural term for the aboriginal people of the Great Lakes.

3   25 U.S.C. 3006.

4   For ease of reading, the word tribe will be used to include Native American tribes, Native Hawaiians and Native Hawaiian organizations, Native Alaskans and Native Alaskan villages.

5   25 U.S.C. 1300k-1300k-7.

6   *Gijigowi Bipskaabiimi* means, in Odawa, "coming back to."

7   25 U.S.C. 3303(e).

8   25 U.S.C. 3004(a)-(b).

9   NAGPRA claims must satisfy the following criteria: (1) fall under one of the NAGPRA categories, (2) cultural affiliation must have been established, and (3) the lineal descendant meets the requirements of the act or the tribe must have standing.

10 I have spoken to some for the manual and others through regular NAGPRA work.

11 MACPRA: Michigan Anishnaabek Cultural Preservation and Repatriation Alliance.

12 Some tribes do not take back remains that have been unearthed, and that is each tribe's prerogative, according to their cultural beliefs.

13 43 C.F.R. 10.2(e)(2), "What does culturally unidentifiable mean? Culturally unidentifiable refers to human remains and associated funerary objects in museum or Federal agency collections for which no lineal descendant or culturally affiliated Indian tribe or Native Hawaiian organization has been identified through the inventory process."

Chapter 4
A Call for Healing from the Tragedy of NAGPRA in Hawaii

E. SUNNY GREER

> "I would recommend and plead with all the people now to respect your *kupuna* [ancestors, elders] ... Give them the best, even when they die."
>
> —Papa Henry Auwae[1]

When my papa said the aforementioned words, the Hawaii State Historic Preservation Division was interviewing him for a video regarding the reburial and care of Native Hawaiian *iwi kupuna* (ancestral bones). Papa was respected for his expertise in life and death issues since he was a *Poʻokela Kahuna Lāʻau Lapaʻau* (foremost medicinal herbalist). He was also noted for his experience in conducting reburial rituals, such as the return of multiple ancestral remains to our sacred healing grounds at Lapakahi. As one of Papa's youngest *haumana hānai* (adopted student), my training in traditional Native Hawaiian funerary customs was enhanced when Papa was invited to participate in the NAGPRA consultation process regarding the "Forbes Cave" controversy,[2] which will be discussed later in the chapter. Our *kupuna* (ancestors) lived above Honokoa Gulch in Kawaihae, where the human remains and cultural objects originated, and where Papa was taken as a young boy.[3] Papa shared with our *ohana* (family) that the ancestors involved were *iwi kahuna* (bones of the priestly class), specifically from the same healing lineage as ours.[4] Papa reasoned that in light of the significant rank and practice of the *kupuna* involved, the objects buried with them (*wewe huna*[5]) were "very powerful and very dangerous ... " He said that he wasn't supposed to reveal these things but he "had to because innocent lives [were] put at risk."[6]

As Papa protected us from the political and social controversies associated with the cultural objects from Kawaihae, he accelerated my training in Native Hawaiian funerary practices. On top of learning additional burial customs and rituals, Papa subtly prepared me for his own death, which he predicted to multiple family members nearly a decade earlier. He repeatedly told us that he would never see the dawning of the new millennium; and as foretold, our ancestors welcomed his ʻuhane (spirit) on December 31, 2000.

In spite of my attempts to steer away from exercising the burial traditions he taught me, circumstances led me to work at the Hawaii State Historic Preservation Division (SHPD) from 2004 to 2006, where I last served as its cultural programs director, providing oversight and support to Hawaii's five island burial councils.[7] The challenges encountered at SHPD further exposed me to controversial repatriation "dichotomies of past versus present, traditional versus contemporary, authenticity versus reproduction."[8] Even my subsequent journey to law school predominantly revolved around burial issues, and I became the first graduate from the William S. Richardson School of Law, University of Hawaii at Mānoa, to obtain dual certificates in Environmental Law and Pacific-Asian Legal Studies, with a specialty in Native Hawaiian Law. I can no longer ignore the fact that both my personal and professional paths converged around Native Hawaiian funerary traditions. In my free time, I serve as a volunteer traditional practitioner of lāʻau lapaʻau (herbal medicine) on two kupuna councils convened under federal and state of Hawaii law to address Native Hawaiian health issues. Like Papa before me, it is quite a humbling experience to serve as an instrument of healing, which sometimes involves death rituals. Thus, it is no coincidence that my doctoral dissertation revolves around traditional Native Hawaiian funerary practices and NAGPRA.[9]

The purpose of this chapter is to briefly discuss the implementation of NAGPRA in the state of Hawaii. Where others might emphasize the successes of NAGPRA, it would be a dereliction of my duty as an academic and cultural practitioner to ignore the fact that in Hawaii, NAGPRA appears to be a source of cultural contention rather than a repatriation remedy. Some would argue that the legal framework divides the Native Hawaiian community and undermines Native Hawaiian funerary traditions. Where other Native peoples experience the healing effects of NAGPRA, why is NAGPRA so problematic in Hawaii that more than half of all disputes addressed by the NAGPRA Review Committee have been Native Hawaiian disputes?[10] In fact, Hawaii's first Native Hawaiian representative on the NAGPRA Review Committee, Colin Kippen, describes its implementation in Hawaii as "particularly difficult."[11] While other Review Committee members portray NAGPRA in Hawaii as "a compli- cated situation"[12] and even an outright "disaster."[13] Although few Native Hawaiians view repatriation under NAGPRA as "positive"[14] others perceive the Act as "a noble effort, [that] has been corrupted."[15] Indeed, such strong sentiments underscore the fact that when it comes to legal claims arising under NAGPRA, "Native Hawaiians have been involved in federal court proceedings more than any other group."[16] Sadly, repatriation under NAGPRA is such a tragedy that Native Hawaiians are "the only group that has had one of their members incarcerated for his repatriation activities."[17]

Hawaii case studies

Two specific cases, the Mokapu[18] and the Forbes Cave controversies, exemplify the difficulty of implementing NAGPRA in Hawaii.[19] Under NAGPRA, Native Hawaiians can submit claims for the repatriation of NAGPRA cultural items as a lineal descendant[20] or as a Native Hawaiian organization.[21] The definition of "Native Hawaiian organization" is "overly-broad,"[22] as evidenced in the first NAGPRA lawsuit in Hawaii, the *Na Iwi o Na Kupuna O Mokapu v. Dalton*[23] case ("Mokapu"). In Mokapu, a Native Hawaiian organization, Hui Mālama I Nā Kūpuna ʻO Hawaiʻi Nei ("Hui Mālama"), sued the Secretary of the Department of the Navy and the Bernice Pauahi Bishop Museum ("Bishop Museum") for multiple NAGPRA violations in connection with the nearly 1,600 human remains excavated from the Mokapu Peninsula. It was "the first large-scale disinterment of a traditional Native Hawaiian burial area"[24] documented in Hawaii. At the time Hui Mālama filed its lawsuit, it "believed itself to be the only group requesting repatriation of the remains . . . [but] fourteen other groups also made claims to the remains."[25] Hui Mālama argued that "the court should recognize the Hawaiian concept of spiritual guardianship"[26] and acknowledge Hui Mālama as the "guardian"[27] of the Mokapu remains, on whose behalf Hui Mālama filed suit. The court not only found "no sound legal basis for granting standing to human remains,"[28] it also held that "nowhere does Hawaiian law acknowledge Hui Malama as the sole guardian for all Native Hawaiian human remains."[29] The court further emphasized NAGPRA's edict with respect to competing claims:[30] "Where claims among several Native Hawaiian groups may conflict, equity would require that all the groups serve jointly as guardian of the human remains for the purpose of negotiating or litigating on the remains' behalf prior to proper repatriation."[31] Thus, with competing claims made by multiple Native Hawaiian organizations, repatriation in the Mokapu case was at a standstill. The failure to repatriate all the human remains in the Mokapu case was a direct result of the "overly-broad" definition of "Native Hawaiian organization," which has since been synonymous with NAGPRA implementation in Hawaii.

Similarly, an infamous case that exemplifies the divisive failure of NAGPRA in the Aloha State involves the removal of human remains and eighty-three cultural items from a burial cave complex in Kawaihae by David Forbes and his colleagues in 1905. The complex was subsequently named after the grave robber and referred to as Forbes Cave. The removed cultural items were later acquired by the Bishop Museum and the Hawaii Volcanoes National Park Museum. The Forbes Cave controversy involved a "loan" of the items from the Bishop Museum to Hui Mālama on February 26, 2000. Members of Hui Mālama reburied numerous sets of human remains and the eighty-three cultural objects without notifying and receiving agreement from the other claimants. As in the Mokapu case, additional Native Hawaiian organizations came forward with claims of cultural affiliation to the cultural items. In opposition to Hui Mālama's stance on reburial, the additional claimants demanded the return of the cultural objects from the unspecified reburial location, and a continuation of the NAGPRA repatriation process.

On August 19, 2005, two of the claimant groups, Na Lei Alii Kawananakoa and the Royal Hawaiian Academy of Traditional Arts, sued Hui Mālama and the Bishop Museum for violating NAGPRA. The lawsuit resulted in a federal court order that demanded an inventory of the cultural items, the specific reburial location, and the disclosure of names and contact information of persons with knowledge regarding the reburial location.[32] Hui Mālama refused to comply with the court order and its board of directors were found in contempt of court on December 27, 2005.[33] The case evolved into a contemporary Hawaiian tragedy, culminating in the three-week incarceration of Hui Mālama member Edward Halealoha Ayau, followed by his release and the subsequent agreement by Hui Mālama to jointly pay the $330,000 for retrieval costs incurred. Of interest, Ayau was "instrumental in drafting the NAGPRA federal provisions requiring consultation with native Hawaiians,"[34] *but was jailed for violating the very laws he helped draft.* This speaks volumes to the problematic nature of NAGPRA implementation in Hawaii. Although there were only four claimant groups[35] to the cultural items in 2000, the number of Native Hawaiian organizations involved as claimants has since increased to nearly thirty today. In light of the strong divergent positions of the Native Hawaiian organizations involved, actual repatriation is doubtful and the cultural items remain in the museums until such time as the claimants "agree upon [their] disposition or the dispute is otherwise resolved pursuant to the provisions of th[e] act or by a court of competent jurisdiction."[36]

Native Hawaiian nationhood

Both the Mokapu and Forbes Cave controversies exemplify the shortcomings in NAGPRA's efficacy with regard to Native Hawaiians. Notably, both cases reveal two fundamental obstacles that NAGPRA cannot overcome in its current form: (1) the absence of a Native Hawaiian sovereign government politically recognized by the United States; and (2) a disregard of traditional Native Hawaiian funerary beliefs and practices in NAGPRA because the provisions to accommodate repatriation claims by Native Hawaiians allow for differential treatment by select groups to assert "their hegemonic cultural practices"[37] in the repatriation process.

First and foremost, "Native Hawaiians are not organized as tribes, and this is the operative category of both NAGPRA and federal Indian law generally."[38] In fact, one of the primary sponsors of NAGPRA, Hawaii Senator Daniel K. Inouye, adamantly stated that NAGPRA "is, indeed, an Indian law, and the federal courts have so stated."[39]

Since Native Hawaiians historically settled in diversified groups with decentralized governments,[40] NAGPRA implementation in Hawaii is quite problematic "partly due to the act being written with tribal considerations in mind when Hawaii has no tribes."[41] Because there is no federally recognized Native Hawaiian government comparable to tribal governments, NAGPRA was intentionally drafted to contain an "overly-broad" definition in order for Native Hawaiian participation in the repatriation process. Case in point: the May 28, 1990, testimony submitted by Hui Mālama president Edward L. Kanahele to the Senate Select Committee on Indian Affairs recommended that there "should be a reference to an 'appropriate Native Hawaiian organization' since we have no recognized sovereign government or entity separate from the State of Hawai'i." With Hui Mālama member Edward Halealoha Ayau clerking at the Native American Rights Fund (NARF) prior to NAGPRA's passage, and later serving as staff counsel, field representative, and advisor to Sen. Inouye,[42] broad Native Hawaiian inclusion into NAGPRA was assured. Although such inclusion "may have been well-intentioned, it does not always make common sense in practice."[43] Indeed, the lack of a federally recognized Native Hawaiian sovereign government, with an agreed-upon structure for organizational leadership and group cohesion, is a significant barrier to effective implementation of NAGPRA in Hawaii. This absence of a sovereign Hawaiian Nation recognized by the United States hinders NAGPRA implementation in Hawaii, resulting in multiple claimants and disproportionate statistics of Native Hawaiian disputes in administrative and court proceedings due to the broad definition of "Native Hawaiian organization."

Burying tradition

Secondly, the very notion of claiming human remains and other cultural items under the moniker of a "Native Hawaiian organization" is not only culturally inappropriate and ineffective in practical application because of the lack of sovereign governmental recognition; it is an affront to traditional Native Hawaiian funerary customs and practices. A brief understanding of such traditions is necessary to comprehend the extent of NAGPRA's incompatibility with Native Hawaiian beliefs. According to the first literate Native Hawaiian historians in the nineteenth century, funerary customs varied by mo'okū'auhau[44] (genealogy), kuleana[45] (authority, responsibility), 'āina (place), rank, and gender.

Funerary customs are dependent foremost on genealogy, and not all Native Hawaiians share the same mo'okū'auhau. "The Kumulipo (one Hawaiian creation chant) is the genealogical beginning to some people, while the Palikū belongs to others, Lolo ['Ōlolo] to others, Puanue to others, and Kapohihi to others."[46] Just as the beginnings of Native Hawaiians vary, so, too, do their beliefs on death and the afterlife.[47] "People differed in their beliefs about the soul and the hereafter."[48] Some believed that after physical death "they would be taken to the bosom of Wākea,"[49] while others "believed that the soul lived forever, and that after the body died the soul would meet its guardian spirits ('aumakua)."[50] Still others believed that "Po (darkness, night) is the place where the spirits of the dead go after their death."[51] No matter what version of the afterlife a Native Hawaiian believed in, it was dependent on their beginning, their genealogy.[52]

Generally, only family members were privy to burial rites, and it goes without saying that "strangers (po'e 'ē) were not welcome in the houses of the deceased."[53] Outsiders were at risk of being put to death if they were near the deceased without authority.[54] Even within a family, those who were the closest relation by blood, "only persons of the same flesh ('i'o ho'okahi),"[55] had authority over certain rituals regarding the dead.

Closely attached to the mo'okū'auhau (genealogy) comes the kuleana (authority, responsibility), which also influenced and led to varied funerary customs. "The worship by the people of the Hawaiian Islands of god images was not the same."[56] Kuleana was not selected by an individual; rather, one's authority and responsibility stemmed from one's mo'okū'auhau, which in turn determined one's kuleana. A Native Hawaiian's blood genealogy or teaching genealogy (practice, discipline) determined his kuleana, particularly the manner in which he showed respect for his gods and the dead. For instance, "You don't take iwi from Kohala and put them in Hilo, that is taking them from Kamapua'a (pig-man demigod) and putting them in the land of Pele (volcano goddess)."[57] Where bird hunters worshiped Kūhuluhulumanu, farmers worshiped Kūka'ō'ō, and medicinal healers worshiped goddesses like Ma'iola.[58] Simply put, a person's kuleana in life determined his place in death, based on his mo'okū'auhau. "If the deep ocean was the kuleana of a man and his family, it was known that his kuleana was there; and if the pit of Pele at Kilauea was the kuleana of a man and his family, it was known that theirs was an irrevocable kuleana (kuleana hemo'ole) to go there."[59]

Moreover, only certain families had kuleana to conduct burials at a particular 'āina (place), because the area was part of their mo'okū'auhau and historically associated with an ancestor. For example, tradition speaks of the god Kumuhonua, who was buried on a mountain called Wai-hon(u)a o Kumuhonua, where only "his children and grandchildren and all his descendants were buried on that hill and it was renamed "The heaping-place-of-bones," O-ke-ahuna-iwi."[60] Indeed, "Hawaiian families from different areas have different customs with regard to burial."[61]

Funerary practices also varied by rank.[62] For example, the kapu following the death of an ali'i (chief) usually lasted ten or more days, while a person of high status (ki'eki'e) lasted three days, and a person of lower status (ha'aha'a) lasted two days until the kapu was freed so the bodies could be laid away.[63] As for the kauwa (outcasts),[64] their funerary customs were inconsequential because rulers, chiefs, and the common people despised them.[65] The *kauwa* were usually killed at will,[66] drowned by having their heads held under water, and laid alive (*hoʻomoe ola*) in the burial places of their masters[67] after being sacrificed.[68] Moreover, the way a corpse was prepared differed by rank. Not all *aliʻi* were buried in the same manner as was common, which was usually to tie a corpse with a rope, with the knees pushed up to the chest into a round shape and wrapped with *kapa* prior to burial.[69] In fact, not all *aliʻi* were equal in rank,[70] so their funerary customs differed as well. Specifically, the death rituals of a ruling chief "were very different . . . They were not like those of all the other aliʻi."[71] Hence, as rank influenced conduct when Native Hawaiians were alive, so, too, did rank affect death rituals.

Funerary practices also varied by gender. In ancient Hawaii, touching a corpse was considered as unclean as women who gave birth or menstruated,[72] for they "were considered to be *haumia* (polluted) and *pōʻino* (defiled)."[73] Moreover, just as one person's belief in particular gods was influenced by *moʻokūʻauhau*, "[w]omen, too, were at odds (*kahi mea kūʻēʻē*) as they worshiped [their] female deities."[74] Women had different *kuleana* than men, and their goddesses were worshipped differently. Furthermore, the "goddess of one woman was different from another woman's. That was the same case for the female *aliʻi*. The god of the high-ranking female *aliʻi* was different from the lower ranking female *aliʻi*. They were not the same."[75]

Undeniably, where *moʻokūʻauhau* (genealogy), *kuleana* (authority, responsibility), *ʻaina* (place), rank, and gender traditionally dictated Native Hawaiian funerary customs, the contemporary NAGPRA process of broadly allowing any Native Hawaiian organization to claim human remains and cultural objects disregards such profound cultural values. A federally recognized sovereign Hawaiian Nation can best facilitate these cultural considerations rather than Congress, the courts, and Native Hawaiian organizations.

Observations

The intent of NAGPRA was to provide healing for native peoples whose ancestral remains and cultural objects were acquired through a tragic history of U.S. colonization and imperialism. There is no greater *kuleana* in the process of decolonization than caring for our ancestral foundation. In spite of the status quo of cultural contention in Hawaii, NAGPRA still offers a healing opportunity for Native Hawaiians, even in its current imperfect form. The ultimate challenge is that since Native consultation and collaboration is a fundamental part of the NAGPRA process, every action becomes a compromise. "The more collaborative the process is, the more of a compromise the product will be."[76] There can be no individual or group healing unless the respect and dignity of the *iwi kupuna* (ancestral bones) is the primary objective. Native Hawaiian claimants should make the expedient and culturally appropriate reburial of the *iwi kupuna* paramount to any other considerations. Moreover, the absence of a federally recognized Native Hawaiian sovereign government does not mean the absence of *kuleana*. The Native Hawaiian entities expressly mentioned in NAGPRA (Department of Hawaiian Home Lands, Office of Hawaiian Affairs, and Hui Mālama I Nā Kūpuna ʻO Hawaiʻi) must be held accountable for their statutorily designated *kuleana* with respect to repatriation of human remains and cultural objects under NAGPRA.

For example, lands administered by the State Department of Hawaiian Home Lands ("DHHL") are considered "tribal lands" under NAGPRA,[77] on par with sovereign tribal reservations. In spite of this fact, DHHL has not established comprehensive written guidelines regarding NAGPRA repatriation on its lands, for review and comment by the Hawaiian Homes Commission or its beneficiaries. Furthermore, DHHL lacks written reports summarizing the total number of NAGPRA cultural items inadvertently discovered and excavated on their lands and the circumstances surrounding their disturbance. For the past twenty-two years, the department has had the opportunity to be a repatriation model for a future Native Hawaiian Nation, but it has failed, and continues to fail, to meet its repatriation potential.

In addition, the deletion of an express recognition of the State Office of Hawaiian Affairs (OHA) and Hui Mālama as examples of a "Native Hawaiian organization"[78] should be considered. As a result of such explicit identification, federal agencies and museums automatically consult with OHA and Hui Mālama, almost to the exclusion of other Native Hawaiians that might be more culturally appropriate. At the very least, their inclusion means that OHA and Hui Mālama are usually culturally affiliated to cultural items when a more definitive cultural affiliation may be more appropriate. In fact, both organizations are the top two Native Hawaiian organizations deemed culturally affiliated to Native Hawaiian cultural items represented in NAGPRA inventories, with Hui Mālama culturally affiliated to Native Hawaiian *human remains* in 93 percent of the total inventories from the act's inception to September 2012, and OHA culturally affiliated 87 percent of the time. Similarly, Hui Mālama was culturally affiliated to an astounding 99 percent of the Native Hawaiian *associated funerary objects* represented in total inventories during the same time period, with OHA culturally affiliated 62 percent of the time. The next highest Native Hawaiian organization culturally affiliated to cultural items represented in total inventories relevant to Hawaii was the Oʻahu Island Burial Council, at 28 percent for human remains, and 32 percent for associated funerary objects. In fact, combining the cultural affiliation percentages for all five island burial councils still fell short of reaching OHA's statistics, for both human remains and associated funerary objects. Such figures lend support to criticism that OHA and Hui Mālama have an unfair advantage over other Native Hawaiian organizations because of their express reference in NAGPRA. In fact, both are the only organizations that have submitted applications for NAGPRA repatriation grants since inception. Moreover, Hui Mālama is the *only* Native Hawaiian organization that was awarded a repatriation grant, with its success rate in receiving repatriation grant awards at an impressive 82 percent. Lastly, 86 percent of the total repatriation grant monies requested by Hui Mālama were awarded, cementing their hegemonic[79] presence in NAGPRA repatriation activities in Hawaii.

Of the two examples of a "Native Hawaiian organization," only OHA is legally accountable to the larger Native Hawaiian community, since it is a state agency with a statutory purpose for the "betterment of conditions for native Hawaiians."[80] Unlike OHA, however, Hui Mālama is a nonprofit organization that is accountable to its board of directors, grantors, and the Internal Revenue Service, *not* the larger Native Hawaiian community. In fact, a 2004 report by the Hawaii State Auditor recommended that Hui Mālama be removed as an example of an "appropriate organization" in Hawaii's state burial laws, "because it suggests singularity and places an official imprimatur on its behavior and practices. Statutory law should avoid references to private organizations."[81] Deletion of both Hui Mālama and OHA as examples of a "Native Hawaiian organization" under NAGPRA should also be considered for this reason.

In light of the problematic and complex nature of NAGPRA implementation in Hawaii, there have been calls to amend the act or to draft a separate statute to address repatriation issues unique to Native Hawaiians. It would be presumptuous of me, however, to advocate for one legislative solution over another, especially when issues regarding the repatriation of ancestors and cultural objects of a people necessitate dialogue on a personal, political, and the nation-state level. As aforementioned, the ideal scenario would be to have a federally recognized Native Hawaiian government offer culturally appropriate alternatives to NAGPRA's current form. In the absence of a sovereign nation, legislative efforts should be held in abeyance until such time that either of the Native Hawaiian organizations mentioned in NAGPRA, or perhaps a new entity, steps forward to engage (as inclusively as possible) the Native Hawaiian community in an informed discussion regarding amendments or alternatives to NAGPRA. After all, a well-intentioned decision made two decades ago by a few Native Hawaiians has resulted in polarizing the larger Native Hawaiian community and prevented repatriation, and will probably continue to do so. It would be premature to offer a preference for amendments or a separate statute at this time when many Native Hawaiians lack an understanding of NAGPRA's existence, implications, and/or potential.

In the meantime, DHHL, OHA, and Hui Mālama should be called to task to educate, notify, empower, and support the larger Native Hawaiian community to participate in the NAGPRA process. Perhaps funding should be appropriated to the named organizations or another entity to provide the outreach needed to inform Native Hawaiian families about NAGPRA. Training of other Native Hawaiian organizations should also be a priority, particularly training to access available NAGPRA grants. From as early as 1993, there were suggestions to place all Hawaii-related NAGPRA consultation and repatriation "notices in newspapers with *statewide* [emphasis added] circulation as well as in the Office of Hawaiian Affairs' newspaper: *Ka Wai Ola O OHA*."[82] There were also requests for Hui Mālama and OHA to "set up toll-free numbers so that people from the outer islands would not have to pay long-distance charges to get information."[83] Notification via colleges and universities was also suggested.[84] Nineteen years have passed since these recommendations were first suggested, but as of November 2012, none of this has happened except the publication of random NAGPRA notices in the *Ka Wai Ola O OHA*, usually at the behest of federal agencies and museums based in Hawaii. Notably, as a Native Hawaiian organization expressly recognized in the law, when OHA receives the initial call from federal agencies and museums to participate in NAGPRA consultation, OHA has not shared all consultation opportunities with the larger Native Hawaiian community through written public notice in their newspaper. Disproportionate statistics that illustrate the hegemony of OHA and Hui Mālama in the NAGPRA process are symptomatic of an uninformed Native Hawaiian community.

Native Hawaiian organizations should not be a substitute for a Native Hawaiian sovereign government. Instead, Native Hawaiian organizations should support efforts toward sovereignty, as well as seeking out, informing, and supporting *families* in the NAGPRA process. Unfortunately, protection and repatriation of Native Hawaiian human remains and cultural objects appears to be a low priority, at least to the state agencies of OHA and DHHL. For example, as a courtesy to OHA and DHHL, I wanted to share my preliminary research on specific NAGPRA information and data as it relates to their organization. Unfortunately, my request to meet with my elected OHA Trustee was referred to the OHA Chief Advocate, and it took six months from my initial meeting request before an actual meeting occurred. As for DHHL, an October 2012 phone request to meet with the director to discuss NAGPRA repatriation issues was met with an entreaty to submit my request in email, which I promptly provided. To date, a reply to my email has not been received, and my verbal and written meeting requests have yet to be accommodated. How can a patient consider different remedies if the patient fails to recognize the *maʻi* (sickness)? It is a shame when the state agencies mentioned in NAGPRA avoid discussions about the law. It is also disheartening when the other Native Hawaiian organization mentioned in NAGPRA, Hui Mālama, has been vilified for the manner in which it has engaged in repatriation efforts. Granted, such criticism may be warranted, but my research suggests that no organization, not even the five island burial councils combined, have the level of expertise Hui Mālama has to navigate through the intricacies of NAGPRA. This leads to the question, *"Na wai e hoʻōla i nā iwi?* Who will save the bones?[85] Most importantly, how can we support those who have the cultural *kuleana* (authority, responsibility) to do so?

> "[F]or reinterment . . . show respect . . . Hawaiians must have love and peace."
>
> —Papa Henry Auwae[86]

Notes

1   *"Nā Iwi Kūpuna,* The Bones of our Ancestors," State of Hawaii Department of Land and Natural Resources, 2003. (on file with author). This article is dedicated to my *kumu* and *kupuna*, Henry Allen Auwae, for always showing me the way. *Na maka o ka hiamoe ke ike.*

2   "Papa Henry Auwae . . . said the Hui Mālama I Nā Kūpuna ʻO Hawaiʻi Nei (Hui Mālama) invited him into this process to support their plan . . . [He] said that he did not want to be used by Hui Mālama." Hawaii Island Burial Council Meeting Minutes, March 24, 2000, at 2–3 (hereinafter "HIBC Minutes").

3   Ibid., 2.

4   Henry Auwae, Remarks at an *ohana* gathering at Waikoloa, Hawaii, April 29, 2000.

5   Papa believed that *moepū* was not the proper word for the objects taken from the burial complex at Honokoa Gulch. Although these specific objects were originally *wewe huna*, their removal from the cave broke the *kapu* and made them *wewe kaulana hoikeike*. Henry Auwae. Remarks at an *ohana* gathering in Honolulu, Hawaii, February 12, 2000. *Accord* HIBC Minutes, *supra* note 2, at 2 and Henry A. Auwae letter to Dr. Elizabeth Tatar, Bernice Pauahi Bishop Museum dated February 14, 2000 (on file with author). The term *moepū*, which is contemporarily used to encompass all funerary objects, is a modern derivative of *moe puʻu,* which was used in the late 1800s in reference to people rather than things. *Moe puʻu* referred to individuals who volunteered or were offered as death companions to lie beside a chief or other notable person of high rank. (Henry Auwae. Remarks at an *ohana* gathering at Waikoloa, Hawaii, April 30, 2000). See also Samuel Manaiakalani Kamakau, trans. Mary Kawena Pukui. *Ka Poʻe Kahiko: The People Of Old* (Honolulu: Bishop Museum Press, 2010), 34.

6   Ibid. Accord HIBC Minutes, supra note 2, at 2. See also George Hueʻeu Sanford Kanahele. *Ku Kanaka: Stand Tall, A Search for Hawaiian Values* (Honolulu: University of Hawaii Press, 1986), 39: "The priests . . . were very kapu."

7   The five island burial councils are the Hawaii Island Burial Council, the Maui/Lanai Islands Burial Council, Molokai Island Burial Council, Oahu Island Burial Council, and the Kauai/ Niihau Islands Burial Council.

8   Angela J. Neller, "From Utilitarian to Sacred: The Transformation of a Traditional Hawaiian Object," in *Pacific Art: Persistence, Change, and Meaning* (Honolulu: University of Hawaii Press, 2002), 137.

9   The author's forthcoming doctoral dissertation, "Burying Tradition: NAGPRA in Hawaii," provides information on traditional Native Hawaiian funerary customs documented in both native and non-native sources from 1778–1870. The project juxtaposes such traditions with the contemporary manner in which they have been applied in the NAGPRA process,

complete with a discussion of the Hawaiian repatriation movement, repatriation data specific to Hawaii, and an evaluation of administrative and legal disputes arising under NAGPRA.

10   Since NAGPRA's inception, seven of the twelve Dispute Findings & Recommendations issued by the NAGPRA Review Committee involved Native Hawaiian organizations, which results in 58 percent of all disputes heard thus far. See http://www.nps.gov/history/nagpra/ REVIEW/Find_and_Rec.htm. (Last accessed October 1, 2012).

11   Statement of Colin Kippen, "Hawaiians have a lot of issues that were particularly difficult to deal with under NAGPRA ... [I] cannot say that Hawaiians have been successful under NAGPRA." NAGPRA Review Committee (hereinafter "NRC") Minutes, October 11–12, 2008, at 21.

12   Statement of Rosita Worl, Ibid. at 13.

13   Statement of Garrick Bailey, "The law doesn't even work that well with the eastern tribes ... And it's even more of a disaster with the Hawaiians." Vicki Viotti, "Decision Today on Hawaiian Artifacts," *Honolulu Advertiser* (March 15, 2005).

14   Edward Halealoha Ayau, "Rooted in Native Soil," in *Implementing the Native American Graves Protection and Repatriation Act,* Roxana Adams, ed. (Washington DC: American Association of Museums, 2001), 53–55.

15   Herb Kawainui Kane, "Don't Let Them Have Hawaiian Treasures," *Honolulu Advertiser* (August 29, 2000).

16   Greg Johnson, *Sacred Claims: Repatriation and Living Tradition* (Charlottesville, VA: University of Virginia Press, 2007), 28.

17   Ibid. Edward Halealoha Ayau of Hui Mālama I Na Kupuna O Hawai'i Nei was incarcerated for contempt of court for defying a court order to disclose the reburial location of eighty-three cultural items involved in the "Forbes Cave" controversy.

18   Na Iwi o Na Kupuna O Mokapu v. Dalton, 894 F. Supp. 1397 (D. Haw. 1995).

19   Portions of this section were previously published in the author's article, "Na Wai E Ho'ōla i Nā Iwi? (Who Will Save the Bones?): Native Hawaiians and the Native American Graves Protection and Repatriation Act," *Asian-Pacific Law & Policy Journal* 14:1 (2012), http:// www.hawaii.edu/aplpj/.

20   An individual tracing his or her ancestry directly and without interruption by means of the traditional kinship system of the appropriate Indian tribe or Native Hawaiian organization or by the common law system of descendance [sic] to a known Native American individual whose remains, funerary objects, or sacred objects are being claimed under these regulations. 43 C.F.R. §10.2(b)(1).

21   Any organization which (A) serves and represents the interests of Native Hawaiians, (B) has as a primary and stated purpose the provision of services to Native Hawaiians, and (C) has expertise in Native Hawaiian affairs, and shall include the Office of Hawaiian Affairs and Hui Malama I Na Kupuna O Hawai'i Nei. 25 U.S.C. §3001(11).

22   Statement of Kina'u Boyd Kamali'i, trustee, Office of Hawaiian Affairs, "A difficulty which we have encountered and bring before you without a clear recommendation for resolve is the overly-broad definition of "Native Hawaiian organization" contained in this act." *Native American Grave Protection and Repatriation Act: Hearing Before the S. Comm. On Indian Affairs,* 103rd Cong., 1st Sess. 45, 50 (1993).

23   894 F. Supp. 1397 (D. Haw. 1995).

24   Statement of Clarence Ching, trustee, Office of Hawaiian Affairs, *Native American Grave and Burial Protection Act (Repatriation); Native American Repatriation of Cultural Patrimony Act; and Heard Museum Report: Hearing Before the S. Comm. On Indian Affairs,* 101st Cong., 2nd Sess. 82 (1990).

25   894 F. Supp. 1405 (D. Haw. 1995).

26   Ibid., 1408.

27   Ibid., 1406.

28   Ibid, 1407.

29   Ibid, 1408.

30   25 U.S.C. §3005(e).

31   894 F. Supp. 1408 (D. Haw. 1995).

32   See Order to Show Cause, at 2, Na Lei Alii Kawanananakoa v. Bishop Museum, No. 05-00540 DAE-KSC (D. Haw. December 22, 2005).

33   See Order Finding Edward Halealoha Ayau, Pualani Kanakaʻole Kanahele, William Aila and Antoinette Freitas in Contempt of Court at 2-5, Na Lei Alii Kawanananakoa v. Bishop Museum, No. 05-00540 DAE-KSC (D. Haw. December 28, 2005).

34   Kunani Nihipali, "Stone by Stone, Bone by Bone: Rebuilding the Hawaiian Nation in the Illusion of Reality," 34 *Arizona State Law Journal* 27 (2002): 2.

35   The original four claimants were Hui Mālama, the Office of Hawaiian Affairs, the Department of Hawaiian Home Lands, and the Hawaiʻi Island Burial Council.

36   25 U.S.C. §3005(e). See also Notice of Intent to Repatriate Cultural Items: U.S. Department of the Interior, National Park Service, Hawaii Volcanoes National Park, Hawaii National Park, HI, 74 *Fed. Reg.* 10756 (March 12, 2009), available at http://www.nps.gov/nagpra/fed_notices/nagpradir/nir0454.html (last visited November 17, 2012).

37   Neller, "From Utilitarian to Sacred," 137.

38   Johnson, *Sacred Claims,* 31.

39   *Native American Grave Protection and Repatriation Act: Hearing Before the S. Comm. On Indian Affairs: Oversight Hearing to Provide for the Protection of Native American Graves,* 106th Cong., 2nd Sess. 2 (2000).

40   Statement of Nathan Napoka of SHPD. NRC Minutes, February 26–28, 1993, 11. Notably, distinct Hawaiian chiefdoms transformed to an absolute monarchy under King Kamehameha I, followed by a constitutional monarchy that was forcefully acquired from King Kalakaua, who acquiesced at gunpoint in 1887. The subsequent 1893 overthrow of the Hawaiian kingdom under Queen Liliʻuokalani resulted in the further dismantling of a Hawaiian sovereign government through the 1898 annexation of Hawaii by a U.S. joint resolution of Congress. Although Native Hawaiians are not a "tribe," had they been allowed to retain their sovereign government in some form, even a diminished "domestic wardship," perhaps the implementation of NAGPRA could be less problematic.

41   Statement of Donald Duckworth, former president, director, and CEO of Bishop Museum. NRC Minutes, November 2, 2004, 10.

42   Burl Burlingame, "Group at Center of Museum Controversy," *Honolulu Star-Bulletin* (December 30, 2000), http://archives.starbulletin.com/2000/12/30/news/story2.html. See also Nihipali, "Stone by Stone, Bone by Bone: Rebuilding the Hawaiian Nation in the Illusion of Reality," 36. "As a young attorney working for Senator Daniel Inouye, [Ayau] used his knowledge of Indian law and applied it to Hawaiian peoples."

43   Georgia M. Helm, Editorial, *Honolulu Advertiser* (April 10, 2000).

44   Mary Kawena Pukui and Samuel H. Elbert, *Hawaiian Dictionary* (Honolulu: University of Hawaii Press, 1986), 254. *Moʻokūʻauhau* means genealogical succession, pedigree.

45   Ibid., 178. "Kuleana" is popularly translated as a right or responsibility. However, kuleana also means authority, interest, and claim.

46   Davida Malo, trans. Malcolm Naea Chun, *Ka Moʻolelo Hawaiʻi: Hawaiian Traditions* (Honolulu: First People's Productions, 2006), 2.

47   Note that there are some common ancestors shared between the different genealogies.

48   S. M. Kamakau, *Ruling Chiefs of Hawaii* (Honolulu: Kamehameha Schools Press, 1992), 214.

49   Kamakau, *Ka Poʻe Kahiko: The People Of Old*. See also Kamakau, trans. Mary Kawena Pukui, *The Works of the People of Old: Na Hana a Ka Poʻe Kahiko*, 132.

50   Kamakau, *Ruling Chiefs of Hawaii*, 200.

51   Martha Warren Beckwith, ed., *Kepelino's Traditions of Hawaii* (Honolulu: Bishop Museum Press, 2007), 48. See also Samuel Manaiakalani Kamakau, trans. by Mary Kawena Pukui, *Tales and Traditions of the People of Old: Nā Moʻolelo a Ka Poʻe Kahiko* (Honolulu: Bishop Museum Press, 2000), 51.

52   Malo, *Ka Moʻolelo Hawaiʻi: Hawaiian Traditions*, 4.

53   Ibid, 76.

54   Kamakau, supra note 5 at 40. Today, we would call this *mahaʻoi*: insolent, presumptuous, brazen. Pukui and Elbert, supra note 44, at 219.

55   Kamakau, *Ka Poʻe Kahiko: The People Of Old*, 40.

56   Malo, *Ka Moʻolelo Hawaiʻi: Hawaiian Traditions*, 66.

57   HIBC Minutes, March 24, 2000, 2.

58   Malo, *Ka Moʻolelo Hawaiʻi: Hawaiian Traditions*, 67.

59   Kamakau, *Ka Poʻe Kahiko: The People Of Old*, 50.

60   Beckwith, ed., *Kepelino's Traditions of Hawaii*, 46.

61   Statement of Glen Kila, member of Koa Mana. NRC Minutes, February 26–28, 1993, 13.

62   Statement of Papa Henry Auwae, "[T]he *kupuna* were buried according to rank." HIBC Minutes, March 24, 2000, 2.

63   Malo, *Ka Moʻolelo Hawaiʻi: Hawaiian Traditions*, 76.

64   Pukui translates *kauwa* as "outcasts" (Kamakau, *Ka Poʻe Kahiko: The People Of Old*, 8), whereas Beckwith translates the term as "slave class" (Beckwith, ed., *Kepelino's Traditions of Hawaii*, 142), thus revealing their divergent disciplines and backgrounds. Pukui was a Native Hawaiian cultural expert and translator, while Beckwith was a folklorist from Massachusetts.

65   Kamakau, *Ka Poʻe Kahiko: The People Of Old*, 8.

66   Beckwith, ed., *Kepelino's Traditions of Hawaii*, 142.

67   Kamakau, *Ka Poʻe Kahiko: The People Of Old*, 8.

68   Beckwith, ed., *Kepelino's Traditions of Hawaii*, 144.

69   Malo, *Ka Moʻolelo Hawaiʻi: Hawaiian Traditions*, 77.

70   Kamakau, *Ka Poʻe Kahiko: The People Of Old*, 39.

71   Malo, *Ka Moʻolelo Hawaiʻi: Hawaiian Traditions*, 82.

72   Beckwith, ed., *Kepelino's Traditions of Hawaii*, 22.

73   Malo, *Ka Moʻolelo Hawaiʻi: Hawaiian Traditions*, 23.

74   Ibid., 66.

75   Ibid.

76   Miriam Kahn, "Not Really Pacific Voices: Politics of Representation in Collaborative Museum Exhibits," *Museum Anthropology* 24 (1) (2000): 57–74, 71.

77   25 U.S.C. §3001(15).

78   25 U.S.C. §3000 (11).

79   Neller, "From Utilitarian to Sacred: The Transformation of a Traditional Hawaiian Object," 137. "[In the NAGPRA process] Hawaiian history and traditional objects are pawns used by

some Native Hawaiians to authenticate their authority over cultural issues to create a contemporary arena for their hegemonic cultural practices."

80   Haw. Rev. Stat. §10-1(a) (2012).

81   The Auditor, State of Hawaii. Rep. No. 04-15 Investigation of the Department of Land and Natural Resources' Process for Developing Recommended Candidate Lists for Appointment to the Island Burial Councils, 50 (2004).

82   NRC Minutes, February 26–28, 1993, 11.

83   Ibid.

84   Ibid.

85   See Pukui and Elbert, *Hawaiian Dictionary*, 104.

86   HIBC Minutes, March 24, 2000, 2.

Chapter 5

Amending Wonder: Museums and Twenty Years of the Native American Graves Protection and Repatriation Act

PATRICIA CAPONE

Hundreds of museums in the United States have implemented the Native American Graves Protection and Repatriation Act (NAGPRA) for more than twenty years. My experience with NAGPRA is based on just one of those museums subject to the act, albeit one which stewards a large and broad collection—the Peabody Museum of Archaeology and Ethnology at Harvard University. This experience includes implementing the act with Indian tribes, Alaska Natives and Native Hawaiian organizations, and collections from nearly every state and most aspects of North America's human history. The collections at the Peabody Museum of Archaeology and Ethnology represent a long history of collecting in the United States, and tend toward systematic collecting. While the size and setting of this museum, within a long-standing university, may be different from more recent academic institutions or small museums, its NAGPRA implementation is of a breadth and scope that resonates with a variety of interests.

While practicing NAGPRA at this museum has been broad in some ways, the breadth of possible NAGPRA experiences reaches far beyond. NAGPRA's application in its many forms unfolds in a spectrum of experiences, from respect for new understanding and its relevance for youth, to learning from past atrocities or malignancies and grieving their scars. NAGPRA's potential for learning resonates in a university museum setting. NAGPRA's contribution to knowledge reaches beyond the collections that museums steward, to raising awareness of the multiple viewpoints regarding them. NAGPRA brings opportunities to develop sustainable intercultural epistemologies. Material objects straddle the physical, metaphysical, and more. In NAGPRA's context, this broadens understanding. Museums' assembling of new ways of thinking, generating new views on assembling objects, and setting themselves as meeting grounds of ideas and incubators of intercultural thought amends museums' wonder. Toward this premise I offer a selected retrospective on twenty years of museums' implementation of NAGPRA and my perceptions of future directions.

Defining museums and explaining the history of American collections sets the context for discussing twenty years of museums and NAGPRA. First, differences between a commonplace definition of museums and NAGPRA's definition of museum require a brief explanation to set out NAGPRA's purview. For much of the history of museums, encounters with objects have evoked a sense of wonder through the physical experience of being with the object and through thinking about the layers of meaning which objects induce.[1] Through time, American museums also revise their approaches to collecting based on a variety of factors, including society's inclinations, intellectual directions, and most recently, NAGPRA. Consequently, NAGPRA revises how museums impart wonder. NAGPRA brings a social and civil conscience to wonder, and in some cases, critical awareness of the dark side to wonder's baggage.

NAGPRA simultaneously extends critical reflection to the practice of stewarding objects and thinking about the uses of heritage in American society. NAGPRA is a tool of consciousness-raising. My experience is that NAGPRA's societal impact can increase the sustainability of stewardship of material objects, and therefore make museums more effective settings for learning and knowledge development.

What is a museum under NAGPRA?

NAGPRA defines museums as institutions which receive federal funding and which are in the United States of America (25 USC 3001). NAGPRA's definition of a museum diverges from a commonplace definition of a museum and that cited by America's largest museum professional organization, the American Association of Museums (AAM). The Association defines a museum as making "a unique contribution to the public by collecting, preserving, and interpreting the things of this world." [2] The Association reckons there are approximately 17,500 museums in the United States,[3] which AAM further describes as: " . . . cultural and educational institutions—community-centered places for remembering, discovering, and learning. They present the best of the world's culture, heritage, and achievement. . . . help preserve the past, define the present, and educate for the future."[4]

One of the main distinctions between NAGPRA's definition of a museum and a common understanding of a museum is NAGPRA's stipulation that a museum receive federal funding. Even where the museum itself may not receive federal funding, if it is governed by a larger entity, such as a university, which does receive funding, the museum could be subject to NAGPRA. Additionally, many institutions, which may or may not consider themselves to be museums, qualify as museums under NAGPRA. For example, a state and/or local history agency or organization, a medical facility, or library may constitute a museum under NAGPRA if it possesses or controls such collections as defined in the act and meets the above criterion of federal funding. Further, a small local cultural entity that receives state funding originating in federal funds might constitute a museum under NAGPRA. These particularities of NAGPRA's definition of "museum" may have taken time to understand and become realized by institutions that do not typically consider themselves to be museums. What does not constitute a museum under NAGPRA? A federal agency does not constitute a museum; neither does a museum outside the United States, or one which does not receive federal funding. This still leaves a large number of institutions subject to NAGPRA.

What does NAGPRA require of museums?

NAGPRA requires that museums summarize, inventory, and repatriate cultur-ally affiliated Native American human remains or cultural items. It also requires that museums make dispositions of culturally unidentifiable Native American human remains as defined in the act. Specifically, NAGPRA defines the following categories of museum holdings as being subject to its requirements: human remains, associated funerary objects, and cultural items.[5] NAGPRA further divides cultural items into three categories: sacred objects, objects of cultural patrimony, and unassociated fu-nerary objects. Failure to meet the requirements of summary, inventory, repatriation, or disposition according to deadlines set out in the regulations could result in civil penalties and jeopardize eligibility for federal funds. NAGPRA allows for museums to request extensions to its deadlines. For museums which are governed by larger entities, the failure to meet NAGPRA's requirements could have ramifications for the entity overall.

NAGPRA regulations pertaining to discoveries that post-date the act are distinct from those for items that are under the possession or control of a museum. The pro-cess is significantly different for human remains and items from recent excavations (post 1990) and those discovered on federal or tribal lands after the 1990 passage of the act. NAGPRA regulations stipulate procedures for these situations which aim toward determining custody and disposition with Indian tribes and Native Hawaiian organizations, and which give priority to the land-owning tribe. Confusion some-times results due to the two different frameworks applied by NAGPRA for these varieties of circumstances. For the most part, today's museums are more frequently involved in the sections of NAGPRA pertaining to items that are already in collec-tions prior to the passage of the Act in 1990. For this reason, I focus here on what is sometimes referred to as "museum NAGPRA."

A similar but separate legislation, the National Museum of the American Indian (NMAI) Act, also affords repatriation of human remains and cultural items to Native American tribes. The NMAI Act preceded NAGPRA by a year, and applies solely to the national museums of the Smithsonian Institution. Because of the Smithsonian's governance, legislation specific to allowing for repatriation within that structure is separate from NAGPRA's purview. The NMAI Act similarly recognized the legitimacy of concerns by Native Americans over equal protection for Native American human remains and cultural items. The collections of America's Smithsonian Institution were among the catalysts for Native American tribes' attention to these concerns.

How did museums come to possess human remains and items of such weighty significance to indigenous Americans?

Museums' implementation of NAGPRA is set within the century-and-a-half history of Unites States museum collections. Most U.S. museums are societal institutions, which are educational in nature and dedicated to the preservation of materials for public accessibility. In acquiring collections, museums both mirror society and aim to contribute to society's improvement through education and through encounters with displays of collections and interpretive programs. Many U.S. museums situate at the intersection of a European and Euro-American history of science and society.

Much of the European and Euro-American history of scientific collecting is borne out in museums and is revisited through NAGPRA's implementation. Furthermore, Russian colonial collecting of Alaska Native and Native American items is evident among early and significant museum collections. Also, some early collecting by Native American scholars and community members is a meaningful setting of collecting history for consideration. Finally, before 1990 there were few tribally run museums, which today diversify museums' purview, and NAGPRA's reach.

Most of the NAGPRA-relevant collections in museums, particularly human remains, were collected during the first century of museums, from about 1870–1970. Systematic collection and study of material remains (artifacts) and the biological remains of humans took place in Western Europe and America, first through sixteenth-century European cabinets of wonder (or curiosities) and later through enlightenment science, mercantile travel, and learned societies.

The advent of American anthropology in the nineteenth century, a time known as the museum-era of anthropology,[6] accounts for many significant collections, which have since become subject to NAGPRA. Archaeology considered human remains and their burial items as settings rich for interpretation. In historical context, these collections were amassed toward evoking wonder, the collecting of aesthetic treasures, and the development of knowledge with the aim of bettering humanity. Consequences to indigenous people were typically (wrongly) not considered within the early contexts of scientific inquiry.

Furthermore, inquiries of the time focused on establishing the boundaries of humanity, as America's and Europe's understandings of geography and the globe's resources were ever-expanding. In other words, whether the human species included indigenous peoples of the Americas and Africa was a central question. Charles Darwin was among the proponents of a notion of a common humanity, in which humanity included all "races" of the time[7]. In this context, collectors, scientists, ship captains, business people, navigators, and explorers amassed human remains and other anthropological collections from around the world—first in private cabinets of curiosities and later in early museums.

Euro-Americans' perplexity over the relatedness of Native Americans to the Americas' large-scale archaeological sites led in part to physically dislocating Native Americans from the nation's early inhabitants. In some cases, such as Cahokia in the Midwest and cliff pueblos in the Southwest, the grandeur and degree of technical achievement was attributed to others—not conceived of as possible to have been built by the area's nineteenth century Native Americans.[8] America's conception of its past grew disconnected from nineteenth century Native Americans, and consequently set the stage for the appropriation of land, and many other resources. The collection of Native American cultural materials was accepted as the property of scientific inquiry rather than as the legacy of sovereign indigenous nations. Racism and Manifest Destiny were among eighteenth and nineteenth century societal contexts in which the early museum collections were taken. From today's lens, these contexts disrespect civil rights, but at the time, they justified colonialist expansion.

Nevertheless, noted early scientists questioned the status quo. An early practitioner of physical anthropology, Samuel Morton, hypothesized relatedness between the Americans being studied through archaeology and nineteenth century Native Americans.[9] Morton argued against the prevailing thought of the time, which related cranial morphology to intelligence and cited no significant difference between Native American and Euro-American cranial morphology. Others had cited distinction in morphology to be an indicator of less-developed intelligence. Early practitioners of archaeology—such as Squier and Davis at the mounds of the Midwest,[10] and Adolph Bandelier[11] in the cliff dwellings of the Southwest—began to chart indigenous origins for the earthworks, architectural monuments, and the societies who created them. Bandelier was also among the early archaeologists to advocate for the protection of America's archaeological heritage, as looting and vandalism began to raise public and governmental awareness of the non-renewable national heritage they represent.

Later in the nineteenth century, anthropologists and federal agencies set out to document what they viewed as the remnants of lifeways of Native Americans. The phenomenon known as "salvage ethnography" took place in the United States and in other countries where post-colonial expansion and modernization were seen to threaten the survival of indigenous people.[12] Native Americans in the path of westward expansion and industrial progress were disconnected in Euro-Americans' imaginations from those who left the wonder of the mound-builders and the cliff-dwellers. Ironically, this mode of collecting simultaneously "preserved and destroyed" what it sought to salvage.[13] Museums became the settings of preservation of the resulting collections.

The colonialist history of archaeology similarly plays a role in archaeology's "controlling the representation of the past" through mechanisms such as attributing the construction of America's great indigenous monuments and earthworks to others, not to Native Americans.[14] Today's post-colonial archaeology in critique points out that Western societies defined themselves through the "representation of others in negative terms."[15] Essentialist representations such as these "reduce complex heterogeneous structures to an inner truth or essence . . . inscribing inferiority . . . Archaeology and museums have played significant roles in the construction of essentialist discourses worldwide."[16]

Scholars of Native American ancestry notably impacted the development of museums and these scholarly fields. In some ways, they bridged the perspectives of collecting cultures and source cultures, while in other ways their roles escape categorization. Their roles in shaping the related academic fields have received attention, while further consideration of their agency vis-à-vis NAGPRA's trajectory and disposition of museum collections is a topic beginning to be noticed. Native American involvement in Western science and art appreciation during the formative years of museum collecting, and the significance of this history, are becoming points of consideration as NAGPRA refocuses attention to the details of collection provenance. The legacies of these scholars are as varied as their individuality and their cultures, and therefore there will not be a singular story, but a complex of interrelated journeys and topics. In what ways do these legacies serve as beacons or dilemmas for today's tribal heritage scholars and museum professionals? Are elements of their early attempts to make heritage sustainable in a multicultural and increasingly global world reference points for today's museums and for designing NAGPRA's architecture?

One example is Arthur C. Parker, of Seneca and Scotch descent who was the first Native American archaeologist. Parker's relevance for a historical modeling of a moral archaeology has recently been detailed.[17] Parker's roles in museums such as the Peabody Museum of Archaeology and Ethnology, New York State Museum, and American Museum of Natural History are significant in the early history of anthropology. Another major contributor, Francis LaFlesch, of Omaha descent, is hailed as the first Native American anthropologist.[18] There are numerous lesser-known contributors to museums who intertwine with NAGPRA's context, such as Theodore B. Pitman of royal Hawaiian ancestry. Pitman's Cambridge, Massachusetts studio researched and fabricated many of the dioramas and models of Native American life for early museums in the Northeast. Legacies such as theirs are directly relevant to reflecting on NAGPRA's trajectory and its future for Native American collections in museums.

Art collecting

In the late nineteenth and early twentieth centuries, art collecting of Native American items for aesthetic purposes relating to senses and emotions (rather than classificatory or descriptive purposes), diverged from anthropological collecting. Art collecting encompassed both scholarly[19] and commercial enterprises, with traders and merchants becoming influential in the future directions of the practice and propagation of Native American material as art. Some items which were collected as art retain more than aesthetic meaning to their originators and have been among some of the most prioritized subjects of requests for repatriation by Native American tribes such as the Ahayu:da or Zuni war gods.[20]

NAGPRA's emergence in historical context

NAGPRA emerges from the intersection of these mainly Euro-American collecting histories with civil rights and scholarly movements such as anthropological relativism, post-colonialism, and philosophies of science which emphasize the notion that principles, behaviors, and understandings are best considered in their local contexts or within the frameworks of understanding that produced them. Anthropological relativism emphasizes acknowledging one's own cultural perspective as a means for heightening one's understanding of another. This approach also involves being conscious to minimize ethnocentrism, to not prioritize (in a dominating way) one's familiar cultural framework in interpreting and assessing another. In this way, reflecting on Euro-American notions of scientific collecting raises awareness to see how some collecting may result in civil rights and other violations.

Today's scholars study these intersections of societal values with scholarship, heritage, and repatriation. [21] Some argue that America's cultural frameworks tend toward litigious problem solving, and therefore gave rise to NAGPRA.[22] Cultural-resource management policy-making, with its roots in non-indigenous perspectives is also cited as a setting for promoting stewardship.[23] Furthermore, NAGPRA's positioning as a means to unraveling society's difficult and specific history relative to museums, the history of science, and American politics has been considered.[24] Some legal scholars consider NAGPRA as human rights law.[25] Still others question the legality of some aspects of NAGPRA. For example, some consider NAGPRA's intersections with freedom of scientific inquiry and notions of an American commonwealth of heritage resources.[26]

Today's production of knowledge by museums stems from contexts in contemporary scholarship described in part above, and from societal counterparts such as the civil rights movement. Museums have been well underway in increasingly self-reflexive pursuits of knowledge. Today's museums engage not only European-derived scientific ideals, but also vary approaches involving both scientific and humanistic co-production of knowledge. Production of knowledge in today's museums values multiple lines of evidence and voices; for example, source communities' perspectives on interpreting collections has been increasing since before NAGPRA's passing, and is becoming commonplace. The notion of voice today also extends to the museum's interested communities, including museum visitors themselves. The Newark Museum's exhibits and programs involving diverse urban religious communities and teen parents are among notable examples of museums exploring authorship and their institution's relevance.

Museums' NAGPRA implementation statistics

Museums account for the majority of NAGPRA implementation when assessed in a national context, which includes federal agencies (reported by the National NAGPRA Program, March 2011). A review of national statistics with an eye toward museum implementation underscores the following:

- National NAGPRA received inventories from 987 implementers: 601 museums, and 386 federal agency units.
- Over 60 percent of the culturally affiliated human remains have been inventoried and reported by museums (947 museums), and 40 percent by federal agencies (34,342 minimum number of individuals [MNI] out of 53,842 combined federal and non-federal).[27]
- Approximately 60 percent of human remains announced in *Federal Register* Notices of Inventory Completion are reported by museums (approximately 22,000 out of 37,000).[28]

Selected twenty-year retrospective from a museum's-eye view

Over the past twenty years, museums have allocated significant resources to implementing NAGPRA, and balance this application of resources with deadlines. In turn, museums have benefited from enhanced knowledge in caring for collections, and from bringing new life to the relevance of museum collections through meaningful dialogues. In doing so, museums' participation in NAGPRA contributes to intellectual trends in the democratization of the production of knowledge, to refining legal analyses regarding cultural property and civil rights, and to balancing the application of resources with meeting deadlines.

Determining cultural affiliation

At the twentieth anniversary symposium "NAGPRA at 20," which was organized by the National NAGPRA Program and the George Washington University in November 2010, a theme pertinent to museums' implementation was that of determining cultural affiliation. A major focus of the discussion was museums' and federal agencies' receptiveness to traditional knowledge and whether traditional knowledge is heard fairly as part of NAGPRA's dialogue for determining cultural affiliation. "Traditional Knowledge as Evidence" formed the topic for one of the panel sessions. Leading up to the panel, struggles have been recounted through the years, which submit that traditional knowledge has not been adequately considered as part of the process of determining cultural affiliation.[29] While "oral tradition" and "other expert opinion," which traditional knowledge encompasses, are among the types of evidence which are required to be considered in the process of determining cultural affiliation (43 CFR 10), a perception persists that traditional knowledge is discounted for other types of evidence. If this sense continues twenty years later, museums have room for improvement in receiving and acting on traditional knowledge and "other expert opinion." Museums can enhance the effectiveness of NAGPRA dialogue, and intercultural dialogue in general, by considering how it is made explicit that this information is received, acknowledged, and, if applicable, acted on. Finally, museums can be attuned to protocols for receiving and managing the information, and be in communication about respecting them.

As previously mentioned, museums are increasingly engaging multiple perspectives in the development and sharing of knowledge. Partnerships are numerous among museums, indigenous communities, and others. These engagements raise awareness and intercultural respect for multiple voices through the updated and often evocative interpretations that result.[30] Professional organizations have made commitments in these directions as well. For example the American Association of Museums, American Anthropological Association, American Association of Art Museum Directors, and Society for American Archaeology all position themselves with codes of ethics and guides for their fields which reflect attentiveness to community, intercultural respect, and dialogue.

Legal study

Legal analyses of NAGPRA now benefit from two decades of research, reflection, and case law, though few cases have been tried. Museums and other NAGPRA implementers alike can utilize these refinements toward considering improved implementation. Much of NAGPRA's legal activity has not related to "museum NAGPRA" but rather to the section of the law relating to removals of human remains or cultural items from federal lands after the passage of the act (section 3). The most well-known case in this area concerns human remains from Kennewick, Washington. While this case does not focus on museum collections, the court's analysis of the determination of cultural affiliation offers some points that might be brought to bear in either section of NAGPRA. Furthermore, the definition of "Native American" as considered in this case raises perplexity about whether the definition corresponds with the intent of Congress. Instead, because there are so few court cases, especially for museum collections, legal-oriented publications may offer special interest for museums in light of the recent legal examinations that focus on more recently regulated areas of implementation such as culturally unidentifiable human remains.[31]

Period of forbearance

A major benchmark for museums in NAGPRA's twenty-year retrospective was the 1995 deadline for inventory completion. The deadline proved difficult for some museums, especially those with large collections of human remains and associated funerary objects. While the statute gave the Secretary of the Interior authority to grant extensions if a museum appealed and could demonstrate a good faith effort toward inventory completion, a number of museums were granted a rather short "period of forbearance" rather than the requested extension. The "period" was granted along with the threat of civil penalties. These institutions concentrated resources over a short period of time in order to implement the requirements. In some cases, this required inventory completion at a rate of 4,000 individual human remains per year. The compression of inventory completion at these institutions resulted in abbreviated consultation periods. For example, tribes who were not ready or otherwise unable to respond to offers of consultation and inventory drafts in the short timeframe were left with their perspectives unrepresented. This situation likely resulted in fewer findings of cultural affiliation than might have been achieved if there had been a timetable more accommodating of complete consultation dialogues.

Museum implementation over the past twenty years

While there is wide variety in how museums have implemented NAGPRA, a brief focus on some of the more common types of cases highlights its scope. The largest category of museum implementation relates to archaeological human remains and funerary objects in systematically collected groupings. These groupings most often resulted from question-driven anthropological investigations, which aimed toward understanding America's past. These investigations tended to focus on broad questions that might be applicable across geographic areas such as social organization, demography, and health. These examples tend to represent most of the large repatriations. For example, at the Peabody Museum of Archaeology and Ethnology, such repatriations included over 2,000 individual human remains from the Pueblo of Pecos,

New Mexico to the Pueblo of Jemez,[32] and over 100 human remains and thousands of funerary objects from the Seneca community, Ganondagan, to the Haudenosaunee Standing Committee on Burial Rules and Regulations. Ganondagan had been excavated in large part by Arthur Parker, the previously mentioned first Native American archaeologist. The role of Native American communities and professionals in the early history of this type of large-scale systematic collecting merits additional reflection in NAGPRA's aim to unravel injustice within contemporary perspective. Some of these large repatriations have given rise to retrospective synthetic studies such as that for the Pueblo of Pecos, which was in part inspired by today's Pueblo's interest in what might be learned through contemporary methods and approaches to human remains.[33] University museums, such as the Peabody Museum, are in settings favorable to exploring research and teaching partnerships such as those that grew from the NAGPRA consultations around Pecos Pueblo, which build toward the goals of various interests and hone intercultural communication.

Early on, NAGPRA regulations recommended that institutions prioritize NAGPRA consultations toward determination of cultural affiliation for Historic period human remains. In some instances, these situations relate to individual leaders and well-known historical events. For example, an early repatriation in 1993 from the Peabody Museum of Archaeology and Ethnology involved Ninigret I, seventeenth century "Sachem of the Iliantics" from present-day Rhode Island.[34] Historic alliances and Native American veterans alike are recognized and brought to rest through NAGPRA. The tragedy of historic military engagements, such as Utah's Black Hawk War of 1865–1872, and a history of disinterment and display from it, are observed and reconsidered through repatriations such as that of Chief Black Hawk to his lineal descendants by the Museum of Peoples and Cultures, Brigham Young University and the United States Forest Service.[35]

Implementing NAGPRA for cultural items, such as sacred objects and objects of cultural patrimony, similarly benefits from close consultation that is conducted with explicit respect for traditional knowledge. Joining together, in part through techniques that follow a tribe's unique methodology of knowledge, results in a hybridity of knowledge and can make for notably effective examples of NAGPRA implementation that lead to new ways of thinking and partnerships.[36]

At one time or another and for a variety of reasons, some Native American communities or individuals selected museums as safeguards of collections. A recent case of the Alaska State Museum raises the nuanced nature of agency by Native American leaders and heritage professionals in attempts to either safeguard or bring new educational appreciation to their people.[37] NAGPRA situations like this highlight a spectrum of Native American agency in assembling a collection and offer opportunity for reflecting on future goals of collections.

Humanizing remains

Much of museums' implementation of NAGPRA for the first twenty years revolved around meeting statutory deadlines for inventorying human remains. Congress selected the term "human remains" to signify what in other contexts or countries might be termed "the dead." The term "human remains" connotes a material quality in its utilization of the word "remains," meaning pieces or fragments present after part is removed. The material connotation of the term "human remains" extends the notion of fragments to refashioned material manifestations such as cremations. Terminology in other laws within the United States, such as state laws pertaining to unmarked human burials also utilize the term "human remains." In Britain, the Human Tissue Act of 2004 serves " . . . to make provision with respect to activities involving human tissue; to make provision about the transfer of human remains from certain museum collections; and for connected purposes."[38] Again, the term "human remains" serves in English within the context of repatriation of individuals who have been dead for a long period of time.

The term "the dead" or "deceased" connotes a sense beyond the material, beyond the state of being alive, and therefore potentially more evocative of a metaphysical realm, and more humanizing. British and U.S. repatriation of individuals recently dead while out of the country tends to utilize the term "deceased." To some extent, in this way, a sense of humanity or personhood is attenuated in English legal terminology in both the United States and Britain when referring to remains from a deeper past.

Reflections on "NAGPRA at 20" and postmillennial directions

Reflections at the "NAGPRA at 20" symposium by two prominent commentators on the act, Suzanne Shown Harjo, advocate for Native American rights, and David Hurst Thomas, anthropologist museum curator, explored their own expanding dialogues during their roles in the development of National Museum of the American Indian. I heard certain aspects of their dialogue as symbols for NAGPRA dialogues overall: as they highlighted elements of a growing process, which involved increased understanding and mutual respect. I found their comments to be suggestive that NAGPRA's dialogues can contribute to the co-development of knowledge in a sustainable multicultural society. Twenty years of NAGPRA have highlighted themes and now evoke directions for museums as stewards and as settings for dialogue. Some of these themes include cross-cultural conceptions of the human body after death, cultural hybridity, and restorative justice. NAGPRA offers museums mutual understanding of collections, and the opportunity to amend wonder by reflecting on justice. NAGPRA coincides with increased awareness of previously quiet(ed) perspectives, and of a multicultural sense of the world. This type of approach is relevant for museums that are positioning themselves as places of dialogue toward co-development of knowledge.

Varied conceptions of human remains and America's potential

Conceptions of human remains vary through time, culture, and space. For example, notions exemplified by recent exhibitions of plastinated human bodies, to centuries-old reliquary practices, and nineteenth-century medical research contrast with the conception of human remains in NAGPRA. While some NAGPRA discourses presume that approaches to human remains share universal elements of dignity and respect, this universality has not been well explored. In situations where a cultural context is ascertainable, dignity and respect as conceived by that culture might be attainable, as is the approach for culturally affiliated human remains. Through shared group identity in cultural affiliation, the perspectives on the dead are guided by living affiliates. However, for culturally unidentifiable collections where, by definition, a relationship of shared group identity to a present-day tribe or Native Hawaiian organization is not yet demonstrated, the perspectives to invoke on their care are not possible to assess. In light of America's multicultural past, in light of the history of museums' goals in amassing collections, and the history and future of tribal agency in America's heritage, what should be considered to be appropriate care for culturally unidentifiable human remains merits a thoughtful pause. America's potential to model a multicultural approach to the situation of culturally unidentifiable human remains may be applicable globally.

NAGPRA's potential to forge new relationships which carry beyond implementation of the act is being well developed in a variety of venues, including in museum exhibits, programs, and literature. Tribally determined museums have increased in number and contribute to this area. New forms of knowledge are developing through the processes of thinking, planning and working together in mutual respect. Finding support for these new directions, especially in times of fiscal constraint and diminished grant funds, will require commitment by institutions.[39] The many examples of these types of NAGPRA-linked projects include: the Harvard Yard Archaeology Project; American Museum of Natural History-Zuni Tribe partnership around digital collections; the historic Alaska kayaks project with the Alutiiq Museum and Peabody Museum of Archaeology and Ethnology; and projects with the Tongva/Gabrielino Tribe around the Santa Barbara Channel Islands with multiple California institutions, including the Fowler Museum, University of California Los Angeles.

From an improved way to conceive of "culture" in cultural affiliation[40] to the creation of post-colonial "third spaces" for discussion and ideas, notions of cultural hybridity gain increasing relevance for NAGPRA's effectiveness. NAGPRA's implementation does not take place in a social, political, or cultural vacuum. Further, in post-colonial studies, the impact of a study is considered and imagined in a global neighborhood, with the "local level" situated as a place to listen and learn.[41] NAGPRA's consultation process, as intended, is an example of an opportunity to reconfigure colonial relationships to post-colonial ones. Twenty years of literally being at the table together has provided settings to listen, respect, learn, and improve. Listening to concern about past practice and thought and the trauma these may draw into the present can be an important aspect to the consultation process. Respecting that present-day views and knowledge may hold new insight that challenges past views and can build more sustainable thought improves practice, relations, scholarship, and society. While much airing and practice remains, it is a step to improve America's approach to its past and to " . . . make sense of the trauma of the present."[42]

International dialogues also consider museums' responsibility in safeguarding world heritage. Philippine gold in Western museums and destruction of archaeological museum items and monuments in the Middle East and Asia over the past twenty years represent puzzles with spurious arguments for paternalistic stewardship. While the irrevocable loss of world heritage raises awareness of the many gray areas in stewardship and global heritage planning, much work remains.

The converse of NAGPRA's healing justice merits mention: the partial dismantling of a field of Western inquiry and its physical evidence. What had previously been conceived of mainly as scientific evidence, interrelated collections of human remains, architectural remains, faunal remains, soils, and so on were gathered to be considered in concert, for their relationships to each other and to the whole. By removing human remains, the web of relationships and future understandings will be altered.

Such revision in light of today's improved understanding of the multiple perspectives on collecting and study directs museums, archaeology, and anthropology to realize informed civic-minded approaches.[43] Increased awareness of mutual understanding along with new types of memory-making also promotes a stage for increased awareness of tribes' rights as sovereign nations. This type of memory-making is taking place, in part in museums, but the potential goes far beyond. These challenges will take commitment and resources by institutions.

Because much public funding will not consider studies of collections that are subject to repatriation under NAGPRA, an unfortunate and possibly unintended result is that collaborative work beyond basic NAGPRA consultation (which is funded by the National NAGPRA Program) is sharply curtailed. This stipulation also contributes to the misperception that collections become inaccessible once repatriation takes place and title is transferred to Native American tribes. While currently, many collections which are repatriated and dispositions which are made under NAGPRA become inaccessible through cultural protocols (for example, through reburial), tribes are increasingly supporting heritage programs. Some situations foster culturally appropriate interpretation and public learning from collections that come into tribal control through NAGPRA. The availability of public funding for this might foster an environment more conducive to tribally directed initiatives around NAGPRA collections. This perhaps unintended perception that NAGPRA collections will no longer play a role in America's learning has not been generally discussed.

Museums as appropriate repositories

An indirect consequence of NAGPRA may have been to influence perception of museums fitness as appropriate repositories for benefitting public good. While this may be a longer-term pattern to observe, short-term observations are possible. First, a problematic perception results indirectly from recently promulgated NAGPRA regulations for section 10.11, disposition of culturally unidentifiable human remains. This regulation requires that all culturally unidentifiable Native American human remains in museums be offered for disposition outside museums. Why are museums—even federal museums—not included among the regulation's options for disposition? The regulation seems almost to say "anywhere but museums." These regulations, in effect, question museums as appropriate stewards of culture and heritage in American society.[44] Curation partnerships between museums and tribes could have been recommended as one of the outcomes of NAGPRA regulations. Would public funding support study if a framework of curation agreements were in place between tribes and museums?

Public dialogue

NAGPRA discourse mainly takes place within a limited arena of implementers and concerned interests. As a law concerned in part with America's heritage and the history of inquiry, relatively few fora have involved broad-based public education and discussion around NAGPRA's public relevance. Some of the new technologies brought to bear in studying the past and in making cultural affiliations are fascinating yet undertold in a public forum. Additionally, the opportunity to utilize NAGPRA's legal backdrops, such as the Trade and Intercourse Act, offers an opportunity to raise awareness about tribal sovereignty and the multilayered implications of tribes' legal rights. It seems a missed opportunity to utilize NAGPRA's goals for remedying human remains and cultural resource infringements as a springboard to related concerns for Native American tribes and Native Hawaiians. Museums, federal entities, and tribes could partner in these efforts to generate public awareness and, potentially, action.

These disjunctions raise questions about whether NAGPRA's unintended consequences could be more rigorously explored without appearing to criticize

NAGPRA's basic aims. As Ames[45] relates in his urging of museums to take risks of relevance, his question might be reframed for NAGPRA: Is NAGPRA doing the right thing while doing the thing right? Museums are increasingly concerned with doing the right thing,[46] for which NAGPRA is in part responsible. Perhaps NAGPRA can model multipartisanship of tribes, museums, and federal entities, and inspire models for developing shared goals and sustainable intercultural action. While the ancestor relationships of NAGPRA connect to legacy populations and implore compassion and respect, the legacy of their placement in museums belongs to all Americans, and will lead to wider social change if its disentangling and resolution involves more of us in considering and acting toward disentanglement together. By amending a historically damaging wonder, museums can inspire new wonders based in part in NAGPRA's justice.

Acknowledgments

I warmly acknowledge generosity of dialogue with the community of NAGPRA practitioners I have the privilege to learn from in all settings and situations—educational, museum, tribal, governmental, and beyond. The viewpoints expressed here represent my own and do not represent any institution with which I am affiliated. Misunderstandings and mistakes are my own. Special thanks to Sangita Chari and Jaime Lavallee, who so ably led our journey toward the work of this book.

Notes

1   Stephen Greenblatt, "Resonance and Wonder," *Bulletin of the American Academy of Arts and Sciences* 43, No. 4 (1990): 11–34.

2   "American Association of Museums, What is a Museum?," American Association of Museums [now American Alliance of Museums], last accessed October 30, 2011, http://www.aam-us. org/museumresources/ethics/coe.cfm.

3   "American Association of Museums, About Museums, How Many," last accessed October 30, 2011, http://www.aam-us.org/aboutmuseums/abc.cfm#how_many.

4   "American Association of Museums, About Museums," last accessed October 30, 2011, http://www.aam-us.org/aboutmuseums/.

5   25 U.S.C. 3001(2) and 43 C.F.R. 10.2.

6   George Stocking, ed., "Objects and Others: Essays on Museums and Material Culture," in *History of Anthropology, volume 3* (Madison: University of Wisconsin Press, 1985).

7   Charles Darwin, *On the Origin of Species by Means of Natural Selection* (London: John Murray, 1859).

8   Kier Sterling, *Rafinesque: Autobiography and Lives* (New York: Arno Press, 1978).

9   Samuel G. Morton, *Crania Americana; or, A Comparative View of the Skulls of Various Aboriginal Nations of North and South America: To Which is Prefixed An Essay on the Varieties of the Human Species* (Philadelphia: J. Dobson, 1839).

10   E.G. Squier and A.M. Davis, *Ancient Monuments of the Mississippi Valley*. Smithsonian Contributions to Knowledge, vol. 1 (Washington, D.C.: Smithsonian Institution, 1848).

11   Adolph Bandelier, *Contributions to the History of the Southwestern Portion of the United States*. Archaeological Institute of America, American Series number 5 (Cambridge, 1890).

12   Steven Conn, *History's Shadow: Native Americans and Historical Consciousness in the Nineteenth Century* (Chicago: University of Chicago Press, 2004).

13   Janet Berlo, *The Early Years of Native American Art History* (Seattle: University of Washington Press, 1992).

14   Matthew Liebmann, "Postcolonial Cultural Affiliation: Essentialism, Hybridity, and NAGPRA," in *Archaeology and the Postcolonial Critique*, (Lanham, MD: Altamira Press, 2008), 6.

15   Ibid., 6.

16   Ibid., 6.

17   Chip Colwell-Chanthaphohn, *Inheriting the Past: The Making of Arthur C. Parker and Indigenous Archaeology* (Tuscon: University of Arizona Press, 2009).

18   Robin Ridington, "A Sacred Object as Text: Reclaiming the Sacred Pole of the Omaha Tribe," *Omaha Heritage E-texts,* http://omahatribe.unl.edu/etexts/oma.0021/index.html.

19   Franz Boas, "The Decorative Art of the Indians of the North Pacific Coast," *New York Bulletin of the American Museum of Natural History,* Vol. 9 (1897).

20   T.J. Ferguson and Barton Martza, "The Repatriation of Ahayu:da Zuni War Gods," *Museum Anthropology* 14, No. 2 (1990).

21   See David Hurst Thomas, *Skull Wars: Kennewick Man, Archaeology and the Battle for Native American Identity* (New York: Basic Books, 2000); Laurajane Smith, *Archaeological Theory and the Politics of Cultural Heritage* (London: Routledge, 2004); Laurajane Smith, *Uses of Heritage* (London: Routledge, 2006); Liv Nillson Stutz, "Caught in the Middle: An Archaeological Perspective on Repatriation and Reburial," UTIMUT: Past Heritage—Future Partnerships—Discussions on Repatriation in the 21st Century, Doc. No. 122 (Copenhagen: IWGIA, 2008), http://emory.academia.edu/LivNilssonStutz/Papers/103402/Caught_in_the_Middle._An_archaeological_perspective_on_repatriation_and_reburial.

22   Smith, *Archaeological Theory,* 2004.

23   Ibid.

24   Thomas, *Skull Wars,* 2000.

25   See Jack Trope and Walter Echo-Hawk, "The Native American Graves Protection and Repatriation Act: Background and Legislative History," *Arizona State Law Journal* 21, No. 1 (1992); C. Timothy McKeown and Sherry Hutt, "In the Smaller Scope of Conscience: The Native American Graves Protection and Repatriation Act Twelve Years After," *UCLA Journal of Environmental Law* 21, No. 153 (2003).

26   See Douglas W. Owsley and Richard L. Jantz, "Archaeological Politics and Public Interest in Paleoamerican Studies: Lessons from Gordon Creek Woman and Kennewick Man," *American Antiquity* (September 2001); Ryan Seidemann, "Altered Meanings: The Department of the Interior's Rewriting of the Native American Graves Protection and Repatriation Act to Regulate Culturally Unidentifiable Human Remains," *Temple Journal of Science Technology and Environmental Law* 28 (2009); Margaret J. Schoeninger et al., "Unexamined Bodies of Evidence," *Science* 20 (May 2011): 916.

27   National NAGPRA report statistics, National NAGPRA Program Midyear Report, 2011, www.cr.nps.gov/nagpra/DOCUMENTS/Reports/NationalNAGPRAMidYear2011final.pdf, 16. Note that this number differs by about 100 individuals between pages 8 (53,816) and 15 (53,742) within the report. No reason is given in the midyear report for the inconsistency.

28   Ibid., 16.

29   Examples are frequent in NAGPRA Review Committee meetings; see Review Committee transcripts for more information on where and when tribes have discussed this matter. www.nps.gov/nagpra.

30   See Laura Peers and Alison Brown, *Museums and Source Communities: A Routledge Reader* (London: Routledge, 2003); Lucy Fowler Williams, William S. Wierzbowski, and Robert W. Preucel, eds., *Native American Voices on Identity, Art, and Culture: Objects of Everlasting Esteem* (Philadelphia: Museum of Archaeology and Anthropology, University of Pennsylvania, 2005). Richard West, *The Changing Presentation of the American Indian* (Washington DC: Smithsonian Institution, 2000).

31   Seidemann, "Altered Meanings," 2009.

32   Patricia Capone, "Pecos Pueblo: The Natural, Cultural, and Historical Settings," in *Pecos Pueblo Revisited* (Cambridge: Peabody Museum of Archaeology and Ethnology, 2010), 9–18.

33   Michele E. Morgan, ed., *Pecos Pueblo Revisited* (Cambridge: Peabody Museum of Archaeology and Ethnology, 2010).

34   58 *Fed. Reg.* 27309 (May 7, 1993).

35   61 *Fed. Reg.* 3459-3460 (January 31, 1996).

36   Martha Graham and Nell Murphy, "NAGPRA at 20: Museum Collections and Reconnections," *Museum Anthropology* 33, No. 2 (2010): 105–124.

37   "Dispute: Sealaska Corporation and Wrangell Cooperative Association, and Alaska State Museums, NAGPRA Review Committee Meeting Minutes, November 17–19, 2010," 9–16, last accessed October 30, 2011, http://home.nps.gov/history/nagpra/REVIEW/meetings/RMS043.pdf.

38   "Act of Parliament of the United Kingdom, Human Tissue Act 2004, Introduction," last accessed October 30, 2011, http://www.legislation.gov.uk/ukpga/2004/30/introduction.

39   Rubie Watson, "Culturally Sensitive Collections: A Museum Perspective," in *Stewards of the Sacred* (Washington DC: American Association of Museums, 2005), 113–122.

40   Liebmann, "Postcolonial Cultural Affiliation."

41   Uzma Rizvi, "Decolonizing Methodologies as Strategies of Practice," in *Archaeology and the Postcolonial Critique* (Lanham, MD: Altamira Press, 2008), 109–128.

42   Homi K. Bhabha, *The Location of Culture* (NY: Routledge, 1994).

43   Barbara Little and Paul Shackel, *Archaeology as a Tool of Civic Engagement* (Lanham, MD: Altamira Press, 2007).

44   Comment on Rule: Native American Graves Protection and Repatriation Act Regulations: Disposition of Culturally Unidentifiable Human Remains, http://www.regulations.gov/#!documentDetail;D=DOI-2007-0032-0181.

45   Michael Ames, "Why Post-Millennial Museums Will Need Fuzzy Guerillas," in *Academic Anthropology and the Museum* (Oxford: Berghahn Books, 2001), 200–210.

46   Ames, "Why Post-Millennial Museums Will Need Fuzzy Guerillas," 203.

Bibliography

Ames, Michael. "Why post-millennial museums will need fuzzy guerillas." *Academic Anthropology and the Museum.* Edited by Mary Bouquet. Oxford: Berghahn Books, 2001.

Bandelier, Adolph F. *Final Report of Investigations among the Indians of the South-western United States.* Papers of the Archaeological Institute of America. Cambridge, MA: John Wilson and Son, 1890.

Berlo, Janet. *The Early Years of Native American Art History*. Seattle: University of Washington Press, 1992.

Collins, Mary B. and William Andrefsky Jr., *Archaeological Collections Inventory and Assessment of Marmes Rockshelter (45FR50) and Palus Sites (45FE36 A, B, C): A Compliance Study for the Native American Graves Protection and Repatriation Act*. Center for Northwest Anthropology, Project Report Number 28, Washington State University, Pullman, 1995.

Colwell-Chanthaphohn, Chip. *Inheriting the Past: the Making of Arthur C. Parker and Indigenous Archaeology*. Tucson: University of Arizona Press, 2009.

Conn, Steven. *History's Shadow: Native Americans and Historical Consciousness in the Nineteenth Century*. Chicago: University of Chicago Press, 2004.

Darwin, Charles. *On the Origin of Species by Means of Natural Selection*. London: John Murray, 1859.

Ferguson, T.J. and Barton Martza. "The Repatriation of Ahayu:da Zuni War Gods." *Museum Anthropology* 14, No. 2 (1990).

Fowler Williams, Lucy, William S. Wierzbowski, and Robert W. Preucel, eds. *Native American Voices on Identity, Art, and Culture: Objects of Everlasting Esteem*. Philadelphia: University of Pennsylvania Museum of Archaeology and Anthropology, 2005.

Graham, Martha and Nell Murphy. "NAGPRA at 20: Museum Collections and Reconnections." *Museum Anthropology* 33, No. 2, (Fall 2010).

Greenblatt, Stephen. "Resonance and Wonder." *Bulletin of the American Academy of Arts and Sciences* 43, No. 4 (January 1990).

McKeown, C. Timothy and Sherry Hutt. "In the Smaller Scope of Conscience: the Native American Graves Protection and Repatriation Act Twelve Years After." *UCLA Journal of Environmental Law* 21, No. 2 (2003).

Liebmann, Matthew. "Postcolonial Cultural Affiliation: Essentialism, Hybridity, and NAGPRA." *Archaeology and the Postcolonial Critique*. Edited by M. Liebmann and U. Rizvi. Lanham, MD: Altamira Press, 2008.

Little, Barbara and Paul Shackel. *Archaeology as a Tool of Civic Engagement*. Lanham, MD: Altamira Press, 2007.

Morgan, Michele, ed. *Pecos Pueblo Revisited*. Cambridge: Peabody Museum of Archaeology and Ethnology, 2010.

Morton, Samuel G. *Crania Americana; or, A Comparative View of the Skulls of Various Aboriginal Nations of North and South America: To Which is Prefixed An Essay on the Varieties of the Human Species*. Philadelphia: J. Dobson, 1839.

National NAGPRA Program. *National NAGPRA Program Midyear Report, 2011*. Washington DC: National Park Service, 2011. http://www.cr.nps.gov/nagpra/DOCUMENTS/Reports/NationalNAGPRAMidYear2011final.pdf.

Owsley, Douglas W. and Richard L. Jantz. "Archaeological Politics and Public Interest in Paleoamerican Studies: Lessons from Gordon Creek Woman and Kennewick Man," *American Antiquity* 66, No. 4 (2001).

Peers, Laura and Alison Brown. *Museums and Source Communities: a Routledge Reader*. London: Routledge, 2003.

Rizvi, Uzma. "Decolonizing Methodologies as Strategies of Practice." *Archaeology and the Postcolonial Critique*. Edited by M. Liebmann and U. Rizvi. Lanham, MD: Altamira Press, 2008.

Schoeninger, Margaret J., Jeffrey L. Bada, Patricia M. Masters, Robert L. Bettinger, and Tim D. White. "Unexamined Bodies of Evidence." *Science* 20 (May 2011).

Seidemann, Ryan. "Altered Meanings: the Department of the Interior's Rewriting of the Native American Graves Protection and Repatriation Act to Regulate Culturally Unidentifiable Human Remains." *Temple Journal of Science Technology and Environmental Law* 28 (2009).

Squier, E.G. and A.M. Davis, "Ancient Monuments of the Mississippi Valley." *Smithsonian Contributions to Knowledge*, Vol. 1 (1848).

Sterling, Kier. *Rafinesque: Autobiography and Lives*. New York: Arno Press, 1978.

Stocking, George, ed. "Objects and Others: Essays on Museums and Material Culture." *History of Anthropology*, Vol 1. Madison: University of Wisconsin Press, 1985.

Stutz, Liv Nillson. "Caught in the Middle: An Archaeological Perspective on Repatriation and Reburial." *UTIMUT: Past Heritage—Future Partnerships—Discussions on Repatriation in the 21st Century*, Doc. No. 122. Copenhagen: IWGIA, 2008.

Thomas, David Hurst, *Skull Wars*. New York: Basic Books, 2000.

Trope, Jack and Walter Echo-Hawk, "The Native American Graves Protection and Repatriation Act: Background and Legislative History." *Arizona State Law Journal* 24 (1992).

Watson, Rubie. "Culturally Sensitive Collections: A Museum Perspective." *Stewards of the Sacred*. Edited by Alison Edwards and Lawrence Sullivan. Washington DC: American Association of Museums, 2005.

West, Richard, *The Changing Presentation of the American Indian*. Washington, DC: Smithsonian Institution, 2000.

Chapter 6
Federal Agency Perspective

C. TIMOTHY McKEOWN, EMILY PALUS, JENNIFER RIORDAN,
and RICHARD WALDBAUER

The federal agencies who must comply with NAGPRA have a variety of missions that are defined in the statutes that created them. Often those missions are characterized as "conservation" or "multiple-use" when it comes to their responsibilities for the public lands over which they have authority. Though they all have preservation of cultural heritage as part of their missions, or are mandated by law, the various approaches that federal agencies take are affected by the structure and functions of their mission-oriented organizations. So when NAGPRA was enacted in 1990, each federal agency had an organization in place, with policies and operations, which could be tasked with the new requirements. While they all recognized the significance of NAGPRA, they also brought different perspectives on the best ways to accomplish the statutory purposes.

In this chapter, we examine NAGPRA implementation from the origins and development of those programs in federal agencies. Specifically, the programs of the U.S. Army Corps of Engineers, the Bureau of Land Management, and the National Park Service are addressed. They each have distinct missions. They each have important differences in their organizations. They each brought distinct approaches to the initial phases of implementation. Together, their accomplishments can be viewed as essential contributions to the national efforts to achieve the purposes of NAGPRA.

We begin with a federal agency that welcomed the enactment of NAGPRA as a critical component of its strategic goals and centralized administration for one part of its cultural heritage program on behalf of its far-flung organizations. The U.S. Army Corps of Engineers had provided significant support for this centralized approach, so the ability to describe the new requirements was aided greatly by the skilled technicians and program management already functioning effectively within the agency. Almost immediately, the corps program became a model that other federal agencies sought to learn about. Their sturdy record in auditing collections and analyzing curation programs helped set standards that other federal agencies were able to use.

The U.S. Army Corps of Engineers' NAGPRA program

Introduction. The U.S. Army Corps of Engineers (corps) administers a centralized NAGPRA compliance program that is unique within the Department of Defense. Established in 1992, the program is managed by the St. Louis District's Mandatory Center of Expertise with direction provided by corps headquarters. This chapter outlines the history of the program, discusses the compliance strategy employed, then highlights the successful repatriation of Native American human remains and funerary objects dating between 800 and 10,000 years before present (ybp).

History of the corps's NAGPRA program. In 1802, Congress formally created the U.S. Army Corps of Engineers. In the Continental United States, the corps is currently comprised of 38 district offices organized within eight regions. In total, the corps administers or manages nearly 11 million acres of public land. Prior to construction or groundbreaking projects conducted on corps lands, archaeological investigations are often necessary. These investigations have been conducted by professional archaeologists, university research programs, and archaeological contractors, and the resulting surveys and excavations have resulted in archaeological collections that total more the 47,000 cubic feet. The collections often remained with the investigators doing the work or were transferred to local museums and historical societies. Thus, corps collections are now stored in a diverse array of universities, museums, offices, and storage facilities.

When NAGPRA was enacted in 1990, the corps recognized the critical importance of the legislation, but also knew compliance would be complicated by the dispersed nature of the archaeological collections. To address the complex compliance issues, corps leadership took the bold steps of requesting line-item funding specifically for NAPGRA compliance and centralizing the management of compliance. The line item funding provides a consistent stream of funding dedicated to NAGPRA compliance. Additionally, to manage the effective use of the resources, to track compliance across the corps, and to provide technical experts to assist districts, a centralized program was established.

To initiate this program, corps headquarters looked to the St. Louis District, which a few years previously had united a group of technical specialists to address archaeological collections management needs. It soon became obvious that success would follow the union of the St. Louis technical focus and the agency's NAGPRA compliance. The technical center in St. Louis was elevated to a national extension of the corps headquarters and designated a Mandatory Center of Expertise (MCX) for the Curation and Management of Archaeological Collections (CMAC). The MCX was chartered to deliver centralized management, administration, and policy devel-opment in corps-wide compliance with NAGPRA.

NAGPRA process. The corps's centralized program developed a step-by-step compliance process that is based on a clearly defined incremental approach. This ap-proach begins with identifying the collections universe, that is, districts first identify the location, extent, and contents of archaeological collections through an in-depth review of the archaeological records associated with district properties. Districts use this data to complete summary reporting requirements, and to identify those collec-tions that contain Native American human remains and funerary objects. The second step of the process is the physical inspection, or inventory, of the collections with Native American human remains and funerary objects.

Concurrent with the first two steps, corps districts consult with Indian tribes. Consultation is central to the identification of cultural items and the determination of cultural affiliation for the human remains and cultural items. Information provided by tribes during consultation is used in concert with other information gathered by the district through research done by both district staff and contracted experts and professionals. To make a determination of affiliation, districts evaluate the totality of evidence and circumstances pertaining to the connection between a claimant and the material being claimed. Once determinations are made, the final steps prior to repatriation—the preparation, submittal, and publication of the necessary compli-ance documents—are completed.

The means and manner of repatriation are determined between the claimant tribe and the district. An important aspect of the corps's program is the authority for districts to rebury the repatriated human remains and funerary objects on corps property, if the materials had been previously removed from corps property. The Water Resources Development Act of 2000 contains section 208, *Reburial and Conveyance Authority*,[1] which authorizes the Secretary of the Army to recover and rebury Native American remains that were discovered on Civil Works project land and have been rightfully claimed by a lineal descendant or Indian tribe. The secretary is also authorized to set aside Civil Works land to rebury these Native American re-mains and convey these set-aside lands to an Indian tribe for use as a cemetery. Corps headquarters has endorsed the use of corps funds for certain reburial expenses.

In addition to providing funding and staff support to districts for NAGPRA inventories, consultation, and cultural affiliation, the MCX is the central repository for copies of compliance documents and tracking of NAGPRA compliance data across the corps. MCX also serves as the technical point of contact within the corps for NAGPRA-related issues. Having worked with NAGPRA since the early 1990s, the technical staff at the MCX provides districts with expert, timely, and efficient assistance that is not available through any other resources. Lessons learned and issues encountered in one district can be used as a template to assist another district. The policy guidance distributed by the central program ensures that a level of standardization in practice is reached throughout the corps.

The process outlined above has lead to significant progress in NAGPRA compliance across the U.S. Army Corps of Engineers. All districts with archaeological collection have completed the summary reporting requirements. Results of the inventories show that there are over 5,000 Native American individuals and 275,000 cultural items in collections from twenty-seven corps districts. Because the inventories conducted at each district were preceded by an in-depth review of the collections' documentation, the corps has a high level of confidence that we have located the full extent of our collections with known Native American human remains and funerary objects. Districts with Native American human remains and cultural items are in consultation with Indian tribes, and corps districts began repatriations in 1996.

To highlight key aspects of the corps's NAGPRA program, an overview of the repatriation of Native American human remains and cultural items from the Marmes site within the Walla Walla District is provided below.

Repatriation of the Marmes collection. The Marmes site (45FR50), located in Franklin County of southeastern Washington State, is a fundamentally important site in Pacific Northwest archaeology and an important location for tribes in the region. The site is a shallow rock-shelter, the slope in front of the rock-shelter, and a floodplain area in the lower Palouse River Canyon just north of its confluence with the Snake River. Archaeological work began at the site in 1962 as part of a survey and testing program meant to document human occupation in the area that would, seven years later, be inundated by Lower Monumental Dam. The land is owned by the Walla Walla District. The initial excavations at the site were carried out within the rock-shelter between 1962 and 1964. The rock-shelter excavations uncovered human remains, including human remains features or burials that contained both human remains and funerary objects. The burials were sequentially numbered from Burial 1 to Burial 22, and the human remains collected were fragmented and fragile. In addition to the human remains in the numbered features, fragments were also found in other areas of the rock-shelter. The human remains from the rock-shelter were not directly dated by radiocarbon, but samples from strata where the remains were excavated yielded dates ranging from 800 years before present (ybp) to 8,170 ybp (Hicks 2004:390).

After 1964, there was a break in excavations within the rock-shelter, and a small amount of stratigraphic analysis was done at the site in 1965. In 1968, a second major data recovery was conducted that included the excavation of a cremation hearth feature within the rock-shelter and the floodplain area. The cremation hearth feature yielded a significant number of small human bone fragments, and dating of the cremation strata produced results of approximately 8,425 ybp to 11,280 ybp. The floodplain deposits were also found to contain scattered human remains, but no defined burial features were recorded. The human remains from the floodplain were collected from strata dating between 9,520 and 10,120 ybp (Hicks 2004:390).

The archaeological collections from the Marmes site are stored at Washington State University (WSU), while Walla Walla District maintains control of the collections. In 1995, WSU produced an assessment and inventory of the Marmes collection at Walla Walla District's request. That assessment concluded that "the great antiquity of the human remains and funerary objects from the Marmes site precluded our being able to discern the identity or tribal affiliation of any of these individuals" (Collins and Andresfky, Jr. 1995:66).

In 1996, soon after the completion of the initial inventory for the Marmes collection, human remains were discovered on Walla Walla District property along the Columbia River in Kennewick, Washington. These remains, commonly referred to as Kennewick Man, became the subject of a lawsuit, and the legal decisions in that case forever impacted the NAGPRA process within the Walla Walla District. The legal case of Kennewick Man resulted in the determination that the Kennewick Man remains were not Native American as defined by the law and therefore, NAGPRA did not apply [*Bonnichsen v. United States*, 217 F. Supp. 2d 116 (D Or. 2002) ("Bonnichsen I"), and affirmed by 367 F.3d 864 (9th Cir. 2004) ("Bonnichsen II")].

Based on these decisions, Walla Walla District was bound to review the Native American determinations for all their collections, and this included the human remains within the Marmes collection. In 2004, Hicks completed an extensive report on the Marmes Site and noted that "because the Marmes human remains were recovered from strata that span some 10,000 years, the results of the Kennewick Man court cases will need to be weighed in the Corps of Engineers' decision-making and repatriation process on the Marmes site collections" (Hicks 2004:421).

In April 2006, the Columbia Plateau Inter-Tribal Repatriation Group submitted a joint claim for the human remains and NAGPRA cultural items within the Marmes site collection. At that time, Walla Walla District began a multi-step process to determine if the human remains in the Marmes collection were Native American and, therefore, subject to the provisions of NAGPRA. As part of this process, Walla Walla District requested MCX assistance in conducting a complete accounting of the human remains within the collection. MCX completed this accounting in August 2007, with members of the Confederated Tribes of the Colville Reservation present during the process. Concurrent with this, Walla Walla District initiated an extensive review of the factors necessary to establish the Native American origin of the collection, if possible. The initial determination was that the human remains recovered from the human remains features within the rock-shelter met the substantial evidence required of the Ninth Circuit Court of Appeals to be determined Native American, and therefore NAGPRA applied. However, information gathered for the human remains from the floodplain and the cremation hearth did not, based on factors considered at that time, satisfy the definition of Native American as required by *Bonnichsen I* and *Bonnichsen II* (USACE 2008).

With the Native American decision made for the rock-shelter remains, the corps continued working with the tribes to make a determination of cultural affiliation for these remains. Archaeological evidence from both regional and local contexts provided the most complete information for this cultural affiliation determination. Geographical and anthropological evidence supported the archaeological evidence (Hackenberger et al., 2009:112–113). Based on a detailed analysis of the lines of evidence, in April 2009, Walla Walla District determined that the rock-shelter burials were culturally affiliated with the Confederated Tribes of the Colville Reservation, the Confederated Tribes of the Umatilla Indian Reservation, the Confederated Tribes and Bands of the Yakama Nation, and the Nez Perce Tribe, collectively the "Claimant Tribes" (USACE 2009a). The Wanapum Band, a non-federally recognized tribe, was also consulted during the process. After publication of the appropriate notices in the *Federal Register*, a minimum number of 45 individuals were repatriated to the Claimant Tribes, along with over 2,000 associated funerary objects and 176 unassociated funerary objects on September 22, 2009. The repatriated collection was reburied on corps lands.

This reburial, however, did not end the NAGPRA process on the Marmes collection. The corps was cognizant of the fact that the tribes did not agree with the original Native American determination for the floodplain and cremation hearth remains and never closed the door to further review and study. The tribes expressed frustration and believed the corps was being overly cautious in their interpretations; they felt that the corps, at that time of the September 2009 repatriation, had enough information to change the original determination that there was not enough evidence to support that the floodplain and cremation hearth remains were Native American.

In 2009, four groups within the corps began a review of the original Native American determination for the floodplain and cremation collections: Walla Walla District, Northwest Division, MCX, and corps headquarters. Tribal members were consulted throughout the process and provided valuable input during the many discussions. The focus was to review the evidence to see if it was possible to establish a demonstrable connection between the older Marmes remains (cremation hearth and floodplain remains) and a presently existing tribe, people, or culture, as required by *Bonnichsen I* and *II*. The new review looked at the cremation and floodplain human remains in the context of the entire site, considering them as part of the sites assemblage as a whole, and where applicable, within the context of the Columbia Plateau region. The study expanded and built upon the Walla Walla District's original 2008 analysis, and also used new information that had been gathered during the process of determining cultural affiliation for the rock-shelter burials. The four groups within the corps were essential to the process, with each office providing specific expertise and assessments. The 2009 evaluation led to a decision by Walla Walla District in December of that year that the floodplain and cremation hearth remains were Native American and that NAGPRA applied (USACE 2009a).

Walla Walla District immediately began the process of determining affiliation for the cremation and floodplain remains. Again, the tribes expressed their frustration at the corps's insistence that this step required another layer of documentation and review. However, cultural affiliation is a stricter inquiry than determining whether remains are Native American. The determination of Native American origin is made on a finding that substantial evidence is available to support the decision that remains are related to a tribe, people, or culture that is indigenous to the United States. Substantial evidence is a lower threshold of proof than preponderance of the evidence, which is required for cultural affiliation. Substantial evidence is essentially a reasonableness standard ("such evidence as a reasonable mind might accept as adequate to support a conclusion"), whereas preponderance of the evidence requires the conclusion being drawn to be more likely true than not true. Second, to be Native American under NAGPRA, there needs to be only a connection to a presently existing tribe, people, or culture. For cultural affiliation, there needs to be shared group identity with a tribe. A tribe, people, or culture is significantly broader than only a tribe; likewise a "connection" is more ephemeral than a "shared group identity" (USACE 2009b). The corps could not simply take the information used for the Native American determination as evidence for a determination of cultural affiliation, nor could it only use the rock-shelter burials' cultural affiliation as evidence of affiliation for the cremation hearth and floodplain remains.

In early 2010, the corps received a report by Dr. Darby Stapp entitled *A Professional Opinion on the Cultural Affiliation of Early Materials from the Marmes Rockshelter (45FR50)*. The report had been contracted by the Claimant Tribes. Considerable review was given to all evidence put forth in the Stapp document, and Walla Walla District weighed the totality of the circumstances and evidence available from the previous research that pertained to the connection between the Claimant Tribes and the Marmes cremation and floodplain remains. In April 2010, based on the evaluation of available literature, site records, reports, statutes, regulations, and case law, Walla Walla District determined that human remains and identified funerary objects from the cremation hearth and floodplain were culturally affiliated with the Claimant Tribes. Following publication of the appropriate notices in the *Federal*

Register, the second repatriation of Marmes material occurred in August 2010, with the repatriated human remains and cultural items reburied on corps lands.

The account of the Marmes collection highlights the complexities of the NAGPRA process for the corps and showcases the importance of the larger NAGPRA program in support of this effort. The corps program at the MCX and corps headquarters was able to bring together cultural resources and legal experts within and outside the corps, while providing funding, professional opinion, and technical review. Dedication at all levels of the corps in addressing the concerns raised by the Claimant Tribes enabled the corps to successfully support a cultural affiliation determination for remains that date prior to 10,000 ybp.

In summary, the many layers of the NAGPRA process require much work across the corps, from the cultural resources staff at the district level to the policy review at headquarters. In the 2009 to 2010 Government Accountability Office (GAO) audit of federal agency NAGPRA compliance, the corps was cited among the top tier of federal agencies for compliance and was noted as a successful program in the GAO presentation before the Senate Indian Affairs Committee in June 2011. The corps's national approach has greatly enhanced its NAGPRA compliance, by providing for a level of standardization and information sharing that is unparalleled in the federal agency response to NAGPRA.

We now turn to a federal agency that approached implementation of NAGPRA by tackling the enormous work of identifying its collections made over a span of more than one hundred years. During that time, the discipline of archaeology itself as a method of both scientific and humanist research changed dramatically. The Bureau of Land Management (BLM) recognized the critical need to unravel the ensuing administrative complexities to develop an inventory that would be both comprehensive and effective. They understood as well that there should be a multiplier effect of accomplishing this work, such that the agency's mission would be addressed through improved project planning and completion. Further, the BLM has been a leader in the protection of cultural heritage through its enforcement program, so their approach to implementation included comprehensive efforts to incorporate those elements of NAGPRA. This has helped to broaden the understanding of NAGPRA as not only Indian law, but also its role within the suite of laws that preserve cultural heritage.

The Bureau of Land Management

Overview. The Bureau of Land Management maintains an active NAGPRA program as part of the agency's Cultural Resource Management program, focusing on three principle activities: (1) inventory and repatriation of Native American human remains and cultural items recovered from the public lands since 1906 and held in museums and universities, supporting sections 5, 6, and 7 of the act; (2) planning for intentional excavations and responding to inadvertent discoveries, in support of section 3 of the act; and (3) pursuing criminal violations involving Native American human remains and cultural items, in support of section 4 of the act. This section provides an overview of the BLM's NAGPRA compliance efforts and a discussion of the opportunities and challenges the agency has faced in implementing this important statute.

About the BLM. The BLM is an agency within the U. S. Department of the Interior that was established in 1946, with the merging of the Grazing Service with the General Land Office (GLO). The BLM is a multiple-use land management agency with the mission "to sustain the health, productivity, and diversity of America's public lands for the use and enjoyment of present and future generations." Mandated through the Federal Lands Policy Management Act of 1976 (FLPMA), the BLM manages resources on these public lands for a variety of uses, such as energy development, livestock grazing, recreation, and timber harvesting, while protecting a wide array of natural, cultural, and historical resources. Today, the BLM manages 245 million acres, most of which are located in the twelve western states and Alaska, and 700 million acres of sub-surface mineral estate throughout the nation. BLM is a tiered organization, with twelve state offices, under which there are 46 districts and 133 field offices.

BLM's NAGPRA program. Implementation of NAGPRA within the BLM is assigned to the Cultural Resources Program, which includes management of the cultural and paleontological resources on the public lands, as well as the associated museum collections, records, and data, and oversight of BLM's tribal relations. At the policy level, implementation of NAGPRA is coordinated by the Washington office under the Assistant Director for Renewable Resources and Planning, in the Division of Cultural, Paleontological Resources, and Tribal Consultation. This division provides technical assistance, training, and coordination for the BLM's NAGPRA implementation efforts.

The BLM's twelve state offices are responsible for primary operational compliance for new discoveries of Native American human remains and cultural items found on lands currently under their jurisdiction[2] and for collections of Native American human remains and cultural items removed from the public lands prior to 1990 when NAGPRA was enacted[3] (sections 5–7 of NAGPRA).

Compliance with NAGPRA is one of many duties assigned to BLM cultural specialists. These staff primarily review land-use proposals that may affect historic properties in compliance with Section 106 of the National Historic Preservation Act (NHPA). The BLM processes more than 13,000 section 106 actions per year. BLM issues approximately 500 cultural resource use permits annually; most, but not all, of which are for non-collection survey conducted by consultants to land-use proponents to conduct section 106 compliance. Nearly nine percent of the 245 million surface acres of public lands managed by the BLM have been inventoried for cultural resources.

With an average ratio of 1.5 million acres of public land per cultural specialist, the focus of the BLM's management of cultural resources is directed toward NHPA section 106 compliance review, on-the-ground inventory, monitoring, and stabilization of archaeological sites and historic properties, and public outreach, interpretation, and education initiatives. Most proactive cultural resource work is accomplished through cost-share partnerships with state, local, and nonprofit organizations.

Implementing the "New Discoveries" requirements of NAGPRA, section 3. The BLM has integrated the requirements for planning for intentional excavations and responding to inadvertent discoveries in its land-use activities, including correlation with NHPA section 106 review and notifications under the Archaeological Resources Protection Act (ARPA). It is BLM's policy to leave burial sites and their contents undisturbed whenever possible (BLM 2004, p. II-9). Incorporating NAGPRA Plans of Action into discovery and treatment plans for archaeological resources and section 106 compliance projects is routine. Through April 2012, the BLM has published thirty-four Notices of Intended Disposition, documenting the planned transfer of 182 sets of Native American human remains, 5,211 associated funerary objects, and three sacred objects.

Implementing the "Collections" requirements of NAGPRA, sections 5–7. Per the requirements of the Antiquities Act of 1906 and ARPA, collections made from the public lands were deposited in public museums, and today, most BLM collections are maintained in non-federal museums and universities. When NAGPRA was enacted in 1990, the BLM Cultural Resource Program mobilized to locate and document archaeological collections recovered from BLM and predecessor agency public lands. This process proved challenging due to the broad dispersal of collections in multiple museums, limited land jurisdiction information in museum records, and the changes in land status over time, as federal lands were conveyed, transferred, and acquired. The agency also faced limited access to records on past collecting activities, because prior to 1984, first the Department of the Interior (DOI) and then the National Park Service (NPS) issued permits for study and collection of archaeological resources under the Antiquities Act and ARPA from the public lands. The Office of the Secretary within the Interior Department issued permits for all agencies from 1906 through 1968. From 1968 until 1984, permitting authority was assigned to the departmental consulting archaeologist in the NPS. It was not until 1984 when the Secretary of the Interior issued secretarial order 3104 that individual agencies, including the BLM, were delegated authority to issue permits for archaeological activities on their own lands. Therefore, the agency did not have a complete record of permitted activities on the public lands.

The complexities of tracking BLM collections are also due to the long history of archaeological work conducted on the public lands and the varied curation of the resulting collections. Federal collections are curated in public museums, universities, and other repositories at the direction of the Antiquities Act of 1906 and ARPA. Both statutes direct agencies to permit only qualified professionals affiliated with reputable institutions to conduct excavation and collection of archaeological resources, which includes Native American human remains and cultural items, and state that any collections are to be permanently preserved in public museums.

Under the Antiquities Act, "the examinations, excavations, and gatherings are undertaken for the benefit of reputable museums, universities, colleges, or other recognized scientific or educational institutions, with a view to increasing the knowledge of such objects, and that the gatherings shall be made for permanent preservation in public museums" (16 U.S.C. 432). Under ARPA, "The archaeological resources which are excavated or removed from public lands will remain the property of the United States, and such resources and copies of associated archaeological records and data will be preserved by a suitable university, museum, or other scientific or educational institution."[4]

Both statutes require that collections be placed in museums in order to ensure preservation, research, and public access. Neither statute allocated resources or explicitly authorized allocation of resources for curation. Collections from public lands were not placed in museums as a service contract with the federal government. Instead, most collections were placed in the museum facility of the researcher that conducted the work, or another museum eager to have collections from that project, whereby immediate access would be available to the interested researchers.

Federal regulations regarding how agencies should oversee and manage these collections were not issued until September 1990, two months before NAGPRA was enacted. This rule, 36 CFR 79, Curation of Federally Owned and Administered Archeological Collections, requires that agencies be "responsible for the long-term management and preservation of preexisting and new collections subject to this part. Such collections shall be placed in a museum with adequate long-term curatorial capabilities."[5] Prior to promulgation of 36 CFR 79 and enactment of NAGPRA in 1990, as long as collections were deposited in a public museum, the permit conditions were considered to have been met. There were no requirements or resources for the agency to track, monitor, oversee, or otherwise coordinate with the museums regarding curation.

As a result of these collections management practices, museums might be in possession of collections that were removed from public lands, but unaware of the federal connection. Such collections include those that were not deposited in the museum identified in the permit, or were exchanged or transferred among museums without DOI involvement or notification. Collections also include those that were from public lands without a permit and donated by private individuals, or collected by museum researchers without authorization. Also, many museum documentation systems (paper and automated) do not identify the agency as the owner and do not have land jurisdiction identifiers in data systems, making it very difficult to identify federal collections from museum records. This challenge is further complicated by the fact that repositories are not required to notify the federal agencies for which they hold collections.

The history of permitting further complicates agency efforts to locate collections. As such, the BLM, like other agencies and DOI bureaus and offices, does not have complete permit records, since these activities took place at a level above them in the DOI or by the NPS. When NAGPRA was enacted in 1990, each of the twelve BLM state offices initiated a search of archaeological collections from public lands under their respective jurisdictions. To do this, the BLM compiled information and coordinated with museums known to hold, or thought to hold, BLM collections.

To aid in the effort to locate archaeological collections, the BLM has made great use of the DOI and NPS permit records, which span 80 years and are housed at the National Archives and Records Administration and the Smithsonian's National Anthropological Archives. These permit files record which museum was proposed to receive the collections and would be responsible for curating them in perpetuity. However, these archives only include applications and permits. Few of the files include copies of the final report submitted at the completion of the work conducted under the permit.

BLM funded the NPS Archeology Program to review these permit files and help populate a permit database. The approximately 2,660 permit records found that were issued by DOI and the NPS between 1906 and 1984 were entered in the National Archeological Database–Permits (NPS n.d.; NADB–Permits), most of which were for non-collection survey activities. About 80 percent of the permits were for work conducted on BLM public lands, or its predecessor agency, the GLO. Reports run from the permit database were provided to individual BLM state offices for follow-up and research to identify local and out-of-state museums that potentially held BLM collections.

The BLM also contracted with the U.S. Army Corps of Engineers' Mandatory Center of Expertise for the Curation and Management of Archaeological Collections (MCX-CMAC), St. Louis District to locate collections removed from

BLM's western lands but curated in eastern museums. The report prepared by the corps provided the BLM with leads that enabled further NAGPRA inventory and reporting (Barnes 1998).

Using the archived permit database and MCX-CMAC report to find information on collections, as well as the BLM's own records and information, the BLM procured assistance from non-federal museums through contracts and assistance agreements. From this endeavor, the BLM was able to inventory and report on a significant amount of material subject to NAGPRA.

Through April 2012, the BLM has completed inventories of Native American human remains and cultural items held in five BLM facilities and thirty-six non-federal museums in seventeen states. These inventories report on 2,065 sets of Native American human remains, 19,840 associated funerary objects, and 446 unassociated funerary objects. Of the inventoried NAGPRA items, 1,583 sets of Native American human remains and 19,026 associated funerary objects have been culturally affili-ated with present-day Indian tribes, which have been published in sixty Notices of Inventory Completion in the *Federal Register*. Of the culturally affiliated NAGPRA items, 1,074 Native American human remains and 14,261 associated funerary ob-jects have been claimed and repatriated.

The BLM also has inventoried 483 sets of human remains and 623 associated funerary objects determined to be culturally unidentifiable. This includes two sets of remains and 202 associated funerary objects that were subsequently affiliated with present-day Indian tribes and reported in a Notice of Inventory Completion. In ad-dition, the BLM has transferred 10 sets of remains under 43 CFR 10.11, Disposition of Culturally Unidentifiable Human Remains.

Of the summaries provided to Indian tribes, 446 items have been identified as unassociated funerary objects, which have been culturally affiliated and published in three Notices of Intent to Repatriate. The only sacred objects and objects of cul-tural patrimony in BLM collections were recently released to the BLM by the U.S. Marshals Service. They were seized and forfeited as part of BLM law enforcement in-vestigations, and the necessary NAGPRA summaries are currently being completed.

Much of the inventory and documentation of NAGPRA collections was com-pleted in the 1990s, resulting in the publication of thirty-four Notices of Inventory Completion between 1996 and 2001. However, the BLM continues to prepare in-ventories and submit notices for publication as previously unreported NAGPRA col-lections are identified in museums and universities. The Secretary of the Interior and the NPS recognized that agencies (and museums) would have ongoing compliance in promulgating the NAGPRA regulations at 43 CFR 10.13, Future Applicability, issued on March 21, 2007. This rule acknowledges the reality that agencies and mu-seums will continue to locate previously unreported collections,[6] and it established timelines by which agencies and museums must prepare inventories and summaries after the statutory requirements had passed.

Since 2008, the BLM has published eighteen Notices of Inventory Completion for collections removed from BLM public lands and in the possession of a museum, but as of 2006, the BLM was not aware of them. As the BLM continues to work with museums to locate and document collections that originated from BLM public lands, the agency will complete summaries and inventories pursuant to the timelines established in 43 CFR 10.13, Future Applicability.

Enforcing prohibition on trafficking of Native American human remains and cultural items (section 4). The BLM's Office of Law Enforcement and Security is dedicated to the preservation and protection of cultural and natural resources on the public lands. NAGPRA is one of many statutes enforced by the BLM. Most investigations involving Native American human remains and cultural items involve several other statutes as well, including ARPA and federal property authorities. These other statutes apply to burial locations and archaeological sites, while section 4 of NAGPRA is limited to trafficking activities. The BLM Cultural Resource Program provides support to law enforcement on investigations involving Native American human remains, cultural items, archaeological sites, artifacts, and other cultural resources.

Annually, the BLM pursues violations of laws protecting cultural resources. In recent years, the agency has pursued two large-scale, multi-year investigations, Operation Bring 'Em Back in Oregon, and Cerberus Action in the southwestern Four Corners states, which have so far resulted in 39 convictions and the recovery of hundreds of thousands of Native American artifacts. As the collections are released from Law Enforcement, inventory of the collections will be completed pursuant to the timelines established in 43 CFR 10.13, Future Applicability, or following procedures for New Discoveries in 43 CFR 10.3-7, if the materials were removed from the public lands after NAGPRA was enacted in 1990.

The BLM has hosted many consultation meetings with Indian tribes, which have aided in initial identification of some items, as well as recommendations on care and handling while artifacts are in agency custody. The BLM is dedicated to repatriating the Native American human remains and cultural items to affiliated Indian tribes, and managing the non-NAGPRA collections for public benefit.

Reburial. Although not a component of NAGPRA, reburial is often a preferred activity following repatriation or transfer of custody. Prior to September 2006, BLM policy prohibited reburial of Native American human remains and cultural items on the public lands. In October 2006, the BLM issued new policy that allows authorization of reburials on a case-by-case basis (BLM 2006). Reburial is a discretionary author-ity, and due to the complexities and demands of multiple-use land management, con-siderations must be made regarding the selection of the site and future management needs. It is BLM's policy to rebury as close to the original location as possible, when possible. It is not always possible due to subsequent or planned development, or high risk of natural or unauthorized human disturbance. BLM evaluates land selection and status, National Environmental Policy Act (NEPA) and NHPA requirements, tribal access, legal and physical protections, and budget concerns. The BLM policy requires that disposition be concluded (meaning BLM has completed repatriation or transfer of custody) prior to reburial. To date, the BLM has received eight requests to rebury Native American human remains and cultural items, all of which were ap-proved and successfully concluded.

Looking forward. The BLM's NAGPRA activities focus on integrating NAGPRA responsibilities for new discoveries in land-use activities, completing NAGPRA documentation on collections removed from the public lands and held in non-federal repositories as they are identified, and pursuing protection of NAGPRA cultural items through law enforcement activities. In 2006, the BLM integrated a NAGPRA training module into its cultural resource fundamentals curriculum developed by the National Training Center in 2006. To further expand BLM staff's basic understanding of NAGPRA requirements, the BLM developed a one-day NAGPRA workshop in 2009 to improve understanding of key responsibilities and support effective decisions regarding NAGPRA. NAGPRA requires thought-ful and respectful consultation and documentation to identify Native American human remains and cultural items and determine cultural affiliation, leading to-ward repatriation or transfer of custody. This process can be difficult, painful, and time-consuming. The BLM remains dedicated to continuing the work necessary to implement NAGPRA.

Finally, we examine the approach by a federal agency to take early steps to comply with the spirit of NAGPRA. In the decade before NAGPRA became law, federal agencies were central participants in the nationwide discussion about the issues eventually addressed in the act's components. They sponsored conferences, conducted seminars, convened their staffs to consider policies and procedures, and reviewed and revised agency guidelines and handbooks. The National Park Service (NPS) was among these agencies, and recognized the significance of the coming law. Early on, they undertook actions that, using existing authorities such as the Archaeological Resources Protection Act, provided practical experience in what might be part of effective implementation. Given this preparation, when NAGPRA became law, the NPS had staff in parks, regional offices, cultural resources centers, and at headquarters who were available and prepared to accomplish the first steps of preparing summaries and inventories.

National Park Service

The National Park Service (NPS) was established in 1916 to promote and regulate the use of the fourteen national parks and twenty-one national monuments then under the administration of the Department of the Interior in a manner that conserved and provided for their enjoyment by future generations.[7] While the scope of the NPS mandate has grown steadily to now include 394 parks, monuments, parkways, preserves, seashores, recreation areas, battlefields, historic sites, and several archaeological centers, the conservation goal of NPS stewardship for its lands and collections remains the same. Large-scale construction, mining, logging, and agriculture activities that occur on other types of federal land are uncommon on the 84.4 million acres of land under NPS control. Unlike many federal agencies that rely on non-federal repositories to curate archaeological and historical collections recovered from agency lands, most of the NPS's 32 million archaeological and ethnographic items remain in agency possession.

The NPS began compilation of an inventory of Native American human remains before NAGPRA's enactment. In 1989, the Native American Rights Fund requested information on the number of Native American human remains in NPS custody or control (Echo-Hawk 1989). NPS Associate Director Jerry Rogers' response of February 28, 1990, provided an eight-page, unit-by-unit survey of the remains of 3,539 Native American individuals, showing their present location and tribal or cultural affiliation (NPS 1990). Rogers explained that the survey results from fifty-nine different park units were only preliminary, and he anticipated that additional human remains and associated funerary objects might be found before a final inventory was completed the following year.

NAGPRA was enacted nine months later, requiring each museum and federal agency to prepare a written summary of unassociated funerary objects, sacred objects, and objects of cultural patrimony in its possession or control by November 16, 1993. The act also required, in consultation with tribal government and Native Hawaiian organization officials and traditional religious leaders, an inventory identifying the geographical and cultural affiliation of Native American human remains and associated funerary objects by November 16, 1995. Each federal agency was also required to determine the ownership or control of Native American human remains, funerary objects, sacred objects, or objects of culturally patrimony that might be excavated or discovered on federal or tribal lands in the future. Some of NAGPRA's administrative duties that were assigned to the Secretary of the Interior were subsequently delegated to the NPS, including preparing regulations, providing staff support to the Native American Graves Protection and Repatriation Review Committee, and publishing notices in the *Federal Register* (see Chapter 2). At the time, placement of NAGPRA administrative responsibilities within NPS ensured that the agency would meet both the summary and inventory deadlines; however it also planted the seeds for allegations of conflict of interest and a series of administrative reorganizations to address the perceptions.

While most federal agencies prepared separate summaries for each administrative unit or region, the NPS headquarters office chose to compile data from all 341 units then part of the park system into a single 103-page document (NPS 1993). Eighty-two park units identified items in their collections totaling 1.4 million items, with the remaining 259 park units reporting no items. The summary did not identify whether a particular item was an unassociated funerary object, sacred object, or object of cultural patrimony, instead offering that the compiled list "may" include such items. Conversely, the culturally affiliated Indian tribe or Native Hawaiian organization was identified for most items. Nearly half of the reported items, mostly pottery fragments and chipped stone, were reported by Ocmulgee National Monument in Georgia, and the twelve reporting park units in the Southeast Region accounted for 89 percent of the service-wide summary total (see Table 1). Park units in the Intermountain Region accounted for another 10 percent of the service-wide summary total. In November, 1993, the service-wide summary was sent to over 800 Indian tribes (including Alaska Native corporations), Native Hawaiian organizations, and non-federally recognized Indian groups.

Preparation of inventories of Native American human remains and associated funerary objects was delegated to each park unit superintendent. In May 1996, inventories from 100 individual park units and the accompanying notifications of inventory completion were distributed to 139 culturally affiliated Indian tribes and Native Hawaiian organizations. Praising the hard work of NPS ethnographers, curators, Indian liaison officers, archaeologists, and historians, NPS Director Roger Kennedy affirmed that "the repatriation process demonstrates our commitment to the common ground and common purpose we all share as Americans" (McKeown 1996: 17). Ultimately, 103 park units reported the remains of 6,221 Native American individuals and 99,371 associated funerary objects (see Table 2). Over 25 percent of the human remains were reported by Mesa Verde National Park in Colorado, and the 46 reporting park units in the Intermountain Region accounted for over 75 percent of the total number of human remains in NPS possession or control. Park units in the Southeast Region accounted for another 19 percent of the total number of human remains (NPS 2011a & 2011b).

NPS compliance with the summary and inventory requirements was exemplary for multiple reasons. Both documents were completed within the deadlines

Table 1: NPS Summary and Notices of Intent to Repatriate

NPS REGION	NPS COLLECTIONS[1]		SUMMARY[2]	NOTICES OF INTENT TO REPATRIATE[3]			
	Archeology	Ethnography		Unassociated Funerary Objects	Sacred Objects	Objects of Cultural Patrimony	Sacred Object/ Cultural Patrimony
Alaska	1,185,034 (3%)	759 (4%)	45 (0%)	0	0	2	0
Intermountain	8,296,280 (24%)	7,848 (37%)	151,260 (10%)	350	2,514	0	22
Midwest	3,107,939 (9%)	3,522 (16%)	421 (0%)	7	12	0	0
National Capital	1,714,245 (5%)	2 (0%)	32 (0%)	0	0	0	0
Northeast	6,852,338 (19%)	238 (1%)	1,219 (0%)	76	0	0	0
Pacific West	4,511,188 (13%)	8,530 (40%)	4,878 (0%)	3,200	4	0	0
Southeast	9,548,677 (27%)	504 (2%)	1,306,995 (89%)	0	0	0	0
Washington Headquarters	67 (0%)	23 (0%)	0 (0%)	0	0	0	0
Total	35,215,768 (100%)	21,426 (100%)	1,464,850 (100%)	3,633	2,526	2	22

Source   [1] As of June, 2011. Ronald Wilson, NPS Chief Curator (personal communication)   [2] NPS (1993)   [3] NPS (2011d)

proscribed by Congress, allowing the NPS to begin repatriations before many other federal agencies. In addition, the summary was comprehensive, identifying those park units believed to hold unassociated funerary objects, sacred objects, and objects of cultural patrimony, as well as those for which no such items were identified. NPS success in completing the summaries and inventories was due in part to the fact that most of its museum collections were in agency possession instead of scattered among non-federal repositories.

The statute required each museum and federal agency to send a copy of the inventory and notification of cultural affiliation to the Secretary of the Interior, who was required to publish the notification in the *Federal Register*. Since NAGPRA was enacted, ninety-six NPS Notices of Inventory Completion were published, of which seventy-three are decisions regarding the repatriation of human remains and associated funerary objects to culturally affiliated Indian tribes, Native Hawaiian organizations, or lineal descendants; fourteen are decisions regarding the disposition

Table 2: NPS Inventories and Notices of Inventory Completion

NPS REGION	Human Remains 1990[1]	Human Remains 1997[2]	Human Remains 2010[3]	% Culturally Affiliated[3]	Associated Funerary Objects, 2010[3]	% Culturally Affiliated[3]
Alaska	46	32	30	100%	44	100%
Intermountain	2,201	4,179	4,357	86%	10,510	84%
Midwest	285	319	329	16%	14,483	92%
National Capital	0	0	1	0%	0	NA
Northeast	48	55	63	94%	5,571	100%
Pacific West	348	175	248	90%	13,392	100%
Southeast	207	1,285	1,193	29%	55,371	77%
Washington Headquarters	0	0	0	NA	0	NA
On loan to NPS	404	0	0	NA	0	NA
Total	3,539	6,045	6,221	72%	99,371	84%

Source	[1] NPS (1990)	[2] NPS (1997)	[3] NPS 2011a & 2011b	[3] NPS 2011a & 2011b

of culturally unidentifiable human remains; and nine are corrections of previously published notices (NPS 2011c). The chronology of notice publications reflects changes in NPS administration of its NAGPRA obligations over the past twenty years (see Figure 5). Following an initial increase in publication, corresponding to the 1995–1996 inventory and notification deadlines, subsequent publication spikes followed establishment of the "General NAGPRA" (later National NAGPRA) program separate from the Archeology and Ethnography Program in 2000 (NPS 2000a), and separation of the Park NAGPRA program from the Archeology and Ethnography Program in 2004 (NPS 2004). The sharp decline in published notices in 2007 corresponds to the withdrawal of twelve notices from the publication process (NPS 2007b). In May 2011, fifteen years after the original notification was sent to culturally affiliated Indian tribes and Native Hawaiian organizations, eight park units in Arizona, Utah, and Nevada had still not published the required notices in the *Federal Register*, although project funds had reportedly been identified to support additional tribal consultation, update the inventory, and finalize and publish the notices (GAO 2010: 88).

Unlike the delays shown in the publication of notices for culturally affiliated human remains, the NPS set a national example in its proactive approach towards the disposition of culturally unidentifiable human remains. From January 6, 1996, to May 14, 2010, regulations required museums and federal agencies to retain possession of culturally unidentifiable human remains unless legally required

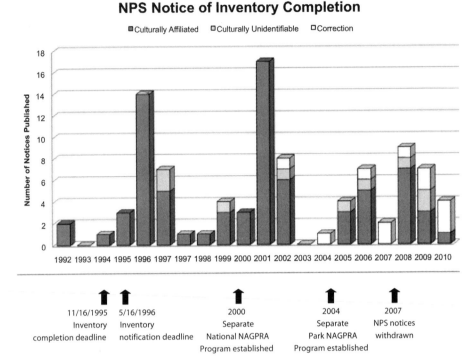

Fig. 5. NPS Notice of Inventory Completion

or recommended to do otherwise by the Secretary of the Interior.[8] During that period, thirteen park units requested such a recommendation from the secretary through the Review Committee and published notices representing the remains of 259 culturally unidentifiable human remains and 244 associated funerary objects. Disposition of the culturally unidentifiable human remains was based on relationships of aboriginal land, cultural relationship, or geographic proximity, and all of the dispositions by these thirteen park units were to federally recognized Indian tribes except one by Fort Vancouver National Historical Park where disposition was to a coalition that included both Indian tribes and a non-federally recognized Indian group (NPS 2009b).

One of the most controversial NPS Notices of Inventory Completion was published by Chaco Culture National Historical Park, determining the remains of 265 Native American individuals and 743 funerary objects to be culturally affiliated with 20 different Indian tribes (NPS 1999). The Hopi Tribe, one of the 20, disputed the park's determination of cultural affiliation, alleging that the park's consultation procedures and standard for weighing the evidence were improper. The Review Committee considered the matter at three different meetings before issuing its recommendations and findings, recommending that the park withdraw the notice and reassess its determination of cultural affiliation to include a site-by-site assessment of the specific data available, conduct separate consultation with each tribe when requested, and retain a qualified independent contractor to critically evaluate and carefully weigh all available evidence (Native American Graves Protection and Repatriation Review Committee 2000). The park superintendent and intermountain regional director declined to revise the notice and stood by their original determination of cultural affiliation, causing the Review Committee to comment that "the situation has done little to build confidence in the commitment of the National Park Service to NAGPRA" (Native American Graves Protection and Repatriation Review Committee 2001: 9).

In the wake of the Chaco Culture National Historical Park dispute, NPS Director Robert Stanton requested that the National Park System Advisory Board conduct a service-wide review of the process used by the NPS to make determinations of cultural affiliation of human remains and associated funerary objects. Information was collected from thirty-five park units that had previously published Notices of Inventory Completion in the *Federal Register*, detailing the chronology of activities, cost, and administrative record for their decisions. Twenty-five park units provided financial information indicating total costs of $1.7 million, with an average cost of slightly over $550 per each individual inventoried. Thirty-three percent of the total costs were incurred by Chaco Culture National Historical Park. The board concluded that the process used by the NPS to make determinations of cultural affiliation met the standards of the statute, but thought that the process could be improved by revising agency guidance to clarify the meaning of cultural affiliation and encouraging individual tribal consultation and precise determinations of cultural affiliation (National Park System Advisory Board 2002).

Consideration of the Chaco dispute also highlighted a potential conflict of interest in having a NPS employee serve as the Review Committee's designated federal officer when NPS was also a party in a dispute. The Review Committee changed its dispute resolution procedures to have the designated federal officer recuse him or herself in such situations, with those duties passing to another federal employee who does not appear to have a conflict of interest. When the Hopi Tribe again requested the Review Committee's assistance in addressing the still unresolved Chaco situation, as well as two new disputes with Aztec Ruins National Monument in New Mexico and Mesa Verde National Park in Colorado, NPS briefly appointed a designated federal officer from another agency for those disputes. Ultimately, however, the Assistant Secretary of the Interior stepped in to tell the Review Committee that its consideration of the Hopi appeal and two disputes was not needed (Native American Graves Protection and Repatriation Review Committee 2004: 16).

While the notices announcing the cultural affiliation of human remains and associated funerary objects were required within six months of the completion of an inventory, Notices of Intent to Repatriate were not prepared until a culturally affiliated Indian tribe or Native Hawaiian organization submitted a valid claim to repatriate an unassociated funerary object, sacred object, or object of cultural patrimony. In the twenty years since NAGPRA was enacted, thirty NPS Notices of Intent to Repatriate were published, accounting for 3,633 unassociated funerary objects, 2,526 sacred objects, two objects of cultural patrimony, and twenty-two cultural items that are both sacred objects and objects of cultural patrimony (NPS 2011d). Over 70 percent of the unassociated funerary objects listed in the NPS notices came from ten archaeological sites at a single park, Lake Roosevelt National Recreation Area in Washington (NPS 2008b). Over 85 percent of the sacred objects listed in the NPS notices are part of a bundle delivered anonymously to Chaco Culture National Historical Park in New Mexico and believed to have been recovered originally from a container, sealed room, or a dry cave at the park (NPS 2005). Park units in the Southeast Region, which accounted for 89 percent of the items listed in the service-wide summary, published no Notices of Intent to Repatriate.

Three of the thirty Notices of Intent to Repatriate were controversial. In 1995, religious leaders from the Cochiti Pueblo reviewed collections at Bandelier National Monument in New Mexico and identified a number of items, including fifty-three projectile points, as specific ceremonial objects needed by traditional Native American religious leaders for the practice of traditional Native religion by present-day adherents. When the park submitted the notice, NPS officials in Washington refused to forward it to the *Federal Register* for publication, arguing that the fifty-three projectile points did not fit the definition of "sacred object." The pueblo requested the assistance of the Review Committee, which recommended publication of the notice (Native American Graves Protection and Repatriation Review Committee 1998a). The Notice of Intent to Repatriate for the fifty-three projectile points was eventually published (NPS 1999).

In 2001, the Navajo Nation claimed three buffalo-hide shields in the collection of Capitol Reef National Park in Utah (NPS 2001). The shields were originally found hidden in a rock crevice by a local resident who took them home, but they were eventually recovered and returned to federal custody. Over the years, various studies of the construction and decoration of the shields identified them as prehistoric Fremont or historic Pueblo, Ute, Plains, Apache, or Navajo. In making his claim, a traditional Navajo religious leader identified the shields' makers by name, recounted the circumstances of the shields being hidden in the rock crevice, and described their use in the *Naayee* (Protection Way) ceremony which provides individuals with a protective barrier behind which they may regain strength, harmony, and balance after a physical or mental illness. Following publication of the Notice of Intent to Repatriate in the *Federal Register*, additional claims were made by the Ute Indian Tribe of the Uintah and Ouray Reservation, Paiute Tribe of Utah, Kaibab Band of Paiute Indians, Southern Ute Tribe, and Ute Mountain Ute Tribe (Threedy 2009: 98). Descendants of the discoverer also asked the Review Committee to review the park's decision. After careful consideration of the various claims, the park eventually agreed to the Navajo request and repatriated the shields. The descendants' request to the Review Committee was declined since they had no property interest in the shields.

In 2005, the Review Committee considered another NPS dispute involving a claim by Hui Mālama I Nā Kūpuna ʻO Hawaiʻi Nei for five items in the collection of Hawaii Volcanoes National Park. The items, recovered in the early 1900s from a cave on the Island of Hawaii, included a carved wooden statue, a "Hawaiian checkers" (*konane*) game board, a cutting tool made from a human clavicle with an embedded shark's tooth, a gourd vessel, and a bone button. While the Review Committee's dispute procedures now allowed for delegation of the designated federal official duties, both Hui Mālama and the park agreed to let a NPS employee serve in that position. The Review Committee found that the park had been very slow in going through the NAGPRA process and that the number of potential claimants of the items had increased with the passage of time. While the Review Committee chose not to issue a finding of fact regarding the identity of the five objects, it encouraged the park to move forward to complete the repatriation process by the end of 2005 (Native American Graves Protection and Repatriation Review Committee 2005). In 2006, the park took the unusual step of determining that the human clavicle was not human remains, relying on a misconstrual of a regulatory provision regarding the cultural affiliation of cultural items that incorporate human remains (NPS 2007a). A Notice of Intent to Repatriate was finally published in 2009 determining that the five unassociated funerary objects were culturally affiliated with fourteen different Native Hawaiian organizations, but that the park could not determine by a preponderance of the evidence which requesting party was the most appropriate recipient and would retain possession of the five cultural items until the claimants could mutually agree on the appropriate recipient (NPS 2009a).

Starting in 1996, federal agencies were also required to publish a third kind of notice regarding the disposition of cultural items newly discovered on federal lands. Fourteen park units have published twenty Notices of Intended Disposition accounting for the remains of 165 Native American individuals, 140 funerary objects, and four objects of cultural patrimony (NPS 2011e). Most of these notices account for one to four cultural items each, a small number consistent with the inadvertent nature of many of these discoveries during construction projects or exposure by erosion. The exceptions are the remains of 142 individuals reported by Tumacacori

National Historical Park in Arizona as part of planned data recovery preceding stabilization of the San Miguel de Guevavi and San Jose de Tumacacori missions (Burton 1992; NPS 2009c), and 135 funerary objects recovered from a single burial at Kings Canyon National Park in California (NPS 2000b). Dispositions of excavated or discovered cultural items were based on relationships of cultural affiliation, aboriginal land, and/or tribal land, and all of the twenty dispositions were to federally recognized Indian tribes, except one involving a coalition that included Indian tribes and a non-federally recognized Indian group at Yosemite National Park in California (NPS 2003).

External evaluations of NPS compliance have been generally good, particularly regarding the agency's preparation of summaries in 1993 and inventories in 1995. In its report to Congress for 1995–1997, the Review Committee commended the NPS for "its singular dedication to full compliance" (Native American Graves Protection and Repatriation Review Committee 1998: 4). The Government Accountability Office found that the NPS, along with the U.S. Army Corps of Engineers and the U.S. Forest Service, did the most work and had the highest confidence that all its NAGPRA items had been identified and that the NPS repatriated 84 percent of the human remains identified in published Notices of Inventory Completion (GAO 2010: 19, 46). NPS was also very proactive in effecting the disposition of culturally unidentifiable human remains. On the other hand, more disputes involving the NPS have ended up before the Review Committee than for any other federal agency or museum. It is a testament to the hard work of NPS field staff that most of these disputes were eventually resolved. The human remains from Chaco Culture National Historical Park, Aztec Ruins National Monument, and Mesa Verde National Park were eventually repatriated, as were the 53 projectile points from Bandelier National Monument and the three shields from Capitol Reef National Park. Allegations of a conflict of interest between park units and the NAGPRA Program have continually surfaced, resulting in changes in the way park units determine cultural affiliation, modifications to the Review Committee's dispute procedures, and NPS organizational changes.

Conclusions

These case studies demonstrate the profound ways that federal agencies' NAGPRA programs have affected the comprehensive implementation of the law. From summaries and inventories, through cultural affiliation work, to sensitive repatriation and heritage protection via enforcement, federal agencies have explored the many aspects of NAGPRA and made important accomplishments in each. They have all addressed the matters related to straightforward compliance, and they have all strived to achieve more in the intercultural relations fostered through NAGPRA.

Notes

1   33 U.S.C. § 2338.
2   These are found in section 3 at 25 U.S.C. 3002.
3   These are found in sections 5–7, 25 U.S.C. 3003–3005.
4   16 U.S.C. 470cc(b)(3).
5   36 C.F.R. 79.5.
6   43 C.F.R. 10.13(b)(1).
7   16 U.S.C. § 1.
8   43 C.F.R. §10.9 (e)(6).

Bibliography

Barnes, James E. *Bureau of Land Management Museum Collections: Select Status Report.* Archaeological Curation—Needs Assessment Technical Report No. 12. U.S. Army Corps of Engineers, St. Louis District, 1998.

Bureau of Land Management. "Guidelines for Conducting Tribal Consultation." *BLM Handbook* H-8120-1, 2004.

———. "Reburial Policy on BLM Lands." Instructional Memorandum 2007-002 (Oct. 13, 2006).

Burton, Jeffrey F. *San Miguel de Guevavi: The Archeology of an Eighteenth Century Jesuit Mission on the Rim of Christendom.* Tucson, AZ: Western Archaeological and Conservation Center, 1992.

Carroll, Mary, Park NAGPRA Program. Emails to Jaime Lavallee, National NAGPRA Program, regarding notice draft withdrawals (Nov. 20 and 29, 2007).

Culturally Affiliated (CA) Native American Inventories Database. http://grants.cr.nps.gov/CAI/index.cfm (accessed October 5, 2011).

Culturally Unidentifiable (CUI) Native American Inventories Database. http://grants.cr.nps.gov/CUI/index.cfm (accessed October 5, 2011).

Echo-Hawk, Walter R. Letter to Jerry L. Rogers, Associate Director for Cultural Resources, re: Request for Baseline Information on Dead Indian Bodies (Dec. 22, 1989).

Government Accountability Office. Native American Graves Protection and Repatriation Act: After Almost 20 Years, Key Federal Agencies Still Have Not Fully Complied with the Act. GAO-10-768 (July 28, 2010).

Hackenberger, S., L. Henebry-DeLeon, S. Campbell, and L. Tisdale. *Recommendations Regarding Cultural Affiliation of Human Remains and Funerary Items from Marmes Rockshelter.* Report prepared by HDR Engineering, Inc. for the U.S. Army Corps of Engineers, Walla Walla District. 2009.

Hicks, B.A. *Marmes Rockshelter: A Final Report on 11,000 Years of Cultural Use.* Pullman, WA: Washington State University Press, 2004.

Kenney, Roger G. Letter to "friends" (Oct. 27, 1993). National Park Service, Servicewide Summary of Unassociated Funerary Objects, Sacred Objects and Objects of Cultural Patrimony (Oct. 20, 1993). [author's note: data from the 1993 summary have been recalculated using the post-1995 NPS regional boundaries].

McKeown, C. Timothy. "National Park Service Sends Inventory of Remains to Tribes, Native Hawaiian Groups." *Anthropology Newsletter* (Sept. 1996).

National Park Service. "Archeology & Ethnography Program Changes." *Archeology E-Gram.* Archeology Program (Dec. 15, 2004). http://www.nps.gov/archeology/pubs/egrams/0412.pdf (accessed October 5, 2011).

———. National Archeological Permit Database (NADB)—Permits. http://www.nps.gov/archeology/tools/permits/intro.htm (accessed July 2011).

———. Notice of Intended Disposition: Kings Canyon National Park. *Auberry Mountain Press, Dinuba Sentinel, Orange Cove Mountain Times, Porterville Recorder, Reedley Exponent, Sanger Herald.* 2000.

———. Notice of Intended Disposition: Tumacacori National Historical Park. *Arizona Daily Star,* September 18, 2009; *Arizona Daily Star,* September 23, 2009; *Nogales International,* July 10, 2009; *Nogales International,* July 17, 2009.

———. Notice of Intended Disposition: Yosemite National Park. *Mariposa Gazette,* June 25, 2003; *Mariposa Gazette,* July 2, 2003; *Union Democrat,* June 20, 2003; *Union Democrat,* June 27, 2003.

———. Notice of Intent to Repatriate Cultural Items: Chaco Culture National Historical Park, Nageezi, NM. 70 Fed. Reg. 31522-31523 (June 1, 2005).

———. Notice of Intent to Repatriate Cultural Items: Hawaii Volcanoes National Park, Hawaii National Park, HI. 74 Fed. Reg. 10755-10756 (March 12, 2009).

———. Notice of Intent to Repatriate Cultural Items: Intermountain Region, Santa Fe, NM. 73 Fed. Reg. 41375- 41379 (July 18, 2008); 73 Fed. Reg. 42827 (July 23, 2008); and 73 Fed. Reg. 64366-64367 (Oct. 29, 2008).

———. Notice of Intent to Repatriate Cultural Items: Lake Roosevelt National Recreation Area, Coulee Dam, WA. 73 Fed. Reg. 51509-51510 (Sept. 3, 2008).

———. Notice of Intent to Repatriate Cultural Items in the Possession of Bandelier National Monument, Los Alamos, NM; Correction. 64 Fed. Reg. 30354-30355 (June 7, 1999).

———. Notice of Intent To Repatriate Native American Cultural Items in the Possession of the U.S. Department of the Interior, Capitol Reef National Park, Torrey, UT. 66 Fed. Reg. 63554-63557 (Dec. 7, 2001).

———. Notice of Inventory Completion: Fort Vancouver National Historic Site, Vancouver, WA. 74 Fed. Reg. 24874-24875 (May 26, 2009).

———. Notice of Inventory Completion for Native American Human Remains, Associated Funerary Objects, and Unassociated Funerary Objects in the Possession of the National Park Service, Chaco Culture National Historical Park, Nageezi, NM. 64 Fed. Reg. 12344-12349 (Mar. 12, 1999).

National Park System Advisory Board. Recommendations Regarding the National Park Service Process for Making Determinations of Cultural Affiliation under the Native American Graves Protection and Repatriation Act. (June 12, 2002).

Native American Graves Protection and Repatriation Review Committee. Minutes of the 16th Meeting. Santa Fe, NM. December 10–12, 1998.

———. Minutes of the 27th Meeting, September 17–18, 2004, Washington, DC.

———. NAGPRA Review Committee Advisory Findings and Recommendations Regarding Human Remains and Associated Funerary Objects in the Control of Chaco Culture National Historical Park. 65 Fed. Reg. 6621-6622 (Feb. 10, 2000).

———. Native American Graves Protection and Repatriation Review Committee Findings and Recommendations Regarding a Dispute Between Hui Mālama I Nā Kūpuna ʻO Hawaiʻi Nei and Hawaii Volcanoes National Park. 70 Fed. Reg. 31520-31521 (June 1, 2005).

———. Report to Congress: 1995–1997.

———. Report to Congress on 1998 Activities.

———. Report to Congress for 1999, 2000, and 2001.

Notice of Intent to Repatriate Database. http://www.cr.nps.gov/nagpra/fed_notices/nagpradir/index2.htm (accessed October 5, 2011).

Notices of Intended Disposition Database. http://grants.cr.nps.gov/nid/index.cfm (accessed October 5, 2011).

Notices of Inventory Completion Database. http://www.cr.nps.gov/nagpra/fed_notices/nagpra-dir/index.html (accessed October 5, 2011).

Orlando, Cindy, Superintendent, Hawaii Volcanoes National Park. Letter to Edward Ayau (August 24, 2007).

Robbins, John. Memorandum to National Center for Cultural Resources Stewardship and Partnership Programs staff, regarding staffing to implement a NAGPRA restructuring (Mar. 29, 2000).

Rogers, Jerry L. Letter to Walter R. Echo-Hawk, Senior Attorney, Native American Rights Fund (Feb. 28, 1990). Native American Human Remains in the National Park Service: A Preliminary Survey—August 1988 (Updated February 1990) (Feb. 26, 1990). [author's note: data from the 1990 preliminary survey have been recalculated using the post-1995 NPS regional boundaries].

Threedy, Deborah L. "Claiming the Shields: Law, Anthropology, and the Role of Storytelling in a NAGPRA Repatriation Case Study." *Journal of Land, Resources & Environmental Law*, Vol. 29, No. 1. (2009).

U.S. Army Corps of Engineers, Walla Walla District (USACE). "Cultural Affiliation Determination and Decision Document for the Floodplain Human Remains and Cremation Hearth Human Remains and Other Cultural Items from 45FR50, Lower Monumental Dam, WA." 2010.

———. "Cultural Affiliation Determination for Burial 1 through 22, Small Unnumbered Cast, and Human Remains Features MCX1, Rice 05, and 64–6 in the Marmes Rockshelter (45FR50) Collection." 2009.

———. "Factors Considered to Determine Applicability of the Native American Graves Protection and Repatriation Act: Human Remains and Funerary Objects Associated with the Marmes Collection (45FR50)." 2008.

———. "Marmes Rockshelter (45FR50) Collections Native American Determination Decision Paper," May 2008.

———.. "Native American Determination for Floodplain Human Remains and Cremation Hearth Human Remains from the 45FR 50 Collection, Lower Monumental Dam, WA." 2009.

Chapter 7
NAGPRA's Impact On Non-Federally Recognized Tribes

ANGELA NELLER, RAMONA PETERS, and BRICE OBERMEYER

Introduction

The Native American Graves Protection and Repatriation Act (NAGPRA)[1] gives standing to federally recognized Native American tribes, Alaska Native villages, and Native Hawaiian organizations. There is no statutory basis under NAGPRA for the repatriation of human remains, funerary objects, sacred objects, or objects of cultural patrimony to a non-federally recognized Indian group or tribe that has stated a claim based on a relationship of shared group identity. Their status as non-federally recognized does not give them the right to make decisions about repatriation even if the ancestors and cultural items are culturally affiliated with them. However, this does not exclude non-recognized Indian groups from participating in the NAGPRA process. Nothing in NAGPRA prevents a museum or agency from including a non-federally recognized Indian group in the consultation process or a non-federally recognized tribe from participating in decisions about Native American human remains or cultural objects.

Federally recognized tribes are those tribes that appear on the list of federally recognized tribes maintained by the Bureau of Indian Affairs (BIA) and published in the *Federal Register*.[2] There are three possible routes that a tribe can follow in order to be included on the BIA list and thus hold status as a federally recognized tribe. A tribe can be acknowledged to hold a government-to-government relationship with the United States through the passage of a congressional bill. Another option is to pursue recognition through the federal courts as a judicial ruling that confers or upholds federal recognition for tribal governments. The final possibility is to achieve recognition through the executive branch either by executive order or by successfully petitioning for federal recognition through the federal acknowledgment process (FAP). Although congressional and judicial routes are still available to tribes, the FAP has largely secured a primary place as the model for tribal recognition.[3]

The FAP was established in 1978 within the BIA to investigate the validity of tribal petitions for federal recognition or acknowledgment. The assessment of tribal petitions was first carried out by the Federal Acknowledgment Project office in 1978. The FAP was later renamed the Branch of Acknowledgment and Research (BAR) (Miller 2004:44). The BAR was later reorganized and became the Office of Federal Acknowledgment (OFA) and was recently moved to the Office of the Assistant Secretary of Indian Affairs within the Department of the Interior. Petitioning tribes must meet seven criteria in order to be acknowledged through the FAP; failure to meet any one of the criterion will result in a negative finding for the potential tribe. The first two criteria ask the petitioner to demonstrate that it has existed as an Indian community from historic times to the present (now revised to have existed from 1900 to the present), and that its existence is identified by outsiders and insiders alike as being distinct from other non-Indian and Indian communities. The final criterion, referred to as termination criterion, requires that neither the petitioner nor its membership be the subject of any legislation that terminated federal recognition. The middle four criteria deal with the characteristics of the tribal government. The governmental criteria require that the petitioning tribe (1) show evidence of a governing body that has maintained authority over its membership, (2) possess a governing document or rules for political organization, (3) demonstrate that its membership consists of individuals that descend from an Indian tribe that functioned as an autonomous entity, and (4) is comprised principally of persons not already enrolled in a federally recognized tribe.

Non-federally recognized Indian groups either cannot meet the FAP criteria (often as a result of assimilation pressures that coerced groups to forgo the very characteristics that are now sought as proof of federal recognition), were refused federal recognition based on their inability to meet the FAP criteria, or had their tribal status revoked through various forms of governmental mischief. In some cases, non-federally recognized Indian groups chose not to give up their inherent rights as sovereign entities by choosing not to sign treaties with the federal government. Thus, while federally recognized tribes make up a significant portion of the Native American population, they do not represent the breadth of Native American communities, and do not possess the closest cultural affiliation to many Native American individuals currently in museums and federal agencies. In fact, the NAGPRA Review Committee has noted that cultural affiliation would in many instances be established with a non-federally recognized Indian group as a more appropriate claimant.[4]

Since NAGPRA requires federal agencies to consult government-to-government with federally recognized tribes, federal agencies may find it difficult to include non-federally recognized Indian groups in NAGPRA consultations if the federally recognized tribes do not want non-federally recognized Indian groups included.

Additionally, some agency staff take the consultation requirement literally and refuse to include non-federally recognized Indian groups even in instances when it would be more culturally appropriate to do so. In some cases non-federally recognized Indian groups are treated like the general public, with no acknowledgment of their historical relationship or vested interests. However, as this chapter demonstrates, this is not always the case. Museums, as well as federal agencies, have included non-federally recognized Indian groups in the consultation process with positive results for everyone.

Likewise, non-federally recognized Indian groups have found ways to actively engage in NAGPRA and repatriation. These case studies highlight the way three distinct, non-federally recognized Indian groups have worked to not only be involved with NAGPRA, but to embrace it in a manner that gives them a voice in decision making. The diversity of the tribes and their unique customs, histories, and perspectives shape the way these Indian groups have successfully and, at times, not successfully engaged in NAGPRA. Angela Neller examines how the Wanapum Band of Priest Rapids in Washington State has been able to maintain their obligation to care for their ancestors, a duty they feel is critical to the success of future generations. Ramona Peters illustrates how the Mashpee Wampanoag Tribe, located in Massachusetts, works within a confederation of tribes to address the repatriation needs of their communities by identifying territories and developing policies that guide their work with museums. Brice Obermeyer addresses the political implications of sovereignty, or lack thereof, within the context of the Delaware Tribe in Oklahoma, along with their struggles with federal recognition.

Repatriation has always been as much a priority to non-federally recognized Indian groups as it is to the federally recognized tribes with standing under the law. Including non-federally recognized Indian groups in the process gives them a voice in decisions that are made about their ancestors, their family. The stories that follow show how NAGPRA has impacted non-federally recognized Indian groups and demonstrate the importance of cooperation and coalition-building between non-federally recognized Indian groups and federally recognized tribes for successful documentation and repatriation efforts under NAGPRA.

The Wanapum Band of Priest Rapids

It started with a question: "How do we deal with human remains that are affiliated to more than one tribe?" My response was simple: "Make a joint claim." That was how I began to work on repatriation with the Wanapum Band of Priest Rapids, and, subsequently, the federally recognized tribes of the Columbia Plateau. I was asked that question because I was experienced in NAGPRA, having done research for my master's degree in anthropology as it pertained to Native Hawaiian issues, as well as working on NAGPRA compliance projects for the Bernice P. Bishop Museum, University of Illinois at Urbana-Champaign, and University of Hawaii at Hilo. As a Native Hawaiian, I am particularly interested in the relationship of material culture and history to the identity of Native people, the changing role of objects through history, NAGPRA and its effect on the Hawaiian community, and the role of museums in preserving material culture and perpetuating Native identity. As the curator for the Wanapum Heritage Center, I work closely with the Wanapum to care for the archival, ethnographic, and archaeological collections curated by the Grant County Public Utility District under a long-standing agreement with the Wanapum Band of Priest Rapids. Repatriation is an extension of that work.

The Wanapum care for their ancestors to ensure that their journey is fulfilled, that the promise made to them by the Creator is realized, and that they will go back to the land, into the ground, to where the people started. Repatriation efforts are based upon that belief.

The Wanapum Band of Priest Rapids has lived since time immemorial on the Columbia Plateau. During the treaty period, the Wanapum were led by the dreamer prophet Smohalla. In 1855, a treaty council was held at Walla Walla lasting eighteen days. Spokesmen from the respective bands were invited to negotiate an agreement that would move their bands to reservations. These spokesmen committed to relinquishing ownership of their lands and in return, the bands retained certain rights of

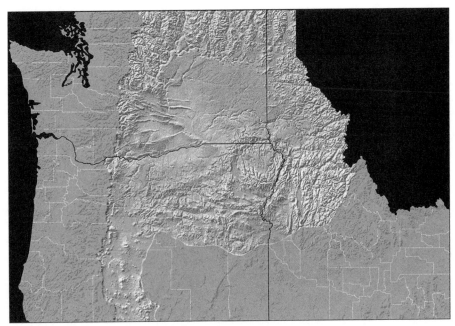

Fig. 6. Map of the Columbia Plateau. Courtesy Wanapum Heritage Center

Fig. 7. Smohalla (1815?-1895), center, in white, Priest Rapids, 1884. Courtesy National Anthropological Archives, Smithsonian Institution (Image No. BAE GN 02903A 06468100)

access to resources on those lands and received money, goods, and provisions. The Wanapum attended the treaty council at Walla Walla but it was clear to Smohalla that under the treaty they would lose most, if not all, of their homelands. Smohalla opposed any treaty that removed the Wanapum from their homeland and the Wanapum walked away, refusing to sign the treaty. As a result, they are federally unrecognized.

Born around 1815, Smohalla foresaw the coming of the railroad, the dams, and the loss of Salmon. He received teachings from the Creator during two near-death experiences and passed those teachings on to his followers, telling them to reject the new Euro-American culture that had come to the plateau and to resist relocation to a reservation. Smohalla was also given a special washat, or dance, and over 120 religious songs for his people to practice. Washat provided an individual with a disciplined way of life that would lead him or her through this world and into the next upon death. Five generations later, the Wanapum continue to live by Smohalla's teachings, with a demonstrated fidelity of belief and practice. Religion and life are one and the same based upon the unwritten laws, teachings, and beliefs, which speak to their responsibilities to the land, to the creatures that live within, on, and above the land, to the ancestors who are buried in the land, and to the ones who have yet to be born. The Wanapum perpetuate their culture by living a traditional life protecting the land, speaking their language, gathering, and preparing traditional foods, attending longhouse services, participating in ceremonies, and passing on their teachings to the next generation.

Values instilled in the Wanapum through their teachings over the generations have shaped the way they respond to the realities of life. The Wanapum work hard to protect the land and all its resources by building relationships with those around them, whether that be federally recognized tribes, federal and state agencies, city and county governments, schools, or the public. Through these and other relationships, the Wanapum share their values about why the land is important, why plants and animals should be allowed to live in harmony, why landforms and archaeological sites are important to preserve, and why cemeteries must be protected. In building these relationships, the Wanapum are kept from being overlooked, are able to stay within their homeland to take care of the land, and have a say in the things that are important to them.

For the Wanapum Band, death is a time, more than any other, when related families come together. Funeral ceremonies are important because people have critical responsibilities that must be carried out to assist the deceased person. An individual's presence on the earth is part of a longer journey, a journey that ties into Smohalla's teachings. This assistance continues with the protection and care of the graves of people who have gone on.

Despite the efforts of the Wanapum Band of Priest Rapids to care for and protect their ancestors, the desecration of burial sites remains a common occurrence, whether due to collectors, development projects, archaeological excavations, looting, or natural events such as erosion. Despite this, the Wanapum Band continues to maintain their responsibility to the ancestors through annual ceremonial visits to ancestors who are still held in museums. For example, in 1924, archaeologists from the Smithsonian Institution excavated a Wanapum cemetery at Wahluke and removed eleven individuals and 486 funerary objects, took them to Washington, DC, and curated them at the National Museum of Natural History. The Wanapum knew about the removal and maintained contact with the museum for years, discussing the return of these individuals, and making visits when possible to conduct ceremonies. Annual visits are also made to the Ancient One,[5] also known as Kennewick Man, housed at the Burke Museum in Seattle, Washington.

Equally important to the Wanapum is the ability to care for the cemeteries within their homeland. Historic records show that Puck Hyah Toot, Smohalla's nephew and subsequent leader of the Wanapum, was particularly concerned about cemeteries the Wanapum were forced to leave behind when they were disenfranchised from their seasonal gathering and fishing areas on the Hanford Reach, where their White Bluffs fishery was located. The fishery and the associated village and cemetery sites were closed off to the Wanapum in 1943 for the Manhattan project by the Atomic Energy Commission. Puck Hyah Toot made multiple attempts to get help from the Atomic Energy Commission to protect the gravesites. He finally succeeded in 1953,

Fig. 8. (left): Puck Hyah Toot, aka Johnny Buck, at Priest Rapids circa 1950s. Courtesy Wanapum Heritage Center (wrap18); (right) with Grant County PUD officials. Courtesy Wanapum Heritage Center (wrap286)

when the Wanapum were allowed to identify and mark the locations so that they could be monitored and protected, a practice that continues today. The Wanapum also maintain an agreement with the Department of Energy to continue to monitor and protect the burial sites on the Hanford Reach. Additionally, Washington State's burial law (HB2624 effective 2008) and corresponding regulations acknowledge the Wanapum Band of Priest Rapids' rights over Indian remains that originate from their areas of interest.

The Wanapum Band and NAGPRA

The Wanapum Band of Priest Rapids' ability to build relationships and educate others about what is important to them allows the Wanapum to be part of the NAGPRA process. As NAGPRA has evolved, the Wanapum Band has been actively involved in repatriation efforts related to the Columbia Plateau, specifically with the Confederated Tribes of the Colville Reservation, Confederated Tribes and Bands of the Yakama Nation, Confederated Tribes of the Umatilla Indian Reservation, the Nez Perce Tribe, and on occasion, the Confederated Tribes of Warm Springs when respective homeland areas overlap. These tribes comprise the Columbia Plateau Inter–Tribal Repatriation Group (CPITRG). Joint efforts by the CPITRG began in 2005 with the repatriation of human remains and funerary objects from the Smithsonian's National Museum of Natural History in Washington, DC,[6] through the National Museum of the American Indian (NMAI) Act.[7] Although this repatriation was done outside of NAGPRA, it was this event that brought the CPITRG together to work through the process and laid the foundation for future collaborative work under NAGPRA.

The CPITRG recognizes that they are descendant communities of the bands of people that have lived on the Columbia Plateau for thousands of years. The bands have been interconnected for many generations as small, autonomous, highly mobile Sahaptain groups that traveled extensively over the landscape, following the seasons and sources of food and moving from place to place to occupy fishing sites and to harvest berries and native plants.[8] Bands came together throughout the year in common, traditional use areas for subsistence, visiting, and marriage. Trading occurred through partnerships and regional trade fairs. These groups continue to be interconnected today, through shared cultural characteristics reinforced by a network of kinship ties developed through a recurring round of visiting and other social activities. For these tribes, the most valued cultural ideals for behavior are cooperation and sharing, closely associated with expectations of reciprocity and responsibility for the welfare of others.

The CPITRG recognizes that many areas overlap as "usual and accustomed" places where cultural practices occur, and that it was the federal government who separated the bands by placing them within reservations with created borders. The CPITRG recognizes that the correct thing to do is to work together to achieve repatriation goals in the most expedient manner.

CPITRG meetings include policy and religious leaders, program staff, and technical staff. On occasion, tribal members attend meetings. The CPITRG practices decision-making in the traditional plateau manner. Historically, the village was the primary political unit with bilateral kinship shaping extended family groups. The bands were led by headmen, whose qualities consisted of wisdom, personal character, and leadership. Headmen positions were semi-hereditary. The headmen were assisted in decision-making by an informal village council of respected men and women. Today, within the CPITRG, decisions are made by an informal "council" of respected men and women who are recognized leaders of their respective tribes and members of their tribal councils or boards. Everyone on the council provides a voice and is heard. Support and information are provided by persons with technical expertise in NAGPRA, museum collection management, and the specifics of particular repatriation efforts. Decisions are made by consensus, with a lead tribe making decisions for those remains and objects that come from sites that are within their ceded areas. By working together, the tribes of the Columbia Plateau stand united.

Aside from the technical staff of each tribe, who are the workhorses of the process, participation is inconsistent from meeting to meeting. This inconsistency at times leads to meetings that seem to repeat what was said in previous meetings, or at times involve individuals who are not as knowledgeable of the process and legalities of repatriation. We work mindfully, respectful of the values and practices of the tribes and individuals involved.

Prior to the creation of the CPITRG, respective tribes made counter claims that were detrimental to the repatriation of the ancestors. Today, repatriation decisions are made by tribal policy and religious leaders. The federally recognized tribes are not without burdens in this process. Each is a sovereign nation, with treaty rights and the right to cultural practice in usual and accustomed places. There are times when each tribe makes it a point to assert those rights during repatriation meetings. Although putting forth a joint claim avoids delays due to competing claims, there is always a risk that a tribe will pull out of the joint claim and make their own claim. However, the objective is to work together to achieve repatriation goals in the most expedient manner. As such, communication is crucial.

The federally recognized tribes of the Columbia Plateau know the Wanapum Band of Priest Rapids as a traditional and religious people with a strong spiritual orientation. As a non-federally recognized Indian group, the Wanapum are neutral, providing a perspective of traditional values and beliefs. The Wanapum are there to support the tribes and participate in the process to ensure that the ancestors are returned. Despite the lack of federal status, the Wanapum Band of Priest Rapids participates equally throughout the NAGPRA progress. Claims are submitted either as one document with all tribes as signatories, or by individual tribes with wording that indicates that the claim is a joint claim with a listing of the tribes working together, including the Wanapum Band of Priest Rapids. Published notices clarify that the Wanapum are a non-federally recognized Indian group but note them as either having a relationship of shared group identity or a cultural relationship with the human remains and cultural items.

Between 2005 and 2011, the tribes of the Columbia Plateau repatriated a minimum number of 1,144 individuals, 30,299 associated funerary objects, 28,889 unassociated funerary objects, and one sacred object from fifty-one institutions. The Palus Cemetery repatriation is a good example of how the Columbia Plateau tribes work together through the NAGPRA process. Last used in 1944, the Palus cemetery was excavated in 1964 by the U.S. Army Corps of Engineers, Walla Walla District as part of a cemetery relocation project due to the construction of several dams along the Snake River. The U.S. Army Corps committed to reburying all named individuals and moving all unnamed human remains and funerary objects to the University of Idaho. Despite assurances otherwise, the Columbia Plateau tribes discovered that most of the named individuals, including Chief Old Bones, his wife, and two of their children, as well as Mrs. Helen Fisher, who was the wife of Sam Fisher, the last resident of the Palus village, had only been partially reburied. The majority of their remains and funerary objects were found within the university's collections. The excavation of the Palus cemetery remained in Palouse descendants' living memory and was of great concern to descendant tribes. The Colville, Nez Perce, Umatilla, Wanapum, and Yakama worked together to finally repatriate the 260 individuals and the 6,220 associated funerary objects that were stored at Washington State University and give them a proper reburial. [9] This 2006 reburial was unique because lineal descendants could be identified for Mrs. Fisher and Chief Old Bones. Their lineal descendants decided not to make formal claims for their ancestors, choosing to allow the tribes to claim them along with the other individuals. The Palus cemetery repatriation was one of the first and largest repatriations that the CPITRG undertook. Not only did the tribes work together, they in turn worked with the lineal descendants of their respective tribes, and followed instructions about the reburial of their ancestors after the repatriation occurred.

Reburying the ancestors

Wanapum teachings hold that an individual's presence on the earth is part of a longer journey. As one elder put it, an ancestor's greatest journey is interrupted when graves are disturbed. Repatriation is not easy. There are physical and spiritual risks. Care must be taken in handling the remains. Care must be taken in the words that are spoken throughout the repatriation process, from consultation to reburial and afterwards. Care must be taken in the feelings that are held while doing the work. Bad thoughts and feelings can bring spiritual and physical harm not only to yourself, but to those around you, including your family. Precautions are taken to ensure that we as individuals are protected, that our families are protected, and that the ancestors are sent back on their journey.

The technical staffs of all member tribes are present to prepare the repatriated human remains for reburial. Oftentimes the Wanapum take the lead in performing the ceremonies associated with the repatriation, including ceremonies that take place before the tribes prepare the collection for reburial, before the collection is transferred to the reburial location, and then again during the reburial. There is never a time that the Wanapum are not there to perform these duties. When another tribe cannot be there to conduct ceremonies, they look to the Wanapum to ensure that the ancestors are prepared for what will be happening to them. Additionally, the Wanapum take the lead in conducting the reburial. This includes preparing the reburial location, transporting the remains, and the actual interment. Wanapum men either dig the reburial site themselves or oversee the excavation by machinery if it cannot be done by hand. They are there to load the remains into vehicles, transport them to the reburial site, and put the bundles into the excavated area for reburial. Finally, the Wanapum take the lead in burning any remaining material, including boxes and museum packaging material such as plastic and paper bags, ethafoam, tags, and the cleaning items used by the technical staff to clean the tables, chairs, floors, and rooms where the remains were stored and prepared for reburial. This is done because part of ensuring the ancestors' ability to go on is to have all things that were associated with the remains, and any residue left behind, taken care of and disposed of properly.

Despite the Wanapum Band's high level of involvement in NAGPRA, there have been instances when the Wanapum have not been able to play an active role in the care of ancestors held by museums and federal agencies because of their status as a non-federally recognized Indian group. Some museums and agencies do not recognize the Wanapum in notices for human remains and objects, even those that come from the Wanapum village of Priest Rapids.[10] Or, it is assumed that the federally recognized tribes represent the Wanapum, and *Federal Register* notices are worded in such a way that they misrepresent or ignore the fact that the Wanapum are equal participants in the process. At times, other tribal members who participate in the process question the Wanapum's role in being there based upon a misconception of history. There are some Wanapum who left the Wanapum Band and are part of the Yakama Nation, a federally recognized tribe. They misunderstand that the Wanapum Band of Priest Rapids is comprised of those folks who not only stayed behind following the edict of their leader, but are also descendants of that leader who continue to practice traditional life ways. The Wanapum tread lightly through these barriers and misconceptions with a singular purpose, and overcome them to care for the ancestors.

Fig. 9. Columbia Plateau Smithsonian Repatriation. Courtesy Wanapum Heritage Center (GroupPhoto_1)

NAGPRA was passed to reinforce and confirm the rights of disenfranchised people over the care of their ancestors, however, it continues to disenfranchise those who have no "standing" under the law. This in and of itself has a much larger consequence. It puts at risk a people's beliefs as well as their right to their identity, to be who they are, to be responsible as they were taught, and to ensure that future generations continue to exist. But non-federally recognized Indian groups are refusing to accept this reality. As Rex Buck, Jr., Wanapum leader, says, "If we recognize the fact that there's an unwritten law that we must live by, then these prophesies too will come to reality. And we will still be here when that time comes, and the last sunrise comes up—and we'll have obeyed what we're supposed to do here."

Wampanoag confederation repatriation and NAGPRA

During the early days of NAGPRA, with all the thought and compromise, non-federally recognized Indian groups like the Mashpee were left out of "legal standing" to repatriate. Despite this, the Mashpee Wampanoag were there, patiently sitting in the audience of the NAGPRA Review Committee, hoping for an agreeable ruling to allow us to rebury our ancestor's human remains.

My name is Ramona Peters, also known as Nosapocket. I am from the Bear Clan, in the Mashpee Wampanoag Tribe. We mostly live in the town of Mashpee on Cape Cod along the coast of Massachusetts. I've been working with NAGPRA for about fourteen years and I'd like to share some of our experiences as a confederation of Wampanoag people responding to this act of Congress.

First, I want to explain how and why I got involved with NAGPRA. Throughout my childhood, the state police and heavy equipment operators would come to our home to see my father. The serious tone and that conspicuous bundle on the step always told us someone had dug up one or more of our ancestors again. My dad, Cjegktoonuppa (Slow Turtle) was the Supreme Medicine Man of the Wampanoag Nation, and also a police officer himself for a time. He was the designated person to receive the unpleasant details of the unearthing: where, who, and how many. They never brought any funerary objects, although we knew our ancestors buried their loved ones with special things. There were times he'd refuse to take certain remains because he felt something potentially dangerous about them. He would insist that the culprit take responsibility for those types of remains instead of risking our family's safety. I recall overhearing him talk about what happened to some people on Nantucket who tried to build a swimming pool in the grave of one of those ancient sorcerers. It was rather disturbing and is painfully memorable so I will not trouble others with the actual story. My father died seven years after the passage of NAGPRA. Cjegktoonuppa chose to be cremated and poured into the Atlantic Ocean, away from all developers and archaeologists. My elder brother and sister have also assisted in dozens of reinterments both before and after the passage of NAGPRA. It's a woeful yet sacred duty that my family has accepted.

The first time I heard of anyone digging up a grave on purpose was while listening to a speech made by Wamsutta (Frank B.) James, an elder Aquinnah Wampanoag. His speech[11] was suppressed at the 1970 Thanksgiving Day festivities at Plymouth by the town leaders who had initially invited him to speak. The speech was given outside in the cold, surrounded by over a hundred Wampanoag and other tribal people. This gathering later became known as "The National Day of Mourning." In his speech, Wamsutta said, "The Pilgrims had hardly explored the shores of Cape Cod for four days before they had robbed the graves of my ancestors and stolen their corn and beans." On January 11, 1999, 379 years later, I personally wrote the NAGPRA claim letter for the Corn Hill site to repatriate those items stolen in 1620.

Historical and cultural overview of the Mashpee Wampanoag Tribe

At the time of European contact there were sixty-nine tribes that belonged to the Wampanoag Nation. This organization of tribes joined in agreement to form one government based on collective peace and cooperation. The totem of the Wampanoag Nation is the Wolf. Grand council meetings were held monthly with all sachems in the nation and the Massasoit.[12]

There were no permanent settlements, tribes moved about within a specific territory adjusting to the seasons; natural resources; social, political, and spiritual gathering sites; and movement of certain migratory species. Before European colonization here in the Northeast, the Wampanoag Nation's domain extended from the Merrimac River north of what is now Boston, west to the eastern shore of Narragansett Bay in Rhode Island, and south through Cape Cod and the nearby islands of Martha's Vineyard and Nantucket. The linguistic distribution of the "N" Algonquin territory equals the political territory of the Wampanoag Nation (Fig. 10).

For approximately 12,000[13] years, Wampanoag semi-permanent villages were strategically located near natural resources such as bodies of fresh water, bays, and rivers. During the fall and winter months, the Wampanoag lived in large villages with long houses.[14] In the spring and summer, they separated into smaller family units and moved to *weety8ômash*[15] near the planting and fishing grounds. The winter villages were surrounded by very high, spiral-shaped palisade walls. This shape allowed ease of egress while offering protection from snow blizzards and cold winds. Wampanoag winter lifestyle in the longhouses meant no real privacy. Living in that environment required tribal members to carry themselves peacefully, with courtesy, and with a generous nature. It is said that hate, greed, jealousy, and envy were not welcomed in the longhouse. This philosophy governed the actions of each individual, clan, or tribe, and allowed for the formation and successful survival of the entire Wampanoag Nation.

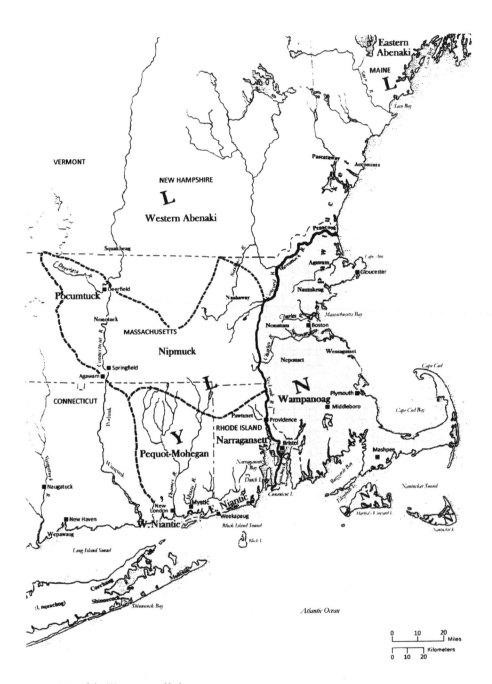

Fig. 10. Map of the Wampanoag Nation

Not unlike most North American tribes who were colonized by Western Europeans, the Wampanoag Nation suffered devastation of disease, war, enslavement, and poverty. The Wampanoag were colonized in the early seventeenth century; hanging on to any speck of the original homelands has been a remarkable effort. Today, there are three surviving Wampanoag tribes (one not federally recognized)[16] that remain on their original homelands. The Assonet, for example, are a band of Wampanoag descendants who live near the Fall River and New Bedford areas of Massachusetts. Other Wampanoag families live within the boundaries of the original Wampanoag Nation territory.

At the time of the passing of NAGPRA, the Mashpee Wampanoag Tribe was not a federally recognized tribe. A lack of federal recognition never deterred the Mashpee Wampanoag from actively participating in the repatriation of their ancestors; the tribe finally gained federal recognition through the FAP in February 2007. However, the foundation of our repatriation efforts was laid in the 1990s, well before that time.

Creating the Wampanoag Repatriation Confederation

The Mashpee Wampanoag Tribe is a surviving tribe of the Wampanoag Nation and therefore responsible for reburying any Wampanoag peoples' remains allowable through NAGPRA. Indeed, even before NAGPRA, the Mashpee Wampanoag felt spiritually obligated to reinter our relatives' remains that were stored as museum collections. However, not having federal recognition meant that museums were not required to send the tribe their summaries and inventories, even if the individuals and cultural objects in the museum were culturally affiliated to the Wampanoag, and despite the Mashpee Wampanoag Tribe's continuous presence in the same village for thousands of years.[17] This did not deter the Mashpee Wampanoag from actively pursuing the repatriation of ancestors through NAGPRA as soon as the law was passed.

The Robert S. Peabody Museum in Andover, Massachusetts, was the only museum to send the Mashpee Wampanoag Tribe an inventory of human remains and associated funerary objects as part of the NAGPRA process when the tribe was still non-federally recognized. This inventory identified Mashpee as culturally affiliated to Wampanoag human remains from a large burial site in Middleboro, Massachusetts. The Mashpee Wampanoag responded to the request to consult; however, because of the tribe's status as unrecognized, the Wampanoag Tribe of Gay Head (Aquinnah), the only Wampanoag federally-recognized tribe at the time, had to provide a letter in support of the repatriation. In addition, the museum had to get approval from the NAGPRA Review Committee to repatriate to the Mashpee Wampanoag due to their status. Therefore, on November 17, 1994, my sister, Mother Bear (Anita Little), and George Green Jr. went before the Eighth Meeting of the NAGPRA Review Committee in Albany, New York, to request the repatriation of ancestral human remains from the Robert S. Peabody Museum. The Review Committee approved the request for disposition to the tribe and the Notice of Inventory Completion was published in the *Federal Register* in February 1995.[18] To my knowledge, the Mashpee Wampanoag were the first non-federally recognized Indian group to repatriate under NAGPRA.

While this initial effort was successful, the tribe quickly realized that the whole process was just not efficient, especially given the costs involved.[19] Meanwhile, the Wampanoag Tribe of Gay Head (Aquinnah) continued to be the only Wampanoag tribe to receive museum inventories. Initially, they did not wish to engage in the NAGPRA process, yet they were inundated with the piles of inventories that poured in as the 1995 museum inventory completion deadline clocked down. The Wampanoag Tribe of Gay Head (Aquinnah) approached the Mashpee and other neighboring tribes for advice and direction. Through the ages, our people formed confederations to facilitate a number of pseudo-treaty functions, including nation-to-nation alliances, trade agreements, resource sharing, and temporary sachem alliances; therefore a confederation to focus on NAGPRA was a logical solution.

The first attempt to form a New England tribal confederacy to respond to NAGPRA was in 1995. This included the Narragansett Tribe of Southern Rhode Island and was called the Wampanoag Narragansett Confederacy. This arrangement did not work out because it was confusing for museums to culturally affiliate to a confederacy that had two different tribal territorial boundaries, cultures, and languages. It became obvious that the confederation must be solely composed of Wampanoag tribal representatives as conflicting claims started to occur.

In 1996, it was determined that the Mashpee Wampanoag, the Gay Head (Aquinnah) tribe, and the Assonet Band of Wampanoag would form a confederation devoted specifically to repatriation efforts on behalf of the Wampanoag Nation. This collaborative group, still exists today, more than fourteen years later, with the original repatriation officers serving. Those repatriation officers are, respectively, Mrs. Edith Andrews of the Wampanoag Tribe of Gay Head (Aquinnah), John Peters Jr. of the Mashpee Wampanoag Tribe, and Chief Kenneth Alves of the Assonet Band of Wampanoag. I have had the pleasure of working with these dedicated individuals as the NAGPRA coordinator and now the NAGPRA director through the years.

Our confederation is acknowledged by the museums we work with and we have had great success in our repatriation efforts. Prior to the Mashpee Wampanoag gaining federal recognition, *Federal Register* notices from museums that culturally affiliated NAGPRA items to the confederation typically used phrases like the following: "Officials of the Robert S. Peabody Museum of Archaeology also have determined that, pursuant to 43 CFR 10.2 (e), there is a relationship of shared group identity that can be reasonably traced between this item and the Wampanoag Repatriation

Confederation, representing the Wampanoag Tribe of Gay Head (Aquinnah), the Mashpee Wampanoag (a non-federally recognized Indian group), and the Assonet Band of the Wampanoag Nation (a non-federally recognized Indian group)."[20]

While our status may differ, we are viewed as equal in matters related to the ancestry and cultural affiliation of our people.

Organizing the Wampanoag Repatriation Confederation

For the purposes of responding to NAGPRA, gatherings of Wampanoag clans, bands, and tribal representatives were convened to determine the appropriate territorial boundaries and identify cultural, spiritual, and political concerns amongst the Wampanoag Nation. Shortly after those gatherings, the Wampanoag Confederation opened council with bordering New England tribes and their representatives, mainly the Narragansett Nation, Abenaki Nation, and the Nipmuc Nation. Our shared histories necessitated collaborative efforts especially in regard to the culturally unidentifiable[21] ancestral human remains that needed to be addressed regionally. In an honorable effort to host the missing tribes once of our Peace Tree and under our same nations' totem of the Wolf, the Wampanoag Confederation reassumed spiritual propriety over ancestral territories prior to European contact.

The next task was to develop a set of policies to guide the confederation's repatriation process. Interviews were conducted with tribal leaders, elders, and medicine people; the information gathered from these interviews became the foundation of the confederation's repatriation policies. The following are the original policies the Wampanoag Repatriation Confederation sent, along with an information packet, to museums upon initiating the NAGPRA consultation process.

> July 22, 1997
> The Wampanoag Confederation Repatriation and Grave Protection Policy
> 1. The Wampanoag Confederation requires that all associated funerary objects from museums and federal agencies be repatriated with the appropriate ancestral human remains simultaneously.
> 2. The Wampanoag Confederation member tribes will host the territory of the Massachuset People, as defined on the official mapped boundaries of the Wampanoag Confederation Repatriation District.[22]
> 3 Under pains of historic responsibility, every member of the Wampanoag Confederation Repatriation Project shall protect and preserve the cultural and intellectual property of the Wampanoag Nation.[23]

4. The Wampanoag Tribal repatriation officers are to be understood as acting under the guidance and on behalf of Wampanoag religious leaders.

5. All of our relations ancestors, and their property, are to include all the indigenous human remains found within our territorial homeland boundaries, without regards to Colonial English or American time orientations such as GMT.[24]

6. Those human remains, which were found in known battleground areas during "King Philip's War," are to be carefully examined to determine racial background prior to repatriation from museums and federal agencies.

7. That human remains of Native persons found at battleground areas (during 1675–1676) shall be repatriated jointly with tribes related in proximity to such battles and known to have participants.

8. That inter-tribal ceremonial reinterment is sought, in respect for the alliances once embraced by neighboring nations and tribes who supported the Wampanoag Confederacy's so-called "King Philip's War."

9. That every effort be made to find suitable reinterment sites closest to the original gravesite of Native persons human remains under the care of the Wampanoag Confederation.

10. That areas known to be Native Burial Grounds be avoided and not used as reinterment sites, unless the locations of individual graves are well defined and will not be disturbed in any way.

11. The Wampanoag Confederation with its proper standing will be the only official Wampanoag organization to receive NAGPRA items per order of public law 101-601.

12. That each tributary tribe of "The Wampanoag Nation," has the right to create and initiate their own repatriation policies, in regard to items repatriated to them, through the Wampanoag Confederation Repatriation Project.[25]

13. The Wampanoag Confederation Repatriation effort will at times seek the option of having certain repatriated items remain in museums and federal agencies for curatorial purposes. An appointed consultant on behalf of the confederacy shall seek scheduling the disposition of such items with museum staff.

The policies reflect more than a set of guidelines for the confederation to follow. They underscore the value system and cultural beliefs that define who we are as

Wampanoag people. They reflect how we understand our relationship and responsibility to our ancestors, our sovereignty and identity, and our enduring connection to our land and history.

Working with museums through the Wampanoag Repatriation Confederation

Since 1996, the confederation has conducted varying levels of consultation with more than seventy museums. The northeastern regional museums are the most familiar and, in most cases, have become friends with the confederation. Members of the confederation serve as Native American representatives and, in one case, as a board member on museum collections committees and advisory councils. It has been a long journey to develop these relationships. I believe both communities benefit from the shared knowledge we now enjoy.

I am constantly reminded of the significant contrast between our tribal value systems and the culturally Western scientific approach that shapes many museum professionals' worldview. It seems that tribal people have always had to adapt to the museum/western culture, without reciprocation the other way. The confederation routinely has to remind museums that as Wampanoag, we are connected to an ancestry that extends back more than 1,000 years, and that the western concepts of time do not apply to how the Wampanoag Nation understands their relation to their ancestors. It is ironic that NAGPRA does not require a museum to justify their decision to designate an individual as culturally unidentifiable, and yet tribes must produce the preponderance of the evidence in defense of our right to claim a connection to our ancestors. We are never asked how we measure time.

We dealt with unexpected resistance from museum staff during the early consultations after the law was passed. Some seemed to regard our ancestors' human remains and funerary objects as their personal property. This so-called property in many cases had been appraised with enormous dollar values on them. The concept of owning someone else, like slavery, where a dollar value is attached to a human being, had a tremendous culture-shock impact on us. Thankfully, because of NAGPRA's requirements, spiritual and philosophical differences have little bearing when it comes to our right to custody in the end.

Another challenge has been finding ways to overcome archaic museum collection practices, particularly those that impeded our efforts to conduct a complete repatriation of total grave content from a single site. The confederation discovered that archaeological teams often divided up artifacts and human remains for their private collections and donated funerary objects to their favorite museums. The same site might also have been impacted for decades by different archaeologists, who often renamed the site after themselves or after an interesting feature they found at that location. Therefore, it is not always the case that all human remains and objects can be found in one museum. It is not uncommon to find that one site has been scattered to seven different institutions all over New England, New York, and Washington, DC. These practices by archaeologists make the task of simultaneously repatriating same-site contents a major undertaking. If any one of the museums involved is slower due to funding, initiative, or confusion about cultural affiliation, it can belabor the process for years. The good news is that we have a team of repatriation officers who are willing to do the research to help the process and nudge museums along. Because we work as a confederation, we have been able to create a database of all the inventories received, allowing us to reassociate the contents of many digs and pinpoint the actual site with a global positioning system.

From the standpoint of the Wampanoag Repatriation Confederation, the museum community is very interesting in an anthropological sort of way. Each museum has a history and unique personality. In general, each seems to operate as an island unto itself, often not communicating with other museums—in fact, we have experienced incredible jealousy between museums. I have found that it can be difficult to navigate the moods and personalities of people in charge; we come from such different cultures. Naturally, the confederation gravitates toward museum staff who are most honest and helpful—often younger staff rather than the older vanguard. This sort of remark may sound inappropriate; however, let me simply say that the confederation has been misled, cheated, and entangled in some complicated political quandaries by staff that I can only describe as malicious. For example, a few museums have submitted inventories with two different cultural affiliations to the same objects. This has created a major strain and incredible delays in the consultation process; in fact, none of those confused culturally affiliated objects have been repatriated in over ten years. One museum NAGPRA staffer contacted our tribal chief, Vernon Pocknett, and faxed him a joint repatriation agreement to sign in an attempt to bypass the confederation (as though it operated independently from the traditional leadership of our people). The chief called and told me he was being harassed and badgered by two individuals whom I will not name. Chief Pocknett was very ill at the time and died shortly after this badgering began. It's deplorable to what lengths people will go to manipulate the process. Neither one of these individuals has apologized, nor have I forgiven them for making my chief's last days so miserable.

We discovered that many museums struggle financially, and learned to consider the financial situations of each museum if we want cooperation and expediency from them. Small museums may insist they do not have to comply with NAGPRA because they do not receive federal funds; this usually means they are understaffed and underfunded. We have started to invite museum staff to our tribal areas instead of going to their facility. This helps develop relationships, shares responsibilities, and creates good faith between us.

In the early years of NAGPRA, we were often asked what we intended to do with the items after they were repatriated. When we answered that we would reinter them as their families had originally done, the questioners were often visibly aghast. One of the worst examples of this was our first consultation meeting with the board of directors of a certain museum. They flatly refused to repatriate the "pretty things," regardless of the fact that those very things came from Wampanoag graves. We walked out of that meeting. I personally have not returned to that museum for any purpose; however, members of our team have voluntarily assisted them with inventorying their collections. It is interesting that this museum primarily houses the collections of the Massachusetts Archaeological Society, a group of amateur and professional archaeologists who dug extensively in Wampanoag territory. I suspect that their resistance to compliance with NAGPRA has its roots in the philosophical differences we encountered during that first consultation meeting.

It has taken some time for me to realize that there are people who place no spiritual value on ancestral human remains. The meeting with that museum's board confirmed that we were up against a deeply held belief that conquest affords certain groups greater authority than others, and that according to these archaeologists, Indian graves have no spiritual importance and carry only scientific or monetary value.

Although the confederation has much remaining work to do with museums, federal agencies have yet to actually engage the confederation with NAGPRA, except for our neighbors at the Cape Cod National Seashore, a National Park Service (NPS) facility. Staff there contracted with local tribal members for the educational content, artifact reproduction, and general design of a new exhibit for their visitor center that opened in March 2011. In addition, the Cape Cod National Seashore entered into a Memorandum of Agreement (MOA) with the Wampanoag Confederation to protect the unmarked reinterment sites that are now on that property. We are hopeful that the confederation will be able to secure a similar arrangement with the Boston Harbor Islands, another NPS property, and work with other federal agencies that may also now have Wampanoag individuals and objects.

Reinterment concerns

One important policy that museums need to understand is that our spiritual leaders have mandated that the confederation find safe reinterment sites before physically repatriating any ancestral human remains. We are not allowed to keep ancestral remains more than one night or to store them in a tribal facility. Our repatriated ancestral remains go directly from museum to the grave.

Federal property like the Cape Cod National Seashore is ideal for reinterment of ancestral remains that cannot be reinterred at their original burial sites. In addition to this partnership, the confederation has made agreements with several Massachusetts townships to use plots in their cemeteries for reinterment of Wampanoag remains. The confederation has developed successful partnerships with community members. In Dartmouth, Massachusetts, an entire seventeenth century Quaker Indian cemetery was unearthed to make a farm for a white Quaker. This cemetery contained thirty-two individuals, including some complete skeletal remains, a rarity in our repatriation experience. We approached the nearest Quaker meetinghouse in that area and requested safe burial sites for these Quaker Indians. We crafted a MOA between the Wampanoag Confederation and the Smith Neck Friends Meeting to facilitate the reinterment and ceremony. We determined it appropriate to invite the Smith Neck Quaker spiritual leader to conduct the reinterment ceremony for these ancestors who had adopted the Quaker faith. Our requests were honored for both the proper protected site and a Quaker style ceremony to place all at rest.

Benefits of operating as a confederation

Working together as a confederation has allowed us to secure funding, volunteers, community support, and greater protection for burial sites. A major challenge for the Wampanoag coalition is that NAGPRA is very poorly suited to protect our burial sites. Even with an act of Congress prohibiting the looting of Indian burial grounds, it still happens.[26] By organizing as a confederation, we are able to access legal protections for our entire ancestral homelands and prevent gaps that might exist between our communities. As a confederation, we were able to create a nonprofit organization to receive funding from sources willing to help us complete our goal to rebury all the ancestors' remains available to us through NAGPRA. Nonprofit status also allows the Wampanoag Confederation to apply for preservation restrictions[27] within the state of Massachusetts, to ensure that reinterment sites remain safe from destructive activity. Any reinterment on private property would be vulnerable to accidental impact if unprotected, which is unacceptable. With preservation covenants, confederation members are informed of any proposed changes to the land near or at the site.

The preservation process places our contact names and board of directors in the Commonwealth of Massachusetts Registry of Deeds for the property where the reinterment site is located. We are then notified in a timely manner of any requests for permits to change the landscape, create additions to the building(s), or add or change signage near our reinterment site. Amendments to the Massachusetts State Unmarked Burial Law that include Native American grave protection on private property were written by my father, Cjegktoonuppa, and Brona Simons, the State Archaeologist/State Historic Preservation Officer (SHPO). The Massachusetts Commission on Indian Affairs and the SHPO can offer homeowners an option for a real estate tax cut when they allow an accidental discovery to stay undisturbed on their property, or allow for reinterment to occur. The Wampanoag Confederation has been provided with state mitigation data on all archaeological sites in Massachusetts since their record keeping began. This data is uploaded into our database so we can cross-check state sites with NAGPRA collections information.

The Wampanoag coalition has taken advantage of grants issued by the National NAGPRA Program to support our repatriation efforts. The Wampanoag Tribe of Gay Head (Aquinnah) received the early grants in the 1990s since they were the only federally recognized tribe, which is a grant requirement. During an early grant cycle, the confederation developed an electronic database to manage the museum inventories and our activities in the process. The program director can easily provide each repatriation officer with updated material to track progress and make reports to their tribal councils. The database was presented at a NAGPRA Review Committee meeting in 1998, which led to a later marketing effort to other tribes. We used the sales proceeds to fund our repatriation efforts, instead of applying for a NAGPRA grant. A recent NAGPRA grant awarded to the Mashpee Wampanoag tribe has allowed the confederation to consult with museums in the New England area. In addition to grants, the confederation has received substantial donations from local supporters who respect our efforts.

The direction we were given by our spiritual leaders and tribal leadership was to first reinter the ancestral human remains and their funerary objects. We have filed 844 repatriation claims and reinterred 187 sets of ancestral human remains and eighty-four funerary objects. There are other New England tribal entities that do not have NAGPRA standing to repatriate on their own. The Wampanoag Confederation has assisted when such a group receives notice of cultural affiliation and needs a federally recognized tribe to sponsor repatriation. The Wampanoag Tribe of Gay Head (Aquinnah), on behalf of the Wampanoag Confederation, has sponsored repatriation for the Abenaki, Chappaquiddic, Herring Pond, and Nipmuc people. The agreed-upon process has generally been for the Wampanoag Confederation to complete the repatriation claim for the group and jointly repatriate the remains from the museums. For example, the confederation has facilitated the Abenaki in recovering as many as thirty-seven of their ancestral human remains from the Peabody Museum at Harvard.[28]

There are a number of Wampanoag people living outside the tribal community. The historical experience of Wampanoag tribes has been fraught with hardship; perhaps the worst was becoming landless. The confederation often requests volunteer interment site monitors for areas that otherwise would not have regular visits by the repatriation officers. These Wampanoag volunteers are invited to the reinterment ceremony, where they experience the reverence placed on the site they are to protect.

One way the Wampanoag Confederation shared the responsibilities of protecting gravesites was to reenlist the power of oral tradition. We spoke at a public gathering sponsored by the Nantucket Historical Society. There are no surviving Wampanoag on the Island of Nantucket, yet there are many gravesites. We shared our feelings about the need to protect the graves there. The gathering was well attended by both children and adults. We asked them to tell others who come to the island to honor the graves of the Wampanoag by keeping a good distance from them. We instructed them to share the importance of showing respect for the people who once lived alone there on Nantucket, raised families, fished in the waters, planted in the fields, and hunted in the woods. We asked the grandparents to tell the stories to their grand-children who will come in the summertime, and tell them to carry on the tradition of protecting Wampanoag gravesites as honorary site monitors for the Wampanoag Confederation. We have forty adult volunteer site monitors on Nantucket today who will contact us if any disturbance occurs or seems imminent.

The Wampanoag Confederation has discussed at great length the manner in which to repatriate sacred items and items of cultural patrimony. NAGPRA is clear about the procedure in which tribes may make appropriate claims for such items. The act of claiming Wampanoag sacred objects poses a conflict regarding intellectual property rights for some tribes within our confederation. We have agreed to create guidelines for museums on a case-by-case basis to avoid revealing unnecessary infor-mation regarding the nature of Wampanoag ceremonial practices. The delicate nature of sharing names and descriptions of sacred ceremonies requires permission from our spiritual leaders, which has not been given to the Wampanoag Confederation repatriation officers in a blanket manner. We have not made any claims for sacred objects or objects of cultural patrimony to date.

Gaining federal recognition

The Mashpee Wampanoag Tribe received federal recognition in 2007. The Mashpee Wampanoag Tribe now houses a NAGPRA department, of which I am the director. The tribe is still an active member of the Wampanoag Repatriation Confederation. At this point, there are two federally recognized tribes in the Wampanoag Confederation, and our most recent *Federal Register* notice reads: "Officials of the Robert S. Peabody Museum of Archaeology also have determined that, pursuant to 25 U.S.C. 3001 (2), there is a relationship of shared group identity that can be reasonably traced between the Native American human remains and the Mashpee Wampanoag Tribe and Wampanoag Tribe of Gay Head (Aquinnah) of Massachusetts. Furthermore, officials of the Robert S. Peabody Museum of Archaeology have determined that there is a cultural relationship between the Native American human remains and the Assonet Band of the Wampanoag Nation, a non–federally recognized Indian group."[29]

The Mashpee Wampanoag received a NAGPRA consultation/documenta-tion grant funded by the National NAGPRA Program in 2009. The previous tribal administration chose to ignore the Wampanoag Confederation and unilaterally applied for a NAGPRA grant. That action caused a rift with the Wampanoag Tribe of Gay Head, and still accounts for a subtle level of mistrust between all the members of the confederation. During the last tribal administration, some folks went on consultation visits to a few local museums. Since we have had over a decade of collaboration with these museums, calls by their staff were made to Wampanoag Repatriation Confederation officers to learn what became of the confederation. It was gratifying to learn that museum staff recognized the Wampanoag Confederation membership's hard work and dedication to this solemn duty. Nothing further came of it, other than a few consultation meetings (with attorneys), and some rather harsh letters to a number of museums. This group of Mashpee Wampanoag had no real clue where to begin, but had the desire to dissolve the Wampanoag Confederation by writing to museums, stating "the Wampanoag Confederation does not exist." What they may have learned before losing the next election was that the *Federal Register* notices of cultural affiliation to the Wampanoag were created by naming the Wampanoag Repatriation Confederation and its membership. It would be a difficult task to undo these notices without creating counter-claims and wasting the resources of all concerned. The Mashpee Wampanoag Tribe received its second grant in 2010, to proceed with its consultations regarding culturally unidentifiable human remains in concert with the other two member groups of the confederation. We were warmly greeted by familiar museum staff as we returned to the spiritual commitment each of us made so many years ago.

Repatriation forces us to be in the center of many losses. It is a long, often difficult process. Not only does the responsibility for a preponderance of evidence rest with the tribes; it often feels like we are also being held disproportionately responsible for others' reckless disregard for the sanctity of Native American gravesites. There are many benefits to working in a confederation. In a confederation, the tribes agree to share equal political power and participate, because we feel it is our moral obligation to rebury those who are of our Wampanoag Nation. It is this foundation that has made us successful regardless of our federal status.

The Delaware Tribe's NAGPRA work during the termination years

The unique history of the Delaware Tribe in eastern Oklahoma and their recent experience with NAGPRA complicates what at first appears to be a simple relationship between tribal repatriation efforts and federal recognition. NAGPRA stipulates that only federally recognized tribes may be culturally affiliated and seek repatriation, and thus, such a provision would seem to automatically exclude potentially affiliated groups who lack federal recognition. This seemingly straightforward provision did significantly limit the Delaware Tribe from participating in NAGPRA-related projects during the years that the tribe lacked federal recognition, but the non-recognized Delaware Tribe was never completely excluded. Their continued efforts under NAGPRA during the termination years can thus provide a perspective on documentation and repatriation from the vantage point of a non-recognized tribal NAGPRA office that was able to remain involved in NAGPRA-related projects despite the loss of federal recognition.

The Delaware Tribe is one of many contemporary tribes that descend from the Unami- and Munsee-speaking peoples of the Delaware and Hudson River valleys, situated within what are today the states of New Jersey, Pennsylvania, New York, and Delaware.[30] First Dutch, then British, and finally American encroachment forced the Unami and Munsee speakers—along with their displaced coastal and interior Algonquian allies such as the Shawnee, Susquehanna, Mahican, Wappinger, Conoy, and Nanticoke—to move further west, to predominately Delaware-established villages at the frontier of European settlement. This series of short but frequent removals began in the late seventeenth century and took what would later become the Delaware Tribe to occupations in what are today the states of Ohio, Indiana, Missouri, Kansas, and, finally, Oklahoma, where the Delaware Tribe is currently headquartered today.

The Delaware Tribe's recent difficulties with sustaining federal recognition began with the tribe's nineteenth-century removal to Indian Territory, which is now roughly the eastern half of the state of Oklahoma. The Delaware Tribe's last removal from Kansas in 1867 was onto lands in Indian Territory within the boundaries of what was then the Cherokee Nation. In order to relocate to the Cherokee Nation, the Delaware Tribe signed an agreement in which they paid for land and membership in the Cherokee Nation. In exchange, the Delaware were given lands within the Cherokee Nation and were to be considered "Native Cherokees." Although the 1867 agreement was signed, the sometimes strained relationship between the two tribes demonstrates that a disagreement has existed over what this agreement actually meant. The Delaware Tribe has always felt that they had paid the dual payments in order to preserve their independence (and thus, federal relationship) while being required to become residents of the Cherokee Nation. The Cherokee Nation, on the other hand, considered the payments to be in exchange for inclusion in the Cherokee Nation, as it would seem contrary for any sovereign nation to include within their boundaries another sovereignty-exerting entity. The actual meaning and intent of the 1867 Agreement has been the subject of five federal court cases, brought by both tribes, some of which were tried in the Supreme Court. Such a long history of federal court cases has yet to clarify this relationship to the satisfaction of either tribe, though both have made recent concessions to allow for the Delaware Tribe's current, but conditional, federal recognition.

This disagreement over the terms of the 1867 agreement in its modern form connects with issues surrounding federal recognition and Delaware tribal membership. When the Bureau of Indian Affairs (BIA) issued the first list of federally recognized tribes in 1979, the Delaware Tribe was left off of the list at the request of the Cherokee Nation. This exclusion occurred despite the long history of government-to-government relations with the Delaware Tribe, even after their 1867 removal. The Delaware Tribe's termination lasted until 1996, when the Delaware Tribe was administratively restored to federal recognition by the Secretary of the Interior, who was ultimately persuaded through the lobbying efforts of Delaware tribal leaders. The 1996 restoration was immediately appealed by the Cherokee Nation on the grounds that the BIA violated the Administrative Procedure Act (APA) by not following the Part 83 process for restoring Delaware recognition. While the Cherokee appeal was being heard in federal courts, the Delaware Tribe remained a recognized tribe and thus eligible for programs, services, and grants available to federally recognized tribes.

It was during these eight years that the Delaware Tribe applied for and was awarded their first NAGPRA grant, in 2000, to work on the documentation and repatriation of the many collections of Delaware human remains and funerary objects stored in museums and federal agencies throughout the United States. Following this work under the 2000 grant, the tribe was awarded another NAGPRA consultation/documentation grant in 2004 to complete a digital database of museum inventories that had already been received, and to begin consultation with two museums that held significant collections of Delaware human remains. That same year, the tribe was also awarded a repatriation grant to support the tribe's effort to repatriate a collection at the State Museum of Pennsylvania that was documented during the 2000 grant.

Unfortunately, 2004 was also the year that the Cherokee Nation's 1996 appeal was ultimately successful and the Delaware Tribe was judicially terminated. Judicial termination meant that the tribe was no longer eligible to operate federal programs and services, and also no longer eligible for grants available to federally recognized tribes. Termination also meant that although many collections had been documented as culturally affiliated with the Delaware Tribe, without recognition, the Delaware Tribe could not legally repatriate such collections by themselves.

Beyond the tribe's status under NAGPRA, termination also meant that for Delaware tribal members to benefit from federal Indian programs and services, they would have to do so as members of another federally recognized tribe. Some tribal members were eligible to claim membership in other tribes and chose to do so, while others simply chose to remain unenrolled and thus ineligible for federal services. Most tribal members lacked descent from another Indian tribe beyond the Delaware and, thus, their only solution was to enroll as members of the Cherokee Nation in order to access much needed programs and services. Based on the Cherokee Nation's interpretation of the 1867 agreement that the Delaware were to become "Native Cherokees," the Cherokee Nation continued to allow all Delaware tribal members to enroll as full members of the Cherokee Nation even if they lacked any Cherokee ancestry.

The Delaware Tribe's NAGPRA program had a similar decision to make following the 2004 termination. There were other federally recognized tribes that were culturally affiliated with the already-documented Delaware collections, such as the Delaware Nation and the Stockbridge Munsee Band. During the years of restored recognition, the Delaware Tribe had developed a strong working relationship with the other Delaware-descended tribes and thus could have potentially pursued documentation and repatriation projects through their offices. Though such a possibility sounded like a simple solution, the reality was that federally recognized tribes are often hesitant to work with unrecognized groups, despite existing or past relationships. Furthermore, other tribes had their own projects and simply did not have the time or resources to add the Delaware Tribe's projects to their list.

A second option was to pursue documentation and repatriation projects through the Cherokee Nation. Since the Cherokee Nation allowed for Delaware membership in the Cherokee Nation, the Delaware NAGPRA office could also pursue repatriation projects through the Cherokee office. Though the legal contact for Delaware collections was the Cherokee Nation following the Delaware Tribe's termination, the Cherokee Nation had no interest in interfering with Delaware-related projects and deferred all comment and action to the Delaware Tribe. However, the Delaware Tribe could not move forward on such projects unless they did so as an extension of the Cherokee Nation. Because of the politically contentious history between the Delaware Tribe and the Cherokee Nation, this was not an attractive option for the Delaware Tribe, as it might give the appearance that the Delaware Tribe had accepted a merger with the Cherokee Nation.

Such obstacles provided significant challenges for the Delaware Tribe during the termination years that ultimately led to a major change in direction and focus. Without federal recognition, the Delaware Tribe's independent documentation efforts and database development effectively ceased when the funding from the 2004 NAGPRA grant ran out. The Delaware Tribe also had to give up on the nearly complete repatriation from the State Museum of Pennsylvania, and return the unspent allocation. Without funding or federal acknowledgment, the NAGPRA office was forced to close, leaving projects unfinished and staff members without employment.

The Delaware Tribe was, however, able to remain marginally in the loop on other repatriation projects as long as such work was done through collaborations with other tribes and without federal or NAGPRA support. Such collaborations ultimately fell into two categories, and the NAGPRA director continued to participate in such collaborations with tribal support, at his own expense. In the first category, the Delaware Tribe continued to participate as interested parties on several joint repatriation projects that were started with the other Delaware-descended tribes before 2004. The most significant project was the repatriation of over 100 Delaware human remains and over 5,000 funerary objects from the Delaware Water Gap National Recreation Area that straddles New Jersey's northwestern border with Pennsylvania. As an interested party, the Delaware Tribe held no voice or decision-making power and was not included on formal consultations. However, the tribe was kept aware of the major developments in this substantial repatriation project.

In the second category, the Delaware Tribe remained active to the extent possible on documentation efforts for those collections identified before 2004 through the Cherokee Nation office. Collections that appeared in *Federal Register* notices during the termination years that were culturally affiliated with the Delaware Tribe were officially listed as affiliated to the "Delaware Tribe on behalf of the Cherokee Nation." This wording meant that ultimately the collections could only be repatriated to the Delaware Tribe if they were formally repatriated to the Cherokee Nation and then passed on to the Delaware Tribe with Cherokee approval. Because the Cherokee NAGPRA office deferred to the Delaware on all Delaware collections and notices, the tribe was able to ensure that the collections were rightfully affiliated with the Delaware Tribe with the intent of correcting the wording once recognition was restored.

Fortunately, federal recognition of the Delaware Tribe was restored in 2009, before any of the joint repatriation projects were finalized. However, there were a handful of *Federal Register* notices that appeared during the termination years, and thus there are some notices that are in need of correction. Correcting the cultural affiliation in the *Federal Register* is important, because the current language implies that the Delaware Tribe is subordinate to the Cherokee Nation, the recognized representative tribe for the Delaware constituency. The Delaware Tribe has long asserted their separateness from the Cherokee Nation and wants to ensure that their government-to-government relationship with the federal government is appropriately recognized in the cultural affiliation notices for identified Delaware remains.

Upon restoration, the Delaware Tribe immediately returned to existing projects. With the support of the NAGPRA Repatriation grant in 2009, the Delaware Tribe was fortunate to be included as full participants in a joint repatriation with the Delaware Nation and Stockbridge-Munsee Band at Delaware Water Gap National Recreation Area.[31] Representatives from the three tribes finalized the reburial of the over 100 remains in September 2009. The Delaware Tribe was also fortunate to receive a 2010 NAGPRA consultation/documentation grant that allowed the tribe to rebuild the NAGPRA office with staff, training, and equipment, as well as to continue previous NAGPRA work focusing specifically on collections that were documented as Delaware, "on behalf of the Cherokee Nation."

While termination led to significant changes to the Delaware Tribe's NAGPRA office and an end to many documentation and repatriation projects, termination did not completely exclude the Delaware Tribe from working cooperatively with other federally recognized tribes. The important role that other tribes played in allowing the Delaware Tribe to continue to remain a part of the NAGPRA processes despite the Delaware Tribe's experience with termination underscores the importance of cooperation and coalition building in consultation and repatriation efforts under NAGPRA. Without the assistance of other tribes, the Delaware Tribe would have been completely left out of important repatriation projects, as well as excluded from those *Federal Register* notices finalized during the termination years. Remaining involved through partnerships with other tribes allowed the Delaware Tribe to participate in important repatriations and set the stage for the tribe to easily correct *Federal Register* notices that can now legally identify cultural affiliation with the Delaware Tribe.

The Delaware Tribe's experience does shed light on a profound limitation in the NAGPRA process. By restricting the repatriation and documentation of cultural affiliation to federally recognized tribes, NAGPRA automatically excludes those groups who lack federal recognition even though everyone (federally recognized tribes, academic community, National NAGPRA, etc.) agrees that there is a shared group identity that can be reasonably traced to a present non-federally recognized Indian group. Privileging political standing over the demonstration of shared group identity places limits on the ability of culturally affiliated groups to repatriate known ancestral collections. The Delaware Tribe and I have witnessed firsthand how such privileging moves the documentation and repatriation process away from the original intent of NAGPRA, which is to return indigenous ancestral burial remains and objects to those who will know best how to properly care for them. The solution to rectify this limitation by allowing documentation and repatriation to non-federally recognized Indian groups may appear to be a simple one. However, it may be difficult to achieve consensus among tribes on how to adequately address this issue without compromising the important position of federally recognized tribes that should continue to be an integral and guiding part of the NAGPRA process.

Conclusion

Repatriation is a sorrowful yet sacred duty that puts descendant communities at the center of loss. A lengthy, difficult process, repatriation makes tribes responsible for others' disregard of ancestral burial sites. Prior to 1990 and the passage of NAGPRA, non-federally recognized Indian groups that were culturally affiliated to human remains were often considered by those interested in repatriation as the most appropriate group to deal with the reburial of ancestors and objects that had been disturbed. Ironically, under NAGPRA, the role of non-federally recognized Indian groups is ambiguous and varies depending upon the non-federally recognized Indian group's history, location, and connection to related tribes and communities. As the case studies demonstrate, although NAGPRA was passed to reinforce and confirm the rights of disenfranchised people to care for related ancestors and their cultural objects, it has taken away the rights of some who are culturally affiliated but have no standing under the law. The current regulatory language cannot legally be used to extend the provisions of NAGPRA to non-federally recognized Indian groups. Legislative actions that amend the statute are needed to give these groups equal footing with federally recognized tribes.

As sovereign nations, federally recognized tribes have retained certain rights that are upheld through a government-to-government relationship with the United States. However, the politics of tribal rights can hinder a non-federally recognized Indian group's ability to care for their ancestors. Some federally recognized tribes refuse to work with non-federally recognized Indian groups, especially in light of perceived notions that sovereign rights will be undermined. Thus, legal systems and politics usurp the inherent human rights of descendant communities to care for their ancestors. One could say that the ancestors become pawns in the game of tribal politics in a manner similar to the ancestors being used as objects in a scientific study.

Museums and federal agencies should take into consideration the historical relationship tribes and non-federally recognized Indian groups have to the individuals in their collections. NAGPRA itself does not explicitly address the issue of cultural affiliation to more than one federally recognized tribe. Indeed, the language within NAGPRA regarding cultural affiliation is universally in the singular. Nowhere, though, does the law prohibit affiliation or repatriation to more than one tribe. Multi-tribe or joint repatriations are becoming more common as museums and federal agencies address the complexity of cultural affiliation between ancestors and the present-day political divisions representing their descendants. Multi-tribe repatriation is an important tool non-federally recognized Indian groups can use to participate in NAGPRA.

Non-federally recognized Indian groups successfully work with federally recognized tribes to develop methods, both formal and informal, that guide the repatriation process. The Wampanoag have developed detailed policies based upon a foundation of knowledge gained from tribal leaders, elders, and medicine people. Territorial boundaries and cultural, spiritual, and political concerns are laid out and provide the framework for interaction. The Columbia Plateau Inter-Tribal Repatriation Group meet together and communicate in a traditional manner giving voice to all, respecting the traditional areas of each, and working together in caring for the ancestors. Key to any process is developing relationships, sharing responsibilities, and creating trust and good faith towards cooperation and coalition building.

As the case studies demonstrate, non-federally recognized Indian groups are savvy in building relationships and working within the bureaucracy of repatriation to be partners in the process. They utilize non-profit status to receive funding or to apply for preservation restrictions to protect reinterment sites, work with the non-Indian community to protect important areas including burial sites, participate in coalitions, build partnerships, share their knowledge and skills with others, and maintain a neutral stance in the face of divisive politics. There are logistical and cultural challenges for tribes conducting repatriation. Although political divisions created by the federal government can lead to multiple tribal perspectives, working together allows descendent communities to overcome these challenges in a manner that reaches the ultimate goal of returning the ancestors to the ground so that they may continue on their journey. This cooperation and coalition building extends to working with museums and federal agencies.

Museums and federal agencies should work with non-federally recognized Indian groups in the NAGPRA process. These groups have a vested interest and can provide much needed guidance and assistance in the care of the ancestors. Positive relationships between museums and federal institutions and non-federally recognized groups can result in mutual trust, strong working relationships, and shared resources that support the preparation, reburial, and ceremonial aspects of repatriation. The benefits of coming together to do the right thing for the right reason extend beyond any one singular purpose, leading to interactions that provide shared knowledge and projects that benefit all communities.

Notes

1   25 U.S.C. 3001 et seq.

2   Pub. L. 103–454; 108 Stat. 4791, 4792.

3   Mark Miller, *Forgotten Tribes: Unrecognized Indians and the Federal Acknowledgment Process* (Lincoln, NE: University of Nebraska Press, 2004). Historian Mark Miller provides the most recent and comprehensive book-length examination of the federal acknowledgment process. Miller describes how the FAP was initially developed in consultation with existing tribal governments, and how the process remains in place precisely because it continues to receive the support of federally recognized tribes. Miller concludes that acknowledged tribes hold an understandable interest in the acknowledgment process and have remained vocal in many of the acknowledgment decisions handed down through the FAP. Such participation by acknowledged tribes is not always antagonistic to petitioning groups, as it is clear that acknowledged tribes have been relatively open to those new groups who can demonstrate a legitimate claim for acknowledgment and meet the established criteria. Federal acknowledgment, however,

whether it is through congressional, judicial, or executive action, has become a process in which federally recognized tribes often voice their support for, or opposition to, the acknowledgment decisions for petitioning tribes, and most dissenting voices from acknowledged tribes reflect the criteria used in the FAP.

4   We are a non-federally recognized tribe. May we still participate in the NAGPRA process? Under NAGPRA, only federally recognized Native American tribes and Native Hawaiian organizations may claim cultural items. NAGPRA does not require museums and federal agencies to consult with non-federally recognized tribes. However, the Native American Graves Protection and Repatriation Review Committee has recognized that there are some cases in which non-federally recognized tribes may be appropriate claimants for cultural items. Museums, if they wish, may consult with non-federally recognized tribes. Museums and federal agencies that wish to return Native American human remains and cultural items to non-federally recognized tribes must make a request for review of a proposed disposition to the Review Committee. http://www.nps.gov/nagpra/FAQ/INDEX.HTM.

5   Commonly known as Kennewick Man, the tribes refer to him as the Ancient One. The July 1996 inadvertent discovery of human remains along the Columbia River led to a legal battle between tribes of the Columbia Plateau and scientists over repatriation and study. The resulting decision of the 9th Circuit Court led to the curation of the remains and subsequent study. Bonnichsen v. United States, 217 F.Supp.2d 1116 (D.Or. 2002), affd. 357 F.3d 962 (9th Cir. 2004), modified and rehearing en banc denied, 367 F.3d 864 (9th Cir. 2004).

6   Laurie E. Burgess, *Inventory and Assessment of Human Remains and Objects from Southeast Washington Northeast Oregon in the National Museum of Natural History* (Washington DC: Smithsonian Institution Press, 2004).

7   20 U.S.C. 80q-1 et seq.

8   Deward E. Walker, Jr., ed., *Handbook of North American Indians: Plateau,* Vol. 12 (Washington DC: Smithsonian Institution Press, 1998).

9   Notice of Inventory Completion: U.S. Department of Defense, Army Corps of Engineers, Walla Walla District, Walla Walla, WA, and Museum of Anthropology, Washington State University, Pullman, WA, and Nez Perce National Historical Park, Spaulding Visitor Center, Spaulding, ID. 71 *Fed. Reg.* 24755-24757 (April 26, 2006).

10   Notice of Inventory Completion: American Museum of Natural History, New York, NY. 70 *Fed. Reg.* 61835-61837 (October 26, 2005).

11   The Suppressed Speech of Wamsutta (Frank B.) James, Wampanoag, to have been delivered at Plymouth, MA, 1970. See: www.informationclearinghouse.info/article21333.htm.

12   *Massasoit:* Wampanoag leadership title meaning "best leader."

13   Date is based on archaeological evidence of Wampanoag presence, 12,000 years before present.

14   Longhouse: called *nuhshquty8ômas,* "a three-fire house."

15   *Weety8ômash:* small dome shaped houses covered with cattail mats or bark.

16   The Mashpee Wampanoag Tribe living on Cape Cod and the Wampanoag Tribe of Gay Head (Aquinnah) living on the island of Martha's Vineyard are federally recognized tribes; the Herring Pond Tribe living in the town of Bourne is a state-recognized tribe. All three live on their original homelands.

17   The Mashpee Wampanoag Tribe has never allowed anyone to disinter any of its burials. No NAGPRA museum inventories of ancestral human remains from Mashpee exist, instead the NAGPRA efforts are aimed at the broader based Wampanoag.

18   60 *Fed. Reg.* 8733-8744 (February 15, 1995), http://www.cr.nps.gov/nagpra/fed_notices/nagpradir/nic0026.html.

19   The Review Committee meetings are typically held in locations where tribes have the expense of travel and being away from home.

20   Notice of Inventory Completion: Robert S. Peabody Museum of Archaeology, Phillips Academy, Andover, MA. 70 *Fed. Reg.* 16839-16840 (April 1, 2005).

21   NAGPRA items have been put in the "culturally unidentifiable" category that lack specific provenience other than the state where they were found. Culturally unidentifiable refers to human remains and associated funerary objects in museum or federal agency collections for which no lineal descendant or culturally affiliated Indian tribe or Native Hawaiian organization has been identified through the inventory process. 43 C.F.R. 10.2(e)(2).

22   Our shared historic allegiance is best understood through The Massachuset and Wampanoag War Pact against The English in 1675 (so-called King Phillips War). The Massachuset suffered near total annihilation in their last effort with us to redeem territory and preserve our traditional way of life. The Wampanoag Confederation will not seek items of cultural patrimony or sacred objects that would belong to The Massachuset People.

23   Sacred and patrimonial aspects of our culture are not to be exchanged for confiscated, stolen, or inappropriately sold objects of our ancestors, held in museums or federal agencies nor private collections. (Per directive of Cjegkitoonuppa.)

24   It is not possible for our confederation of Wampanoag peoples to sever the blood lineage of our existence since our first Mother, for the conveniences of either modern or foreign cultural mores.

25   Traditional Wampanoag confederations protected individual tribal power, giving equal rights and voice to each tribal entity organized under one alignment with the same prime purpose, be it peace, trade agreement, travel privileges, or other purposes.

26   See 25 U.S.C. 3003, which has provided for federal and tribal lands protection since November 16, 1990; and 18 U.S.C. 1170, which punishes illegal trafficking in Native American human remains and cultural items.

27   The Wampanoag Confederation Inc. can legally hold covenants over land use at reinterment sites placed in the Registry of Deeds of Massachusetts.

28   Notice of Inventory Completion for Native American Human Remains and Associated Funerary Objects in the Possession of the Peabody Museum of Archaeology and Ethnology, Harvard University, Cambridge, MA. 66 *Fed. Reg.* 51468-51469 (October 9, 2001).

29   Notice of Inventory Completion: Robert S. Peabody Museum of Archaeology, Phillips Academy, Andover, MA. 73 *Fed. Reg.* 30969-30970 (May 29, 2008).

30   The Delaware Nation headquartered in Anadarko, Oklahoma and the Stockbridge Munsee Band headquartered in Bowler, Wisconsin are the other two Delaware-descended federally recognized tribes.

31   Notice of Inventory Completion: U.S. Department of the Interior, National Park Service, Delaware Water Gap National Recreation Area, Bushkill, PA. 73 *Fed. Reg.* 65876-65879 (November 5, 2008), and Notice of Intent to Repatriate Cultural Items: U.S. Department of the Interior, National Park Service, Delaware Water Gap National Recreation Area, Bushkill, PA. 73 *Fed. Reg.* 65875-65876 (November 5, 2008).

Chapter 8
Implementing NAGPRA at History Colorado: Applying Cultural Property Legacy Collections and Forging Tribal Partnerships
BRIDGET AMBLER and SHEILA GOFF

Introduction

History Colorado (HC, formerly the Colorado Historical Society) is the state history museum. Along with its collection and preservation responsibilities, HC administers educational programming, publications, exhibits, the State Historical Fund (SHF), and the Office of Archaeology and Historic Preservation (OAHP). As a museum institution that receives federal funding, HC is required to comply with the Native American Graves Protection and Repatriation Act (NAGPRA).[1] This chapter provides an overview of the agency's collecting history, our response to implementing NAGPRA, tribal collaborations, and solutions to challenges presented by NAGPRA.

When NAGPRA was passed on November 16, 1990, HC had been collecting American Indian objects and human remains for more than one hundred years. NAGPRA required a full accounting of the HC collections, and also something new—sitting at the table with tribes to discuss our collections as colleagues. As part of our continuing efforts to implement legal compliance and to reflect upon the impact of NAGPRA twenty years after the law's passage, the first and current HC NAGPRA liaisons (Bridget Ambler and Sheila Goff, respectively) share their perspectives here.

Ambler was raised in the American Southwest and spent much of her childhood exploring its hidden landscapes with her family. Her father, John Richard (Dick) Ambler, was a professor of archaeology at Northern Arizona University, who specialized in Ancestral Puebloan culture, and often took the family on field expeditions in Arizona, New Mexico, and Utah. Ambler began working for her father as an archaeological field technician when she was 13, and continued on to pursue degrees in anthropology from Northern Arizona University (undergraduate) and Colorado State University (graduate). She was employed as a contract archaeologist in the Southwest and Rocky Mountain regions, including a number of projects on tribal lands. Her tenure at HC began as an archaeological information specialist and a human osteologist with the Office of Archaeology and Historic Preservation in 1995. Around the same time, the Material Culture department was completing its NAGPRA inventory,[2] and Ambler was recruited to help in that effort. She began working with the NAGPRA coordinator, Roger Echo-Hawk and Assistant Curator Carolyn McArthur. Ambler was hired as the NAGPRA liaison in 1996 while Echo-Hawk transitioned to work at the Denver Art Museum. Ambler continued as NAGPRA liaison until 2005, when McArthur left for other opportunities and Ambler was promoted to curator, which included oversight of the HC NAGPRA program.

Goff's interest in NAGPRA began while she was doing archaeological fieldwork for the United States Forest Service and Bureau of Land Management in the mid 1990s. In 2003, she entered the Museum and Field Studies Program at the University of Colorado, Boulder. At that time, the University of Colorado Museum of Natural History was in the midst of conducting consultations to complete its inventories. Being able to participate in numerous consultations with southwestern tribes fueled her interest in NAGPRA and gave her the experience needed to work at HC.

As HC began its inventory, we first learned about the collection amassed over time that resulted in large numbers of Native American human remains and cultural objects in our possession. Additionally, we learned to understand the relationship between state law and federal law and how to work within both. We recognized that if we were going to address tribal concerns about issues such as the disposition of culturally unidentifiable human remains, we needed to forge collaborative relationships not only with the various departments of HC but also with other state agencies and tribes. We tapped into the expertise and experiences of the National NAGPRA Program, the Review Committee, and other states, like Iowa, that were grappling with the same issues. The work is ongoing. Through NAGPRA, we have improved our knowledge of our collections. Our tribal partnerships have transcended NAGPRA, and have enhanced interpretation in our exhibits and education programs, and we are better able to convey to a general audience what Native American community members want others to understand about them.

Collections history

On August 1, 1879, the Colorado State Historical and Natural History Society was established in direct response to HB134, which sought contributions "particularly from pioneer settlers of the country."[3] The objectives of the new organization were to collect and preserve Colorado's history and natural history, relying largely on memberships throughout the state.[4] After moving to a series of temporary locations, HC eventually found a more permanent home in the State Capitol in 1895. At this point, the organization was little more than an assemblage of cabinet curiosities, but that would soon change.

The Mesa Verde collections

In 1888, Richard Wetherill and Charlie Mason "discovered" Cliff Palace, a large Puebloan cliff dwelling tucked inside the recess of Cliff Canyon, on the southern end of the current Mesa Verde National Park.[5] According to Ute Mountain Ute history,[6] it was Acowitz, a Ute tribal leader who lived at the mouth of Mancos Canyon, who originally told the Wetherill family about the canyon ruins and how to get to Cliff Palace, but credit for the "discovery" went to the Wetherills and Charlie Mason.[7] The Wetherills, including Richard and his brothers Al and Clayton, collected artifacts and incredibly preserved human remains from Cliff Palace and surrounding sites over the years, and made several attempts to sell the artifacts and remains in Durango as "Ancient Aztec Relics."[8] They also approached the Colorado State Historical Society and the Smithsonian Institution[9] in an effort to sell the collection. Later, in 1889, Clayton Wetherill and Mason uncovered a well-preserved, bundled mummy of a child in Mancos Canyon. When the child was put on display locally, it generated fevered public interest.[10] Eager to seize the opportunity to display the collection and child, and feeling public pressure to purchase the "exotic" artifacts, HC purchased the whole collection for $3,000.[11] This was an astounding act for the foundling museum, considering that the entire legislative appropriation for the whole year to HC was $1,500, and that the balance of the purchase was carried personally by staff![12] HC displayed the mummified remains of the child in the Colorado State Capitol building, drawing large crowds that waited in lines extending for blocks to get a glimpse of the objects and the mummified remains. Exhibiting the individuals and artifacts from Mesa Verde marked the first public success for the organization, and was symbolic, too, of the way researchers and visitors perceived Mesa Verde culture as static and disembodied from contemporary Pueblo people.

After a foreigner, Gustaf Nordenskiold, worked with the Wetherills to excavate in the Mesa Verde area and then exported artifacts and human remains to Helsinki, Finland, Coloradoans became outraged that *their* treasures were leaving the state.[13] In response, the Colorado Legislature voted in 1891 to fund expeditions to find artifacts and human remains from the Mesa Verde region and display them at the Chicago World's Fair. Arthur Wilmarth was hired to supervise excavations at a number of large sites, and those artifacts were displayed as the "State Collection" at the 1893 Columbian Exposition at the Chicago World's Fair.[14] Wilmarth later returned the collection to HC. At the same time, Colorado journalist Virginia McClurg, who had visited the ruins and became a passionate advocate to protect the area from looting, formed the Colorado Cliff Dwellings Association. Through the women's organization, McClurg sought to preserve the cliff dwellings as a Colorado State Park. McClurg's proposal lost to another set forth by Lucy Peabody (previously the vice president of the Colorado Cliff Dwellings Association) to establish the area as a national park in June, 1906.[15] Today, Mesa Verde National Park is a World Heritage Site,[16] and the collections at HC represent one of the largest assemblages of artifacts from the Mesa Verde region in the world, including, until recently, a large number of individuals who had died there.[17]

The public fascination with the dead

With the early success from the display of Mesa Verde area relics, HC purchased additional collections (some of which included human remains) and funded its own expeditions into the American Southwest. On April 10, 1905, the Colorado Legislature appropriated $6,000 to purchase the Cecil Deane collection via HB 207.[18] That was a large sum of money to pay for a collection at the time, particularly for a collection lacking documented provenance. Deane dug up burials across the American west, often collecting only crania, which were displayed alongside artifacts at his home in Longmont, Colorado, much like a small museum. [19] Other small-scale archaeological collections (which also included human remains) were purchased, primarily from private collectors. Then, in 1908, HC funded a full-scale excavation of Cannonball Pueblo in southwest Colorado, led by Edgar Lee Hewitt and in collaboration with the University of Colorado and the Colorado Society of the Archaeological Institute of America. Cannonball Ruin was located on federal land, and Hewett, the author of the American Antiquities Act of 1906,[20] applied for one of America's first antiquities permits to excavate the site in 1908.[21]

Public support to acquire and display archaeological objects and individuals was at a peak when, on September 2, 1915, a new museum was constructed on 14th Avenue in Denver, just across the street from the State Capitol. The Cliff Dwellers and Cannonball collections (including human remains) were proudly exhibited as central features in the museum.[22] By the 1920s, archaeological pursuits for burials and objects became a focus of HC, and a new "Archaeology and Ethnography Section" was formed, headed initially by Jean Jeancon. Jeancon led excavations of sites in the Pagosa/Piedra region, along with Frank H.H. Roberts, who went on later to work at the Smithsonian Institution.[23] In 1927, HC relieved itself from its natural history duties and instead devoted its efforts to Colorado's history, changing its name from the State Historical and Natural History Society to the Colorado State Historical Society.[24] During the latter half of the decade (1927–1929), a young archaeologist named Paul Martin was hired to conduct archaeological field research in southwestern Colorado.[25] Martin left Colorado and went on to the Field Museum of Natural History in Chicago; while HC maintains collections he excavated from Lowry and elsewhere, his field notes from those excavations remain missing. His departure from HC marked the end of intensive archaeological research projects initiated by the organization.

During these early years when HC funded active research programs and purchased collections, commensurate funding to document and research the same collections was difficult to come by. Beginning in the 1930s, the nation faced a financial crisis, and HC suffered severe budget cuts. To stay relevant to its constituents in the midst of the Great Depression, HC became the first museum in the nation to institute New Deal programs (primarily funding construction of dioramas). Not immune to the hard times facing the rest of the country, adverse conditions in 1932 forced the Governor's Committee on Unemployment to be housed in the Curator of Archaeology's office (by that time vacant) and Cliffdweller Hall in the state museum.[26] The following year, the archaeological laboratory and exhibit space were repurposed for the Civil Works Administration. In the face of economic disaster, archaeology and scholarly inquiry (and study of the human remains in the repository) seemed the first "luxuries" to go.

After archaeological research was no longer a priority, collections and human remains were acquired through private donations. The largest assemblage of human skeletal remains resulted from a donation by James Mellinger. Mellinger pursued archaeology as a hobby, and collected human remains (almost exclusively crania) and artifacts from sites in Colorado, New Mexico, Utah, Arizona, Wyoming, and South Dakota.[27] All individuals in the Mellinger collection lack site-specific or regional provenience.

In 1973, a state statute governing "Historical, Prehistorical and Archaeological Resources" was passed, thus creating the Office of the State Archaeologist.[28] The primary function of the state archaeologist was "to coordinate, encourage, and preserve by the use of appropriate means the full understanding of this state's archaeological resources as the same pertain to man's cultural heritage, the study and understanding of which within the state of Colorado will result in an ultimate benefit to the citizens of this state."[29] Under that authority, the state archaeologist often received human remains recovered as a result of inadvertent discovery, criminal cases, or excavated by the Office of Archaeology and Historic Preservation (OAHP) for projects on state lands. Between 1973 and 1990, human remains uncovered during archaeological excavations and under the state archaeologist's authority were held either in the OAHP storage area or by other institutions.

While the individuals in the care of HC had been largely unexamined by scholars since the organization was founded, James Hummert took on the ambitious task of cataloging those individuals in 1981.[30] As part of his research strategy, many of the individuals, mostly those representing partial skeletal assemblages, were disarticulated. Like skeletal elements were stored with other like elements. Separating individuals, without documentation and without an accurate accounting to begin with, would prove an immense challenge later on, when HC was charged with reporting the number of individuals in its possession as required by NAGPRA.[31]

Just a month before the passage of NAGPRA, the State of Colorado passed its own law governing inadvertent discoveries of Native American remains from state and private lands in 1990.[32] This statue—along with its rules and provisions—provides the Colorado State Archaeologist–HC Office of Archaeology and Historic Preservation permitting authority for archaeological studies within the state.[33] Part 13 of the law, "Unmarked Human Graves," sets forth provisions for dealing with the discovery, treatment, and temporary custody of human remains and associated objects, including Native American human remains.[34] Although it was written before the passage of NAGPRA, the State Unmarked Burial Law required the State Archaeologist to confer with the Colorado Commission of Indian Affairs (CCIA) to arrange for the reburial of Native American human remains.[35] Under Colorado law, the state archaeologist was, for a brief period of time, able to collaborate with CCIA and the state's two resident tribes, the Ute Mountain Ute Tribe and the Southern Ute Indian Tribe, to accomplish a small number of reburials. As it would turn out, the well-meaning intent of the state law and regulations would soon come face-to-face with its federal counterpart, and the collision would be one with significant consequences.

NAGPRA arrives at the door

When the Native American Graves Protection and Repatriation Act (NAGPRA)[36] arrived knocking on the doorsteps of American museums on November 16, 1990, most answered in their nightclothes, unsure of the strange visitor and certainly unsure of how to accommodate it (and without the financial means to fund compliance).[37] This uncertainty created a hesitant reception among museums and archaeologists, some of whom feared the law would end scholarly inquiry or empty museums of their collections. High profile court cases like "Kennewick Man" (also known as "The Ancient One"[38]) were featured prominently in the media, while the vast majority of museums and tribes worked, without much fanfare, to comply with the administrative requirements of the law. Such was the case for HC.

Beginning in 1990, HC was faced with the Herculean task of compiling information about its ethnographic collections and human remains after over a hundred years of collecting. Original provenience information for items and human remains was sometimes misplaced or lost altogether. In 1989, HC went "electric" and began efforts to download catalog data into a relational, computerized database. Without funding for a database manager or time to develop cataloging standards, data was often entered inconsistently or sometimes not at all. The scenario had the potential for disaster, yet eventually yielded unexpected benefits for the organization.

Other museums in the country faced similar challenges in tracking their collections. By 1990, a "curation crisis" had been declared for federally owned collections.[39] The crisis hit Colorado particularly hard, where museums across the state often lacked staff, funding, and storage to adequately house the archaeological collections in their care, and in light of NAGPRA, were reluctant to accept new collections that might be subject to the law.[40]

Summaries[41] of cultural items were due to tribes under NAGPRA on November 16, 1993,[42] and the inventories[43] were due on November 15, 1995.[44] Faced with new federal mandates and an immense backlog, HC scrambled to organize and summarize its considerable collections. Remains in the Mesa Verde collection, part of the most important founding collections of the organization, had not been systematically cataloged. Ironically, NAGPRA forced the institution to create an organized listing of human remains in its collections, and for the first time in over 100 years, HC conducted systematic examinations of the remains and associated funerary objects, to document very basic information such as age at time of death, gender, and other information that would be helpful to tribes and as required under NAGPRA.[45]

At first blush, the tasks ahead seemed gargantuan: create an inventory of all Native American human remains and associated funerary objects in HC's holdings, and report all cultural items[46] in the collections to potentially affiliated Native American tribes.[47] An initial challenge to implement NAGPRA at HC was figuring out who would be responsible for what; in other words, developing an organizational structure for the administrative responsibilities required for compliance. Because the Department of Material Culture was responsible for museum collections and the great majority of human remains subject to the law were in its collections, institutional compliance with NAGPRA was vested in that department. A NAGPRA team was established to include internal "stakeholders", including the state archaeologist, state historian, registrar, collections manager, assistant curator of material culture, and curator of material culture. Later, the NAGPRA team included the director of collections and library and the executive secretary of the CCIA, who is responsible by statute[48] for duties including coordinating "intergovernmental dealings between tribal governments and this state," reviewing legislation potentially affecting Native Americans in Colorado, and advocating on behalf of the state's two resident tribes—the Southern Ute Indian Tribe and the Ute Mountain Ute Tribe.[49]

To comply initially, Anne W. Bond, then the curator of material culture at HC, and Nancy Blomberg, curator of Native arts at the Denver Art Museum (DAM), forged a National Park Service (NPS) NAGPRA grant partnership to create a shared NAGPRA coordinator to begin compliance efforts. That grant position was filled by Roger Echo-Hawk, who remained in the position until 1996. At the time, Echo-Hawk was completing his graduate work at the University of Colorado, Boulder and was an emerging history scholar studying Native American oral traditions and cultural rights implications.[50] HC Assistant Curator of Material Culture and NAGPRA Compliance Coordinator Carolyn McArthur, a scholar with extensive knowledge of Native American material culture, was responsible for compiling information about the museum's collections. Echo-Hawk and McArthur are credited with laying the groundwork for creating a NAGPRA compliance program that infused current scholarship of legal requirements and academic standards with an aggressive tribal consultation agenda. Creating a NAGPRA program that was proactive rather than reactive took time, energy, and many meetings to assure agency officials that aiming for the highest compliance standards was truly in HC's best interest. Over time, their efforts paid off, and HC has developed numerous NAGPRA documentation and repatriation grants, consulted with Native American tribes from across the nation, and repatriated hundreds of Native American human remains and thousands of associated funerary objects.

Initially, hundreds of tribes were contacted as part of the effort to provide NAGPRA summaries. This was made possible with the help of the Native American Consultation Database provided by the National Park Service. Echo-Hawk researched the evidentiary details associated with the summaries and McArthur researched object context and history. Through extensive collaboration, McArthur and Echo-Hawk sifted through accession lists, donor files, personal notes, newspaper articles, HC archives, catalog records, and correspondence. Pursuant to 43 CFR Subpart C § 10.8 of the NAGPRA regulations, on November 16, 1993, HC provided complete summaries of its collections of Native American objects to lineal descendants (if known) and culturally affiliated Indian tribes and Native Hawaiian organizations. In January 1995, HC held its first tribal consultation under NAGPRA with the Pawnee Nation of Oklahoma. Depending largely on NPS NAGPRA grant funds, HC held many subsequent tribal consultations over the years, sometimes with individual tribes and on other occasions, with groups of tribes. Once the benefits of collaboration could be demonstrated to the agency, each consultation became easier, and the institution as a whole, over time, came to embrace the idea of partnering with tribes to share information about collections and other issues of mutual interest.

On November 15, 1995, HC submitted its inventory,[51] titled, *Indentured Spirits: A Census of Human Remains and Associated Funerary Objects at the Colorado Historical Society*, to the departmental consulting archaeologist, Archeological Assistance Division, NPS.[52] At the same time, the inventory was sent to tribes identified by HC as having potential interest in the disposition of these human remains and associated funerary objects.[53]

The original HC inventory included an accounting of Native American human remains in the museum collections and also those under the purview of the state archaeologist. The state archaeologist is responsible for making decisions about unmarked human burials discovered inadvertently on state and private lands.[54] Initially, Native American human remains under the purview of the state archaeologist were reburied in consultation with the CCIA. Later, in 2004, the relationship was clarified: "The state archaeologist, in consultation with the Colorado Commission of Indian Affairs, will determine if, when, and how Native American human remains and associated funerary objects collected under state permit are reinterred or repatriated in keeping with CRS 24-80-1302 and 1304 and the federal Native American Graves Protection and Repatriation Act (P.L. 101–601, 104 Stat. 3048)".[55]

Over time and with legal clarification, it became clear that once the state archaeologist had assumed decision-making control over Native American human remains removed from state and private lands in Colorado, the State of Colorado was responsible for reporting those individuals as part of our NAGPRA inventory, according to "museum provisions" of the law.[56] This relationship was later verified by the Colorado State Attorney General's office, who determined that the state archaeologist had sufficient possession[57] and control[58] over Native American human remains to trigger NAGPRA's provisions.[59]

The original intent of the state statute regarding authorized excavation of human remains was to provide the state archaeologist with the authority to adopt rules and regulations that would consider the following: (a) the rights and interests of the landowners, (b) the sensitivity of human beings for treating human remains with respect and dignity, and (c) the value of history and archaeology as a guide to human activity.[60]

Tribal efforts to repatriate inadvertent discoveries on state and private lands

To address ongoing interagency responsibilities regarding NAGPRA, including discoveries on state and private lands, HC established the shared position of NAGPRA liaison in November 1998 through an NPS NAGPRA grant partnership with the CCIA. As a decision-making party when Native American remains were discovered on state and private lands, and with the statutory responsibility of serving the needs of Colorado's resident Ute tribes and other American Indians living in the state, CCIA was a natural choice as a grant partner to address matters of mutual interest under NAGPRA. In December 1998, at the CCIA quarterly meeting with the Ute Mountain Ute and Southern Ute Indian tribes, Mr. Terry Knight, Sr., a traditional religious leader for the Ute Mountain Ute Tribe and NAGPRA representative, raised objections to then-Lieutenant Governor Joe Rogers, about the state's inadvertent discovery process. Knight pointed out that because of conflicts with NAGPRA and evidentiary requirements, it was simply taking too long to rebury (and in some cases, making no effort to rebury) those persons that had been disinterred. Knight demanded swift action.

At the time, state agencies faced two major hurdles to accomplish repatriation: (1) there was not yet a functional understanding of how inadvertent discoveries on state and private lands could and would be repatriated according to NAGPRA, and (2) the majority of those inadvertent discoveries were "culturally unidentifiable" under NAGPRA, and the regulations governing disposition of "culturally unidentifiable"[61] remains had not yet been published.[62]

While Colorado regulations articulate the state archaeologist's authority (in consultation with CCIA) to make determinations regarding the disposition of Native American human remains and associated funerary objects, NAGPRA holds the state archaeologist to additional standards.[63] These standards—*Summaries, Inventories, Repatriation, Disposition of Culturally Unidentifiable Human Remains [reserved], and Civil Penalties*—respectively required that before repatriation and reburial could occur, those NAGPRA provisions must be met.[64] Pursuant to these provisions, since 1990, the state archaeologist had annually presented a summary report on inadvertent discovery cases to the CCIA at their annual December meeting. After 1992, the Department of Material Culture also provided inventories of all Native American remains in its custody to tribes in both written and verbal form during NAGPRA consultations. Together, beginning in 1998, CCIA and HC consulted with tribes to develop a dynamic "Tribal Contacts List" (updated annually) that listed contact information of tribes having aboriginal interests in the State of Colorado.[65]

To address Knight's concerns, CCIA formed a Reinterment Committee in 1998, initially composed of three sub-committees: Reburial, Legal Resources, and Hearings. The Reburial sub-committee included tribal practitioners and other partners that would focus on reburial events. The Legal Resources sub-committee focused on changing the Colorado law to expedite repatriation. The Hearings sub-committee was to develop a hearings process to accomplish repatriation under existing Colorado law. Eventually, by 2000, these three subcommittees merged into a single CCIA Reinterment Committee whose focus was NAGPRA consultations with HC and tribes, re-writing the state's burial law, and developing a statewide reburial plan. Members were drawn from a variety of stakeholders, including the tribes, the Native American Rights Fund (NARF), Colorado Department of Natural Resources, Colorado Department of Highways, Colorado Department of Health and Environment, Colorado Department of Labor and Employment, and HC.

Under continued pressure to address Colorado's burial legislation, the CCIA and HC crafted a Memorandum of Understanding (MOU) in 1999 to work together to (1) provide a comprehensive accounting of all Native American individuals in HC collections that might be reasonably culturally affiliated, (2) identify reburial sites, (3) petition the NAGPRA Review Committee to approve a process for disposition of culturally unidentifiable Native American individuals, (4) develop a reburial process, (5) and work together to revise state statutes governing burials.[66] While the MOU lacked regulatory teeth, it was important in that both agencies resolved to work together toward the expeditious repatriation of Native American remains held in HC's collections.

In this dynamic environment, HC and CCIA partnered on an NPS NAGPRA grant to hold a symposium in 2000 to address the cultural affiliation standard of NAGPRA as it applied to Native American remains originating from the Rocky Mountain Front Range and Eastern Plains of Colorado.[67] Tribal experts and academic scholars were invited to discuss the lines of evidence recognized under NAGPRA and the extant legal scholarship regarding determinations of cultural affiliation for this group of human remains (including individuals associated with Plains Woodland and Late Prehistoric era contexts).[68] During the symposium, presentations provided information with the potential for elucidating cultural affiliation for some of these individuals. A crucial presentation by Dr. Sherry Hutt also provided legal clarification of the preponderance of evidence standard, prima facie evidence, and determining cultural affiliation under NAGPRA.[69]

With these legal standards and components of NAGPRA clarified, officials at HC realized that evidence gleaned from previous tribal consultations and scholarly research, in addition to new evidence presented at the symposium, were sufficient to satisfy the cultural affiliation requirements of NAGPRA for many individuals previously designated as culturally unidentifiable under the law. Thus, HC was able to make a determination of shared group affiliation and proceed with repatriation. That decision has been criticized by Roger Echo-Hawk (a panelist and Pawnee Nation of Oklahoma tribal representative at the symposium) as "negotiated cultural affiliation," a decision he asserts was made by HC in order to expedite repatriation and placate participating tribes.[70] In the end, the decision to affiliate the remains was based on the reasonable requirements of the law rather than scientific standards of proof. During that time, numerous institutions preferred declaring Native American human remains as culturally unidentifiable under NAGPRA. Motivation for not determining cultural affiliation varied among organizations; it could be a way to avoid controversial decisions, justify the need for additional study, or delay pending tribal consultation. In many instances, museums were waiting for final regulations to be drafted that would guide repatriation of culturally unidentifiable Native American human remains and associated funerary objects. In our case, HC published two NAGPRA Notices of Inventory Completion for the Native American human remains and associated funerary objects originating from Colorado's eastern Plains (and including those dating to the Plains Woodland era), and without counterclaims, repatriated those remains to claimant tribes who reburied them in 2001 and 2010.[71]

Also in 2001, the NAGPRA liaison grant-funded position shifted from being shared between HC and CCIA to be housed full-time at HC. We realized that the position was critical for ongoing compliance on behalf of the agency and that we could not depend on NPS NAGPRA grant money to fund the position indefinitely. While HC continued with tribal consultations and repatriations, we also initiated efforts to fund a position within the agency. In 2005, HC successfully lobbied the Colorado legislature to create a full-time NAGPRA position. The position was justified based on the agency's continuing responsibilities to comply with the law, and importantly, the consequences of civil penalties[72] that could be applicable if the agency did not comply with NAGPRA. HC and CCIA continued to collaborate on NAGPRA grants and tribal consultations through the NAGPRA team and the CCIA Reinterment Committee.

While the Colorado Ute tribes, CCIA, and HC had accomplished a great deal, the tribes still sought a long-term legal remedy to accomplish repatriation for indigenous human remains removed from state and private lands in Colorado. In the spring legislative session of 2001, the Ute Mountain Ute Tribe and Southern Ute Indian Tribe secured initial sponsorship of a House bill to amend the State of Colorado's burial law.[73] Before the bill was read on the House floor, it was "postponed indefinitely," likely due to fiscal impacts, constituent opposition, and potential conflict with NAGPRA. For three years, the tribes' attorneys worked to develop a viable option. In January 2004, those efforts culminated in Senate Bill No. 04-0666, "A Bill for an Act Concerning Procedures Related to the Discovery of Native American Human Remains."[74] This time, HC had their representative at the attorney general's office review the bill, and he concluded that the bill would conflict with, and thus be pre-empted by, federal law (NAGPRA).[75] Once again, the bill was withdrawn before it could be read on the floor. Understandably, the tribes were displeased.

Frustrated with the legal review, the two Ute tribes reached out to then-Colorado Attorney General Ken Salazar.[76] The tribes persisted in seeking a workable process and presented their preferences to Attorney General Salazar. Ultimately, they asked the attorney general's office to develop revisions to Senate Bill No. 04-0666 to resolve any discrepancies with NAGPRA (a request never pursued by the attorney general's office). Some months later, HC addressed the CCIA, inviting the agency into a cooperative meeting with the tribes to identify a joint agreement.[77] That invitation was met with a counter-invitation by CCIA[78] to have discussions in three tribal consultation regions according to the "Draft Recommendations Regarding the Disposition of Culturally Unidentifiable Human Remains and Associated Funerary Objects" developed by the NAGPRA Review Committee.[79] In addition, CCIA requested that the agencies partner on an NPS NAGPRA grant to develop the process. With encouragement from the attorney general's office, HC took CCIA up on their suggestion, and agreed to partner on a fiscal year 2005 NPS NAGPRA grant to: "host regional consultation meetings with 44 additional Native American tribes with a legacy of occupation in Colorado. The goal of the meetings is to develop a process for consultation and disposition of culturally unidentifiable Native American human remains and associated funerary objects removed from state and private lands in Colorado. Finally, discussants will consider the role of the NAGPRA Review Committee in recommending processes for the disposition of culturally unidentifiable Native American human remains and associated funerary objects (see 25 U.S.C. 3001§ 8(c)(5))."[80]

The plan was ambitious, but with clear goals in mind and strong partnerships, facilitated tribal consultations yielded a process that worked at least to some degree for all of the stakeholders and also worked within both state law and NAGPRA.

Development of the Process for Consultation, Transfer, and Reburial of Culturally Unidentifiable Native American Human Remains and Associated Funerary Objects Originating from Inadvertent Discoveries on Colorado State and Private Lands ("Process")

The Ute Mountain Ute Tribe and the Southern Ute Indian Tribe joined the grant partnership with the CCIA and HC to complete the grant objectives. For management purposes, it made sense to follow CCIA's suggestion to divide the state into three consultation regions: Great Plains, Southwest, and Basin and Plateau, following guidance from the National NAGPRA Review Committee to develop a regional solution.[81] Grant partners hosted three regional consultations, ultimately inviting representatives of forty-five additional tribes with a legacy of occupation in Colorado and with interests in the respective regions. This group included not only the tribes whose "aboriginal occupation" might be recognized by the criteria set forth in 43 CFR § 10.11(b)(2)(ii) for culturally unidentifiable human remains (CUI rule), but also those tribes that HC had identified through extensive research and previous consultations as having ancestral ties to Colorado.

During the course of consultations, extensive, sometimes intense, discussions ensued, but a draft of the "Process" emerged.[82] HC circulated it for comment amongst the consulting tribes by mail, email, and telephone, then revised it and circulated it again. Ultimately, an acceptable final draft was ready for presentation to the National NAGPRA Review Committee, no doubt the result of the extensive 2006 consultations and follow-up, but also because of the already-established relationships HC had from our previous NAGPRA work with tribes.

At the time the grant project was conceived of and awarded, Lieutenant Governor Jane Norton served as the chair of the CCIA, with Karen Wilde as the executive secretary. Mr. Knight was the NAGPRA representative of the Ute Mountain Ute Tribe and chair of the CCIA Reinterment Committee, assisted by Lynn Hartman, cultural resources administrator. Ambler was the HC NAGPRA liaison and Georgianna Contiguglia was the HC president and CEO. Clement Frost was the chairman of the Southern Ute Indian Tribe and Manuel Heart was the chairman of the Ute Mountain Ute Tribe during the development of the Process. Both chairmen served as signatories along with Norton and Continguglia. However, a number of personnel changes occurred prior to the first consultation. Ambler moved into the position of acting curator and Richard H. Wilshusen came on board as the NAGPRA liaison, bringing years of experience working with tribes, including service on the Advisory Council on Historic Preservation (ACHP). Ernest House Jr., a CCIA intern under Wilde and an enrolled member of the Ute Mountain Ute Tribe, assumed the position of executive secretary after Wilde's resignation. Additional changes occurred after consultations. The continued participation from many of the group's original members ensured that the process moved forward.

Representatives from HC, CCIA, and the two Colorado Ute tribes presented the Process before the National NAGPRA Review Committee for their November 3 and 4, 2006, meeting in Denver, Colorado. The delegation included Chairman Heart and Terry Knight (Ute Mountain Ute Tribe), Vice Chairman Matthew Box and Director of Legal Services Monte Mills (Southern Ute Indian Tribe), State Archaeologist Susan Collins, Ambler, and Heather Ahlstrom (the HC NAGPRA liaison after Wilshusen's departure), and House, Jr. (CCIA). The signed Process and letters of support from thirty-three consulting tribes were provided. The Review Committee conditionally approved the Process, pending formal responses from three tribes with traditional interests in Colorado who were recognized by the Indian Claims Commission: the Kiowa Tribe of Oklahoma, the Jicarilla Apache Nation, and the Apache Tribe of Oklahoma. [83]

The Apache Tribe of Oklahoma sent a letter of support immediately after the Review Committee meeting. The Jicarilla Apache Nation responded in August 2007, stating that the tribe was working on a similar project with the State of New Mexico and would not participate in consultation meetings with the State of Colorado at that time.[84] In February 2008, a delegation traveled to Oklahoma to present the Process to the Kiowa Business Committee (KBC) and request a formal response. The group consisted of recently elected Chairman Ernest House Sr. (Mr. House's father), Terry Knight (Ute Mountain Ute Tribe), House Jr. (CCIA), and the new HC NAGPRA liaison, Sheila Goff. Chairman Frost of the Southern Ute Tribe was unable to attend but sent a statement to submit to the KBC. The group appeared to be well received and was told that a response would be discussed during executive session. In April, a response arrived at HC, stating that the Kiowa Tribe of Oklahoma declined to approve the Process,[85] raising objections to some of the language in the document. This came as somewhat of a surprise, in that the Kiowa NAGPRA representative who consulted in 2006 had raised no objections. At present, HC continues dialogue with the Kiowa Tribe of Oklahoma, informing them of and inviting them to consult on all inadvertent discoveries on state and private land. The Kiowa representative participated in consultations in 2009.

With the requested responses in hand, the partners were ready to present before the Review Committee again. By this time, of the forty-seven consulting tribes, thirty-nine had provided letters of support (including the two signatories) and two had provided phone calls of support. One tribe objected to the Process and five tribes were non-responsive. Representatives from HC (Goff and Ambler, working under a new HC president, Edward C. Nichols), CCIA (House, Jr., speaking on behalf of the new lieutenant governor, Barbara O'Brien) and the Colorado Ute tribes (Knight, Chairman Frost, and House, Sr., who provided statements that were read) appeared before the Review Committee in De Pere, Wisconsin, on May 16, 2008, with the information. The Review Committee approved the Process, stipulating that implementation was contingent upon receiving a written letter of authorization to proceed from the Secretary of the Department of the Interior. The letter, dated September 23, 2008, arrived December 2, 2008, and was signed by Lyle Laverty, Assistant Secretary for Fish and Wildlife and Parks.[86] The efforts begun by Terry Knight, Sr. at the 1998 CCIA meeting ten years earlier had succeeded at last.

Success can be attributed to the work and commitment of all parties involved to resolve the issues brought forth by the Colorado Ute Tribes. In addition, success resulted because HC had created a robust NAGPRA program, dedicated to establishing new relationships between the agency and tribes while implementing the law. Consultation was, and remains, its cornerstone. In planning the Process consultations, HC drew upon its experience of having hosted well over 100 consultation meetings with fifty-five tribes by the time of the first regional consultation. Over the years, we have learned many lessons, including the importance of working with tribes from the very beginning in the development of the goals and agenda for a consultation meeting, and to make sure consultation meetings present a dialogue among participants. We have also often found it helpful to have facilitated meetings, in which participants establish guiding principles for respectful communication that encourage expression of all ideas. We strive to be transparent and consistent, and have written "NAGPRA Policies and Procedures for Consultation and Repatriation," which we share with tribes. Finally, we share information openly with delegates, pre- and post-meeting.

What the Process does

In general, the Process is a mechanism for the disposition of culturally unidentifiable (CUI) Native American human remains and associated funerary objects, developed prior to the 2010 promulgation of 43 CFR § 10.11 (often referred to as the "CUI

Rule"). It establishes a timeline HC agreed to follow, so that CUI remains are not held indefinitely by the agency. It includes two points repeatedly emphasized by tribal delegates during consultation. First, tribes prefer that inadvertently discovered remains be left undisturbed whenever possible.[87] Second, if remains must be removed, tribes prefer that all analyses be non-destructive.[88]

The Process is consistent with the Colorado State burial law in that when human remains are discovered, citizens are required to immediately notify the appropriate law enforcement official (police, sheriff, or coroner) and the coroner must examine the remains within 48 hours to determine if there is forensic concern. Failure to do so can result in being charged with a misdemeanor. If the remains are not associated with a crime, the coroner notifies the state archaeologist, who determines if they are over 100 years old and Native American.[89] If they are, the state archaeologist, the executive secretary of the CCIA, a representative of at least one of the Colorado Ute tribes, and the landowner meet to determine a course of action. The addition of a tribal representative to this decision-making step was requested by tribes during consultations and was incorporated into the Process.[90] The day that the state archaeologist is notified of the discovery is critical, because the Process outlines a series of tasks that must be completed within 100 days of the date the discovery is reported to the state archaeologist, as detailed in the following.

After notification, archaeologists from the Office of Archaeology and Historic Preservation, or a designee, begin to conduct a burial investigation. Under state burial law, there are two courses of action: leave the remains in situ or remove them.[91] The Process states that the preferred option is to leave the remains in situ, in response to tribal concerns expressed during consultations.[92] The Process provides an additional option—prompt reburial at greater depth close by, in cooperation with at least one of the Colorado Ute tribes.[93] Finally, if the safety of the remains is threatened or the landowner requests that they be removed, they are disinterred by Day 10, under both state law and the Process.[94] The executive secretary of the CCIA notifies tribes who have expressed interest in the region of the discovery before removal.[95]

If remains must be removed, under the Process, by Day 55, the state archaeologist must receive the findings of the investigation, including a physical anthropological analysis of the remains. The analysis minimally consists of age, sex, pathologies, and cause of death. Most importantly, as previously stated, the analysis is non-destructive, and remains or funerary objects will not be marked or altered in any way. By Day 70,[96] the state archaeologist reviews reports and either accepts them or requests more information. Based on the information available, by Day 75, the Department of Material Culture at HC identifies potentially affiliated tribes and begins the consultation process with them.[97] If there is insufficient evidence to identify potential affiliation, HC consults interested tribes in an effort to obtain additional information, and if unsuccessful, determines that the remains are culturally unidentifiable and prepares a Notice of Inventory Completion referencing the Process.[98]

By Day 100, HC must submit the notice for publication in the *Federal Register*.[99] Thirty-one days after publication, barring any disputes, the remains and associated funerary objects are available for transfer and reburial. Consulting tribes authorized the Southern Ute Tribe and the Ute Mountain Ute Tribe to act as the lead tribes in the transfer and reinterment of remains dispositioned under the Process, if no other tribes come forward.[100] HC, CCIA, and the two Colorado Ute tribes have worked with the Colorado Division of Parks and Outdoor Recreation and the Colorado Department of Natural Resources to identify state land in each of the three regions for reinterment so that individuals can be reinterred more closely to where they were removed. The location of the land is confidential. Culturally unidentifiable remains, associated funerary objects, soil matrix, and any other materials collected from the burial feature are reinterred.[101] The Colorado Department of Transportation has donated services to excavate burial trenches.

HC recognizes that sometimes the 100-day deadline cannot be met. For example, inclement weather may delay a burial investigation. Submitted reports may suggest more research, and so on. When a reasonable situation that may cause a delay presents itself, the Process allows for consultation between HC, CCIA, and the Colorado Ute tribes so that an acceptable new deadline can be established.[102]

HC makes every effort to ensure that all tribes with ancestral ties to Colorado have the opportunity to participate in the Process. Annually, the NAGPRA liaison verifies tribal NAGPRA representatives and contacts tribal leaders so that they can update their regional preferences for notification of discoveries, consultation under the Process, and reinterments. Tribes can express interest in one, two, or all regions. Any tribe who does not respond is still notified of all discoveries, consultations, and reinterments in all regions.

Implementation of the Process

In 2009, HC informed consulting tribes that the Department of the Interior had authorized the Process. HC presented information to tribal leaders and designated NAGPRA representatives about potential culturally unidentifiable Native American human remains and associated funerary objects originating from Colorado State and private lands currently in their custody. HC in collaboration with CCIA and the two Colorado Ute tribes invited tribes to consult by telephone to discuss the individuals and provide information that might lead to a determination of cultural affiliation. No additional information emerged.

HC submitted four Notices of Inventory Completion to NPS. They reported sixty-eight culturally unidentifiable individuals and sixty-three associated funerary objects to be dispositioned under the Process. Notices were published in the *Federal Register* on May 7, 2009.[103] They were not disputed and these individuals and associated funerary objects were transferred and reburied by the Southern Ute Indian Tribe and the Ute Mountain Ute Tribe. In 2012, four more notices were published for the disposition of an additional twenty-four individuals and forty-one associated funerary objects under the Process. These, too, have been transferred and reburied. Between 2009 and 2012, additional inadvertent discoveries on Colorado State and private lands occurred, but they were either left in situ, reburied promptly close by, or affiliated.

Another state that took up the challenge

It is important to acknowledge that Iowa has a lengthy history of addressing tribal concerns for the respectful and timely disposition of culturally unidentifiable Native American human remains and associated funerary objects originating from state and private lands, including the development of a state process. Long before the passage of NAGPRA, Iowa became the first state to respond with legislation to the unequal treatment of inadvertently discovered Native American human remains.[104] Iowa is the home prehistorically and historically to twenty-one tribes. In 1971, Maria Pearson (1932–2003), a Yankton Sioux activist, learned that inadvertent discoveries of Anglo and Native American remains were being treated differently by the Iowa Department of Transportation. The former were reburied quickly, while the latter were removed for study. She voiced her concerns to then-Governor Robert D. Ray, inciting controversy[105] and ultimately, in 1976, the Code of Iowa, the statutory laws of the state, was modified to include protection for ancient human remains (greater than 150 years of age) discovered on state and private lands.[106] The Office of the State Archaeologist (OSA) was charged with implementing the program and established the OSA Burials Program. Ongoing consultation was part of the 1976 legislation and is conducted with the Indian Advisory Council. Between 1977 and 1991, Iowa established four state cemeteries and the OSA was responsible for reinterment of ancient remains in the cemetery closest to the discovery site in collaboration with the Indian Advisory Council. Before the passage of NAGPRA, Iowa conducted regular reburials of Native American human remains once or twice a year and at least 2,000 individuals were reinterred.[107]

In 1990, the passage of NAGPRA presented Iowa with the challenge of how to comply with both state and federal law. Since the CUI rule had not yet been promulgated, Iowa could not continue with the disposition of culturally unidentifiable remains without appearing before the Review Committee for each disposition and reburial.

The OSA endeavored to develop a standing process, so that culturally unidentifiable Native American human remains could have timely disposition.[108] Discussions began in 2001, after waiting four years to accomplish one reburial under NAGPRA.[109] In 2004, with an NPS NAGPRA grant, Iowa held consultations with twenty-one federally recognized and one non-federally recognized tribe with historic interests in Iowa. Again, like Colorado, Iowa consulted more broadly than the criteria currently set forth in the CUI rule. Iowa and consulting tribes developed a draft process, focusing on reburial. They presented it before the Review Committee in 2006 for approval and recommendation to the Secretary of the Interior. The Review Committee provisionally authorized it contingent upon getting signatures from all twenty-one tribes. In 2008, Iowa received formal authorization from the Assistant Secretary for Fish and Wildlife and Parks in the Department of the Interior. The processes in both states are more similar than different.

43 CFR § 10.11 (CUI rule) arrives . . . where does that leave the Process?

On March 15, 2010, the final regulations for disposition of culturally unidentifiable Native American human remains were published in the *Federal Register*.[110] The new regulations altered the implementation of the Colorado Process. HC, CCIA, and the two Colorado Ute tribes met shortly after their promulgation to review the regulations and discuss their impact on the Process. Particularly relevant to the Process are the sections that stipulate with whom HC must consult for the disposition of culturally unidentifiable remains, and to whom HC must transfer control of culturally unidentifiable remains.

Under 10.11(b)(2) of the CUI rule, HC must consult with Indian tribes from whose tribal lands the remains were taken at the time of removal, and from whose aboriginal lands the remains were removed. The issue of tribal lands for the Process is moot, since the Process deals with inadvertent discoveries on state and private lands. With respect to aboriginal lands, the regulations state, "Aboriginal occupation may be recognized by a final judgment of the Indian Claims Commission or the United States Court of Claims, or treaty, act of Congress, or executive order."[111] As previously noted, in the development of the Process, HC identified forty-seven tribes as having ancestral ties to Colorado. This group includes not only tribes that are recognized by the documents listed in the CUI rule, but also tribes HC concluded had aboriginal interests in Colorado, based upon research and information learned in previous consultations. Under the Process, after HC receives remains resulting from inadvertent discoveries on state and private lands, the state archaeologist and the Department of Material Culture evaluate the information acquired during the burial investigation to determine if remains are potentially affiliated or unidentifiable. In the case of the former, consultation with potentially affiliated tribes begins. In the case of the latter, HC has twenty-five days to invite tribes from the larger group it has identified as having ancestral ties to Colorado to consult in efforts to obtain information that may lead to a determination of cultural affiliation. In summary, under the Process, HC goes beyond the requirements of the new regulations for consultation regarding culturally unidentifiable remains. There is no conflict between the Process and the new regulations.

Additionally, 10.11(c) of the CUI rule prioritizes to which tribes HC must offer to transfer control of the culturally unidentifiable remains. Again, it is based upon the area from which the human remains were removed. HC will not be handling remains removed from tribal lands under the Process, as previously stated. The next priority, then, is the tribe or tribes considered "aboriginal" to the land where remains were removed. Criteria for being defined as aboriginal is based upon the same criteria in the law that was quoted above, and for Colorado may include the Navajo Nation, the Jicarilla Apache, the Kiowa Tribe of Oklahoma, the Comanche Tribe, the Apache, the Cheyenne and Arapaho Tribes of Oklahoma, the Northern Cheyenne Tribes, and the Northern Arapaho Tribes,[112] depending upon the location of the discovery. According to 10.11(c)(2), if none of the "aboriginal" tribes agrees to accept control, there are other possibilities for transfer: to other Indian tribes; with a recommendation from the Secretary of the Interior, to a non-federally recognized tribe; or reburial under state or other law. Note that the Process is just that—a process that is consistent with state law, but is not part of state or federal law.

What are the options under NAGPRA for HC and the Process? It would appear that if a discovery occurs on adjudicated land, HC will need to first offer to transfer control to the appropriate aboriginal tribe(s). HC has been advised by David Tarler, National NAGPRA Program,[113] as follows:

> The promulgation of the regulation at 43 CFR § 10.11 does not force the "aboriginal land" and "tribal land" tribes to accept the transfer of human remains. Those tribes are free to furnish you with a document indicating that, until further notice, they do not agree to accept control of culturally unidentifiable Native American human remains that have been removed from their aboriginal lands or from lands that at the time of their removal were their tribal lands. If none of these "tribal land" or "aboriginal land" tribes agrees to accept control of culturally unidentifiable humans remains, then consistent with the "Process", you may transfer control of the remains to the Southern Ute Indian Tribe of the Southern Ute Indian Reservation and the Ute Mountain Ute Tribe of the Ute Mountain Reservation on the 31st day following publication of a Notice of Inventory Completion in the *Federal Register.*

If the discovery does not occur on adjudicated land, HC can move forward per the Process.

Since the promulgation of the CUI rule, there has been only one inadvertent discovery on adjudicated land in Colorado. History Colorado is midway through the consultation process with the tribes on whose aboriginal land the discovery occurred; so far, half of those tribes have indicated that they will not accept control and prefer that the Process be followed.

Conclusion

The Colorado Historical Society did not know where its compliance efforts would lead when it began its work to meet the 1993 deadline for summaries and 1995 deadline for inventories. We got organized and developed policies and procedures for collections, including those subject to NAGPRA. We acquired a tremendous amount of information about our collections, not only from the resources on hand but certainly from all the tribal representatives who have reviewed our collections. We improved our care and handling procedures, specifically with respect to human remains and cultural items in response to tribal concerns. While trying to understand the intersection between state law and federal law, we improved our relationships with other departments in our institution. The trust relationships we built with tribes while engaging in NAGPRA projects have helped us to better understand our collections and improve our exhibits and education programs. Finally, we built strong relationships with state and federal agencies that assist us with our work and vice versa. It has been a challenging, rewarding journey, and it's far from over.

Notes

1   25 U.S.C. § 3001–13. At 25 U.S.C. 3002(8) "museum" means any institution or State or local government agency (including any institution of higher learning) that receives Federal funds and has possession of, or control over, Native American cultural items. Such term does not include the Smithsonian Institution or any other Federal agency.

2   43 C.F.R. §10.9(f).

3   *The Colorado Magazine: A Centennial Legacy* 57 (annual 1980), preface.

4   Maxine Benson, "Bancroft to Smiley," *The Colorado Magazine: A Centennial Legacy* 57 (1980), 2.

5   Frank McNitt, *Richard Wetherill: Anasazi.* Revised edition. (Albuquerque: University of New Mexico Press, 1966), 323–324.

6   Ernest House, Sr., Chairman, Ute Mountain Ute Tribe, personal communication, Ute Mountain Tribal Park, October 3, 2009.

7   McNitt, *Richard Wetherill*, 323. Interestingly, Charlie Mason asserts that "the Indians occupying this portion of the Ute Reservation were not friendly and made it unpleasant for all who came into their country, so no one thought it worthwhile to explore the side canyons."

8   "Catalogue of Ancient Aztec Relics From the Mancos Canyon, La Plata County, South-Western Colorado," *The Durango Herald*, 1889.

9   McNitt, *Richard Wetherill*, 34–37. McNitt points out that the Wetherills originally offered the sale of the collections as "Aztec Relics" in the *Mancos Times* in September, 1894. Apparently, Wetherill was capitalizing on the public concept that the cliff dwellings had been built by the Aztecs, even though he thought otherwise.

10   McNitt, *Richard Wetherill.*

11   *The Weekly Republican*, May 30, 1889.

12   Benson, "Bancroft to Smiley," 10.

13   McNitt, *Richard Wetherill*, 43.

14   S. Gillis, "The Wetherill-Mesa Verde Collection of the State Historical Society of Colorado" (unpublished manuscript, State Historical Society of Colorado, 1983).

15   Polly Welts Kaufman, *National Parks and the Woman's Voice: A History* (Albuquerque: University of New Mexico Press, 2006), 27–30.

16   See "The 1972 Convention Concerning the Protection of the World Cultural and Natural Heritage" of the United Nations Education, Scientific and Cultural Organization. Under the Convention, World Heritage sites are recognized as having "outstanding universal value."

17   See Notice of Inventory Completion for Native American Human Remains and Associated Funerary Objects in the Possession of the Colorado Historical Society, Denver, CO. 69 *Fed. Reg.* 68162-68169 (November 23, 2004).

18   Gillis, "The Wetherill-Mesa Verde Collection."

19   LeRoy R. Hafen, "History of the State Historical Society of Colorado Part III," *The Colorado Magazine*, October 1954, 37–80. Hafen points out that Deane was a private collector, and not a scholar. However, he was well connected with state legislators, and was able to lobby effectively for the sale of his collection.

20   16 U.S.C. § 431–433.

21   On March 21, 2008, HC received a letter from the Bureau of Land Management (BLM) requesting transfer of the Cannonball Collection back to the care of the BLM as part of its efforts to consolidate BLM collections held by outlying museums. That transfer was accomplished in September, 2009, after a deaccession recommendation supported by a copy of the original permit located in the National Archives.

22   Richard H. Wilshusen, "Archaeological Ceramics Collections at the Colorado Historical Society: Their Past Histories and Future Uses in Exhibits, Research, and Instruction," 2004.

23   Benson, "Bancroft to Smiley," 16–18. See also Jean A. Jeancon, *Archaeological Research in the Northeastern San Juan Basin of Colorado During the Summer of 1921* (Denver: Press of the Webb-Kennedy Publishing Co., 1922); Jean A. Jeancon and Frank H.H. Roberts, "Further Archaeological Research in the Northeastern San Juan Basin of Colorado, During the Summer of 1922: The Pagosa-Piedra Region," *The Colorado Magazine*, November 1923, 12-28; Jean A. Jeancon and Frank H. H. Roberts, "Further Archaeological Research in the Northeastern San Juan Basin of Colorado, During the Summer of 1922: The Pagosa-Piedra Region," *The Colorado Magazine*, September 1924, 260–276.

24   Phil Karsh and Georgianna Contiguglia. Letter from the chairman and president in "125 Years of History: The Colorado Historical Society's 2003–2004 Annual Report" (unpublished manuscript, the Colorado Historical Society, 2004): 2. The "split" from natural history at this time is not well documented. Importantly, many of the "natural history" collections (including, possibly, ethnographic and archaeological collections) went to the Denver Museum of Natural History (founded in 1900, it is now known as the Denver Museum of Nature &

Science). The impetus for the split and division of those collections is an important event deserving of additional research.

25 Katherine D. Kane, "Museums and Archaeology: The Collecting Tradition of the Colorado Historical Society and the Potential for Research" (master's thesis, University of Colorado, Boulder, 1985).

26 Hafen, "History of the State Historical Society," 44–45.

27 Virginia Pullen and Dean Krakel, "The Mellinger Archaeological Collection," *The Colorado Magazine*, January 1952, 75–78.

28 C.R.S. 1963: § 131-12-1.

29 C.R.S. § 24-80-403.

30 James Hummert, "The Human Osteological Collection of the Colorado State Historical Society" (unpublished manuscript, Colorado Historical Society, 1981).

31 Also known as Minimum Number of Individuals. See Tim White, *Human Osteology*. Second Edition. (San Diego: Academic Press, 1999), 291–292.

32 C.R.S. § 24-80-1301-1305.

33 8 C.C.R. § 1504-7.

34 C.R.S. § 24-80-1301-1304.

35 C.R.S. § 24-80-1302(f).

36 25 U.S.C. § 300-13.

37 See the "Statement of the American Association of Museums, the Association of American Universities, the National Conference of State Historic Preservation Officers, the Native American Rights Fund, the Society for American Archaeology and the Society For Historical Archaeology on Funding for the Grant Program Established in the Native American Graves Protection and Repatriation Act (P.L. 101-601)" (unpublished manuscript presented to the Subcommittee on Interior of the Committee on Appropriations, U.S. House of Representatives, February 26, 1992).

38 Bonnichsen v. United States, 367 F. 3d 864 (9th Cir., 2004).

39 S. Terry Childs, "The Curation Crisis," *Federal Archaeology* 7(4) (1995): 11–15.

40 Tina Nepstad-Thornberry et al., "Addressing the Curation Crisis in Colorado: An Assessment for the Executive Committee of the Colorado Council of Professional Archaeologists," (unpublished manuscript, University of Colorado, Boulder, 2002).

41 43 C.F.R. § 10.8.

42 23 U.S.C. 3003 § 6.

43 43 C.F.R. § 10.9.

44 25 U.S.C. 3003 § 5.

45 43 C.F.R. §10.9(c).

46 See 43 C.F.R. § 10.8.

47 See 43 C.F.R. § 10.8 (b) (ii) C.F.R. § 10.8.

48 C.R.S. § 24-44-101-108.

49 C.R.S. § 24-44-103.

50 See Roger C. Echo-Hawk, "Kara Katit Pakutu: Exploring the Origins of Native America in Anthropology and Oral Traditions." (master's thesis, University of Colorado, Boulder, 1994).

51 43 C.F.R. §10.9.

52 Roger C. Echo-Hawk, "Indentured Spirits: A Census of Human Remains and Inventory of Associated Funerary Objects at the Colorado Historical Society" (unpublished manuscript, Colorado Historical Society, November 1995).

53   As new information has come to light, the "Inventory" has also changed. In 1981, James Hummert disarticulated many of the sets of human remains in the collection as part of his research on the osteological collection (see Hummert, "The Human Osteological Collection"). When compiling inventories as required by NAGPRA, HC found that an accurate count of the number of individuals in its collections was impacted, because parts of individuals were stored separately. HC used NPS NAGPRA funds (08-00-GP-231) to hire a physical anthropologist to rearticulate the remains. Once skeletal elements were reunited, HC found that fewer individuals were represented than had been originally reported in the "Census" and a revision was submitted to NPS.

54   C.R.S. 24-80 § 1301–1305.

55   OSAC publication #1308b as listed at http://www.coloradohistory-oahp.org/publications/pubs/1308b.pdf, revised January 2004.

56   43 C.F.R. § 10.9. This provision of NAGPRA is distinct from 43 C.F.R. 10.4, which applies only to inadvertent discoveries of Native American human remains and associated funerary objects on federal and tribal lands. When inadvertent discoveries of Native American human remains were made on state and private lands in Colorado and the state archaeologist made a decision about disposition without consulting potentially affiliated tribes, the state made a unilateral decision to take possession and control in the same way that museums do.

57   43 C.F.R. § 10.2(3)(i).

58   43 C.F.R. § 10.2(3)(ii).

59   Susan Collins to Karen Rogers, "Legal Review of LLS No. 01-061.01" (unpublished interoffice memorandum, Colorado Historical Society, October 22, 2001).

60   C.R.S. 24-80 § 1304.

61   43 C.F.R. 10.9 (d)(2).

62   43 C.F.R. § 10.11 (1990).

63   8 C.C.R. § 1504.13.

64   43 C.F.R. § 10.8–10.12.

65   "Colorado Tribal Contacts List" (unpublished manuscript on file, Department of Material Culture, Colorado Historical Society, updated 2010).

66   "Colorado Commission of Indian Affairs and The State Historical Society of Colorado: Memorandum of Understanding" (unpublished manuscript, Colorado Commission of Indian Affairs, 1999).

67   NPS NAGPRA Grant 08-99-GP-197.

68   43 C.F.R. § 10.14(e).

69   "Ancient Peoples of the Rocky Mountain Front Range and Eastern Plains of Colorado: A Symposium." (unpublished transcripts, Colorado Historical Society, October 10 and 11, 2000). Especially important here was the discussion about the "preponderance of evidence" and prima facie evidence. "Reasonable" evidence, lacking evidence to the contrary, can constitute a "preponderance" all by itself.

70   Roger Echo-Hawk, "Keepers of Culture: Repatriating Cultural Items under the Native American Graves Protection and Repatriation Act," (unpublished manuscript, Denver Art Museum, 2002), 74–82.

71   Notice of Inventory Completion for Native American Human Remains and Associated Funerary Objects in The Possession of the Colorado Historical Society, Denver, CO. 66 Fed. Reg. 10906-10909 (February 20, 2001) and Notice of Inventory Completion for Native American Human Remains and Associated Funerary Objects in The Possession of the Colorado Historical Society, Denver, CO. 67 Fed. Reg. 45992-45994 (July 11, 2002).

72   43 C.F.R. § 10.12.

73 LLS No. 01-0161.01.

74 See SB04-066 in *Senate Journal*, 64th General Assembly, State of Colorado, Second Regular Session, January 8, 2004.

75 "Our concerns over Colorado's Inadvertent discovery law," correspondence to Attorney General Ken Salazar from the Ute Mountain Ute Tribal Council and the Southern Ute Indian Tribal Council (June 16, 2004).

76 Ibid.

77 Susan Collins and Georgianna Contiguglia correspondence to The Honorable Jane Norton (October 4, 2004).

78 Jane Norton correspondence to Georgianna Contiguglia (January 14, 2005).

79 "Draft Recommendations Regarding the Disposition of Culturally Unidentifiable Human Remains and Associated Funerary Objects", 60 *Fed. Reg.* 32163-32165 (June 20, 1995).

80 08-05-GP393, "Native American Graves Protection and Repatriation Act FY 2005 Grant Proposal," (History Colorado, March, 2005).

81 "Draft Recommendations Regarding the Disposition of Culturally Unidentifiable Human Remains and Associated Funerary Objects," 60 *Fed. Reg.* 32163-32165 (June 20, 1995); "Draft Recommendations Regarding the Disposition of Culturally Unidentifiable Human Remains and Associated Funerary Objects," 61 *Fed. Reg.* 43071-43073 (August 20, 1996); Notice of Draft Principles of Agreement Regarding Disposition of Culturally Unidentifiable Human Remains-Extended Date for Comments, 64 *Fed. Reg.* 41135-41136 (July 29, 1999); and "Recommendations Regarding the Disposition of Culturally Unidentifiable Native American Human Remains," 65 *Fed. Reg.* 36462-36463 (June 8, 2000).

82 "The Process for Consultation, Transfer, and Reburial of Culturally Unidentifiable Native American Human Remains and Associated Funerary Objects Originating from Inadvertent Discoveries on Colorado State and Private Lands." (on file, History Colorado).

83 "Indian Land Areas Judicially Established 1978, Map Index," http://www.nps.gov/history/nagpra/DOCUMENTS/ClaimsMAP.htm. Accessed July 8, 2011.

84 Letter from President Levi Peseta to Ernest House Jr., on file at HC, dated August 2, 2007.

85 Letter from Dewey Tsonetokoy Sr. to Sheila Goff, on file at HC, dated April 4, 2008.

86 Letter from Lyle Laverty to Edward C. Nichols and Barbara O'Brien on file at HC, dated September 23, 2008.

87 "Process," 2B.

88 C.R.S. § 24-80-1302 (1-4).

89 C.R.S. § 24-80-1302 (1-4).

90 "Process," 2B.

91 C.R.S. § 24-80-1302 (4b).

92 "Process," 2B.

93 "Process," 2C1, 2D1.

94 C.R.S. § 24-80-1302, 4(d) and "Process," 2D.

95 "Process," 2A.

96 "Process," 2D (1-4), 2E.

97 "Process," 3A.

98 "Process," 3B, 4A.

99 "Process," 4A.

100 "Process," 4B, 5A.

101 "Process," 5G.

102 "Process," 2D2.

103 Notice of Inventory Completion: Colorado Historical Society, Denver, CO. 74 *Fed. Reg.* 21385-21388 (May 9, 2009); Ibid, 21391-21393; Ibid., 21393-21395; and Ibid., 21395-21397.

104 "Native American Graves Protection and Repatriation Act," http://en.wikipedia.org/wiki/NAGPRA. Accessed July 8, 2011.

105 "Native." Some credit her with motivating the writing of NAGPRA. http://en.wikipedia.org/wiki/NAGPRA. Accessed July 8, 2011.

106 Code of Iowa, chapters 263B and 716.5.

107 Native American Graves Protection and Repatriation Review Committee, Thirty-second Meeting Minutes, Juneau, AK, (May 30-31, 2006), 18. Available: http://www.nps.gov/history/nagpra/REVIEW/meetings/MINUTES.HTM.

108 Notice of Inventory Completion: Office of the State Archaeologist, University of Iowa, Iowa City, IA and State Historical Society of Iowa, Des Moines, IA. 73 *Fed. Reg.* 59665-5967 (October 9, 2008).

109 Native American Graves Protection and Repatriation Review Committee. Thirty-Second Meeting Minutes, Juneau, AK, (May 30-31, 2006), 18. Available: http://www.nps.gov/nagpra/REVIEW/INDEX.HTM.

110 43 C.F.R. Part 10, 75 *Fed. Reg.* 12378-12405 (March 15, 2010).

111 43 C.F.R. § 10.11(b)(2).

112 "Indian Land Areas Judicially Established 1978, Map Index," http://www.nps.gov/history/nagpra/DOCUMENTS/ClaimsMAP.htm. Accessed July 8, 2011.

113 David Tarler, designated federal officer, National NAGPRA Program, email message to Sheila Goff, HC NAGPRA liaison, July 13, 2010.

Chapter 9
Moving Forward from the Last Twenty Years: Finding a New Balance

SHANNON KELLER O'LOUGHLIN

The twentieth anniversary of the Native American Graves Protection and Repatriation Act (NAGPRA) presented us with a moment to evaluate the past two decades of its implementation and an opportunity to reconsider how we move forward. I would like to take this moment (and this chapter) to describe the planning for, and underlying dilemmas encountered at, the NAGPRA at 20 Symposium held at the George Washington University campus in Washington, DC, November 15 and 16, 2010, and how that symposium reinvigorated my understanding of how important education and activism are for the future implementation of NAGPRA into the powerful legislation it was meant to be.

The NAGPRA at 20 Symposium

NAGPRA celebrated its twentieth anniversary on November 16, 2010. A group of unusual suspects were invited by the National NAGPRA Program to plan the act's twenty-year anniversary conference, the NAGPRA at 20 Symposium. The planning committee was assigned the daunting task of creating an agenda of panels and presenters to mark this important moment in NAGPRA history, as well as an important moment in federal Indian law and policy.

The NAGPRA at 20 planning committee could have been nicknamed (depending on the particular moment we were consumed with our planning activities during the one and a half years prior to the actual event) the "lack of planning" committee, the "what the hell are we getting into" committee, the "can you please tell her to stop it" committee, the "we must plan the impossible and revolutionize the world" committee, and other things that I shall not repeat here (but I will if you ask me in person). We were all excited by the opportunity we had before us, but not always sure how to get there.

The individuals who made up the planning committee are not famous (except maybe for Professor Joe Watkins[1]). I don't believe there were any particular reasons we were chosen by the National NAGPRA Program, but it likely had something to do with the fact that we had extra time to spare . . . because we are not famous. And surely, the National NAGPRA Program knew us to be a group of hard-working individuals from diverse backgrounds involved in various aspects of the "practice" of NAGPRA. The members of the planning committee included:

- Patricia Capone, associate curator at the Peabody Museum of Archaeology and Ethnology at Harvard University
- Sangita Chari, grants and outreach coordinator at the National NAGPRA Program
- Chip Colwell-Chanthaphonh, PhD, curator and NAGPRA officer at the Denver Museum of Nature & Science
- Clay Dumont, Klamath, and a professor of sociology at San Francisco State University. Clay resigned from the planning committee during the course of our planning
- Eric Hemenway, an Anishinaabe from Little Traverse Bay Bands of Odawa Indians, the NAGPRA specialist for the Little Traverse Bay Bands, and a member of the NAGPRA Review Committee
- Jaime Lavallee, Muskeg Lake Cree and the notice coordinator at the National NAGPRA Program
- Kelly Jackson, member of the Lac du Flambeau Band of Lake Superior, and NAGPRA coordinator and tribal historic preservation officer for her tribe. Kelly resigned in the course of our planning
- J. Kehaulani Kauanui, associate professor of American studies at Wesleyan University, who joined the planning committee a few months after we had our first meetings and resigned at the same time as Clay
- Emily Palus, national curator and NAGPRA coordinator for the Bureau of Land Management, who resigned in the course of our planning
- Joe Watkins, a citizen of the Choctaw Nation of Oklahoma, and director of the Native American Studies Program at the University of Oklahoma
- Fred York, regional anthropologist from the National Park Service, Pacific West Region
- Me. I was the attorney in the bunch, and the other citizen of the Choctaw Nation of Oklahoma

Our diverse experiences "practicing" NAGPRA and the reasons we were chosen for this task were not as important as what we were collectively trying to do with this wonderful opportunity and moment in history. We all truly wanted to facilitate something great, exciting, and poignant. In one of our first meetings, we were provided a draft purpose to engage our thinking and planning. It was basic and retrospective: Consider the impact of NAGPRA on Indian Nations, federal agencies, and museums and how NAGPRA has altered the relationships between these parties, and describe what issues NAGPRA has raised over the last twenty years. Of course, the question that always arises when you talk about NAGPRA was also present: How do we balance the Native American and Native Hawaiian perspectives with the institutional perspectives in an appropriate way?

Let's talk about balance for a minute because it is this "balance-of-interests" rhetoric that NAGPRA practitioners have most definitely contributed to NAGPRA over the last twenty years. The passage of the NAGPRA statute on November 16, 1990, was significant to Indian[2] people because it represented (to Indian people at least) a new hope and new public consensus about Native American and Native Hawaiian[3] peoples.[4] No longer would Native peoples'[5] graves be treated differently than a non-Native grave! Finally, Native peoples could find comfort (or so we thought) in the fact that our unmarked graves would no longer be stripped and our ancestors placed in boxes for study! After hundreds of years of theft and forced relinquishment of ancestors, funerary objects, sacred objects, and objects of cultural patrimony, these beautiful and sacred items would return to their rightful places, to rest and to heal and fortify the people as these special objects were meant to do, and as our ancestors had instructed. We celebrated: "The purpose of [NAGPRA] is to provide for the protection of Native American graves and the repatriation of Native American remains and cultural patrimony."[6] We thought the purpose was simple and its meaning understood by all.

However, institutions interpreted and acted on the law much differently than Native peoples expected. You see, the way NAGPRA is structured, institutions have the power to make all determinations of cultural affiliation and whether they will repatriate. By leaving all of the decision-making to institutions,[7] NAGPRA has effectively granted the party with the pecuniary interest in Native peoples' ancestors and objects the ability to delay and obfuscate the protection of Native peoples' graves and the repatriation of ancestors and cultural objects. Native peoples did not understand that institutions would use this power to frustrate the purpose of NAGPRA. Nor did we fully appreciate the creative ways institutions would frustrate the purpose of NAGPRA.[8] The burden of the institutions' decisions, or lack thereof, has fallen unilaterally on Native peoples who still must fight for the purpose of NAGPRA as written in the law.

Institutions and Native peoples therefore have a fierce competition of interests. Three people cemented that competition: Judge Ruggero J. Aldisert, Judge Susan P. Graber, and Judge Ronald M. Gould. These three demonstrated this competition of interests in the well-known case *Bonnichsen v. United States*, stating: "NAGPRA

§ 3002(a) was not intended *merely to benefit American Indians*, but rather *to strike a balance* between the needs of scientists, educators, and historians on the one hand, and American Indians on the other [emphasis added]."[9] Though the statement was in a simple footnote and unrelated to the judges' decision (and not at all a part of the statutory or regulatory language of NAGPRA), it stuck, and boy, is it sticky.

Courts often make decisions by weighing the interests of adversary parties to determine where the burdens and benefits lie in order to resolve a legal dilemma. If the weighing of interests is fair and the decision-maker understands the context of the facts, then this method can be a very healing way of resolving conflicts. Adversary parties are forced into compromise for the betterment of the parties and society. However, competing interests can be so divergent that compromise is unthinkable for both sides. Where interests are skewed, the facts are not understood, and the interests are incommensurable, balance cannot be achieved. Unfortunately, this is the "actual state of things"[10] when institutional property interests are weighed against the cultural and traditional values of Native peoples. And, as when courts have reviewed NAGPRA decisions made by museums and science, institutional interests always win.[11] NAGPRA is not so simple, and not at all what Native peoples expected.

So, back to the symposium planning. I was strongly wedded to the possibility that the symposium could provide an opportunity for all of us to explore whether a new vision of NAGPRA was possible. Would it be possible to create a shared vision of NAGPRA that did not rely on an attempt to balance incommensurable interests? Was there some other magic that we could conjure that would make the practice of NAGPRA simple, and its interpretation undeniable? I looked at the challenge, and my fellow conference planners, with hope that we could find a new vision for NAGPRA.

The planning committee decided that the symposium needed to provide a method for interaction and dialogue, giving participants and panelists an opportunity to communicate their stories and a dedicated time to be forward-looking. We brainstormed an agenda and a vision statement. The symposium would be titled "NAGPRA at 20: Conversations about the Past, Present and Future of NAGPRA," and would present an agenda that remembered and acknowledged our past, critically evaluated our current practice, and then would draw particular focus and effort into (what I hoped would be) a new dialogue that had the potential to lead us into a productive future. An early draft of our vision statement read, "'NAGPRA at 20: Conversations about the Past, Present and Future of NAGPRA' seeks to create an all-inclusive forum in which indigenous peoples and institutions (museums, universities, federal agencies, and other institutions) can have critical conversations and transparent dialogue . . . 'NAGPRA at 20' committee members sincerely hope that this conference will motivate the creation of a shared vision between Indian Nations and public institutions and continue the healing that NAGPRA was intended to promote."

We all had large and good intentions. Carrying out those intentions, however, was not as easy as brainstorming a vision statement. Our planning committee had its share of conflict, which was apropos considering that the deadlocks we would find ourselves in as we planned the symposium mirrored the inability to balance the incommensurable interests of Native peoples and institutions. At the same time, we agreed that we wanted to use the forum of the symposium to find a path out of this deadlock.

But of course, the deadlock that occurred with the planning committee is what has happened to all of us that work with NAGPRA. This deadlock of interests between institutions and Native peoples has left the purposes of "protection" and "repatriation" (as the act is titled) empty, and all of us completely useless to do good. If you are a NAGPRA practitioner, then you have probably heard the stories and gossip surrounding NAGPRA and its implementation: NATHPO and the National NAGPRA Program can't get along; Indian nations cannot find resolution among themselves and argue in public about ownership of ancestors and cultural items; Native Hawaiian organizations argue with one another about the same things; the Government Accountability Office (GAO) investigates the National NAGPRA Program; and various archaeological associations use their financial resources to lobby Congress and influence decision-makers. Are these the "protection" and "repatriation" activities that promote the purpose of NAGPRA? Throughout our daily NAGPRA practice, our interactions with one another are often politicized and adversarial. Indian nations have had to hire lawyers to be successful on basic NAGPRA repatriation claims (ask me how I know). How can the purposes of "protection" and "repatriation" cause so much conflict and lack of balance?

Thus, the large and good intentions of our planning committee, to provide a forum to develop a shared vision of our future, were not fulfilled, in my opinion. We were stuck within our incommensurable interests and we could not maintain a shared vision and unity among ourselves to push each other out of the status quo. I suppose you could say we caved in to the comfortable rubric of our positions. Instead of working through the discomfort, some of our planning committee members vocally resigned from the committee and others quietly fell away. But the planning progressed, and for the last three or four months prior to the event date, we all were just trying to get the event organized in a way that was useful. Ultimately, it was easier to fall into the known rhetoric and old habit than to take a risk and have faith that something better would appear out of our discomfort. I kept my fingers crossed that by some miracle or epiphany a new spark of a hopeful future would be activated in the process.

And there was controversy otherwise. In the planning of the conference, many Native traditional speakers and Native leaders could not attend because there was not enough funding to get them to Washington, DC. So, the symposium lacked a full regional representation of Native leadership and Native NAGPRA practitioners. Some of us were also criticized for wanting to pull controversial Native peoples into the symposium as speakers; others on the planning committee were not able to get their controversial museum or archaeology speakers in the schedule because those speakers had boycotted the symposium. There were rumors that individuals from the museum and scientific communities were boycotting the symposium because they felt an equal balance of interests would not be presented. I wish those who boycotted would have attended, so that their concerns would have risen above more than just gossip. But of course, the symposium was full of various egos on both sides, many of whom I respect for their decades of work creating the path in which we are all embedded.

It was so easy for us to forget that we were trying to rise above the controversial and embedded status quo and create sessions that endeavored to pull out something new, whatever that was. We were stuck to the middle road, trying to balance opinions, positions, and expectations. In my opinion, we missed the mark—and an opportunity.

However, there was one Native leader whose words and actions continue to inspire me, who spoke during the "Traditional Knowledge as Evidence" panel. Richard (Rick) Hill, Tuscarora, and coordinator of the Indigenous Knowledge Center in Six Nations Territory in Canada, said that he used to argue about the ethics and morality of NAGPRA, then he realized it was a waste of his time, that it has not worked out very well for us anyway. He said the bottom line is that we believe different things. For me, the simple acceptance that we believe different things, instead of forcing ourselves to compromise our responsibilities and beliefs, is a starting point for a new vision. The second phase is to recognize our differences.

Rick made it clear that traditional knowledge is still not recognized as valuable in balancing the weight of these competing interests. He said, "If I pour my heart out to you, if I open up this book of spiritual knowledge for you to judge whether it's valid or not, it is just another form of victimization and colonization," and he was not going to do it anymore. Rick talked about the need to balance Western science's new and ever-changing theoretical knowledge with old indigenous knowledge—biology has learned to do it to understand how to protect our dwindling resources; medicine has learned to do it to find ways to promote a healthy body. For some reason, we have not been able to do it in NAGPRA. Rick discussed the importance of the treaty relationship and how it taught respect and how to resolve disputes between cultures. He said many powerful things, but in the end, it came down to a simple proscription: "The end goal is about making this right. Don't take things that don't belong to you, apologize, and don't do it again. We can't rest in the injury of the past. We have to move forward and do the right thing."[12]

The symposium ended with the final session "The Future of NAGPRA." I was unsure what anyone was left with after the final session, but relieved somewhat that the symposium could be forgotten through a diabetic coma from overindulgence in cupcakes and champagne at the U.S. Department of the Interior building (not quite the appropriate food groups for us tribal peoples) that followed the final session. I was sad and embarrassed that my hopes to encourage dialogue for a new future of NAPGRA did not materialize. Is the opportunity gone?

What did you think about the symposium?

There were two different surveys completed during the symposium. The responses provided evidence of the audience's expectations for the symposium and of NAGPRA. Namely (do I have to repeat it?), that NAGPRA requires a "balancing of interests" between Native peoples and institutions. The first survey was a general evaluation survey given in the registration packet for the symposium asking the surveyor to rate whether his or her expectations were met and allowing the surveyor to provide other written feedback—in general, and for each specific panel. Out of over 250 attendees, forty-one evaluations were returned. The second survey was provided in the session titled "Strengthening the Purpose of NAGPRA: Exploring Ways to Increase Accountability" and requested narrative answers to specific questions.

The first session of the symposium, "The Beginning: Remembering Our Past," featured Suzan Shown Harjo[13] and David Hurst Thomas.[14] One survey responder noted: "Perhaps the only session that exhibited any balance whatsoever." For the session "NAGPRA in the Courts and in Practice," another survey responder stated: "There was a precision of language and ideas that was absent from all other sessions. It provided an interesting background and perspective that I've never heard before. That said, still heavily skewed towards tribes."

For the "Science as Evidence" panel: "I thought this session would discuss the benefits of scientific research used in conjunction with traditional knowledge. But it seemed as though the speakers were more concerned with saying why science is not good to help with repatriations." And, in response to the last panel of the symposium, "The Future of NAGPRA," a responder said, "should have been more balanced."

Other survey commenters provided the following specific feedback:

> You achieved a very good balance between Native and Anglo views, no small feat. Granted, the Anglo crowd is the choir, but (hopefully) are the future of their disciplines, whether anthropology, museum studies, or law. This was the best meeting/conference/symposium that I have attended in a very long time.

> Participants were more than cheerleaders for National NAGPRA. Major voices for science and museum organizations were absent completely. Most museum participants represented smaller museums with

far less experience than those of larger museums. Also, little diversity of opinion—not a real forum for discussion of complex issues but the advancing of an agenda.

"The AAM [American Association of Museums] or other prominent museum organizations should have been included on the program."

"Appreciated multiple perspectives, hopeful and optimistic attitudes."

"I work with NAGPRA daily at an institution that knows and respects NAGPRA as the hard-won compromise it was. These sessions did not demonstrate such knowledge or respect for the law as it is written, but for some ill-defined 'spirit' of the law—a concept and sentiment entirely removed from the framer's intents (ask them!). Events such as this one do nothing other than provide a 'pep rally' for those who share this ill-conceived view of the law."

"Taught the importance of respect and building trustful, lasting relationships."

"More balance for 'NAGPRA at 25' please."

It seems from this small sample, the expectation and even demand from the audience was that a balance of interests must be shown between Native peoples and institutions. In fact, some of the responses reflect how polarizing and inflexible this expectation can be.

The second survey for "Strengthening the Purpose of NAGPRA" session on the last day of the symposium resulted in twenty-one surveys returned. The responders included an equal mixture of Native American individuals, museum professionals and archaeologists, and students. The survey asked four specific questions:

1. Who benefits from NAGPRA and what are those benefits?
2. Who is harmed by NAGPRA and what are those harms?
3. How can we improve accountability among repatriation participants?
4. What do you want to say to the National NAGPRA Program that will improve accountability among repatriation participants, in the National NAGPRA Program, and/or with NAGPRA as a law?

Responses to this survey once again demonstrated how deeply embedded the balance-of-interests rhetoric represents the way we understand NAGPRA. There were also some compelling previews of a potential future. Most of the responders answered questions one and two about harms and benefits similarly, stating that Native Nations, as well as institutions, were benefited and harmed by NAGPRA for reasons that fall within the spectrum of Native peoples' human rights to museum property rights. In response to questions three and four regarding accountability, some responders noted a need for something beyond NAGPRA that would provide a universal concept or umbrella, under which we could all come together. Interestingly, a couple of these responders referred to this universal concept as stronger enforcement mechanisms and penalty provisions. In other words, the only way to improve accountability was to increase enforcement against those who have not yet complied with the provisions of NAGPRA.

The students provided the most compelling previews for the future. One student in particular recognized that the balance-of-interests rhetoric will never work productively for anyone:

> This is not to deny the struggles and victories of activists who have fought hard for the passage of NAGPRA and other human rights laws but to ask people to think critically about why, twenty years later, we are still struggling to work together. I think it speaks more to a need to rethink democratic practices and Native sovereignty as a whole so that we cannot simply give Native people a place at the table that exists, but walk somewhere else together and build an entirely new table. I'm not quite sure what the design will be, but that's just a thought. The basic rights seem to be the most difficult to recognize.

Why are we still struggling to work together twenty years later? Perhaps balance is not what we should be expecting.

What gave me hope about the future of NAGPRA was the time I was able to spend with bright and enthusiastic students from various universities. These students have not spent decades investing in the possession of Native peoples' ancestors and cultural objects. Though I was terribly dissatisfied that the planning committee could not move one another or the audience at the symposium to the beginnings of a new dialogue and a new era for NAGPRA, I think these students will.

Advice and hope from an attorney

I have always tried to distinguish myself from a "real" attorney. I am a Native peoples lawyer (practicing federal Indian law and being a citizen of an Indian Nation), and I always tell people that being a Native peoples lawyer is different than being a "real" attorney. Native peoples lawyers exist in a schizophrenic world, pledging allegiance to more than one constitution and constantly rallying between divergent values and interests, and never, ever, forgetting history. Did you know that we Native peoples lawyers still believe that the U.S. Constitution means what it says, and what our ancestors were told when we conceded our territories? Yes, even though law and policy have demonstrated ambiguous and strained reasoning over time, we still believe that treaties are the "Supreme Law of the Land,"[15] and these special agreements are righteous and will stand forever, as long as the grass is green and rivers flow.

I also view NAGPRA in my Native peoples lawyer, schizophrenic way. Regardless of how the last twenty years have played out, I will always advocate that legislation passed for the benefit of Native peoples will actually benefit Native peoples and be interpreted broadly for the benefit of Native peoples.[16] I will always advocate that nowhere in the text of the statute or its regulations does NAGPRA require a balance of interests between Native peoples' spiritual responsibilities and institutional property rights.

And, I will always advocate that it is from our treaties that NAGPRA arose. Many treaties between the United States and Indian nations generally proscribed a "bad man" provision, so that if an American citizen did bad acts to Indians, the United States would act to mitigate or punish the bad acts and bad actor.[17] The enactment of NAGPRA and its regulations are keen examples of remediating the damages caused by U.S. citizens against Indian nations and their citizens.

American citizens have long been looting and grave robbing, and "purchasing" our human remains and other significant cultural items from Native peoples under duress. (Just look at the history of the George Gustav Heye Museum, the predecessor of the National Museum of the American Indian.[18]) NAGPRA is legislation that seeks to protect Native peoples from the past, current, and future harms caused by bad citizens. Somehow, the last twenty years of NAGPRA history has morphed these basic federal Indian law principles and our righteous treaties so that our most basic cultural and human rights must be on equal footing, and balanced against property interests of institutions that have profited from the looting, grave robbing, and unconscionable purchases.

There is absolutely nothing wrong with finding balance where it can be gained through transparent consultation, and full and informed consent. A collaborative approach between Native peoples and institutions can work. There have been wonderful stories in NAGPRA's history where the parties have not had to struggle against incommensurable positions and everyone walks away in the end with a good mind and resolution from an injured past. Some of those positive repatriation experiences are expressed in this book. But after twenty years, finding that balance is not guaranteed, and in my experience is not the norm. It is my strong opinion that we have undergone a fruitless effort in the last twenty years to forge an alleged balance as a goal of NAGPRA. How long will we continue to believe that a balance-of-interests approach between spiritual responsibilities and institutional property rights will be successful? As Rick Hill said, "We believe different things."

What is the consensus today?

A lot has changed in our collective thinking that brought us to the passage of NAGPRA twenty years ago; much has changed since. For instance, many more students have been raised with a realistic representation of Native peoples' history and have not become invested in decades of hoarding Native peoples' human remains and cultural items. We must continue to encourage and support our new students and emerging NAGPRA practitioners.

Also, consider the birth of a new perspective on indigenous peoples' human rights: by an overwhelming vote of 143 states of the international community, indigenous peoples' rights were explicitly recognized and confirmed when the United Nations General Assembly adopted the Declaration on the Rights of Indigenous Peoples on September 13, 2007.[19] Even Australia, New Zealand, Canada, and the United States, countries with large indigenous populations who initially voted against the declaration in 2007, have now endorsed it. As the U.N. special rapporteur has confirmed, the declaration embodies *long existing international norms*. The declaration represents "an authoritative common understanding, at the global level, of the *minimum* content of the rights of indigenous peoples," which "does not attempt to bestow indigenous peoples with a set of special or new human rights, but rather provides a contextualized elaboration of *general human rights principles and rights* as they relate to specific historical, cultural, and social circumstances of indigenous peoples [emphasis added]."[20]

Included in the declaration's international norms are Articles 11, 12, and 31, which specifically call out indigenous peoples' rights to repatriation and control of their ancestors and cultural objects.[21] These articles recognize that indigenous peoples' rights to repatriation and control of their ancestors and cultural objects are the norm, "nothing more" than general human rights; these rights are not unusual, new or special. These rights enumerated in the declaration are understood as an "authoritative common understanding, at the global level."

Within the declaration, there is no balance of interests and no controversy concerning institutional property rights to these objects. There is no need to balance such interests within the declaration, because a strong rubric of the declaration integrates the right of self-determination and to free, prior, and informed consent, which is expressed in Articles 1, 12, 20, 27, and 30. The right to free, prior, and informed consent is a necessary aspect of the right of self-determination, a right of all peoples which was enshrined in Article 1 of the United Nations Charter in 1945[22] and is "widely acknowledged to be a principle of international law."[23] Self-determination is also a right well enshrined in United States federal Indian law.[24]

When Native peoples' graves, temples, special secret containers, masks, wampum belts, and other cultural and sacred items were taken to fill museums, for trade and for souvenirs, the taking most often occurred without the free, prior, and informed consent of the Native Nation governments, special societies, or individuals whose responsibilities were to protect such items for the community. If NAGPRA truly is considered "graves protection" and "repatriation" legislation that was passed for the benefit of Native peoples, it must also be read with the declaration as guiding interpretation: In line with the recognized rights of self-determination and free, prior, and informed consent, NAGPRA seeks to remedy the failure of individuals and institutions to obtain Native peoples free, prior, and informed consent and reinstitute Native peoples self-determination over their millions of cultural objects, including ancestors' remains and grave goods. In fact, the current language of NAGPRA supports this international norm of free, prior, and informed consent mandating that an institution cannot obtain the "right of possession" over an object without the voluntary consent of the individual or group that had the authority to alienate the object in the first place.[25]

It is further appealing for me to consider that graves protection and repatriation to Native peoples is an international norm. In other words, if you do not read NAGPRA as legislation that was meant to provide a process by which institutions that did not obtain the free, prior, and informed consent of Native peoples for human remains, funerary objects, objects of cultural patrimony, and sacred objects would repatriate those items, then you are outside the accepted global norms of our society. No balance of interests needed.

Activism and education

In law, sometimes precedent becomes more important than societal norms, and at other times law will overturn outdated precedent.[26] Resistance to change usually comes from the fact that it is old people who have made the rules and who have become invested in those positions. So I am waiting for some of you old thinkers to, you know, die, and for our new thinkers to take your place![27]

In the meantime, I challenge all of us to rethink the next twenty years of NAGPRA and whether a "balance of interests" continues to be an acceptable rhetoric. We do not have to believe the same thing to do the right thing. The advocacy and education required of us is simple and universal: Do not take things that do not belong to you, apologize, and do not do it again. We cannot rest in the injury of the past. We have to move forward and do the right thing.

Notes

1   Professor Watkins is a member of the crew "Time Team America" on PBS. See http://www.pbs.org/opb/timeteam/.

2   The term "Indian" is a legal term of art and is defined by various statutes. It is generally limited to individuals whose tribe is recognized by the United States; in other words, a citizen of a federally recognized tribe. My use of the term "Indian" here refers only to citizens of federally recognized tribes. Therefore, citizens of non-federally recognized tribes did not find much, if any, comfort in the passage of NAGPRA because NAGPRA did not give non-recognized tribes any standing to obtain repatriation of affiliated ancestors, funerary objects, sacred objects or objects of cultural patrimony. For more information on some limited ways that these non-federally recognized tribes have used NAGPRA, see Chapter 7 of this book.

3   The terms "Native American" and "Native Hawaiian" are defined by NAGPRA, 25 U.S.C. § 3001(9) and (10): "Native American" means of, or relating to, a tribe, people, or culture that is indigenous to the United States; "Native Hawaiian" means any individual who is a descendant of the aboriginal people who, prior to 1778, occupied and exercised sovereignty in the area that now constitutes the State of Hawaii. The term "Native American" is broader than the term "Indian" because it is not limited to federally recognized tribes.

4   Paraphrasing Mr. Rennard Strickland, quoted by Steven Gunn in "The Native American Graves Protection and Repatriation Act at Twenty: Reaching the Limits of Our National Consensus," *William Mitchell Law Review* 36 (2010): 505.

5   I will use the term "Native peoples" to be inclusive of all Native American and Native Hawaiian peoples indigenous to what is now known as the United States including Alaska and the Hawaiian Islands.

6   Select Committee on Indian Affairs, "Providing for the Protection of Native American Graves and the Repatriation of Native American remains and Cultural Patrimony," September 26, 1990.

7   I use the term "institution" or "institutions", which is not defined by NAGPRA, instead of "museum" and "federal agency," which are defined by NAGPRA. I wanted to broaden the term to include not only those institutions that understand they are a "museum" under NAGPRA, but call into question all institutions—public and private—who have any type of pecuniary interest in maintaining cultural objects.

8   In my practice of NAGPRA on behalf of Indian nation governments, I have heard the following reasons from institutions in response to why repatriation could not occur:

- We have not had a chance to [study, perform DNA testing, gather additional information, request funding from NAGPRA] as required by our museum board. So [without consultation] we have inventoried the remains as culturally unidentifiable.
- The tribe has not given us enough information about why they need this object and how it is involved in a ceremony. Please give us an affidavit from your traditional religious leader stating how he/she uses the object.
- All we have is geographic site information so we will have to do further study outside of the documentation we currently have to determine affiliation.
- The remains are from about 1100-1300 AD, so we [the museum] have determined that they are too old to be affiliated with a present-day tribe and therefore we have not consulted with any tribes.
- Can't we loan you the remains? Or perhaps bury them in a protective case that we can access when new scientific technologies become available?

- The anthropologist purchased that sacred object from a person who said he was an Indian in 1830, before it was acquired by a military captain, and then somehow wound up for sale at Sotheby's, so clearly the museum has rightful possession.
- You only want affiliation for those remains to prove your land claims.

9   367 F.3d 864, note 14 (9th Cir. 2004).

10   See Robert A. Williams, Jr., "The Algebra of Federal Indian Law: The Hard Trail of Decolonizing and Americanizing the White Man's Indian Jurisprudence," *Wisconsin Law Review* (1986): 219 (presenting how federal Indian law consistently advances Eurocentric ideology over Native peoples' world views).

11   There is an African proverb that says: Tales of the hunt shall always glorify the hunter. In *A History of Livingston County New York: from its part in the war for our Union: with an account of the Seneca nation of Indians, and biographical sketches of earliest settlers and prominent public men*, the author compares this moral to how Indian stories have been told: "It was a dictate of policy, during the Revolution, to paint the Indian as black as possible in crimes and cruelty, and to hold him often responsible for deeds of which it might easily be shown the British were alone guilty. Since then, the prejudice has been adroitly fostered by those whose selfish ends it subserved. That the Indian committed excesses and barbarities, it would be vain either to deny or to palliate. But how far he was justified in waging the only system of war-fare known to his race, as a measure of retaliation, it is for the moralist to say. If the whole story were told, if the Indian could tell his side, how then would stand the record? The lion in the fable disputes with the man as to which was the braver and stronger of the two. The latter exultingly points to a marble statue of a man strangling a lion, in proof of the superiority of his kind. 'That,' answered the lion, 'is your version of the story; let us be the sculptors, and we will reverse the positions; the lion will then stand over the man.' Is not the moral applicable here?" Lockwood L. Doty, "A History of Livingston County New York: from its part in the war for our Union: with an account of the Seneca nation of Indians, and biographical sketches of earliest settlers and prominent public men," 1876, 65-66, accessed November 5, 2012, http://archive.org/stream/historyoflivings00doty#page/n7/mode/2up. (Thank you George McIntosh!)

12   NAGPRA at 20 video, "Traditional Knowledge as Evidence," November 16, 2010.

13   Suzan Shown Harjo is a well-known Cheyenne and Hodulgee Muscogee advocate for American Indian rights, including protecting sacred sites and challenging stereotypical images of Indian people. She is a poet, writer, lecturer, curator, and policy advocate, who has helped Native peoples recover over a million acres of land. She serves as president of the Morning Star Institute, a national Native American rights organization based in Washington, DC.

14   David Hurst Thomas is a curator in the Department of Anthropology at the American Museum of Natural History and an adjunct professor at Columbia University and the City University of New York.

15   The Supremacy Clause of the United States Constitution, Article VI, Clause 2, establishes the U.S. Constitution, U.S. treaties, and federal statutes as "the supreme law of the land." The text of the supremacy clause decrees these to be the highest form of law in the U.S. legal system.

16   See Morton v. Mancari, 417 U.S. 535, 554 (1974), holding that the Court will uphold specific legislation for the benefit of Indians "[a]s long as the special treatment can be tied rationally to the fulfillment of Congress' unique obligation toward the Indians." Let's not forget federal Indian law interpretation principle #1: "The standard principles of statutory interpretation do not have their usual force in cases involving Indian law. The basic Indian law canons of construction require that treaties, agreements, statutes, and executive orders be liberally construed in favor of the Indians; and all ambiguities are to be resolved in favor of the Indians."

Felix Cohen, *Cohen's Handbook of Federal Indian Law*, 5th ed. (Albuquerque, NM: American Indian Law Center, Inc., 2005) 119–122. (Citations omitted.)

17 Article 1 of the Treaty with the Northern Cheyenne and Northern Arapaho, May 10, 1868, 15 Stats., 655; Article VII of the 1794 Treaty of Canadaigua; Article 1 of the Fort Laramie Treaty of 1868; among others.

18 Edmund Carpenter, *Two Essays: Chief & Greed*. (North Andover, MA: Persimmon Press, 2005).

19 To see the voting record go to: http://unbisnet.un.org:8080/ipac20/ipac.jsp?profile=voting &index=.VM&term=ares61295#focus.

20 Human Rights Council, Special Rapporteur on the situation of human rights and fundamental freedoms of indigenous peoples, *Promotion and Protection of all Human Rights, Civil, Political, Social and Cultural Rights, including the Right to Development: Report of the Special Rapporteur on the situation of human rights and fundamental freedoms of indigenous people, S. James Anaya*, 85–86, U.N. Doc. A/HRC/9/9 (August 11, 2008).

21 United Nations Declaration on the Rights of Indigenous Peoples, September 13, 2007:

Article 11:

1. Indigenous peoples have the right to practise and revitalize their cultural traditions and customs. This includes the right to maintain, protect and develop the past, present and future manifestations of their cultures, such as archaeological and historical sites, artefacts, designs, ceremonies, technologies and visual and performing arts and literature.
2. States shall provide redress through effective mechanisms, which may include restitution, developed in conjunction with indigenous peoples, with respect to their cultural, intellectual, religious and spiritual property taken without their free, prior and informed consent or in violation of their laws, traditions and customs.

Article 12:

1. Indigenous peoples have the right to manifest, practise, develop and teach their spiritual and religious traditions, customs and ceremonies; the right to maintain, protect, and have access in privacy to their religious and cultural sites; the right to the use and control of their ceremonial objects; and the right to the repatriation of their human remains.
2. States shall seek to enable the access and/or repatriation of ceremonial objects and human remains in their possession through fair, transparent and effective mechanisms developed in conjunction with indigenous peoples concerned.

Article 31:

1. Indigenous peoples have the right to maintain, control, protect and develop their cultural heritage, traditional knowledge and traditional cultural expressions, as well as the manifestations of their sciences, technologies and cultures, including human and genetic resources, seeds, medicines, knowledge of the properties of fauna and flora, oral traditions, literatures, designs, sports and traditional games and visual and performing arts. They also have the right to maintain, control, protect and develop their intellectual property over such cultural heritage, traditional knowledge, and traditional cultural expressions.
2. In conjunction with indigenous peoples, States shall take effective measures to recognize and protect the exercise of these rights.

22 Article 1(2) of the United Nations Charter provides that a purpose of the United Nations is "To develop friendly relations among nations, based on respect for the principle of equal rights and self-determination of peoples, and to take other appropriate measures to strengthen universal peace."

23   S. James Anaya, *Indigenous Peoples in International Law*, 2nd ed. (New York: Oxford University Press, 2004), 97.

24   See Indian Self-Determination and Education Assistance Act of 1975, Pub. L. No. 93-638, 88 Stat. 2203 (1975).

25   25 U.S.C § 3001(12).

26   Brown v. Board of Education of Topeka, 347 U.S. 483 (1954), which outlawed segregation and overturned Plessy v. Ferguson, 163 U.S. 537 (1896), which upheld state segregation laws.

27   Teasing is a method of control of social, and other, situations by Indian people. Vine Deloria, Jr., "Indian Humor" in *Custer Died for Your Sins* (Norman and London: University of Oklahoma Press, 1988), 147. I am teasing . . . kind of.

Chapter 10
Navigating a Colonial Quagmire: Affirming Native Lives in the Struggle to Defend Our Dead

CLAYTON W. DUMONT JR.

> "The most significant challenge of our generation is to safeguard what remains."
>
> —Wallace Coffey[1]

For Native peoples, the Native American Graves Protection and Repatriation Act (NAGPRA 25 U.S.C. 3001) is about protecting the physical remains, the graves, the spirits, and the dignity of our ancestors. Yet there is something even more fundamental at stake. NAGPRA is about our very survival as Native peoples. It is about our ability to maintain our own identities, to define our worlds and histories for ourselves, to know and to teach our children who we are. The future of NAGPRA is inextricably tied to Native peoples' ability to resist political, judicial, and epistemological attacks on our status as sovereign peoples. NAGPRA is about power.

Defending NAGPRA's integrity, as Indian law designed to protect Native ways of knowing and being from the aggressions of hostile archaeologists and physical anthropologists, is resistance to forced assimilation. Attacks on NAGPRA actively erase Native peoples as distinct cultures and political entities. Resisting requires contesting the naturalization of anthropological narratives. To challenge the colonial power of scientists, we must point to the cultural and historical, and not panhuman, bases of their desires, beliefs, and self-perceptions. We will not win in the courts and halls of government without confronting their cultural stories, including their tales of "objectivity."

As Natives, should we fail to recognize and interrogate the thoroughly colonial qualities of the cultural domains where the battle to define NAGPRA is occurring, we risk ceding our right to self-representation, and ultimately our self-understandings, to non-Indians.

I begin by introducing myself and describing how I came to the battle for this law. I then consider some of the not-always-obvious complexity of insisting on

Natives' cultural and political uniqueness, complexity that comes to light when we acknowledge the overwhelming power of American colonialism to influence Native self-understandings. Next I sketch out a modest portion of the cultural history that gave birth to our scientific opponents' desires. I locate epistemological longings of contemporary American archaeology and physical anthropology in the politics and history of Europe. My goal is to show that the passions of these scientists originate, like all human political articulations, from the cultural intrigues of specific times and places. I then assess the double standard afforded the scientists' cultural constructs in the courts, where the future of NAGPRA will almost certainly be decided. Finally, I conclude with a brief suggestion of strategy for organizing ourselves as Native peoples and allies to confront the most obstinate NAGPRA resisting scientists and institutions.

Introduction

Waq lisi (Hello.) *gew ?a seesas Clayton Dumont.* (My name is Clayton Dumont.) *noo ?a ?ewksiknii* (I am Klamath.) I am also a professor of sociology at San Francisco State University. I have been studying and writing about NAGPRA for a little more than a decade. My motivations are personal, tribal, pan-Indian, and academic.

My first experience with the horror of grave desecration happened while I was a teenager. I had driven to one of the reservation cemeteries where many family members, including my great-grandparents, are buried. The sound of my pickup bouncing up the dirt road brought a tribal member and his very large dog from a nearby house out to greet me. The sight of recently disturbed graves and freshly turned dirt explained his vigilance. I remember feeling sick to my stomach as I walked among the violated burials, looking at the familiar names of tribal families on the headstones. Many of these ancestors were dead before I was born, but I felt like I knew them from the stories I had heard from elders. Not too many years later, my uncle told me of "some asshole" who knew that "an Indian lived in the house" he rented in Springfield, Oregon, and so knocked on his door trying to sell contents of Indians' graves. When this same uncle was younger, we kids joked that he would one day pack his guns and head off to join the American Indian Movement (AIM). As a young adult, that rather animated conversation in Springfield helped me understand why he could be so stridently serious about being Native.

Almost a decade later, I was a newly minted PhD, interviewing for a job at the small university near our traditional lands in southern Oregon. In my application letter, I had written of my desire to be close to the Klamath Tribes and of my hope that a strong tradition of tribal youth attending the campus could be created. After the morning preliminaries, I was taken to lunch by the resident archaeologist. The department to which I was applying was a joint sociology/anthropology faculty, and he wanted to know how I, as a potential colleague, felt about the still new NAGPRA. The Klamath Tribes had regained our federal recognition only a few years earlier, but our Culture and Heritage Department officers were already using the statute to frustrate his desire to "excavate" in our country. I forgot where I was and responded to his questions in a blunt Klamath way, breaching the norms of upper-middle-class, academic culture.

When we returned to campus, the whole hiring committee was waiting to conduct the main interview. I was led into a room with human remains stacked in open boxes and laid out on shelves surrounding the table where I was invited to sit. I was caught off guard and the intensity of my survey of the room was no doubt noticed. (Given the location of the university, I thought there was a strong possibility that these dead could have been my relatives.) It was not long before we were discussing how I felt about the prospect of coming to a joint department. This led to a long discussion of the racist history of anthropology. I stayed academically polite this time, but it was clear to all that the discussion did not help my case as an applicant for the job.

Although less intense, many graduate school experiences left me curious about the cultural origins of scientific hubris. How was it possible that these folks were so bloody sure that they alone were called to access the real, the true, and the "objectively empirical"? Only among some Christians had I encountered such self-assured zeal. These experiences led to my ongoing academic interest in the politics and cultural history of science, particularly the human sciences. I have spent much of the last twenty years studying the cultural genealogy of the scientific self. NAGPRA, as a site of cross-cultural knowledge politics, fits naturally within this pursuit.

Hard honesty about what remains and how we safeguard it

At first glance, Mr. Coffey's call in the epigraph to "safeguard what remains" appears straightforward. No one need explain to Native peoples why it is imperative to protect what remains of our languages, our oral histories, our ceremonies, and knowledge of our ancestors' ways. Yet, if not read carefully, the assumption of a tidy intellectual separation between the Native and the non-Native world that it must be protected from is both naïve and dangerous. Such a careless reading mistakenly assumes the possibility of a relationship of exteriority between these existences.

In other words, an unscrutinized and assumed separation conjures the fantasy that centuries after contact, some untouched "authenticity" is holding on, some quickly drying reservoir of the purely Native that must be preserved and replenished. But Native studies scholars have long since pointed to the links that this imagery shares with the racist history of anthropological desire and with the romantic nationalism of centuries of European American popular culture.[2] Indeed, a central function of our still-unique National Museum of the American Indian (NMAI) is to expose, interrogate, and contest the power of non-Native expectations of and about Natives.[3]

Sometimes I imagine how a conversation with my great, great, great grandfather, who made his mark on our treaty with the United States in 1864, might go. How would Kilo'kaga (translated as: "warrior of small stature" by the 1890 ethnographer Albert Gatschet[4]) or "Kellogue," as his identity was recorded on the treaty, understand "authenticity," "tribe," "tribal chairman," "Culture and Heritage Department," and "blood quantum"? Or for our more specific concern with the future of NAGPRA, how would he decipher "preponderance of the evidence," "culturally unidentifiable," and "a relationship of shared group identity which can be reasonably traced historically or prehistorically"? Imagining the maddening if not prohibitive discordance of such a conversation, it seems to me, begins to get at the thoroughly permeating power of colonialism that underwrites the cultural spaces we now inhabit.

In her brilliant, some would say heretical, text, *Native Acts*, Lenape scholar Joanne Barker has proclaimed, "I do not believe that there is an authentic tradition to be revitalized from a past that transcends 'Western Ideology.'"[5] She is not suggesting that Native peoples are or have ever been without distinct ways. Nor is she saying that there are no "real Indians" left. Rather she means to encircle that whole line of questioning with a careful consideration of how Native peoples have been constructed in the narratives of the colonizers. Barker means to assert an inevitable relationship of conceptual interiority between Native and non-Native cultural spaces in the early twenty-first century.[6] She is cajoling us, warning us against underestimating the impact of colonialism on (what we should *not* consider "inauthentic") contemporary Native thinking.

My great, great, great grandfather probably articulated responses to mid-nineteenth century American cultural constructs. These were no doubt fashioned, not in the ways of "the tribe," but of his s?aaMaks (relations). He and his relations lived in a specific place near ?ews (Klamath Lake), and they were distinct from ma'klaks (other, now "Indian" people) who lived elsewhere on the lake, on ya'aga (Lower Williamson River), and from the e'ukshi ma'klaks (Klamath Marsh people). But he and all the once-distinct communities that became the federally recognized Klamath Tribes (the Klamath, Modoc, and Yahooskin peoples) had to learn to see themselves in ways that mattered to the United States.

Anthropology, including archaeology, has a long history of serving the interests of the federal government and American nationalism.[7] Prestigious and racist scientists asserted the biological inferiority of indigenous peoples as justification for the theft of Native homelands by the United States. Indeed, much of the anthropological invention (and thus desperate pursuit) of "authentic" Natives came from scientists' belief that Darwin had foretold our demise through natural selection.[8] We were inferior, this thinking went, so it was natural that our racial and cultural superiors should take what we had; but it was also anthropologists' duty to "objectively" record the "authentic" qualities of "full bloods" so that future generations could have access to that "knowledge."

"Race," a now discredited invention of earlier generations of scientists, was put to use by the United States to subjugate non-white peoples.[9] The racialized "Indian" became part of what Gerald Vizenor has called a "literature of domination,"[10] deployed by self-congratulatory European Americans as they actively destroyed the ways of those who inhabited North America before their own immigration. "Blood quantum" is a colonial creation closely connected to the invention of race. Inasmuch as it is said to measure true "Indian-ness," it institutionalizes and apparently documents the demise of the anthropologists' "authentic" Natives.[11] It thus serves the interest of the United States and current generations of Americans by hastening the end of their constitutional and treaty obligations to Native peoples.

As the survivors of this cultural genocide, living Natives must confront the ongoing privilege and power attached to these concepts and the stories they propagate.[12] Consequently, I think it makes sense for us to be careful about how, when, and why we employ cultural constructs that have been inherited from this colonial history. Which is not to say that we can avoid them. (This is what I meant above when I said it is naïve to assume the possibility of a relationship of exteriority.) Certainly some tribes/nations retain more of their own languages and the cultural differences that reside there than others. But English, the prestige of science, and the dictates of constitutional law now pervade Indian country. Nevertheless, we *can* work to understand why these foreign cultural constructs were developed, where and when they originated, and how they were and are being used against us. We can thus learn to be strategic about how and when we choose to deploy or contest them.

As late as the 1930s, my great grandfather and his brothers were still translating our tribal council meetings from English to Klamath because the elders' thinking remained in their own language. But bigotry, greed, boarding schools, Christianity, and ultimately the Termination Act did their work.[13] Now, in our council meetings we fight over the legal meaning of "*our* Constitution" and parliamentary procedure.

It is right to feel despair about this, about having lost so much. However, it is a mistake to feel bad about it because we think we are no longer "authentic." Our traditions *are* who we are as Native peoples. They *are* that important. But this is not the same thing as being persuaded that we have lost what were *always only* colonial concoctions, admixtures of what earlier generations of anthropologists, government agents, and missionaries expected and demanded from their encounters with our ancestors. We need to insist that *we are* the Natives! As one of my favorite parts of our NMAI exhorts in a way that strikes me as beautiful, dry Native humor: "We are the EVIDENCE."

The point of Joanne Barker's words, quoted above, is that we can no longer definitively separate understandings of our ancestors' ways from anthropological renderings carried out for unfriendly political purposes. (I doubt that our pre-contact Native ancestors foresaw their coming status as anthropologists' "evidence.") As she says, " 'the Native' and 'traditions' are conditional . . . they are made meaningful and relevant again and again in specific contexts in which they are articulated."[14] This, I argue below, is precisely the complexity from where the future of NAGPRA will be decided.

Despite the fact that NAGPRA was passed to protect Native peoples from archaeologists and physical anthropologists, we are being called on to *be* the colonizers' anthropologically authentic Indians. We are being told that anthropological ideals of "material culture," "biologically distinct populations," and scientific "reliability" must be met and approved by scientists, or they will not return the dead whose graves they justify violating using these same constructs. In short, we are being told (yet again) to make ourselves "meaningful and relevant" for the anthropologists, archaeologists, and the courts, using terms and concepts they currently value, if we are to continue successfully using a law designed to protect us from these same scientists.

It is important to continue working to "safeguard what remains" of our political and cultural independence. Fighting to stop the Society for American Archaeology (SAA), the American Association of Physical Anthropologists (AAPA), and the American Association of Museums (AAM) from twisting NAGPRA into a caricature of itself is part of this work.[15] We can succeed, it seems to me, in safeguarding what remains of our cultural independence, including our responsibility to our deceased ancestors, by studying the European development of the American colonizers' intellectual gaze.

I want to suggest that we should learn to narrate this history for them. By confronting current generations of NAGPRA resisting archaeologists and physical anthropologists with the often contentious, political births of their sacred (anthropological, nationalist, moralizing) stories, we can denaturalize and disturb their authority. Locating scientists' desires in philosophy, theology, and politics that are specific to their own societal backgrounds, and not to Natives' histories, destabilizes their megalomaniacal claims to panhuman relevance.

Through these efforts, we also make ourselves aware of the role that colonial agendas (conceived alongside European self-appraisals) play(ed) in the development of our own agencies (selves) as Native peoples. This awareness allows us to make more informed and strategic choices about how we negotiate our own identities, both within our tribal communities and in our dealings with outside governments.[16] Knowing the colonizers' epistemological history and, when necessary, teaching it to them may begin leveling the political playing field and help us extend greater control over how our self-presentations are read by non-Natives.

Confronting the cult of value-neutral "objectivity"

The belief in "objectivity" or the quest to be "unbiased" is a form of idol worship that Native peoples attempting to protect our dead must continuously confront. Many biological anthropologists and archaeologists simply assume that these (ultimately faith-based) pursuits transcend culture.[17] For the deepest believers, the social and political origins of their objectivity pilgrimage are invisible and irrelevant.

Lauraelyn Whitt describes this inability to critically assess their own cultural ways: "[T]he ideology of western science, wedded as it is to the thesis of value-neutrality, insists that issues of power do not enter into knowledge making or shape the dynamics of knowledge systems. The relations of domination and assimilation which characterize imperialism (whether in its historical or contemporary variants), and which facilitate biocolonialism, are thus neither acknowledged nor acknowledgeable."[18]

Much of American archaeology remains anachronistically mired in what scholars who study the history of science recognize as "positivism." Positivism is a philosophy of science that arose in the nineteenth century and sought to erase all ideology and indeed all human influence from what proponents assumed would become purified depictions of the natural and social worlds. Positivists believed that knowledge could be purged of preconceptions; scientists would learn to record only what existed before the prejudices of perception interjected themselves. Despite Whitt's simplifying and homogenizing label ("the ideology of western science"[19]), positivism has relatively few adherents among contemporary social scientists. Nor is such extreme "mechanical objectivity"[20] widely and uncritically invoked across disparate natural sciences. As the progressive archaeologist Tamara Bray has observed, "Hiding behind the trousers of positivist science, one notes a stubborn determination on the part of the archaeological establishment to cling to antiquated notions of objectivity, the search for truth, and the neutrality of scientific practice—features that most of our sister social sciences have long since rejected. To date, there remains something of a vacuum in the theorization of knowledge production within the field (2007:81)."[21]

While far too expansive and complex to do justice here, it is important to my argument that readers get a glimpse of the political and cultural origins of assertions of value neutrality in the human sciences. While the intellectual genealogy of these assumptions extends as far back as ancient Greece and the early Christian church, the most immediate political utility of such assumptions was manufactured from the strife generated in the European Enlightenment.

In only a few centuries (roughly the seventeenth and eighteenth), the intellectual authority of the Catholic church and political power of the monarchies that it validated were successfully challenged. Political authority threatened to, and sometimes did, break down. (Thousands of French citizens were guillotined in the civic chaos that wealthy classes across Europe feared could inundate their own borders.) Eventually, constitutional governments (like the United States) codified the rights of "individuals," regardless of whether they were born noble or common.[22] These rights included the unbridled pursuit of wealth through commerce and private property.

By the nineteenth century, industrial capitalism and urbanized, gross economic inequality had followed. In the United States, in particular, the gap between the wealthy and the poor was ethnic, racial, and too proximate to avoid. Newly crowded cities lacked adequate infrastructure. They were hastily built, dirty, and disease ridden. Factories employed children, were not governed by safety codes, and there was no eight-hour day or minimum wage. Urban rivers, lakes, and air were horribly polluted. Unequally distributed misery meant that the potential for political unrest was always at hand. Revolutionaries promoting an array of hostile political solutions were plentiful.

Nineteenth century positivists claimed they could cut through politics, religion, and ideology. They endeavored to ease the societal unrest wrought by the Enlightenment with pure, value-neutral scientific methodology. Auguste Comte, one of the founding proponents of this philosophy, asserted that positivism would "establish a general harmony in the entire system of ideas."[23] It would do so "by imposing a series of indisputable scientific conditions on the study of political questions."[24] Despite vowing to admit "only well-prepared and disciplined minds" who would uncover "the fundamental law of continuous human development,"[25] positivism was a dismal failure.

Nineteenth and early twentieth century positivists simply validated the prejudices of their gender, social class, and "race." Indeed what we now recognize as bigotry was wholly invisible to their "disciplined minds." They assumed that their sexist and racist beliefs *were reality* and that they were merely observing and documenting the natural order of things. Comte, for example, claimed that positivist science would "prove that the equality of the sexes, of which so much is said, is incompatible with all social existence."[26]

Claims to value-free social science were thoroughly discredited by the late middle twentieth century. The influx of women and racialized minorities into universities, both as faculty and students, during the civil rights era reduced positivists to a relatively small and marginalized camp. Although value-free objectivity remains the stated goal of most American social scientists, very few claim that they can achieve it. More importantly, there is now a large corpus of scholarship detailing and debating the gendered, racialized, cultural, hetero-normative, and class-based qualities of social scientific knowledge.[27] But as Bray noted above, positivism maintains a curious hold on mainstream archaeology and physical anthropology, particularly among the most vehement resisters of NAGPRA.

Yet change is afoot. Writing loosely under the title "Indigenous Archaeology" is a growing collection of Native and non-Native scholars who as Stephen Silliman says, "seek to interrogate, repair, and hopefully move beyond the colonial origins of the discipline and its treatment of Native people."[28] This is overdue, Michael Wilcox points out, because "the privileged position" of researchers, so carefully interrogated by cultural anthropologists decades ago, was "brought to the attention of archaeologists by the passage of repatriation legislation" but "has never been adequately addressed by many archaeologists, particularly in North America."[29]

Chip Colwell-Chanthaphonh and T.J. Ferguson, long time proponents of taking Native criticisms of archaeology and physical anthropology seriously, are equally clear that less progressive colleagues must learn to think critically about the politics of their own ways of knowing: "Data, the basis of archaeological knowledge, were long thought to be self-evident, simply 'discovered' through scientific study. A raft of scholarship in recent decades, however—principally following from Foucault's critique of power/knowledge—has shown that knowledge derived from archaeological work is itself a social, political, and economic process, constructed through selective interpretive strategies throughout a research project."[30]

Such sentiments are exactly the kind of honorable humility that can lead to an ever more productive relationship between scientists and Indians. Most of the Native people that I know are not against archaeology per se. But we are against colonialism. When biological anthropologists and archaeologists assume the mantle of extra-cultural purveyors of "objectivity," they are behaving like colonizers. The way forward is for them to stop chasing their own tales of "value-neutrality" at Indians' expense and consider how their own cultural history has led them to what *they* consider imperative questions.

Epistemological anxieties themselves, worries over techniques and their limits in a quest to accumulate empirical facts, are not traditional concerns of peoples outside of Europe and its diaspora. The scientific quest for essential structure in the world and a singular logic that organizes it originates in Christian monotheism and Greek philosophy. Indeed, scientists did not begin openly asserting their independence from Christianity until the nineteenth century.

In its Neo-Platonist and Enlightenment era forms, the theological and scientific pursuit of the logic of the biblical Creation required extreme attacks on the body and physical senses.[31] In between, Christian Aristotelians, who dominated the European Middle Ages, jealously and zealously debated relationships between the parts of the Creation, even as half the planet remained unknown to them.[32] No wonder that this European history is littered with the blood of "heretics," those whom their prosecutors deemed insufficiently able to discipline themselves in pursuit of the light of the one true God and orthodox truth. Once beyond the shores of Europe, this mission became what Vizenor has called "the puritanical destinies of monotheism."[33] Science and Christianity were the complimentary twin engines of colonialist expansion and missionary-ism across the globe.

My purpose in all too briefly citing this history is not to assert that modern, NAGPRA-resisting archaeologists and physical anthropologists are deists. Nor do I think they are literally missionaries or believe themselves "racially" superior to Native peoples. Rather, I think they have failed to interrogate the role this extended cultural history continues to play in their desires and assumptions. I am suggesting that there are unexamined, metaphysical (faith-based) presuppositions at work in their stated needs and self-appraisals. I think that all of us, Natives and scientists, will get farther down the road toward genuinely respectful collaborations, if and when members of the scientific community can be persuaded to look carefully at the intellectual genealogy of their own epistemological quests.

Sociologists sometimes describe the difficult work of recognizing one's own cultural assumptions as "fish trying to see water." Yet even a few weeks' study of Plato's dialogues, of René Descartes' *Meditations on First Philosophy*, or Francis Bacon's *Advancement of Learning* could help modern positivists recognize culturally inherited presuppositions at work in their own narratives. For example, there is a remarkable overlap, given that they are approximately 2,400 years apart, between Plato's attack on the oral historians of ancient Greece (the "poets") and Ronald J. Mason's scientific dismissal of Native oral histories.[34]

Plato assumed that the oral keepers of the community's past (the storytellers/poets) were dangerous. In *The Republic* he warns of the "magic of poetry."[35] Oral history is dangerous, he admonishes, because "its hearers [should] fear its effects on the constitution of their inner selves."[36] Plato distrusts feelings, and the empathy for others cultivated by oral re-collections of ancestors' lives is sure to breathe unwanted passion and sentiment into the self-governance and moral regulation of the community. As he says, "Very few people are capable of realizing that what we feel for other people must infect what we feel for ourselves."[37]

For most Native peoples, this warning is not just curious; it seems kind of crazy. Why would any sane person not want the young members of their community to feel deeply, particularly in consideration for the well-being of others? After all, the community is the source of one's own identity and its health is the basis of our own well-being. However, Natives who have repeatedly been told to control our emotional pining for our dead ancestors will also recognize that Plato's disdain for feelings, which he recognizes are experienced by the body, is one clear source of the colonizers' cultural belief that important decisions must be governed by rationality and "objectivity." As Plato warns, upon hearing "the sweet lyric or epic muse, pleasure and pain become your rulers instead of law and rational principles."[38]

For Mason, orally re-collecting the episodes of ancestors' lives, including the empathy-based moral lessons that they carry, is an embrace of "folkloric chaff" and a "wasteful diversion in the search for a trustworthy past."[39] Stories about "when mother was a girl," "before the old chief's house burned down," or "the dream time," are the product of "limited horizons and short tenure."[40] Presumably his reference to "limited horizons" and "short tenure" is an assertion of Native parochialism. He is saying that we Natives are limited by the close-up needs of and feelings for our communities. But science, he is suggesting, is not so encumbered. "Western science and historiography have achieved a hitherto and elsewhere unparalleled independence from religious and other extraneous considerations in the pursuit of objective knowledge."[41]

Both Plato and Mason are claiming to defy feelings and emotions in the service of a way of knowing that exceeds the needs of any one group, place, or time. They are both saying that they may speak for all peoples because they alone have developed a capacity to cut through the humanity that limits the rest of us. In Mason's own words: "I do mean to assert the epistemological superiority of Western or Euroamerican achievement in reconstructing human (and indeed universal) history over all its predecessors and contemporary would-be rivals. The former is and does what the latter are not and cannot do: it is critically reflexive and evidence-bound, and it is capable of comprehending the others in their own terms while concurrently deconstructing them in a search for whatever of their component elements may be testable by independent methods."[42]

Ironically, Mason's claim to "critical reflexivity" and "independence from religious and other extraneous" influences is neither. His "pursuit of objective knowledge" is firmly rooted in the theology of his cultural ancestry, and the fact that he is apparently unaware of this epistemological inheritance belies his claim to "independence." Further, if he is unaware of the roles his cultural ancestors continue to play in his self-understanding, then he is wrong about being "critically reflexive." That is, he is unable to think critically about his own assumptions. As Whitt said above, "The relations of domination and assimilation which characterize imperialism . . . and which facilitate biocolonialism, are thus neither acknowledged nor acknowledgeable."

"Objectivity," as we now understand the word, is only as old as the mid-nineteenth century.[43] It has had multiple cultural incarnations, most of them steeped in the metaphysics of theology.[44] However, one historical constant is concern with the impact of the sensual self on what the scientist believes s/he perceives. Often, this took the form of an ascetic purging characterized by severe self-disdain.

For example, Descartes' self-loathing reads like a window into neurosis. His desperate attempt to free himself from prejudice leads him to assert that he will stop his ears, shut his eyes, and withdraw all bodily senses. And those sense-based perceptions that he cannot finally purge, he will force himself to regard as "vacuous and false."[45] At one point he goes so far as to question whether he really exists, even entertaining the possibility that an evil demon is present and merely tricking him into thinking that he can think. Ultimately, he solves his inability to crawl outside his own skin with his faith in his God. "I know by experience that there is in me a faculty of judgment which, like everything else which is in me, I certainly received from God. And since God does not wish to deceive me, he surely did not give me the kind of faculty which would ever enable me to go wrong while using it correctly."[46] "If I were unaware of God," this foundational figure in the development of the modern scientific self proclaims, "I should thus never have true and certain knowledge about anything."[47]

Think about this for a moment. It is not at all obvious that Descartes' theological justification for "true and certain knowledge" is unrelated to Mason's "pursuit of objective knowledge." On the contrary, given the similarity of their stated desires, I do not think anyone should simply accept Mason's, or his archaeological colleagues', claims to being only "evidence bound." All of us, Natives and scientists, should be asking whether Mason and his positivist colleagues can really muster better than theological reasons for claiming that they can escape the prejudicial experiences of earthly living. And if, as I believe, it can be shown that scientists are mere mortals, living human lives with human concerns rooted in human values and prejudices, then we should also be asking why they are not reflexively rethinking their penchant for chasing their own metaphysical aspirations.

Mason says he is "capable of comprehending others [Natives] in their own terms while concurrently deconstructing them in a search for whatever of their component elements may be testable by independent methods." It seems to me that this "capacity" to be value free ("independent"), which he says spells the "epistemological superiority of Western or Euroamerican" ways of knowing, is an unexamined inheritance of the faith-based assertions of Plato and Descartes.

Consider that, much like Mason today, Plato thought that the poets/oral historians of ancient Greece taught only context specific lessons. For example, they moved listeners to understand how Odysseus felt as he fought on the beaches outside Troy. Good storytellers involved the bodies of their listeners, helping them to smell the salt air, feel the hot blood of wounds, and experience the pride that rippled through the Greek ranks when Hector was slain by Achilles. But, Plato charged, they never asked what is pride *itself*, outside of and beyond any context. The poets were dangerous, he asserted, because their listeners were so enraptured by feelings that they never asked about the non-story-based reality of events and people. Plato's remedy was indicated with the Greek word *eidos*, which would become the Latin *forma* and eventually the English "essence."

Plato claimed that an abstract world of essences existed behind the physical life available to the senses. There were many individual chairs in the world, this thinking went, but there was also an essential "chair-ness." In short, he posited a world of context-independent truths (essences) available only to the mind. And these truths could only be obtained by disciplining the subterfuge of the body and its confusing emotions.

Mason's asserted ability to "search for whatever of their [Native oral traditions] component elements may be testable by independent methods" is a direct cultural descendent of Plato's claim to gain independence from feelings and contexts in pursuit of "essences." Mason is asserting that he can measure ("testable") essential qualities in Natives' oral traditions. As he says, "while there is no substitute for indigenous North American oral traditions in all their singularities . . . so also is it true that none of them can be properly understood in geographical or single disciplinary isolation. They are all variable instances of a universal phenomenon."[48] Again, let us think carefully about this claim. Mason is asserting that all the real earthly stories told in all the different and evolving languages for all the daily reasons over thousands of years by all the different peoples that became the Europeans' "Indians" can be reduced to: "variable instances of a universal phenomenon."

Such a dubious assertion prompts the question: Has anyone ever seen an essence? How is the claim that all these differences can be reduced to some ghost-like essence/"universal phenomenon" not a metaphysical/faith maintained claim? If essences really exist, why do careful scholars repeatedly qualify their analyses with warnings against assuming them: "There is no singular scientific community" and "Natives are a diverse population of different cultures"? Once again, then, I think Mason and his like-minded colleagues should look carefully and critically at the philosophical and theological origins of their beliefs. Native peoples whose oral traditions Mason claims to "comprehend in their own terms" using "independent methods" have a right to some serious explanation. Why is this European-derived story of an invisible world of universal essences gleaned from a disembodied mind (Descartes' "faculty") anything more than the faith-based invocations of a powerful cult of true believers?

To be clear, I think Native peoples, because we are constantly on the receiving end of scientists' pious appeals to "objectivity," have a right to expect some genuinely reflexive thinking from our scientific antagonists. How, exactly, do contemporary archaeologists and physical anthropologists understand their cultural links to the phantasms of Platonist, Cartesian, and Christian metaphysics?

Assessing the threat to "oral traditional" evidence in NAGPRA

It is clear that the future success of NAGPRA will depend on Native peoples' ability to defend the status of our oral histories as legitimate "evidence" in disputes with scientists. Despite the fact that Congress placed "oral traditional" evidence side by side with scientific ways of knowing in the statute, many archaeologists and physical anthropologists insist that (because of their scientific credentials) they expect to be the final judges of the value of our oral histories.[49] Never mind that the whole purpose of NAGPRA is to protect Indians from scientists. These critics have made it a priority to convince the courts that it remains their right to determine what Indians do and do not understand about our own histories.

As most readers of this book know, more than two decades after the passage of the law, only about 25 percent of the ancestors being held by federally funded institutions have been returned to the control of their closest living relatives. It is increasingly evident that there are specific institutions and even specific individuals within those institutions that are responsible for resisting the return of the approximately 120,000 deceased Natives who remain stranded in the drawers, boxes, and laboratories of these archaeologists and physical anthropologists.

Of the thirty-two institutions reporting the possession of more than 1,000 Native dead, thirty are responsible for labeling more than 73,000 as "culturally unidentifiable." Sixteen of these museums claim that 90 to 100 percent of the ancestors in their possessions are culturally unidentifiable. Five declared a full 100 percent of those they hold to be so. Nine of the eleven institutions holding the largest numbers of bodies (each with more than 2,400) maintain that in excess of 85 percent are culturally unidentifiable. These nine museums alone are holding more than 45,000 Indian dead.[50] Given that we know where these relatives are, it is now a matter of coming together as Native peoples and allies to insist that the wishes of their closest living relatives are followed. Looking briefly at two major court cases, each of which has gone against the tribes and moved to erase the legislated importance of Native "oral traditional" evidence, can help us understand the extent of the colonial power that we will confront in the coming months and years.

In *Bonnichsen v. United States*,[51] Judge Ronald M. Gould returns hostile scientists to their pre-NAGPRA position of unchecked colonial power.[52] He permits Native ways of knowing to be reduced to objects for positivist scientists' Platonic and Cartesian gaze. By returning the Columbia River tribes to the status of scientific specimens whose only real significance derives from anthropological narrations, the judge destroys the legislated attempt to award Native ways of knowing a small measure of equality with those of the scientists. The following rather long quote from near the end of the decision illustrates this mistake.

> But evidence demonstrates that oral histories change relatively quickly,
> that oral histories may be based on later observation . . . and deduc-
> tion (rather than on the first teller's witnessing ancient events), and

that these oral histories might be from a culture or group other than the one to which Kennewick Man belonged. . . . [W]e conclude that these accounts are just not specific enough or reliable enough to show a significant relationship of the Tribal claimants with Kennewick man. Because oral accounts have been inevitably changed in context of transmission . . . because the value of such accounts is limited by concerns of authenticity, reliability, and accuracy . . . we do not think that the oral traditions . . . were adequate to show the required significant relationship.[53]

This passage is then footnoted with the judge's thanks to two anthropologists who provided him with this scientific rendering of Native oral traditions. "We find of considerable help the explanations of the uses and limits on oral narratives as explained and documented with scholarly authority by amicus curiae Dr. Andrei Simic . . . and Dr. Harry Glynn Custred."[54] The footnote includes a lengthy list of accolades attesting to the anthropologists' ability to demarcate "the role of folklore and oral tradition in developing cultural identity of ethnic groups."

The tone of these passages effuses privilege. There is not a hint of self-interrogation, of reflexive self-awareness. There is zero evidence that the judge or the scholars he cites are conscious of their own cultural presumptions or their history. These are pronouncements made by and for fellow believers, for other members of the cult of value-neutral objectivity in conversation among themselves. They assume and expect that their own representations of Natives will function as ground zero reality for everyone involved. This *is* colonialism.

Of course no extra-cultural evaluation of the court's assertions is possible. Claiming to possess such a superhuman capacity is precisely the culturally derived fantasy of the judge and the "scholarly authority" he relies on. As I have tried to show, this faith descends to them from their Greek and Christian ancestors. I want, then, to advance a more modest critique. I want to consider whether these judicial and scientific narrations can stand up to their own criticisms. Imagining for a moment that the court was able to honestly apply the same criteria it invokes in its attack on Native knowing, to a consideration of the value of scientific traditions, how would the archaeologists' and anthropologists' stories fare?

Judge Gould questions the "reliability" of Native oral histories because they "have been inevitably changed in the context of transmission" and "may be based on later observation . . . and deduction (rather than on the first teller's witnessing of ancient events)." The scientists whose credentials he cites make the same criticism. "[O]rally transmitted narratives change over time to meet the evolving needs and aspirations of the people who tell them."[55]

Although Natives from the Columbia River area, where the ancestor they call "the Ancient One" was found, are faulted for change and evolution in stories that are thousands of years old, do not anthropological narratives also change often, sometimes in the course of a single scholar's lifetime? And can anyone seriously dispute that this "change over time [is] to meet the evolving needs and aspirations of the people who tell them"? Even a cursory review of the last 100 years of scientific claims about Native people shows indisputably that archaeologists and physical anthropologists have altered their "truth" over and over again, depending on cultural and political contexts. Scientists themselves do not dispute this failure of "reliability." (Scientific reliability is the ability to obtain a consistent result when repeating a scientific investigation.)

Glancing at the first page of the first chapter of a randomly chosen introductory archaeology textbook, I found the following:

> The history of archaeology is . . . in the first instance a history of ideas, of theory, of ways of looking at the past. . . . The main thing to remember is that every view of the past is a product of its own time: ideas and theories are constantly evolving. . . . When we describe the archaeological research methods of today we are simply speaking of one point on a trajectory of evolution. In a few decades or even a few years time these methods will certainly look old fashioned and out of date. This is the dynamic nature of archaeology as a discipline.[56]

If scientists are allowed to change and grow, then why not Indians? Archaeologists admit that their own "ideas and theories are constantly evolving" and that their "every view of the past is a product of its own time," but the court chastises the modern descendants of the Ancient One "because oral accounts have inevitably changed in the context of transmission." The fact is all human understandings change, and all of our "histories [are] based on later observation . . . and deduction (rather than on the first teller's witnessing of ancient events)." No one now living met Abraham Lincoln or was an eyewitness to anything he did or said. Despite the fact that he has only been dead for about 150 years (far from "ancient") and that we have pictures and documents penned in his own hand, historians continue to debate and change their minds about the meaning and significance of multiple parts of his biography.

If things were reversed, if Indians had the power and felt the need to hoard important "artifacts" of early American history, the logic outlined in the court's decision could not be relied upon to force their return to modern American citizens. Capable and determined Native lawyers could easily show that modern interpretations of earlier U.S. history are "based on later observation . . . and deduction (rather than on the first teller's witnessing . . . events)." It would be a simple matter for Native attorneys to demonstrate that the history told and re-told by American scholars "changes relatively quickly."[57] If they could muster enough audacity, a well-paid Native legal team could argue that this obvious instability of narrative leads to "concerns of authenticity." Indians could claim that because the Americans' stories continue to change they lack "reliability" and therefore are not "adequate to show the required relationship" between contemporary Americans and their own ancestors.

The issue of "authenticity," of whether contemporary Natives are "from the same culture" as the dead ancestors that they want returned has also surfaced in a high profile court dispute between the Northern Paiute peoples and the Nevada office of the Bureau of Land Management (BLM).[58] Archaeologists desecrated ancient burials from a cave in Northern Paiute territory in 1940. Despite admitting that these dead are Native people and from the traditional lands of the Northern Paiute, the BLM refuses to return them. The scientists argue that Paiute country "shows significant cultural changes through time" and "evidence of discontinuity in material culture, settlement patterns, and subsistence strategies" over the past ten millennia.[59] To support their finding that "the culture history of the western Great Basin shows a pattern of changes in cultural adaptations . . . over the last 10,000 years," the scientists point out that the textiles found in burials in Paiute country are not static over the past 100 centuries.[60] This evolution, they claim, proves that these dead are "not the same culture" as modern day Northern Paiute.

What if George Washington's grave had been disturbed by Natives who were now arguing in court that the clothes ("textiles") he was buried in were significantly different from those found in contemporary Americans' burials? No doubt a mere 213 years since Washington's death is sufficient to show a "discontinuity in material culture." Obviously, clothing styles and grooming habits have changed. (Was Washington buried in a wig?) New materials (e.g., nylon) and new production techniques unimaginable in Washington's time are now common. Although I am not an expert on American mortuary history, I suspect that physical preparation of bodies has also evolved. What about the vessels in which the deceased were laid to rest? Are these the same now as they were in 1799 when Washington passed? What about the laws governing burials, and therefore the techniques and locations permitted then and now? (If I desire it, can I be buried, as Washington is, on my estate, i.e., in my backyard?)

It is no more difficult to prove that American "settlement patterns and subsistence strategies" are far different in the early twenty-first century than they were in 1799. In the late eighteenth century, 90 percent of the American workforce was rural farmers. Most ate what they grew and what others grew regionally. There was no refrigeration. Outside of salt, modern preservatives were unavailable. Livestock was not filled with antibiotics and there were no genetically modified organisms.

Like the Paiute and the Columbia River tribes, then, American culture also "shows a pattern of changes in cultural adaptations." Given that this obvious "evidence of discontinuity in material culture, settlement patterns, and subsistence strategies" has occurred over barely two centuries, how is it fair to expect Natives to remain static Platonic essences for 100 centuries?

In their amicus curiae brief in support of the scientists seeking to hold and study the Columbia River tribes' ancient ancestor, Glynn Custred Jr. and Andrei Simic register their concern for "diffusion" in oral traditions. These anthropologists maintain that "even if an element [of a Native oral history] can be associated with a specific geographic region, there is no assurance that it was not borrowed from earlier inhabitants."[61] Worse still, they argue, "North American Indian narratives also include elements and tales borrowed from European sources."[62] The Indians' stories, then, "cannot be dated and are clearly the result of diffusion."[63]

I think this criticism of Native ways of knowing is the most ridiculous of all of the scientific "evidence" I have cited. The idea that Custred's and Simic's narratives are not similarly a product of "diffusion" and "borrowed" from earlier societies is ludicrous. They are writing in English! Their English words are diffused from older Greek and Latin languages. The Constitution governing their country (a fairly important element of "material culture") is indisputably an outgrowth of the European Enlightenment and the French revolution.[64] As I have already argued, their science is an outgrowth of ancient Greek philosophy and Christian theology.

If all human societies change, evolve, and borrow from each other, then these scientists and the courts that rely on their "scholarly authority" are demanding that Indians present ourselves as the unobtainable, faith-based ideals of their own inherited desires. Despite the human impossibility of doing so, as Barker said above, we are being told to be "the Native and traditions" that the scientists demand lest they refuse to deem us "meaningful and relevant."

After all, there has never been any "objective" place where one culture begins and another leaves off. For example, how does one decide which parts of American culture are *purely* American and which ones are contaminated ("diffused") by the ways of earlier peoples and other societies? (Most would agree that salsa derives from south of the American border, but it is now reportedly the most popular American condiment, outselling even ketchup.) What about the differences that exist *within* American society? Are these all part of one culture or are they each distinct? Rural Georgia, where I have visited, is cultural light years away from San Francisco, where I work. But if these are distinct cultures, where should we draw the line between them? Perhaps we should use speech patterns? Political opinions? Diet? Religion? Even if we can come to agreement about these criteria, there are always more (non-objective) decisions to address. *Exactly* how must a southern drawl be articulated before it is *authentically* Georgian, and not diffused from, say, North Carolina and Alabama?

In other words, all such decisions are arbitrary and therefore political choices. Diffusion and change among human cultures is a constant, multidirectional process and as such "cannot be dated." Yet in the world of Custred, Simic, and the courts ruling against Natives in these two cases, cultures are static, isolated, Platonic essences that scientists with disembodied Cartesian minds can reliably and objectively assess. If Native cultures do not resemble this scientific fantasy, they are said to lack "authenticity." As Pawnee scholar and activist James Riding In observes, "It is as if those individuals had lived in cultural isolation, having never intermarried with outsiders and having never shared their technologies, ceremonies, and worldviews with others."[65]

Again, why should anyone, except on the basis of unexamined faith, accept such goofy claims? Riding In's observation that "this scenario is a convenient rationale devised by institutions to circumvent the reburial intentions of the repatriation laws" is a distinct possibility.[66] Another, as I have tried to argue here, is that these scientists are largely ignorant of their own intellectual history. Consequently, they seem wholly unaware that they are perpetrating what should be a ridiculously obvious double standard.

Simic and Custred assert that "the authenticity and accuracy of oral narratives can only be determined by critical analysis"[67] and that this "analysis should be as objective as possible."[68] They warn against seeking to "justify a preconceived conclusion."[69] If, as I claim, preconceptions are a consequence of life among humans, then it is fair and right to cast doubt on these anthropologists' invocation of an unobtainable ideal.

One of these scholars, Custred, has a long record of working against the interests of racialized minorities. In addition to his service to the scientists working to disembowel NAGPRA, he co-authored California ballot measure 209 which outlawed state-based affirmative action programs in 1996. He also publicly endorsed Proposition 54, a 2003 measure designed to force the state to cease tracking racial inequalities.[70] In 2005, he published an attack on Mexican immigrants in the right-wing periodical, *American Spectator.* There he blamed immigrants for abusive "consumption of tax supported services . . . due to their high fertility," charged that "illegal aliens account for 95 percent of all outstanding warrants for homicide," and blamed them for "pushing down wages" for Americans. He also accused the Mexican government and military of complicity because ostensibly Mexican migration is "a potential means for manipulating the American political system."[71]

Therefore, the history of at least one of the scholars relied upon by the Ninth Circuit Court of Appeals in its anti-Native ruling suggests that he may have "preconceived conclusions" about the status of brown and black peoples in American society.

Again, no one is "objective." No one has ever been. I do not fault Custred for this; I fault him and his colleague for not recognizing and admitting that their scientific narratives rely on faith-based fantasy diffused to them from their own cultural ancestors.

The way forward?

Many NAGPRA-resisting members of the scientific community are fond of asserting warm and growing relationships between the tribes and their own NAGPRA-implicated institutions. Sometimes these assertions are genuine. In those instances, we can all feel some relief that great injustices are finally being honorably addressed. However, as the numbers reported above (of ancestors labeled "culturally unidentifiable" by scientists) indicate, too often this amounts to "happy talk" designed to obscure resistance to NAGPRA.

As I have tried to show, this resistance to the law is often grounded in a lack of cultural reflexivity. That is, scientists and the courts that have so far agreed with them appear incapable or unwilling to seriously examine their own cultural genealogy. They have yet to carefully consider scientific ways as cultural phenomena. Consequently, they remain unable to critically examine, or even recognize, the implications of theological and metaphysical assumptions that they have inherited from earlier generations of European intellectuals.

I think it is important that Native peoples, struggling at this moment with specific institutions for the return of their ancestors, have confidence asserting that science, although powerful, provides no supernatural access to any secrets of human existence. Despite the megalomaniacal claims of some archaeologists and physical anthropologists, they have no superhuman insight into reality. Like Natives, scientists are mere mortals, limited and enabled by their cultural histories and their humanity. Moving forward requires that they admit this.

Genuine collaboration between equals is only possible when both scientists and Natives are humble enough to recognize that our own ways of knowing are not panhuman imperatives. Despite the welcome and relatively recent inroads of "indigenous archaeology," thus far, this self-awareness has been grossly one-sided. When scientists espouse such colonial hubris, they are not only validating the desecration of Indian dead, they are also insisting that Native peoples accept scientific agendas as the basis of our own self-understandings. They are insisting that we participate in completing our own forced assimilation. And let there be no illusions. Failing to insist on our cultural independence will further threaten our political sovereignty.

I would like to close with a suggestion for further discussion. What if Native peoples and our allies, from Alaska to Maine to Florida to Hawaii, organized some form of an electronic/technological central location where we could share and compare our experiences with specific institutions and their personnel? (When I made this suggestion at the NAGPRA at 20 Symposium in November of 2010, one prominent archaeologist angrily compared me to Senator Joseph McCarthy hunting communists.) It seems to me that organizing ourselves in this way could allow us to identify specific problems with specific institutions that, as Natives and allies working to free Indian dead, we may have in common. At the same time, there would be no requirement that any culturally inappropriate revelations be made. All entries of information would be voluntary and explicitly "opinions."

Sharing experiences would allow defenders of NAGPRA around the nation to identify any behavioral inconsistencies at individual institutions dealing with multiple tribes. Should consultation-based push come to legal shove, such knowledge might be useful. Sharing experiences would also allow us a way to gain some insight into the interpretations of the statute, character, and cooperativeness of specific museum personnel, before setting foot on the premises. In other words, knowing something about the quality of the relationships between other Native peoples and a museum's staff could help us prepare our own NAGPRA claims on the same institutions.

All of this might eventually function as a kind of informal check on the behaviors of these museums. Knowing that Native peoples around the country might gain access to knowledge of ill treatment or genuine collaboration could be an incentive to behave in an honorable way. Finally, such sharing of experiences might further develop a community of intellectual and emotional support among those doing the NAGPRA work for their tribes and nations. Ultimately, this could lead, when appropriate and necessary, to political collaborations and shared strategy targeting specific museums.

Regardless of whether others think this an idea worth pursuing, I feel honored to have been asked to share my thoughts here about our responsibilities to our deceased ancestors. *Mak'laks* (Native people) and allies, please contact me if I can be of any NAGPRA related help to you. *sepk'eec'a* (Thanks.)

Notes

1 Quoted in Rebecca Tsosie and Wallace Coffey, "Rethinking the Tribal Sovereignty Doctrine: Cultural Sovereignty and the Collective Future of Indian Nations," *Stanford Law and Policy Review* 12 (2001): 191–210.

2 See Robert Berkhofer, *The White Man's Indian: Images of the American Indian From Columbus to the Present* (New York: Random House, 1978); Phillip J. Deloria, *Playing Indian* (New Haven, CT: Yale University Press, 1998); Paige Raibmon, *Authentic Indians: Episodes of Encounter from the Late Nineteenth Century Northwest Coast* (Durham, NC: Duke University Press, 2005); and Gerald Vizenor, *Manifest Manners: Narratives on Postindian Survivance* (Lincoln, NE: University of Nebraska Press, 1994).

3 See Joanne Barker and Clayton Dumont, "Contested Conversations: Presentations, Expectations, and Responsibility at the National Museum of the American Indian," *American Indian Culture and Research Journal* 30, No. 2 (2006): 111–40.

4   Albert Gatschet, *Contributions to North American Ethnology Vol. 2, Part 2: The Klamath Indians of Southwestern Oregon, Dictionary—Klamath-English* (Washington DC: Washington Government Printing Office, 1890), 130.

5   Joanne Barker, *Native Acts: Law, Recognition, and Cultural Authenticity* (Durham, NC: Duke University Press, 2011), 15.

6   The idea here is that there is no longer any absolute externality. Being Native is understood, in part, as being other than white. That is, the non-Native has become a ubiquitous and inevitable reference point for Native-ness. It is therefore part of the possibility of Native self-definition. And this co-determined "white/Indian" binary has been a fundamental source of self-understanding for many generations, reflecting colonial ideas about who and what Indians were and are in every American political era since contact.

7   See Robert Bieder, *Science Encounters the Indian: 1820-1880* (Norman, OK: University of Oklahoma Press, 1986) and *A Brief Historical Survey of American Indian Remains* (Boulder, CO: Native American Rights Fund, 1990); Tsosie and Coffey, "Rethinking the Tribal"; Alice Kehoe, *The Land of Prehistory: A Critical History of American Archaeology* (New York: Routledge, 1998); Nancy Parezo and Don D. Fowler, *Anthropology Goes to the Fair: The 1904 Louisiana Purchase Exposition* (Lincoln, NE: University of Nebraska Press, 2007); Laurajane Smith, *Archaeological Theory and the Politics of Cultural Heritage* (New York: Routledge, 2004); Rebecca Tsosie, "Indigenous Rights and Archaeology" in *Native Americans and Archaeologists*, Nina Swidler and Kurt E. Dongoske et al., eds. (Walnut Creek, CA: Alta Mira Press, 1997), 64–76.

8   Douglas Cole, *Captured Heritage: The Scramble for Northwest Coast Artifacts* (Norman, OK: University of Oklahoma Press, 1985); James Riding In, "Repatriation: A Pawnee's Perspective," *American Indian Quarterly* 20, No. 2 (1996): 238–50; Michael Wilcox, "Dialogue or Diatribe?: Indians and Archaeologists in the Post-NAGPRA Era" in *Spirit Wars: Native North American Religions in the Age of Nation Building*, Ronald Niezen, ed. (Berkeley, CA: University of California Press, 2000), 190–93.

9   Tomas Almaguer, *Racial Fault Lines: The Historic Origins of White Supremacy in California* (Berkeley, CA: University of California Press, 1994); James Davis, *Who is Black: One Nation's Definition* (University Park, PA: University of Pennsylvania Press, 1991); Carl Degler, *Neither Black Nor White: Slavery and Race Relations in Brazil and the United States* (Madison, WI: University of Wisconsin Press, 1971); Cheryl Harris, "Whiteness as Property," *Harvard Law Review* 106, No. 8 (1993): 1710–91; Michael Omi and Howard Winant, *Racial Formation in the United States: 1960s to the 1990s* (New York: Routledge, 1994).

10   Vizenor, *Manifest Manners*.

11   J. Kehaulani Kauanui, *Hawaiian Blood: Colonialism and the Politics of Sovereignty and Indigeneity* (Durham, NC: Duke University Press, 2008); Kimberly Tallbear, "DNA, Blood, and Racializing the Tribe," *Wicazo Sa Review* 18, No. 1 (2003): 81–108.

12   Robert Warrior, *Tribal Secrets: Recovering American Indian Intellectual Traditions* (Minneapolis: University of Minnesota Press, 1995).

13   House Concurrent Resolution 108 passed in 1953. It "terminated" the federal recognition of more than 100 tribes and 11,000 Natives.

14   Barker, *Native Acts*, 21–22.

15   Jon Daehnke and Amy Lonetree, "Repatriation in the United States: The Current State of the Native American Graves Protection and Repatriation Act," *American Indian Quarterly* 35, No. 1 (2011): 87–97; Clayton Dumont, "Contesting Scientists' Narrations of NAGPRA's Legislative History: Rule 10.11 and the Recovery of 'Culturally Unidentifiable' Ancestors," *Wicazo Sa Review* 26, No. 1 (2011): 5–42; James Riding In, "Decolonizing NAGPRA," in

For Indigenous Eyes Only: A Decolonization Handbook, Angela Wilson and Michael Yellow Bird, eds. (Santa Fe, NM: School for Advanced Research Press, 2005), 53–66; and "Graves Protection and Repatriation: An Unresolved Universal Human Rights Problem Affected by Institutional Racism," in *Human Rights in Global Light: Treganza Museum Anthropology Papers* 24-25, Mariana L. Ferreira, ed. (2007–08): 37–42.

16   Barker, *Native Acts.*

17   Tamara Bray, "Repatriation and Archaeology's Second Loss of Innocence: On Knowledge, Power, and the Past," in *Opening Archaeology: Repatriation's Impact on Contemporary Research and Practice,* Thomas Killion, ed. (Santa Fe, NM: School for Advanced Research, 2008), 79–90; Kehoe, *The Land of Prehistory*; Smith, *Archaeological Theory*; Larry Zimmerman, "Multivocality, Descendant Communities, and Some Epistemological Shifts Forced by Repatriation" in *Opening Archaeology,* Killion, ed., 91–108.

18   Laurelyn Whitt, *Science, Colonialism, and Indigenous Peoples: The Cultural Politics of Law and Knowledge* (New York: Cambridge University Press, 2009), 219.

19   This is also why Barker places the phrase "western ideology" in quotation marks in the first passage I cited: "I do not believe that there is an authentic tradition to be revitalized from a past that transcends 'Western Ideology.'"

20   Lorraine Daston and Peter Galison, *Objectivity* (New York: Zone Books, 2007).

21   Bray, "Repatriation and Archaeology's," 81; See also Ann Kakaliouras, "An Anthropology of Repatriation: Contemporary Physical Anthropological and Native American Ontologies of Practice," *Current Anthropology* 53, No. 5 (2012): 210–221. Apparently equally frustrated, Kakaliouras observes that "counter to the hopes of indigenous archaeologists and their allies" twenty years of experiences with repatriation by archaeologists and physical anthropologists have not "transformed the basic positivistic and universalist premises with which these sciences operate," 212.

22   At the time it was authored, these "individual" rights applied only to white men who owned property.

23   Quoted in Irving Zeitlin, *Ideology and the Development of Sociological Theory* (Saddle River, NJ: Prentice Hall, 1997), 84.

24   Ibid., 85.

25   Ibid., 84–85.

26   Ibid., 87.

27   Clayton Dumont, "Toward A Multicultural Sociology," *Teaching Sociology* 23, No. 4 (1995): 307–20, "The Analytical and Political Utility of Poststructuralism: Considering Affirmative Action," *Canadian Journal of Sociology* 23, Nos. 2–3 (1998): 217–37, *The Promise of Poststructuralist Sociology: Marginalized Peoples and the Problem of Knowledge* (Albany, NY: SUNY Press, 2008); Russell Ferguson and Martha Gever et. al., *Out There: Marginalization and Contemporary Cultures* (Cambridge, MA: MIT Press, 1990); Sandra Harding, *The Science Question in Feminism* (Ithaca, NY: Cornell University Press, 1986), *Feminism and Methodology,* ed. (Bloomington, IN: Indiana University Press, 1987), *Is Science Multicultural? Postcolonialisms, Feminisms, and Epistemologies* (Bloomington, IN: Indiana University Press, 1998); Susan Hekman, *Gender and Knowledge: Elements of a Postmodern Feminism* (Boston: Northeastern University Press, 1990); Patricia Hill-Collins, *Black Feminist Thought: Knowledge, Consciousness, and the Politics of Empowerment* (Boston: Unwin-Hyman, 1990); Paul Hirst and Penny Woolley, *Social Relations and Human Attributes* (New York: Tavistock Publications, 1982); Ernesto Laclau and Chantal Mouffe, *Hegemony and Socialist Strategy* (London: Verso, 1985); Michael Mulkay, *Sociology of Science: A Sociological Pilgrimage* (Bloomington, IN: Indiana University Press, 1990); Steven Seidman, *The Postmodern Turn*

(Cambridge, MA: Cambridge University Press, 1994), *Queer Theory/Sociology* (Cambridge, MA: Blackwell, 1996), "Relativizing Sociology: The Challenge of Cultural Studies" in *From Cultural Studies to Sociology,* Elizabeth Long, ed. (Malden, MA: Blackwell, 1997), 37–61; Dorothy Smith, *The Everyday World as Problematic: A Feminist Sociology* (Boston: Northeastern University Press, 1987); Linda Smith, *Decolonizing Methodologies: Research and Indigenous Peoples* (London: Zed Books, 1999); Trinh Minh-ha, *Woman, Native, Other: Writing Postcoloniality and Feminism* (Bloomington, IN: Indiana University Press, 1989); Stephen Woolgar, ed., *Knowledge and Reflexivity: New Frontiers in the Sociology of Knowledge* (London: Sage Publications, 1988).

28   Stephen Silliman, "The Value and Diversity of Indigenous Archaeology: A Response to McGhee," *American Antiquity* 75, No. 2 (2010): 217–20, 219.

29   Michael Wilcox, "Saving Indigenous People From Ourselves: Separate But Equal Archaeology is Not Scientific Archaeology," *American Antiquity* 75, No. 2 (2010): 221–27, 223.

30   Chip Colwell-Chanthaphonh and T.J. Ferguson, "Introduction: The Collaborative Continuum," in *Collaboration in Archaeological Practice: Engaging Descendant Communities,* Chip Colwell-Chanthaphonh and T.J. Ferguson, eds. (New York: Alta Mira, 2008), 14. See also: Sonya Atalay, "Indigenous Archaeology as Decolonizing Practice," *American Indian Quarterly* 30 (2006): 280–310 and "Community Based Participatory Research: Methods and Applications for Archaeological Collaboration," presented at the annual meeting of the Society for American Archaeology (2008); Bray, "Repatriation and Archaeology's"; Chip Colwell-Chanthaphonh, "Opening America's Skeleton Closets," *Denver Post,* May 9, 2010, http://www.denverpost.com/opinion/ci; Jon Daehnke, "A Strange Multiplicity of Voices: Heritage Stewardship, Contested Sites, and Colonial Legacies on the Columbia River," *Journal of Social Archaeology* 7, No. 2 (2007): 250–75; Alan Goodman, "Racializing Kennewick Man," *American Anthropology Association Newsletter* 38, No. 7 (1997): 3–5; Dorothy Lippert, "In Front of the Mirror: Native Americans and Academic Archaeology," in Native Americans and Archaeologists, Swidler and Dongoske et al., eds., 120–27; Larry Zimmerman, "A New and Different Archaeology," *American Indian Quarterly* 20, No. 2 (1996): 297–307, "Public Heritage, A Desire for a 'White' History of America, and Some Impacts on the Kennewick Man/Ancient One Decision," *International Journal of Cultural Property* 12 (2005): 265–274, and "Multivocality, Descendant Communities, and Some Epistemological Shifts Forced by Repatriation."

31   Francis Bacon, *Advancement of Learning* (Chicago: Encyclopedia Britannica, 1605/1952); Susan Bordo, *The Flight to Objectivity: Essays on Cartesianism and Culture* (Albany, NY: SUNY Press, 1987); René Descartes, "Meditations on First Philosophy" in *The Philosophical Writings of Descartes,* vol. 2 (Cambridge: Cambridge University Press, 1641/1994); Dumont, The Promise; Michel Foucault, *The Politics of Truth* (New York: Semiotext(e), 1984); Eric Havelock, *Preface to Plato: A History of the Greek Mind* (Cambridge, MA: Harvard University Press, 1963); Werner Jaeger, *Early Christianity and Greek Paideia* (Cambridge, MA: Harvard University Press, 1961).

32   Morris Berman, *The Reenchantment of the World* (New York: Cornell University Press, 1981); Lorraine Daston, "Baconian Facts, Academic Civility, and the Prehistory of Objectivity," *Annals of Scholarship* 8 (1991): 337–63; Richard Rubenstein, *Aristotle's Children: How Christians, Muslims, and Jews Rediscovered Ancient Wisdom and Illuminated the Dark Ages* (Orlando, FL: Harcourt, 2003); Arthur Lovejoy, *The Great Chain of Being: A Study of the History of an Idea* (Cambridge, MA: Harvard University Press, 1936).

33   Vizenor, *Manifest Manners,* 16.

34   Ronald Mason, *Inconstant Companions: Archaeology and North American Indian Oral Traditions* (Tuscaloosa, AL: University of Alabama Press, 2006).

35 Plato, *The Republic*, Desmond Lee, Tr. (New York: Penguin Books, c. 427-347 BCE/1974), 601.

36 Ibid., 608.

37 Ibid., 607.

38 Ibid.

39 Mason, *Inconstant Companions*, 9.

40 Ibid., 2.

41 Ibid.

42 Ibid., 6.

43 See generally, "Symposium on the Social History of Objectivity," *Social Studies of Science* 22 (1992).

44 Daston, "Baconian Facts"; Daston, *Objectivity*; See also Lorraine Daston and Peter Galison, "The Image of Objectivity," *Representations* 40 (1992): 81–128.

45 Descartes, "Meditations on," 24.

46 Ibid., 37–38.

47 Ibid., 48.

48 Mason, *Inconstant Companions*, 97.

49 Peter Jones, *Respect for the Ancestors: American Indian Cultural Affiliation in the American West* (Boulder, CO: Bauu Institute Press, 2005); Stephen Ousley, William Billeck, and Eric Hollinger, "Federal Repatriation Legislation and the Role of Physical Anthropology in Repatriation," *Yearbook of Physical Anthropology* 48 (2005): 2–32; Andrei Simic and Harry G. Custred Jr., Motion for Leave to File Brief of Amicus Curiae in Support of the Plaintff-Appellees. Bonnichesen vs. United States Nos. 02-35996 (2004): District Court No. 96-1481 (D.Or.).

50 Lauren Miyamoto, public presentation at NAGPRA Review Committee Meeting (November 19, 2010, Washington DC). These nine institutions are, in descending order, starting with those holding the largest number of ancestors: Phoebe A. Hearst Museum of Anthropology, University of California, Berkeley; Peabody Museum of Archaeology and Ethnology at Harvard University; Ohio Historical Society; Illinois State Museum; University of Alabama Museums, Office of Archaeological Services; University of Kentucky, William S. Webb Museum of Anthropology; University of Tennessee, Knoxville, Frank H. McClung Museum; University of Missouri, Columbia; University of Tennessee, Knoxville, Department of Anthropology. (If the two University of Tennessee units are combined, they rank 4th in the number of deceased Indians held.)

51 Robson Bonnichsen et al. vs. United States of America et al., and the Confederated Tribes of the Colville Reservation, et al. (2004): United States Court of Appeals for the Ninth Circuit No. 02-35994, D.C. No. CV-96-01481-JE.

52 Walter Echo-Hawk, "Testimony Before the United States Senate Committee on Indian Affairs," July 28, 2005.

53 *Bonnichsen*, 1607.

54 Ibid., n.23: 1607.

55 Simic and Custred Jr., Motion for Leave, 3.

56 Colin Refrow and Paul Bahn, *Archaeology: Theories and Methods* (New York: Thames and Hudson, 2005), 19. As part of some very helpful criticism, an anonymous reviewer of an earlier draft of this chapter suggested that my illustration of the instability of archaeological truth is much like the claim advanced by Vine Deloria Jr. in *Red Earth, White Lies: Native Americans and the Myth of Scientific Fact* (Golden, CO: Fulcrum Publishing, 1997). Like all

Native academics I owe a great debt to Professor Deloria, whom I never had the high honor of meeting, but I am not a fan of this particular book. At least as I read, he seems to be saying there that archaeologists are simply wrong. This is not my claim, at all. Rather I am arguing that scientific selves and self perceptions, desires and questions, methods and interpretations, are of an extended cultural genealogy originating in Europe and its cultural histories. Although a source of powerful explanations, there is therefore no pan-human reason to assume that archaeologists' desires and questions are relevant for living well on the earth. Arguing "truth" with archaeologists, then, is not wholly unlike pagans entering a church to debate scripture with fundamentalist Christians. Indeed, I remember that my concern as I turned the pages of *Red Earth, White Lies* was that it could be read as implying that more research could determine who was right.

57   There are now more than 14,000 published biographies of Lincoln. One scholarly documentation of his malleability through time is Barry Schwartz, *Abraham Lincoln in the Post-Heroic Era: History and Memory in Late Twentieth-Century America* (Chicago: University of Chicago Press, 2008).

58   Fallon Paiute-Shoshone Tribe v. United States Bureau of Land Management, United States District Court for the District of Nevada (2006).

59   Pat Barker, Cynthia Ellis, and Stephanie Damadio, "Summary of the Determination of Cultural Affiliation of Ancient Remains From Spirit Cave, Nevada" (Bureau of Land Management Nevada Office, July 26, 2000).

60   Ibid., 97.

61   Simic and Custred Jr., Motion for Leave, 28.

62   Ibid.

63   Ibid., 32.

64   The evidence is strong that the U.S. Constitution and its precursors (The Albany Plan of 1754 and the Articles of Confederation) were in part modeled after the governance structure found among the Six Nations. In other words, American governance is at least partly diffused from Native tradition. David Wilkins, *American Indian Politics and the American Political System* (New York: Rowman and Littlefield, 2007), 129–130; Vine Deloria Jr., "Anthros, Indians, and Planetary Reality" in *Indians and Anthropologists: Vine Deloria Jr. and the Critique of Anthropology*, Thomas Biolsi and Larry Zimmerman, eds. (Tucson, AZ: University of Arizona Press, 1997), 217.

65   Riding In, *Graves Protection*, 39.

66   Ibid.

67   Simic and Custred Jr., Motion for Leave, 3.

68   Ibid., 11.

69   Ibid.

70   Justin Jones, "Prop 209 Co-Author Glynn Custred Endorses Prop 54," *Free Republic*, 2003, accessed June 28, 2010, http://www.freerepublic.com/focus/f-news/971051/posts.

71   Glynn Custred, "Where are My Juice and Crackers?" *The American Spectator* (July/August, 2005), 2.

Chapter 11
The Impact of NAGPRA on Communities
JAN I. BERNSTEIN

"We are all connected—even if you can't see how, just being in the world changes the world."

—Douglas Brooks[1]

NAGPRA is nothing new

What do we as human beings desire more than anything else? After our basic needs of food, shelter, and clothing are met, we desire to be recognized as human, and in that recognition we want to be treated with dignity and respect, to be seen as nothing less than human. The history of the United States is filled with chapters in which groups of people were marginalized and had to fight for the same basic rights that were afforded to the dominant culture. Among those groups are blacks, women, and immigrants including Irish, Italians, and Jews who were discriminated against, and in some cases treated as property. Native Americans were not only marginalized, but also demonized and targeted for extinction. They literally had prices put on their heads.

It took a civil war to end slavery and a civil rights movement filled with conflict to gain a semblance of parity for black Americans. It took the sacrifices of the women's suffrage movement for women to get the right to vote, and on August 26, 1920, the Senate ratified the Nineteenth Amendment to the U.S. Constitution. And it took the Native American Graves Protection and Repatriation Act (NAGPRA) to give Native Americans and Native Hawaiians the same rights that everyone else in the U.S. possessed over their ancestors and cultural items. NAGPRA did not bestow new rights or special rights, instead it simply codified rights that, under common law and property law, should have been extended to Native Americans and Native Hawaiians. U.S. law is based on French, English, and Spanish common law and under common law we all have the right of disposition of our dead relatives and their funerary objects. Until NAGPRA, this right was denied to Native Americans and Native Hawaiians when their relatives were discovered either inadvertently or during an intentional excavation, and then collected, curated, studied, and exhibited. Prior to the signing of NAGPRA on November 16, 1990, basic property law protections were frequently denied to Native Americans and Native Hawaiians, when they would seek return of religious items and items of central cultural import from museums and governmental agencies. What does it say about a people who do not extend the same rights and protections to all citizens?

Giving voice to untold stories

I am neither a scholar nor academic. I do not have a thorough grasp of the scholarship, nor have I read all of what has been written about NAGPRA over the past twenty years. What I do bring to this chapter is over two decades of experience working in NAGPRA compliance. In 1986, I was selected by Dr. Robert Kautz to join his team at the State of California Parks Department, which was charged with reporting on their holdings of Native American human remains and funerary objects. When that project was completed, I moved to New York City in 1988, where I worked as an assistant curator at the Brooklyn Children's Museum. Before I left the museum, it was poised to repatriate wampum to the Haudenosaunee Confederacy. In 1990, I moved to Denver, Colorado, where I still reside. After completing a graduate degree in museum and field studies at the University of Colorado, Boulder, and partnering in a museum consulting business, I joined the staff of the University of Denver Museum of Anthropology in 1995. I served for eight years as collections manager and NAGPRA coordinator, and as adjunct faculty in the Department of Anthropology's Museum Studies graduate program. By the time I left the university, in 2003, I knew that I wanted to focus exclusively on NAGPRA, and that is how I came to found Bernstein & Associates NAGPRA Consultants.

To begin the process of writing this chapter, I interviewed the people who, like me, have worked in NAGPRA for many years, and who also implement it. Out of those interviews, as you might expect, came stories of how NAGPRA has had a profound impact on the lives of those of us who work on its implementation on a daily basis. But, what you might not expect, are the stories of how NAGPRA has touched the lives of people who have nothing to do with its direct implementation.

In the telling of these stories, you will also see how NAGPRA has cast a light on the collection practices of museums and federal agencies that have acquired Native American human remains and cultural items over the past 150 years, and how NAGPRA has been a force for change. The voices in this chapter have the power to raise consciousness about the often-untold stories behind the acquisitions and use of Native American and Native Hawaiian human remains and cultural items. They are often painful reminders of the social, ethical, and moral consequences of laws that were enacted by federal and state governments, as well as policies and procedures of museums, and the attitudes and behavior of collectors, dealers, scientists, and members of the general public toward the indigenous people of what is now the United States of America.

How does NAGPRA accomplish this? On its face, the act facilitates the repatriation of Native American and Native Hawaiian human remains, funerary objects, sacred objects, and cultural patrimony, but it also brings together people who might not have otherwise encountered one another. In coming together to work through the NAGPRA process, new communities are created. Hopefully, they will be a force for positive change, not only in the ways in which living and deceased Native American and Native Hawaiians are viewed and treated, but also in the way we see and treat each other.

Why are Grandma's bones housed in the museum?

Based on a very non-scientific analysis, I have come to conclude that the vast majority of people in the United States are unaware that Native American human remains and items, some of which are of great spiritual import, are in the possession of museums and federal agencies. If people are aware, they do not have a full understanding of the ways in which the remains and items were acquired. My conclusion is based on conversations I frequently enter into when meeting people during social occasions, after I explain to them what I do for a living.

People are often shocked and appalled when I tell them about the ways in which the human remains came into the possession of museums and federal agencies; and how so much of it stems from the institutionalized dehumanization of Native Americans. From the moment European explorers arrived, Native American graves were looted and some eventually ended up in museums. Examples of grave robbing can be found from coast to coast, from the Mashpee Wampanoag on Cape Cod to the Yurok in Northern California, as well as Alaska and Hawaii. Besides robbing graves directly, there are a myriad of other ways in which museums and federal agencies came into possession of Native American human remains and cultural items. For example, the U.S. Surgeon General's Circular Number 2 of 1867 called on military medical officers to collect crania together with specimens of Indian weapons, dress, implements, diet, and medicines.[2] That is how the skulls of Cheyenne and Arapaho people who were massacred at Sand Creek in 1864 ended up in the Smithsonian Institution.[3] Large and small collections were acquired and continue to be acquired as a result of archaeological excavations and inadvertent discoveries. People are often taken by surprise to hear that Native American human remains, when discovered, were, and often still are, taken to museums, while those of non-Natives are reburied, often at taxpayer expense.[4]

However, collections are not limited to human remains and funerary objects. Collections also include sacred objects and those of central cultural importance (under NAGPRA, called "objects of cultural patrimony"). There are two examples that come readily to mind. First, in the late 1800s, there were individual collectors, such as George Gustav Heye. His extensive private collection of approximately one million items became the basis for the National Museum of the American Indian (NMAI), which is under the Smithsonian and has its own repatriation law. Second, institutions also collected materials directly. For example, one institution (what is now the Field Museum in Chicago), collected by employing agents who traveled to Indian reservations to "purchase" cultural items. I put the word in quotes because these were often sales under duress, which made them illegal sales. The people on the reservations were barely subsisting and were believed to be a "dying race," and hence their objects needed to be collected and preserved for future non-Native generations.

The many atrocities inflicted on the first peoples of what is now the United States of America were an assault on "We the people." I know this might sound a bit hokey, but we are all degraded when we degrade those we perceive as "the other." What can be more degrading than having your basic beliefs disrespected to the degree that they become objects of curiosity and museum display? In my experience and opinion, NAGPRA is above all else human rights law, as its goal is to right the past wrongs of collecting the deceased and cultural items of "the other." When a disenfranchised group of people gains basic human rights, such as the right over the disposition of their ancestors' remains and protection of their graves, as well as the right to items of central importance to their culture and spiritual practices, we all benefit, for in returning those rights we restore our humanity. As such, the passage of NAGPRA was a major human rights victory.

Getting reacquainted

The human rights victory of NAGPRA's passage provided an opportunity for museums and federal agencies to begin to develop a new kind of relationship with Native Americans and Native Hawaiians, who are the descendants of the people whose scalps, skeletons, mummified remains, funerary objects, sacred objects, and objects of cultural patrimony are in the museums and repositories. However, not only was it the present state of dispossession that was recognized, it was also the methods of acquisition of the remains and objects that had occurred, some of which were at the time clearly violations of common law and property law, that helped to build the new relationship. The recognition that these methods of acquisition are (now) considered by many (although there were some that believed back then) to be immoral and unethical, is also part of the human rights victory. The protection, enfranchisement, and recognition were not without challenges. The challenges were daunting as representatives of museums, Indian tribes, and Native Hawaiian organizations began to learn how to navigate the NAGPRA process (and in so doing began to forge relationships of trust and mutual respect), where before there were feelings of distrust, suspicion, misconceptions, and sometimes anger or hostility.

I spoke with two tribal representatives about their early experiences under NAGPRA and how things have changed over the years, and these are their stories.

John (Jim) Peters Jr., repatriation officer of the Mashpee Wampanoag Tribe[5] and executive director of the Massachusetts Commission on Indian Affairs, described his first NAGPRA consultation, "We have all come a long way since those early days. . . . We were sitting with a Harvard curator with a British accent. We were doing consultation but we didn't know what consultation was about. We didn't want to show that we didn't know anything and so we talked about the weather; and they didn't know how to deal with us."

Jim went on to describe how the process has evolved for him and the other members of the Mashpee Wampanoag NAGPRA Committee. "It has been quite a journey for us to go through . . . the learning curve . . . to really find out what's there (housed in the museums). It's opened my eyes to see how, over the years, people have robbed our graves, compiled them, and studied them, and to go through the records." Today, he and his sister, Ramona Peters, NAGPRA director for the Mashpee Wampanoag Tribe,[6] and the other two members of their NAGPRA Committee have what Ramona referred to as, " . . . sort of a tag-team approach . . . each of the four has a different style . . . all have strengths they bring to the consultations. One of our officers does a lot of research beforehand and he might ask a very pointed question about an inventory or something irregular. And we have an elder woman; she keeps things from getting too heated. She will start a conversation or break in and talk about what's on the stage or something (to diffuse the situation). She reminds us that part of our cultural roots is keeping peace.

Jim described how "we are left to bury the dead after the carnage, so to speak. It is really difficult to look at that history and be with the people emotionally, intellectually." Ramona adds, "To touch them, to be with them, make prayers. There may be some anger, some fear." Jim went on, "To be with them, to touch them—it sends shivers through you." Today, Jim and Ramona reinter the remains of their ancestors sometimes with the help of student interns who in the past might have instead been excavating Mashpee Wampanoag graves. The interns also conduct research on the original burials, which Jim and Ramona then use to reinter the remains and funerary objects in a way that, as closely as possible, approximates the way in which they were first interred, which is the preferred method of reburial for the Mashpee Wampanoag.

NAGPRA—choice or imposition?

For those of us who happened to be employed by museums in the early 1990s, we did not choose to work in NAGPRA. It was something that had to be done because it was the law. We did not aspire to the work in NAGPRA, unlike those embarking on careers today. Depending on your perspective, you could say that NAGPRA either chose us or was imposed upon us. For some, especially those who were more advanced in their careers in 1990, NAGPRA could feel like an imposition. For me, NAGPRA presented an opportunity to make a positive difference in people's lives and in so doing, facilitate healing in the world. Many others share this perspective.

Deborah (Debbie) Confer, who some thirty-five years ago embarked on a career, first in archaeology and then in museum collections management, described how she came to NAGPRA and what it came to mean to her:

> I vividly remember the first time I encountered human remains in an archaeological context. I was in field school in northern Arizona, long before the passage of NAGPRA. We were digging an Ancestral Puebloan village site and found an adult female skeleton on the floor of a kiva, which was very unusual. Since she was not in a traditional burial position, and there was evidence the village had burned while occupied, we wondered if this woman's burial in the kiva had been accidental. Contemplating her death, I was both moved and excited by the possibility that we could tell her story when reporting on the site. Our field crew included Navajo men, who refused to excavate human remains, but it never occurred to me that native people might not think the same as archaeologists about removing and documenting the burial. That consideration was just not part of my consciousness thirty-five years ago. After working in museums for more than twenty years now and consulting with representatives from more than forty tribes, I find it hard to believe it didn't occur to me that tribes wouldn't welcome research on their ancestors' remains, but it didn't. I actually consider the NAGPRA compliance process to be applied museum anthropology. To me, it's one of the most interesting aspects of museum work.

Like Debbie, I too came to the realization that NAGPRA is the most rewarding aspect of museum work; in fact, I could no longer justify spending my days on other aspects of my vocation. Museum collections management work is incredibly important, but it no longer spoke to me like the human rights work that happens with NAGPRA.

On a fairly regular basis over the past five years or so, graduate students have asked me how I came to work in NAGPRA, and how I created a NAGPRA consulting firm. More often than not they say, "I want to be you. I want to do what you do." As I said, this is a fairly new phenomenon. Today's graduate students never experienced the pre-NAGPRA museum and seem to have nothing but enthusiasm for working together with Native Americans and Native Hawaiians to facilitate repatriation.

Ray Gonzales is the cultural specialist for the Santa Rosa Indian Community of the Santa Rosa Rancheria (Tachi-Yokut),[7] and for twenty years he worked as a prison chaplain; many of those years at Corcoran, a maximum-security state prison in Kings County, California. The prison is not too far from the Santa Rosa Rancheria, which is only a few miles north of the California wine regions of Sonoma and Napa. During his time there, Ray had to fight for basic rights for the Native American prisoners including the right to worship. Ray described how the corrections officers, sometimes willingly and sometimes extremely begrudgingly, allowed him, along with his friend and current supervisor, Lalo Franco, cultural specialist and NAGPRA coordinator for the Tachi-Yokut, to erect the structure, light the fire, heat the rocks, and lead not only his Native American brothers but also men of many faiths, into the warm embrace of the sweat lodge. So much was dependent on the correction officers who had control over every aspect of their lives, the inmates as well as the chaplain. But one thing the corrections officers did not have control over was what Lalo and Ray told the inmates in the sweat lodge. They told the prison inmates at Corcoran about their NAGPRA successes and those successes gave the inmates hope. "It made them feel good in a place that was primarily about punishment rather than rehabilitation," Ray said, describing the impact of NAGPRA on that community. As an introduction to his story, he simply stated, "I spent twenty years in prison." He was making a point about the conditions he had worked under, but he just as easily could have been referring to the imprisonment of the Native American human remains in museums and repositories, which, thanks to NAGPRA, now have a process under which they will be set free.

Incarceration undoubtedly has a profound effect on one's life; it certainly curtails one's ability to make personal choices. For some, the demands of NAGPRA compliance may have felt like a prison sentence. For one thing, seismic-scale shifts in institutional priorities had to be made to meet the deadlines. Steve Lekson, curator of anthropology, who in 2003 assumed responsibility for NAGPRA compliance at the University of Colorado Museum, described his experience:

> NAGPRA has changed me, professionally. And, I suppose, personally . . . My principal role in the process was to determine cultural affiliation of ancient remains and thus enable affiliated tribes to request repatriation (or unaffiliated tribes to object to their exclusion). I did my work in consultation with tribes, considering a range of evidence, of which archaeology was only one category. But the remains were mostly obtained through archaeology, so my particular field of study shaped how affiliations were reached. And that was a problem. The archaeology

evidently required for "cultural affiliation" as spelled out in NAGPRA was the archaeology of the 1920s and 1930s—a credulous, naïve, quasihistorical style of archaeology that my field had long since passed by. Pots, I was taught, do not equal people. And I was taught correctly, I think; yet NAGPRA required me to equate pots (and other funerary objects) with people, indeed with specific tribes! I was caught up in arguments over tribal affiliations of seventh-century pithouses—a topic that would have flunked me out of grad school. . . . As a curator, I . . . turned off the archaeology side of my brain . . . NAGPRA isn't archaeological law . . . NAGPRA is human rights law, or property law, or Indian law. Whatever: It's the law, so we did it. . . . Doing NAGPRA was rough on my archaeological psyche. Apologizing to tribe after tribe for a century of archaeology; receiving more than a few dressing-downs, very specifically about archaeology's sins; but, more than those discomforts, wondering if perhaps the Indians were right. Maybe archaeology was not worth the hurt it caused native peoples. That, more than the scolding, wore me down. NAGPRA made me hard on myself—and my field."[8]

Steve described how he as an archaeologist became a whipping boy for his profession's activities, but how it was also a learning process. That experience as an archaeologist, in my opinion, pales in comparison to those of the people who, through the NAGPRA compliance process, are reminded again and again and again of the plethora of atrocities that were inflicted on the living Native Americans and Native Hawaiians and their ancestors. NAGPRA impacted Steve's life both personally and professionally. However, it certainly has had a very profound impact on the lives of the individuals and families who have had their relatives repatriated.

Impact on lives

How NAGPRA goes beyond repatriation and begins the process of healing.
Lalo Franco, Tachi Yokut cultural specialist and NAGPRA coordinator, described to me the impact that NAGPRA has had on him and his people:

> NAGPRA is helping to heal only one of the many wounds inflicted on Native Americans. Removing the dead from their resting places were only some of the wounds inflicted on Native Americans. But the wounds are all related: the taking of the land, the new arrivals to the land who acted without respect for the people they met, the loss of the language, the boarding schools that removed the children from their families, their culture, and their language, and the declining health of

the people in recent times. The wounds are all related and NAGPRA addresses one of the deeper scars. NAGPRA reminds us of the power people had over us, the disregard. The Great Spirit set the cycle in motion. We don't believe humans have the right to interrupt the cycle. The interruption of the cycle and the NAGPRA processes is [sic] like a wound that just begins to heal when it is ripped open again. With every new consultation, the activities of the past must be exposed and re-examined so the healing can begin again.

The Comanche, the Navajo, and other groups have cultural prohibitions against speaking of the dead and coming into contact with the dead and their possessions. Despite these and many other challenges associated with repatriation, there is a shared sentiment that NAGPRA is vitally important to Native American and Native Hawaiian communities. Jimmy Arterberry, Comanche tribal historic preservation officer (THPO) and tribal historian, described to me how his tribe came to terms with the dilemma of repatriation and reburial as they began to participate in the NAGPRA process. He began with the comment: "You tell them that they have forever scarred and altered our traditions and that can never be corrected. We inherently knew when the time was to gather to pay respects to those people. We didn't need a calendar or a clock . . . We knew when it was time to revisit those places and honor the dead . . . it didn't have to be talked about."

Jimmy says that his eldest aunt told him this before he left for Washington, DC, where he was invited to testify before a U.S. Senate Subcommittee, which was holding a hearing on protecting Native American sites. Jimmy noted: "NAGPRA not only forced the Comanche people to confront the reality of the wrongs that were committed against our people but it also forced us to change our traditional ways. It forced the Comanche people to talk about the dead. It changed our traditions. It altered our traditional life-ways. When people passed, Comanche tradition was to not mention them again. When people passed it was the traditional way to let the dead go and not speak of them. . . . Still today some people don't want to talk about them."

But others like Jimmy do talk about them because of NAGPRA. They not only talk about them, but they read about them in the museum records. They read about the decapitations, about how they were taken from their graves, about how they were boiled down, about how they were sent to museums and put on display. Jimmy's aunt told him to tell the senators about the "scarring and altering":

NAGPRA is very positive in that we are finally able to deal with it [the Comanche on the shelves and the knowledge of how they got there], but at the same time on the other side of it, yes, it altered our traditions.

But that negative effect does not outweigh the positive impact. It's something we've learned to live with and address in an altered fashion. When we retrieve the people we sometimes know their names and other times we just know they are our kin. There are burdens that have resulted from NAGPRA that are spiritual and economic . . . that the Comanche have had to incorporate into our traditional ways.

NAGPRA's impact reaches the tribal, cultural, and traditional, as well as the personal and familial. It makes us face our past and allows us to look toward a more equitable future. All of this and more is encapsulated in this story of the return of human remains collected as a direct result of the U.S. Surgeon General's Circular Number 2 of 1867,[9] which promoted the removal of crania of Native Americans killed on the battlefield. W. Otis Halfmoon, liaison at the National Trails Intermountain Region of the National Park Service and member of the Nez Perce Tribe, described, in an email to me, how it impacted him, his mother, and his tribe when the remains of his warrior great grandfather who was killed in a battle with U.S. soldiers and Bannock scouts were repatriated:

Back in 1877, the soldiers made an attack on the Nez Perce people along the Big Hole River in Montana. To make a long story short, the soldiers were beat back . . . and my great grandfather, Pahkatos Owyeen (Five Wounds), was killed. The Nez Perce warriors could not recover his body being it was too close to the soldier positions. Once the Nez Perce left the battlefield General O.O. Howard arrived with 500 plus soldiers. They saw the body of Pahkatos and recovered the head . . . the reason I say "recovered" is that the Bannock scouts mutilated his body. The soldiers kept the head and it ended up in Washington DC. After much research, paperwork, and discussion, it was determined that the skull could be returned back to my family and Tribe. My mother was alive still, she was in her 90s, and she was honored that she could receive the skull of her Grandfather. It was a sad affair but at least his skull was returned. The skull represented much . . . just how close in years that this war took place . . . only 133 years ago. It showed my family the bloodlines of Nez Perce warriors that go through our veins. It showed the Nez Perce Tribe that this happened only yesterday.

Twenty-one years after the passage of NAGPRA, some scientists, especially those who have based their careers on the study of Native American culture, skeletal material, and cultural items, have not had an easy time of it. Some have gone so far as to take legal action to stop repatriations. The named litigant in *Bonnichsen v. United States* (a.k.a. the Kennewick Man case),[10] Robson Bonnichsen, who has since passed away, was quoted as saying, "Repatriation has taken on a life of its own and is about to put us out of business as a profession."[11] Tim D. White, a professor in the Department of Integrative Biology at the University of California, Berkeley, in his recent book, *Human Osteology*[12], wrote:

> Human osteologists interested in continuing to curate and study human skeletal remains have been marginalized and demonized within their own intellectual settings and denied access to the very collections they once curated. Curators of human osteological collections have literally been locked out of the collections by their own anthropologist colleagues and isolated from the NAGPRA consultation process with Native Americans. Meanwhile, untrained, formerly unemployed archaeologists have lined their pockets with federal and institutional money under the guise of conducting inventories of remains required by NAGPRA and under bogus extensions to the NAGPRA deadline granted by the National Park Service. No wonder this unforeseen and unfortunate turn of events has resulted in the widespread abandonment of skeletal biology by museums and other institutions of higher learning, and parallel exodus of researchers and students from human osteology.

Based on my conversations with younger physical anthropologists and osteologists, I think the attitudes of Drs. White and Bonnichsen may be generational, and certainly not all members of their generation share their views about how NAGPRA has gone too far and had such extreme and negative consequences for their professions. Conversely, there are people who believe that NAGPRA has not gone far enough. Many Indian tribes have expressed great concern over the omission of associated funerary objects in 43 CFR 10.11, the rule for the disposition of culturally unidentifiable human remains. Others such as James Riding In and the Hopi Tribe have expressed an interest in applying NAGPRA to intellectual property. Groups that are not federally recognized Indian tribes do not have standing under NAGPRA, which has created friction between federally recognized and non-recognized groups when they disagree on such matters as disposition, and when a museum or agency refuses to consult or transfer control to non-recognized groups.[13] Some believe that NAGPRA has not gone far enough in that it does not directly cover discoveries on state and private land.[14] Others have expressed a desire for it to apply to private collectors and museums that do not receive federal funds.

The Emotional Toll. By its very nature, NAGPRA work can be fraught with emotions. That should come as no surprise, for when we deal with NAGPRA, we are in the realm of death and spirituality. As we work through the NAGPRA process, people can and do get emotional. It happens during consultations when, as Lalo said, old wounds are reopened. And it happens during repatriations, when those wounds begin to be healed. But nowhere have I seen more heated exchanges and more heightened emotions than when the NAGPRA Review Committee hears disputes.

I have witnessed two Native Hawaiian NAGPRA representatives exchange death threats during their testimony before the Review Committee.[15] On the twentieth anniversary of NAGPRA, the Review Committee heard two disputes on the same day, both of which involved Alaska Native groups. The atmosphere was electrified when the testimony of one group began with dancing, singing, and drumming in traditional garb, and ended with the chairman losing control of the process. The testimony was so wrought with emotions that by the end, I felt as if my insides had been clawed to shreds. That evening during dinner with colleagues, everyone agreed that they, too, felt drained. On at least two occasions, I witnessed Western Apache elders, stoic former military men, reduced to tears as they revealed information about the Gaan, which they explained should never be revealed to the uninitiated but were doing so to support their case. Because they felt they had to, they were explaining that Gaan dance items meet the definitions of both sacred objects and cultural patrimony—not just sacred objects, which the Denver Art Museum[16] and Field Museum[17] had determined.

How do we navigate the challenges?

Prior to NAGPRA, reinterment was an alien concept from a traditional cultural perspective to most tribes and groups with standing under the act. The people had burial practices, but they did not have reburial practices, and many drew a distinction between the two. Likewise, most did not try to preserve cultural items in perpetuity, as museums do as part of their missions. During consultations, traditional religious leaders often will describe how their cultural items have a natural life cycle that includes an eventual return to the earth. When, in the autumn of 2000, I inquired among culturally affiliated tribes whether it would be appropriate to repair a 1,000-year-old ceramic vessel that was damaged during the rehousing of the University of Denver Museum of Anthropology collection, to a person, I was urged to refrain from doing any repairs. One tribal NAGPRA representative said the damage was a part of the life cycle and it should be allowed to continue on this path toward reintegration with the earth. Coming to terms with these opposing worldviews is just one of the challenges faced by those who work in NAGPRA.[18]

Challenges: spiritual health and safety

The power associated with some sacred objects and cultural patrimony can also be of great concern to Native Americans and Native Hawaiians. The care and handling of these items is often strictly bound by tradition, but tradition often does not address the care and handling of items that have been disassociated from the traditional care-taker, in some cases for decades or generations. I have been told that certain sacred objects and cultural patrimony pose a great threat when they are not properly cared for, and illnesses, deaths, and devastating fires have been attributed to the mishan-dling of these powerful items. To protect their communities from harm, traditional religious leaders have had to be creative in their efforts to handle these items as they are repatriated.

In the early years of NAGPRA, the Zuni Tribe decided that they would not repatriate or rebury human remains because they do not have a reburial ceremony and would not adopt one. Then, about ten years after the passage of NAGPRA, the Zuni Tribe began to submit repatriation requests for human remains and funerary objects that would then be reburied by another tribe. It is my understanding that former Councilman Arden Kucate initiated this change. Today, the Zuni Tribe, along with the Hopi Tribe, Pueblo of Acoma, and Pueblo of Zia are referred to as the "four repatriating Pueblos." Jointly they request repatriation of human remains identified as "Puebloan," "Ancestral Puebloan," and "Anasazi." They do this with the support of the other seventeen Pueblos.[19] When the four repatriating Pueblos request repatria-tion, either the Pueblo of Acoma or Hopi Tribe will then take the lead on the reburial typically.

Although it took them a few years to start the repatriation of human remains, the Zuni were at the forefront in addressing the dangers associated with items with strong spiritual power. The Zuni started with the repatriation of Zuni war gods called Ahayu:da, which meet the NAGPRA definition of cultural patrimony. They had been repatriating Ahayu:da from public and private collections around the world for sev-eral decades prior to the passage of NAGPRA; therefore, it came as no surprise when the first two NAGPRA Notices of Intent to Repatriate were for Ahayu:da. The first was published by the Peabody Museum of Archaeology and Ethnology at Harvard University on March 15, 1993,[20] and the second was published on June 29, 1993,[21] by the Portland Art Museum.

Because the Ahayu:da are considered to be extremely powerful, and require proper handling, the Zuni Tribe did not want them to be physically transferred directly to Zuni. Ed Ladd, who has since passed away, was not only a member of the Zuni Tribe, but also a curator at the Laboratory of Anthropology (LA) in Santa Fe, New Mexico, putting him in a unique position to come up with a solution. The repa-triated Ahayu:da were delivered to the LA, where they were received by traditional religious leaders who drove over three and a half hours from Zuni, New Mexico, to receive and prepare them for transport back home. This process was developed to ensure the safety of all concerned.

Challenges: physical health and safety

NAGPRA workers not only take into consideration the spiritual consequences of repatriation, but they also take into consideration the real physical dangers posed to tribal members by museum preservation practices. For decades, museums and private collectors applied pesticides to items that were made with organic materials such as fur, feathers, skins, hair, and plants, in an effort to preserve them. They used organic pesticides such as DDT and inorganic compounds made with heavy metals such as arsenic and mercury, all of which are toxic to humans. These practices had a devastating effect on the Hopi Tribe when items that were unknowingly treated with pesticides were repatriated and reintroduced into traditional use. Leigh Kuwanwisiwma, director of cultural preservation, described how, soon after he returned repatriated masks and other items to traditional religious leaders at several of the Hopi villages, the traditional religious leaders became ill, and one died. Leigh attributes the illness and death directly to the pesticides that were later found to have been applied to the items, since the items were stored in the traditional way, in the same room as the food. It was heartbreaking for all concerned. After working so hard to repatriate them, Leigh decided it was imperative that the repatriated items be removed again. Today they sit in boxes, encased in several layers of plastic, sealed with tape, in a secure location where they await a way in which the pesticides can be removed. According to Leigh, because of this incident, the Hopi Tribe placed a moratorium on the repatriation of sacred objects and cultural patrimony that may contain pesticides. For the last few years, he has been working with Nancy Odegaard at the Arizona State Museum and others to find ways to detect and remove the toxic substances, so that repatriated items will no longer pose a physical risk.

Ongoing impacts from repatriation

The goal of NAGPRA is repatriation, but along the way, during consultations, relationships develop that can sometimes blossom into partnerships that have the potential to be catalysts for positive changes. In May of 1999, human remains representing a minimum of 1,922 individuals and 534 associated funerary objects were reburied at Pecos National Historic Park in New Mexico. They were repatriated to the Pueblo of Jemez by the Robert S. Peabody Museum of Archaeology and the Peabody Museum of Archaeology and Ethnology at Harvard University. Between 1915 and 1929, Alfred V. Kidder excavated the site when it was under private ownership. In working through the NAGPRA process, a partnership was formed between the Pueblo of Jemez, Pecos

National Historic Park, and Phillips Academy, an elite private boarding school in Andover, Massachusetts, that operates the Robert S. Peabody Museum of Archaeology. The relationships that developed during the NAGPRA process led to creation of the Pecos Pathways program, a hands-on educational program for high school students, in which students from the Pueblo of Jemez and Phillips Academy work and live one week at the pueblo, one week at the park, and one week in the Andover-Boston area. Under the program, students get hands-on experiences in archaeological survey, site recording using sophisticated electronic equipment as well as simple tools, pottery making, archaeological excavation, pottery identification, stone tool identification, museum cataloging of artifacts, researching traditional uses of plants in northern New Mexico, bread making and baking in an *horno* (outdoor oven). They have also maintained a restored floodplain on Glorieta Creek, and used GPS equipment in the field to record locations of the Santa Fe Trail ruts. The Pecos National Monument staff finds that an important result of the continued relationship with the Pueblo of Jemez is having the benefit of their frequent involvement in park activities and events. For many families at Jemez, this was their ancestors' homeland for centuries and a place to which Pecos descendants stay connected throughout each year. [22]

The road ahead: costs and benefits

There is much work to be done and limited resources to do it. That is as true today as it was in the early 1990s. In a survey sent to museums in early 1993, the American Association of Museums (AAM) asked for information about the ability of museums to implement NAGPRA.

In its response, the University of Colorado Museum (UCM) estimated that it had 65,000 catalog entries of Native American cultural items representing 700,000 individual items; their estimate for Native American human remains was 300 individuals; they could not estimate the number of associated or unassociated funerary objects. UCM was unable to come up with precise numbers because the collection had not been fully catalogued; this was particularly true for the archaeology collection at the object level. Not only had the items not been fully cataloged, they were not computerized, and instead were in hard-copy formats. In response to a survey question about the estimated total cost to comply with the act, UCM responded: "$100,000 (4 years to comply and 2 years to follow up)." UCM went on to say, "This figure is probably unrealistically low."[23] Unfortunately, the inability of UCM to provide accurate numbers and descriptions was not unique and sadly, for many museums, this is still the case.

For years to come, there will be NAGPRA work that needs to be done, including collections management work required to support consultation. But without funding, that work will slow down or even come to a halt, which would be a violation of the act. It is up to those of us who care to keep NAGPRA in the forefront as an

Fig. 11. Reinterment at undisclosed location. Photo by Leah A. Hight.

institutional and funding priority. This means that significant resources are needed to see the NAGPRA process through to completion. For many Indian tribes, Native Hawaiian organizations, museums, and federal agencies, completion is a long way off. Consultation on millions of cultural items has yet to occur to determine if they are covered by NAGPRA and whether they will be claimed. Tens of thousands of human remains have yet to be repatriated and of those whose control has been transferred, thousands sit in boxes and drawers in the possession of museums and federal agencies awaiting reinterment.

A lack of money is not the only thing that slows down the process. A lack of land for reinterment can stop some Indian tribes, such as the Hopi Tribe, from requesting repatriation. For other Indian tribes, it does not stop them from making repatriation requests of culturally affiliated human remains and disposition requests for culturally unidentifiable remains, but it does mean that they remain in the possession of museums and federal agencies after the transfer of control has been completed. In other words, the Indian tribes are legally in control, but are unable to take physical possession of the remains and complete the repatriation process and reburial. Currently the Colorado College, University of Colorado Museum, History Colorado (formerly the Colorado Historical Society), and the Denver Museum of Nature & Science are in possession of human remains representing nearly 700 individuals whose legal control has been transferred to Indian tribes, but have not yet been physically transferred because there is currently no place to reinter them. In his recent book, *Grave Matters*,[24] Tony Platt has suggested that reinterment sites that also serve as memorials be established across the country, not only to solve the problem of insufficient land, but to memorialize and recognize the genocides and dehumanization that lead to the acquisitions in the first place.

The NAGPRA community and its impact on humanity

> "I hear a lot of talk from here [pointing to his head] but I don't hear any
> talk from here [pointing to his heart]."[25]
> —Unknown participant at "Ancient Peoples of the Rocky Mountain
>   Front Range and Eastern Plains of Colorado: A Symposium"

I approached the writing of this chapter with great trepidation. At first, I hesitated, because I did not feel like I was a member of a community that had been impacted by NAGPRA; I thought I was an outsider whose role is to facilitate the process; I thought the communities impacted by NAGPRA were those who have standing, such as the lineal descendants, Indian tribes, and Native Hawaiian organizations, and those that are required to comply, the museums and federal agencies. I also hesitated to write this chapter because of concerns I had about betraying trusts. For example, sensitive information is often shared during NAGPRA consultations and details about reinterments often should not be revealed as there is a real threat of looting and also for cultural reasons of secrecy under some circumstances. But what I've come to understand is that I am part of a new community, the NAGPRA community, because "NAGPRA is really about the quality of the people involved. Good people with good hearts can make the law work. And the reverse is also true."[26]

The NAGPRA community is comprised of the people whose stories have been given voice in this chapter, the other authors who contributed to this book, as well as hundreds of others who believe in the spirit of the act. When we recognize the humanity in others, we restore our own humanity. When we fail to recognize the humanity in others, our own humanity is diminished, which can only lead to suffering. It is NAGPRA that connected our communities and made a new one so that we can see how the world changes to encompass the rights of all, both the living and dead.

Acknowledgments

I would like to thank the following people who generously agreed to share with me the impact of NAGPRA: Jimmy Arterberry, Comanche Nation THPO, tribal historian, artist, and activist; Lalo Franco, cultural specialist and NAGPRA coordinator, Santa Rosa Rancheria of Tachi-Yokut Indians; Raymond Gonzales, former cultural specialist, Santa Rosa Rancheria of Tachi-Yokut Indians; W. Otis Halfmoon, Nez Perce, tribal liaison, National Trails Intermountain Region, National Park Service; Lynn Hartman, Ute Mountain Ute Tribe; Terry Knight, THPO and NAGPRA coordinator, Ute Mountain Ute Tribe; John "Jim" Peters, executive director, Commission on Indian Affairs at the Commonwealth of Massachusetts and an official NAGPRA representative of the Mashpee Wampanoag Tribe; Ramona Peters, NAGPRA director, Mashpee Wampanoag Tribe; Deborah Confer; and Stephen Lekson. I am extremely grateful to Sangita Chari and Jaime Lavallee who asked me to write the chapter and guided me through numerous drafts, as well as to my readers, especially Clay Dumont, Skye Griffith, and Ronald Smith. And lastly, I am eternally grateful to be here now on this path that has provided me the opportunity to do important human rights work, and where I am blessed to spend time with so many wonderful people who listen to their hearts.

Notes

1   Dr. Douglas Brooks said this during a series of lectures he gave on various topics related to Tantric philosophy, in Estes Park, CO, September 19–26 2010. Dr. Brooks is a scholar of Hinduism, south Asian languages, and the comparative study of religions who lived in India with his teacher, Dr. Gopala Aiyar Sundaramoorthy, for many years studying and practicing Srividya, Auspicious Wisdom, and the modern traditions of goddess-centered Tantra. Currently Professor of Religion at the University of Rochester, he holds both a Masters and his doctoral degrees from Harvard University.

2   The Surgeon General's Order is reproduced in full in Robert Bieder, *A Brief Historical Survey of the Expropriation of American Indian Remains* (1990) at 319–320.

3   "United States Army Medical Museum, Anatomical Section, Records Relating To Specimens Transferred To The Smithsonian Institution" http://www.nmnh.si.edu/naa/guide/_uv.htm.

4   "Colorado Rev. Stat. §24-80-401, et seq." repealed and reenacted in 1973, amended 1990, 1991, 1995. Section 13 of the Historical, Prehistorical and Archaeological Resources Act establishes a procedure with regard to unmarked human graves. Upon discovery of human remains, the coroner and sheriff, police chief or land managing official are notified and have 48 hours to determine if forensic study is necessary. If not, the coroner contacts the state archaeologist who determines if the remains are over 100 years old and if they are Native American. The Indian Commission is notified if the remains are Native American. Excavation of remains takes place unless all parties agree unanimously to leave them in situ. The State Archaeologist has 10 days to complete the excavation and assumes custody of the remains. Analysis is allowed for up to one year. The State Archaeologist consults with the Indian Commission on reinterment and pays for the disinterment and analysis of remains from state lands and of remains from private lands, if no one else is willing. If human remains are discovered during an anthropological investigation, the archaeologist will determine the age and, if possible, cultural affiliation. If the remains are less than 100 years old, the coroner is notified; if the remains are over 100 years old, the State Archaeologist is notified. Anyone who knowingly disturbs an unmarked human burial commits a Class 1 misdemeanor; any person who has knowledge that an unmarked human burial is being unlawfully disturbed and fails to notify the local law enforcement official commits a Class 2 misdemeanor. Any person who discovers on any land suspected human skeletal remains or who knowingly disturbs such remains must immediately notify the coroner of the county wherein the remains are located and the sheriff, police chief, or land managing agency official.

5   This is the tribe of the Thanksgiving story. In the 1600s when encountered by the English, the Wampanoag lived in southeastern Massachusetts and Rhode Island, as well as within a territory that encompassed current day Martha's Vineyard and Nantucket. They are also known

for their resistance to colonial encroachment. King Philip's War (1675–1676) against the English colonists resulted in the deaths of 40 percent of the tribe. Most of the male survivors were sold into slavery in the West Indies. Many women and children were enslaved in New England. Survivors remained in their traditional areas and continued many aspects of their culture, while absorbing other people by marriage and adapting to changing economic and cultural needs in the larger society. Although the last native speakers of Wôpanâak died more than 100 years ago, since 1993 the tribe has been working on a language revival project that is producing new native speakers, the first time this has been achieved in the United States. The chief groups of Wampanoag began to re-organize their governments in the late twentieth century, although only one federally recognized tribe has reservation land. Sources: Author interview with Ramona Peters and Jim Peters Jr., www.mashpeewampanoagtribe.com, and http://en.wikipedia.org/wiki/Mashpee_Wampanoag.

6   Ramona Peters is also a contributing author in Chapter 7 of this book, titled "NAGPRA's Impact on Non-federally Recognized Tribes" by Angela Neller et al.

7   "Our History" http://www.tachi-yokut.com/history.html. In the Tachi Yokuts' own words: "The Tachi Yokut inhabited the fertile San Joaquin valley of California for centuries. They farmed, hunted, fished, and gathered grains, nuts and fruits in the valley and up into the foothills. But, with the arrival of the American settlers, they lost the land and sometimes the people were killed for a bounty. By the end of the 19th century, the Tachi Yokut Tribe was split across the central and southern parts of California. The Citizenship Act of 1924 gave all Indians American citizenship rights while allowing them to retain their tribal citizenship but it made little difference in the way they were treated by the government. As part of their integration into white society, the Federal government sent their children to government schools, their religion was banned, and the teaching of their language and culture was all but forbidden. Even after the land grabs and removal efforts had ceased, the damage had been done. The division of our people, the suppression of the Indian culture, and the influence of white society left the people with few ties to the past. Aspirations for the future were being destroyed by the resulting economic hardships and prejudice. For generations the people tried to support themselves as seasonal field laborers. Government regulations produced long term economic stagnation on the reservation, resulting in 85 percent unemployment, a crumbling infrastructure, and a cycle of poverty that ground away at the hope for a better future for our children. Finally in 1988, with the passage of the Indian Gaming Regulatory Act, the Tachi-Yokut Tribe had the mechanism to become self-sufficient and exercise self-determination. Today all of that has changed for the better first with a Bingo hall and then with the Tachi Palace Hotel & Casino."

8   Stephen H. Lekson, "My Adventures in Zuni-and Kykotsmovi and Window Rock and . . ." *Museum Anthropology* 33, No. 2 (September 2010): 180–193.

9   Supra at note 2.

10   367 F.3d 864 (9th Cir. 2004).

11   George Johnson, "Indian Tribes' (sic) Creationists Thwart Archaeologist," *New York Times*, October 22, 1996,. http://www.nytimes.com/1996/10/22/science/indian-tribes-creation-ists-thwart-archeologists.html?src=pm.

12   White, T.D., Black M.T, Folkens, P.A. (2012) *Human Osteology*, 3rd Ed. at 366.

13   See Angela Neller et al., Chapter 7 of this book, "NAGPRA's Impact On Non-federally Recognized Tribes," for more on the discussion about how non-federally recognized Indian tribes are working (or not) under NAGPRA.

14   NAGPRA can apply under 43 C.F.R. 10.13, if the state or private land removals come under a museum's control.

15   Twenty-seventh meeting of the NAGPRA Review Committee, September 17–18, 2004, Washington, DC.

16   Twenty-third meeting of the Review Committee, May 31, June 1–2, 2002, Tulsa, OK.

17   Thirty-third meeting of the Review Committee, November 3–4, 2006, Denver, CO.

18   See Patricia Capone, Chapter 5 of this book, "Amending Wonder: Museums and Twenty Years of the Native American Graves Protection and Repatriation Act," for more about changes that have occurred in museums.

19   The other 17 Pueblos are Ohkay Owingeh, Pueblo of Cochiti, Pueblo of Isleta, Pueblo of Jemez, Pueblo of Laguna, Pueblo of Nambe, Pueblo of Picuris, Pueblo of Pojoaque, Pueblo of San Felipe, Pueblo of San Ildefonso, Pueblo of Sandia, Pueblo of Santa Ana, Pueblo of Santa Clara, Kewa Pueblo (formerly Pueblo of Santo Domingo), Pueblo of Taos, Pueblo of Tesuque, and Ysleta del Sur Pueblo.

20   Notice of Intent to Repatriate a Cultural Item in the Possession of the Peabody Museum of Archaeology and Ethnology. 58 *Fed. Reg.* 13796-13797 (March 15, 1993).

21   Notice of Intent to Repatriate Cultural Items in the Possession of the Portland Art Museum. 58 *Fed. Reg.* 34818 (June 29, 1993).

22   Malinda Blustain, Director and Bonnie Sousa, Registrar/Senior Collections Manager, Robert S. Peabody Museum of Archaeology. Email message to author January 5, 2012.

23   UCM was correct, not only were the funding needs underestimated, but also underestimated were the number of individuals represented by the Native American human remains. By the end of 2012, UCM will have consulted with 240 Indian tribes about human remains representing a minimum of 645 individuals and 732 funerary objects; that is more than twice as many human remains as were reported in the AAM survey. The price tag for the consultations and repatriations of those remains and associated funerary objects is over ten times the predicted amount totaling upward of $1,049,675, of which $669,675 (64 percent) came from 13 grants that were awarded to UCM between 2004-2011 by the National NAGPRA Program; the other 36 percent came from UCM. These figures do not include the funds expended by UCM after the May 1996 deadline and before the first NAGPRA grant in 2004. Still to come are years of consultation about items identified in NAGPRA summaries that have been sent to more than 300 Indian tribes and Native Hawaiian organizations.

24   Tony Platt, *Grave Matters: Excavating California's Buried Past* (Berkeley California: Heyday, 2011).

25   Author's notes taken during "Ancient Peoples of the Rocky Mountain Front Range and Eastern Plains of Colorado: A symposium", which was organized by the Colorado Historical Society (now History Colorado) October 10–11, 2000. The statement is unattributed and was not recorded in the meeting transcription. During the writing of this chapter, the author asked others who were in attendance, but no one could remember who said it, although they do remember it being said, possibly by Clement Frost, then NAGPRA Representative of the Southern Ute Indian Tribe, who is now deceased.

26   Clay Dumont, Klamath and Professor at San Francisco State University, wrote this in his comments on a draft of this chapter.

Index